THE NEW DO-IT-YOURSELF HANDBOOK

THE NEW DO-IT-YOURSELF HANDBOOK

MARSHALL CAVENDISH

Published in 1995 by Bookmart Ltd,
Desford Road, Enderby,
Leicester LE9 5AD.
Produced by Marshall Cavendish Books
(a division of Marshall Cavendish Partworks Ltd),
119 Wardour Street, London W1V 3TD

Copyright © Marshall Cavendish 1995

ISBN 1 85435 838 3

Printed and bound in Malaysia

Some of this material has previously appeared in the Marshall Cavendish partwork *ProFile*.

Contents

THE NEW DO-IT-YOURSELF HANDBOOK

INTRODUCTION

The Complete Do-It-Yourself Handbook is the ultimate manual for the home improvement enthusiast. In easy-to-follow, step-by-step photographs, beginners and experts alike can learn to assess, plan and carry out the jobs that make a house more of a home. Armed with a few basic techniques and a handful of carefully selected tools, even relative newcomers to DIY can tackle surprisingly ambitious projects. And, as the book will show you, doing it yourself doesn't mean that you have to compromise when it comes to the quality of the results.

Many common DIY projects can be accomplished with the help of only a few important skills. These skills can be applied to a whole range of tasks inside and outside the house. By concentrating on thoroughly explaining these essential techniques, *The Complete Do-It-Yourself Handbook* provides the reader with the skill and knowledge to take on virtually any job with confidence. Complicated tasks are made as easy as possible; large projects are broken down into simple steps; and the mystery is taken out of materials and specialized tools.

But *The Complete Do-It-Yourself Handbook* is more than simply a tutorial. It is also a reference manual for dealing with common household repairs and emergencies, telling you how to fix most things around the home. Whether you have problems with fuses or with plumbing; dripping taps or smashed windows; coping with damp or insulation problems;

even soundproofing – *The Complete Do-It-Yourself Handbook* tells you what to do. Again, step-by-step photographs and clear, easily followed instructions will take the beginner from the early planning stages through to the perfect finish. Shortcuts and tips from the professionals will help more experienced DIYers achieve a better, quicker result.

USING THIS BOOK
The Complete Do-It-Yourself Handbook is arranged in five practical chapters – Tools, Decorating, Repairs, Carpentry and Plumbing. Each is full of advice, with the emphasis on practicality and economy. In the first chapter, for example, you will learn about the range of tools available on the market, and what each one does. As tools often represent a major financial outlay, the advice on how to select and look after your set of tools is invaluable in helping you avoid unnecessary expense.

Perhaps the quickest and easiest way to improve the appearance of your home is by decorating. Chapter 2 takes you from the earliest steps such as using a paint roller or stripping old wall paper through to advanced techniques of papering stairwells and ceilings, or achieving special effects with paint. The chapter covers flooring, too, showing you, for example, how to tile awkwardly shaped rooms.

The following section, Repairs, provides a reference manual for maintaining the appearance of your home by coping with everyday problems: fixing rotten window frames, for example, mending tears and holes in carpet, or replacing electrical fuses. For a whole range of indoor and outdoor repairs, Chapter 3 provides the most efficient and practical solutions.

Traditional woodworking remains one of the most useful and adaptable tools in the DIY armoury. In Chapter 4 you will learn the basic skills of carpentry; and how to achieve professional results in wood joints, allowing you to create shelves, cabinets, or a host of other projects. The chapter also contains valuable tips on often overlooked skills, such as cutting wood, using a chisel, and accurate drilling. A section on selecting timber gives you a basic working knowledge of wood, essential for understanding how to get the most out of your materials.

The chapter on planning explains how the different plumbing systems in your house work, making you aware of how individual jobs and repairs may affect other parts of the system. From the basic techniques of working with piping to specific projects such as installing a new shower, we show you how to repair and improve your home's plumbing.

Together, the five chapters of *The Complete Do-It-Yourself Handbook* build into a complete guide to virtually all the essential tools, materials and techniques of effective DIY. Whatever improvements or repairs you have in mind, this book contains all the information you need to complete home repairs and improvements with the minimum fuss and expense, and maximum success.

WARNING

Many electrical and plumbing tasks are governed by official regulations. This book reflects the regulations applicable in the UK and Australia. Should you be using the book in other countries, we advise you to seek advice on any local regulations that might apply. Wherever you are working, if you have any doubts about the safety of a project, you should consult a professional. Reputable builders, plumbers and electricians should be able to give you up-to-date advice on any changes in regulations that might affect any projects you undertake.

TOOL STORAGE

Tools are expensive, and unless you provide somewhere to store them when they're not in use they will soon get lost or damaged. There's a wide choice of fixed and portable storage ideas.

Probably the most useful basis on which to judge your storage needs is by where the tools are used. Those tools which you carry around from job to job, or want to keep in your car, need different types of storage from those you use only in a workshop.

If you need to carry a selection of tools with you to the job, one of the simplest answers is a **metal tool box**. These have lift-out and cantilevered trays which fold out as the box is opened, allowing you to keep different tools separate. They're cheap and very strong, and can usually be locked for security, but can be heavy to carry around when full.

The other disadvantage with metal tool boxes is that there is no protection for individual tools, which can rattle about within the box. The solution here is to store them in individual **tool rolls**.

These are made from stout fabric or plastic, and have small pockets to take the tools. A range of different sizes is available.

If you want to carry just a few simple tools and fixings to the job, a **tool belt** is a good choice. Stout pockets and tool loops hold everything you need, and leave both hands free. A carpenter's apron performs the same function if you are working mainly at your bench.

Storage within your workshop needs

Below: *Metal or plastic tool boxes with cantilevered trays provide neat storage for a wide range of tools, and can be easily carried to the job*

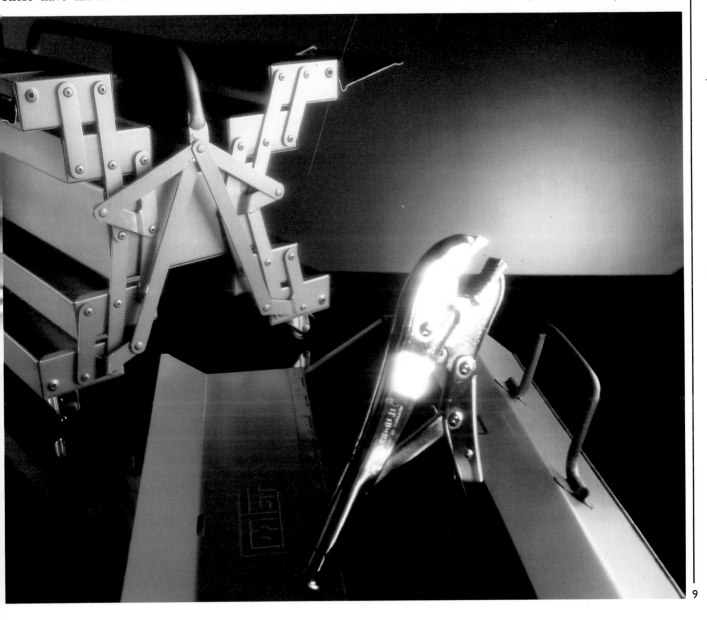

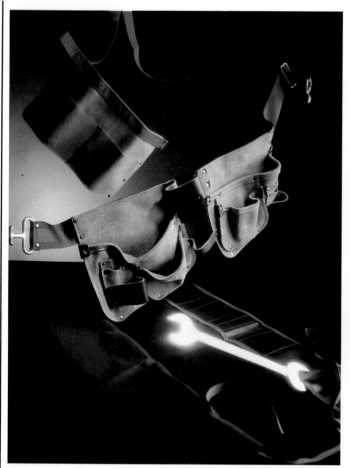

Above left: *Tool belts and aprons are useful for storing odd tools on the job. Tool rolls provide protection for small tools in your tool box*

Above right: *In the workshop, you can keep your tools in a lockable tool cabinet, or display them on the wall using adjustable storage racks*

Below: *For storing small tools, a wooden tool chest with felt-lined drawers or a metal one with plastic compartments is ideal*

to be able to cope with a larger array of tools. One option is to choose a wall-mounted **tool cabinet**. These are fitted with a range of brackets and clips, allowing you to store a wide range of tools, and most are lockable—a useful extra security feature.

An alternative is to go for one of the proprietary wall-mounted **display boards**, which allow you greater flexibility and mean that you can see at a glance where each tool is. Some have sturdy metal backing plates; others use pegboard. Both feature a range of movable clips and brackets.

You can store smaller tools, especially bladed tools such as chisels and gouges, in a wooden **tool chest** with individual felt-lined drawers. These can also be carried to the job. However, they are comparatively expensive. A variation on this idea is the metal storage chest with individual plastic drawers of various sizes, ideal for keeping small tools such as tape measures, punches, bradawls, twist drills and the like in order.

PAINTING TOOLS

Whether you're painting a window frame or re-decorating the whole house, you need something to get the paint out of the can and onto the surface. Knowing the best tool to use helps you get a professional finish every time

Brushes

Brushes are still the most popular tools for applying paint. They are long lasting, easy to clean and are more versatile than rollers and pads. Standard brush sizes go from 15 to 150mm (½ to 6in)—choose the size to match the work to be done.

Below: *Selection of paint brushes, including special purpose varieties*

Paint should be applied quickly, evenly and at the right consistency. If it's laid on too thickly it will sag or run; if it's too thin it will not cover the old finish and will not dry to an even sheen. Brushes, rollers and pads all have their virtues and merits.

1 Large, 150mm emulsion brush for walls. Used to cover large areas.
2 General purpose 100mm brush for emulsion or eggshell paint on walls.

3 Small, 15mm brush for narrow areas.
4 Angled cutting-in brush. The slanting bristles are designed for cutting-in on internal angles on window frames, architraves and skirtings, or where two colours meet.
5 General purpose gloss brush for woodwork.
6 General purpose gloss brush for larger areas of woodwork.
7 Thin, fine-lining brush for delicate and fiddly work or for painting decorative lines on furniture.
8 Radiator brush for painting inaccessible places behind radiators and pipes—an invaluable tool if you want a really professional finish to your decorating.

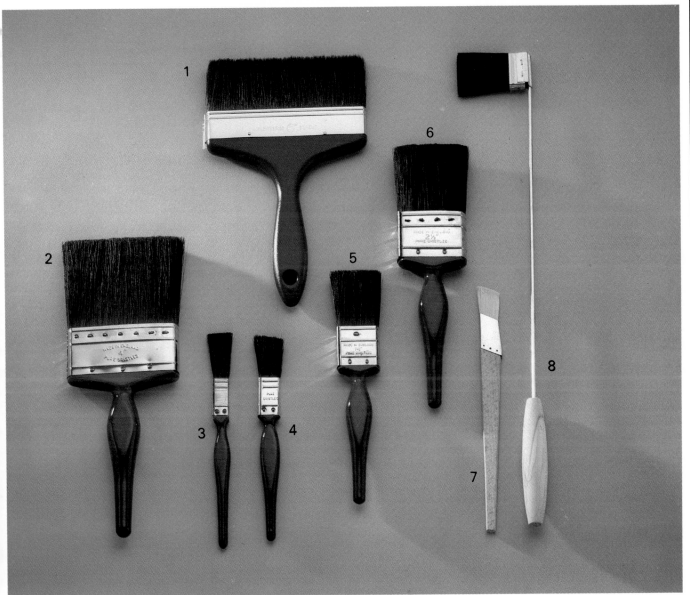

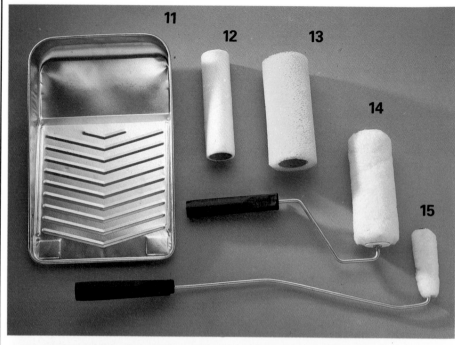

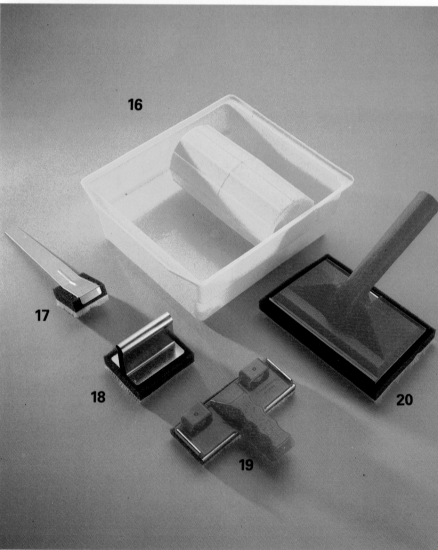

Above: *Paint kettles and tray*
Left: *Selection of paint rollers*
Below left: *Paint pads and tray with roller*

Kettles and trays

Paint kettles are used to hold paint while you work—decant a little at a time and keep the lid shut on the paint tin.
9 Plastic and tin kettles are suitable for all types of paint. Use the butchers hooks for hanging them on ladder rungs to leave your hands free.
10 Standard plastic tray for paint rollers.

Rollers

Rollers are quicker than brushes and are ideal for large areas of walls and ceilings. They are good on rough or textured surfaces, but it is hard to paint to a neat edge and you will still need a brush for cutting-in.
11 Pressed tin paint tray—the sort favoured by professionals—with a deep paint well and ridged loading area.
12 Smooth, short pile roller suitable for gloss, eggshell, undercoat and primer.
13 Textured roller made of foam for stippled finish with texture paints.
14 Deep pile roller for emulsion and masonry paint on rough surfaces such as textured wallpaper and brickwork.
15 Slim long-handled roller for reaching into awkward areas behind radiators.

Pads

Paint pads have a short fabric pile bonded to a foam backing pad. They give an even paint coverage with gloss or emulsion.
16 Paint tray with roller to load the pad evenly without having to dip it into the paint. This is part of a kit along with pads 17, 18 and 20.
17 Small pad, sometimes called a sash wand, used for window frames.
18 Medium sized pad (70 × 55mm) for smallish areas of wall or woodwork.
19 Special edging pad for internal angles. The two small wheels run against the surface not to be painted.
20 Large pad (160×100mm) for emulsion paint on walls.

ELECTRICAL TOOLS

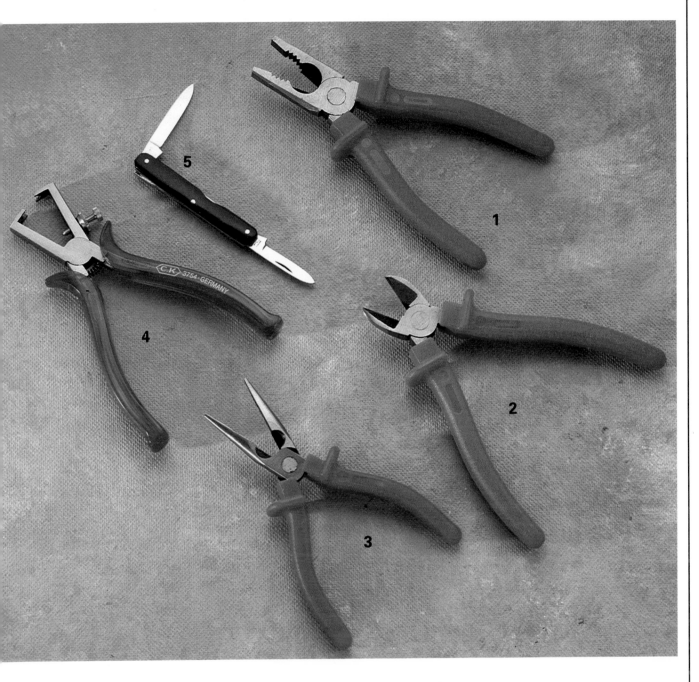

Everyone needs to be able to cope with simple electrical repairs within the home, as well as the occasional emergency. Having the right tools to hand will save you a lot of time and trouble

An electrical toolkit

1 Combination pliers have a square nose and a serrated hole which can be used for holding small nuts and bolts. They also have blades at the centre which can be used to cut through cable. Electricians' pliers have insulated handles which give useful protection in case of an accident, but you should never knowingly work on a live circuit.

2 Wire cutters are useful for cutting through thick cable and flex. Again, the electricians' version has properly insulated handles.

3 Long nose pliers are particularly useful for electrical work. They can be used in confined spaces and the pointed nose helps bend the cores when making connections—the large cores in power cables are virtually impossible to bend with your fingers. They also have a 13

cutting blade, like the combination pliers, and some have a serrated hole as well.

4 Wire stripping pliers are used to cut through the insulation sleeve without damaging the copper core. The brass screw is used to adjust the depth of cut for different thicknesses of flex and cable.

5 A pocket penknife is handy for cutting through the outer sheathing on cable and flex to expose the cores.

6 Wire strippers and cutters are an inexpensive alternative to wire stripping pliers. They are adjustable to suit all core thicknesses and will also cut the wire. The handles on this version also act as spanners to turn small nuts and bolts often found in plugs and electrical appliances.

7 A small hammer is useful for fixing cable clips.

8 A floorboard saw is designed to cut into floorboards without damaging adjoining boards. You'll need this if you're planning a complete rewire.

9 A bolster is used to prise up floorboards without damaging the edges.

10 A handyman's knife is useful for stripping the outer sheathing from cable and flex.

11 Two sizes of electrical screwdrivers should be sufficient for most jobs—a

Above: *Adjustable wire strippers save time and effort*
Left: *If you're planning extensive rewiring you'll need a floorboard saw to cut through floorboards and a bolster to lift them up. Other essential tools are a handyman's knife and electrical screwdrivers*

small one for wiring up plugs and a larger one for switches, sockets and other electrical fittings. Some have neon bulbs in the handles so you can test if a circuit is live before you attempt to work on it.

Most electrical tools are just insulated versions of standard tools you'll find in any toolkit. You can make do with ordinary tools for simple jobs such as fitting a plug, but if you plan more extensive work such as rewiring the house then you'll find the job is quicker and easier—and safer—if you kit up properly before you start.

It's a good idea to put together a special electrical toolkit to deal with emergencies. This should consist of a torch (complete with batteries), a pair of long-nosed pliers, an electrical screwdriver (the type with a neon bulb in the handle and an insulated shaft), a roll of insulation tape, some spare fuses for plugs (3A, 5A and 13A), and rolls of fuse wire (or cartridge fuses, if appropriate) of different ratings suitable for your consumer unit.

MEASURING TOOLS

Most do-it-yourself jobs involve measuring and marking out, and for a professional-looking finish it's essential that you have the right tools. Some are useful extras; others are indispensable

Measuring things so you can cut and shape them to the size you want is one of the most basic do-it-yourself jobs, and one that isn't confined to woodwork. For short measurements you can get by with a straight ruler, but a metre stick or a folding rule will be more useful for bench work. However, most people prefer to use a retractable steel pocket rule, which can contain a tape measuring from 2m to 5m long. The handiest types have a spring-loaded return to draw the

tape back into the holder, and also a tape lock so you can lock the tape out to take and check measurements. Some also allow you to take internal measurements such as inside drawers.

Most of your marking out will be lines at right angles to straight edges, and the tool to use for this is the try square. It can also be used to check squareness along the length of a piece of wood. The mitre square is a variation of this, and has its blade set at 45° to the stock so you

can mark out mitre joints accurately. A combination square combines the features of both try and mitre squares, and its headstock can slide along the rule so that internal angles can be checked as well as external ones. For angles other than 45° or 90°, you need a tool called a sliding bevel. This has a slotted steel blade attached to the stock with a wing nut, so it can be set to any angle with the aid of a protractor. The slot in the blade allows the blade length to be varied.

Below: Marking tools include a mitre box (1), a mitre square (2), a try square (3), a combination type (4), a sliding bevel (5) and a protractor (6)

MEASURING TOOLS

A mitre box is a cutting jig designed to allow you to make 45° cuts in wood and decorative mouldings up to about 50mm wide. The wood to be cut is held in the base of the box on a block of scrap wood and the saw is placed in opposite slots that keep it on line. The scrap wood ensures a clean cut and protects the box itself from damage. Some mitre boxes also contain a pair of slots for making the right-angled cuts.

The other operation for which marking tools are essential is making lines parallel to an existing edge. The marking gauge is the simplest type, and has a stem of wood with a pin set in one end and a stock which slides along the stem and can be locked in position at the required distance from the pin. The cutting gauge is similar, but has a small blade instead of a pin. The mortise gauge is used for marking out mortise and tenon joints, and has two pins. One is set on a slide so you can alter the distance between it and the fixed pin.

Right: *Common measuring tools include the metre rule (1), steel rule (2), tape measure (3), counter rule (4), surveyor's tape (5), straightedge (6) and folding rule (7).*
Below: *Marking tools include the marking gauge (1), cutting gauge (2), mortise gauge (3), compasses (4), dividers (5) and beam compass (6)*

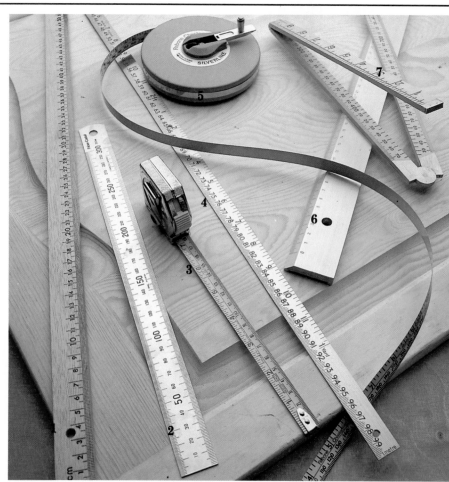

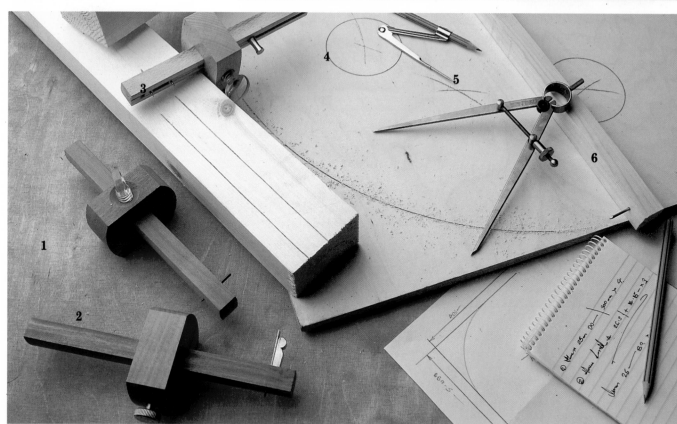

SCREWDRIVERS

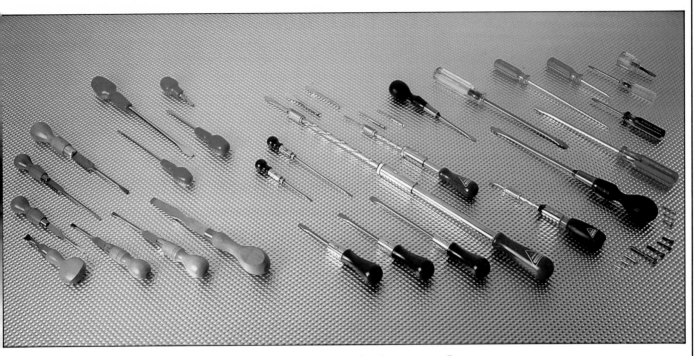

Screws come in an enormous range of sizes and several different types, and each requires the right screwdriver if it is to be driven properly without damage to screw or workpiece.

There's a huge array of screwdrivers designed to cope with all sorts of different jobs. You will need a selection to cope with most everyday jobs, plus a few specialist tools for unusual fixing situations.

Plain screwdrivers have a shaped handle fixed permanently to a steel blade, with a tip shaped to fit a slotted or cross-headed screw. The two commonest traditional handle shapes are the cabinet and the engineer's patterns.

The **cabinet** handle used to be of wood, but plastic has largely replaced it nowadays; it is shaped like a flattened pear to allow a good grip with plenty of torque. The **engineer's** pattern is designed with a cylindrical fluted handle, to allow oily hands a positive grip. Both types are made in a wide range of blade lengths and tip sizes, and you will require several to cope with the most widely used screw sizes. A useful type to have is the **stubby screwdriver**, which has a very short blade and a chunky handle. It's ideal for driving screws in confined spaces.

The drawback with ordinary screwdrivers is that you have to keep altering your grip as you work, and driving lots of screws can give you a blistered palm. With a **ratchet screwdriver** there's no need to release your grip on the handle while driving screws; the ratchet mechanism allows you to drive the screw with a series of twists, returning the handle to the original position ready for the next turn. A **spiral ratchet screwdriver** has a similar mechanism, but

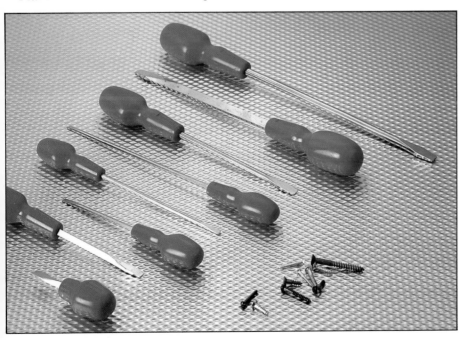

you drive the screws by pumping the handle up and down. Most have interchangeable bits.

For driving cross-head screws you will need special **cross-point screwdrivers**, one for Philips screws and another for Pozidriv and Supadriv screws. Both types are sized according to the dimensions of the recess on the screw head; a No 2 size will cope with the most common screw sizes (gauges 5 to 10). You can also get Philips and Pozidriv heads for ratchet and spiral ratchet screwdrivers.

Amongst specialist screwdrivers, you are likely to need a small, slim one for electrical work (plus possibly one containing a mains tester), and also some hexagonal-shafted Allen keys if you carry out work on domestic appliances and the like. For really stubborn screws, you can always fit a screwdriver bit into an ordinary carpenter's brace; this allows you to exert tremendous torque.

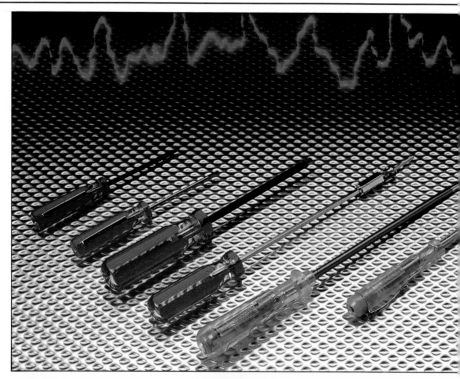

Top right: *Electrician's screwdrivers have insulated handles and blades; some have integral screw-holders. Mains testers include a small neon bulb to indicate live components*

Right: *Cross-head screwdrivers have different tip sizes to match the recesses in screw heads. Ratchet types have interchangeable tips*

Below right: *More exotic models feature such novelties as pistol-grip handles, flexible shafts and interchangeable tips of various types for extra versatility*

Below: *Special-purpose drivers include Allen keys, offset drivers, impact drivers, screwdriver bits for braces and mini-drivers for jewellery and other fine work*

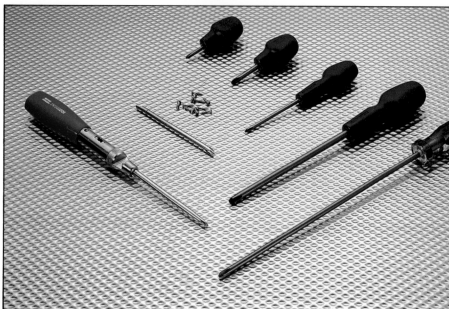

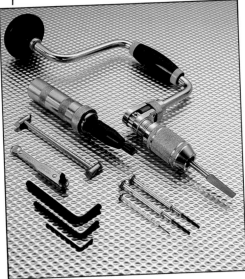

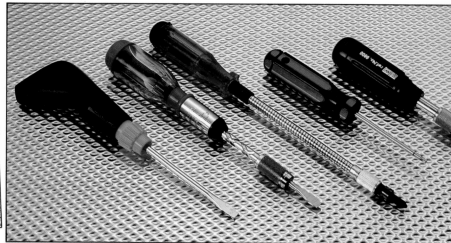

SPANNERS

The right spanner is the key to success with any job where nuts and bolts are involved. There are lots of different types to choose from, and some are more versatile than others.

Below: *The range of spanners available includes socket sets (top right), open-ended ones (bottom right), combination spanners (centre left) and adjustable types (bottom left)*

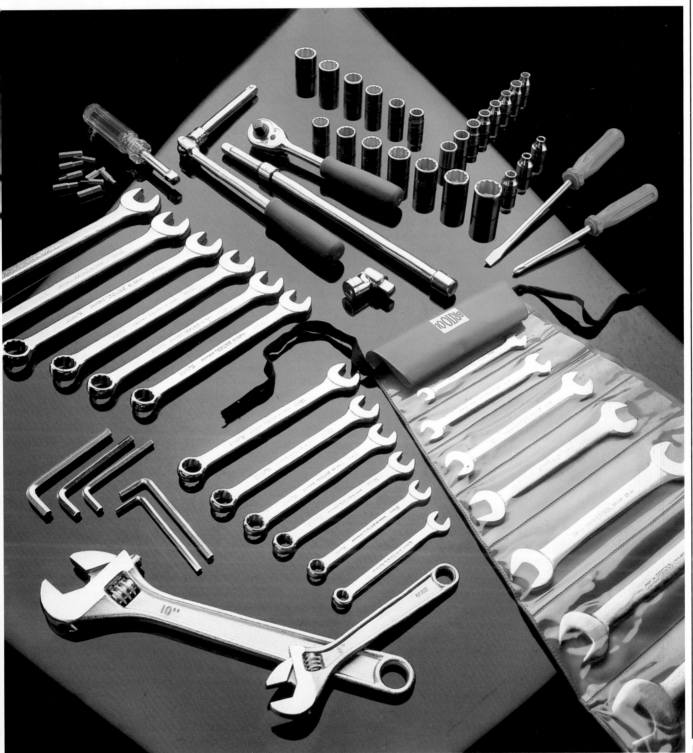

SPANNERS

Open-ended spanners have a flat profile and open jaws at one or both ends. The jaws are set at an angle of about 15° to the handle to make the tool easier to use in confined spaces. They are usually sold in sets, each spanner having a different jaw size at each end.

Ring spanners totally enclose the nut, so they are less likely to slip than open-ended spanners. The inside of the ring is notched to provide a grip on the nut. Most ring spanners have offset heads to help reach inaccessible or recessed nuts. Like open-ended spanners, they come in sets with a different-sized head at each end.

Combination spanners have an offset ring head at one end and open jaws at the other. However, the ring and jaw on each one are the same size, so you don't get the useful dual working capacity.

Adjustable spanners have a movable jaw, and so can be used on bolt heads and nuts of any size within their jaw capacity. There are two main types. The crescent type resembles an open-ended spanner, and has the jaws at an angle of 15°. The other main type—often called a monkey wrench—has the jaws set at 90° to the handle. Both types come in several sizes.

Socket spanners are widely used for car repairs. They come in sets, and are turned with a torque wrench. Box spanners are similar, and are turned with a tommy bar. Even if you don't do any car repairs, a small set of socket or box spanners plus a tommy bar is a

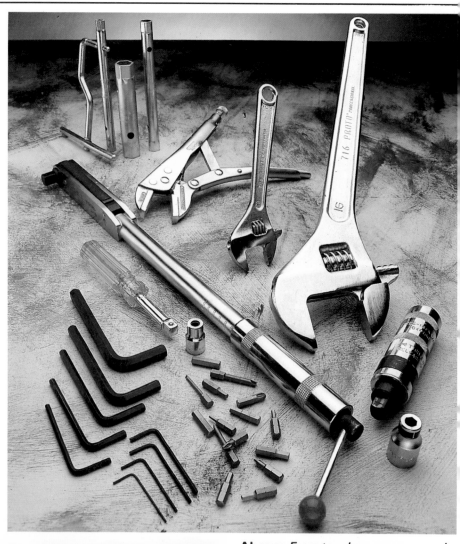

Above: *From top: box spanners and tommy bar, self-grip pliers, crescent adjustable spanner, impact driver for stubborn nuts, torque wrench for sockets, Allen keys (bottom left) for hexagonal socket nuts and bolts*

Left: *A basin or crowsfoot spanner (top) fits taps to basins and baths. An immersion heater spanner (bottom) tightens immersion heaters in place*

useful addition to your tool kit for general-purpose use.

Spanners come in metric and imperial sizes. Metric ones are sized in millimetres according to the across-flats size of the bolt head or nut they will fit. Imperial spanners are more complicated because of the different types of bolt available. UNF and UNC (Unified Fine and Coarse) spanners are sized according to the across-flats measurement of the nut in inches. BA, BSF and BSW spanners are sized according to the thread diameter, again in inches, rather than by head size.

HAMMERS AND MALLETS

Hammers are probably the most widely used tool in the tool box. They're essential for driving nails in woodwork, assembling frameworks, shaping metal and working with masonry, while mallets are useful for all sorts of assembly operations

Below: *Claw hammers may have integral steel handles (top) or traditional hickory ones (second from top). Cross-pein hammers come in several sizes; small, lightweight types (bottom) are known as pin hammers*

Hammers come in a wide range of shapes and sizes, all designed for a particular purpose. Most have a steel head and a separate wooden handle, although steel and glass fibre are becoming more commonplace. Mallets may be of all-wood construction—the traditional carpenter's mallets—or may have striking faces made from materials such as rubber or leather.

Perhaps the commonest and most generally useful hammer is the claw hammer. This has a V-jointed claw opposite the striking face which is used for pulling out nails and pins (and for all sorts of unofficial jobs involving prising and levering). Head weights range from about 450g (16oz) up through 570g (20oz) to 680g (24oz)—heavy enough for all structural carpentry work. Wooden handles can tend to work loose, while steel and glass fibre types are bonded permanently to the hammer head.

Cross-pein hammers, often known as Warrington pattern hammers, have a striking face similar to that of a claw hammer, but instead of a claw there is a cross 'pein' at right angles to the line of the handle which is used to start small pins and nails held between the fingers. This type is used for all joinery work, and has head weights ranging from 170g (6oz) up to around 450g (16oz).

Pin hammers are just lightweight versions of the cross-pein hammer, and are used as their name implies, for driving small fixing pins on delicate work. Head weights are usually around the 100–115g (3½–4oz) mark.

Ball-pein hammers, often known as engineer's hammers, are general-purpose hammers for the metalworker or mechanic rather than the woodworker, although many are used in this way. The flat face is intended for operations such as driving cold chisels and punches, while the rounded ball pein is for jobs such as riveting, bending and shaping metal. Common head weights range from 115 to 680g (4oz up to 3½lbs), although heavier types are available.

The carpenter's mallet is mainly used for two jobs—assembling wooden joints and driving wooden-handled chisels and gouges—where a steel hammer might

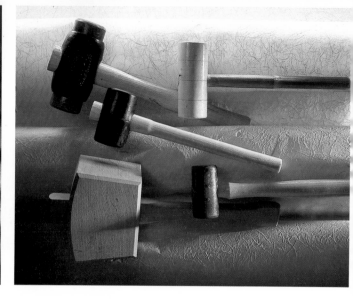

cause damage. It's usually made from beech, and has a square section head between 100 and 150mm (4 to 6in) long.

Soft faced hammers and mallets are most useful for assembly work as an alternative to the carpenter's mallet, and for general shaping work on things like thin sheet metal. Most have interchangeable replaceable heads.

Hammers for masonry work come in three types. The smallest is the club hammer, which is used for jobs like driving cold chisels into masonry and cutting bricks (in conjunction with a brick bolster). It has a square head 100 to 150mm (4 to 6in) long, weighing 2½ to 3 or 4lbs (1.1, 1.4 and 1.8kg), and also has a short wooden handle.

The brick hammer resembles a woodworker's claw hammer in profile, but the 'claw' is solid and is intended for rough cutting and shaping of bricks. Head weights range from 1½ to 4lbs (680g to 1.8kg).

The sledge hammer is really just a large, heavy-duty club hammer, and is used for jobs like breaking up concrete, driving posts into the ground and so on. The shaft is around 750mm (2ft 6in) long, and the square-sectioned head may weigh between 4 and 14lbs (1.8–6.4kg).

Hammers can be dangerous tools, so care and common sense are needed if accidents are to be avoided.

Top: *The most widely used hammers for masonry work are the club hammer (top and bottom), used for driving cold chisels and brick bolsters, and the heavyweight sledge hammer (centre), for breaking up concrete, and driving posts into the ground*
Above left: *Ball pein hammers (centre) are used mainly for metalwork, but make adequate general-purpose hammers. Soft-faced hammers are often used when working with thin sheet metal*
Above: *The wooden carpenter's mallet (bottom) is essential for assembling wood frameworks and driving wood-handled chisels.*

SAWS FOR WOODWORK

You need several different types of saw for woodwork, depending on the type of cut you are making —straight, curved or enclosed. Within each group there are several important variations.

Above: *The flooring saw is designed for cutting floorboards only, while the versatile tenon saw is used for lightweight sawing and joint-cutting jobs. The dovetail saw is a smaller version*

For most jobs a straight cut is normally all that's required, and for this you need either a hand saw or a back saw. There are several kinds of hand saw, but for most general-purpose work a panel saw will prove most useful. This gets its name from its traditional job of cutting up panels for wardrobes, drawer bottoms and the like. It has a thin, flexible blade and will cut chipboard, plywood, hardboard and natural timber. A typical length is around 560mm, and the blade will have around 10 tooth points per

inch (known as 10ppi).

The rip saw is a larger version of the panel saw, and is intended for ripping— cutting wood fast along the grain. It's a little longer than the panel saw, and has a coarser cut—commonly 4 to 6ppi.

Back saws are easily identified by the steel or brass stiffener running along the top of the blade. This has two functions: it keeps the blade rigid along its whole length, and also provides weight and stability when the saw is being used. The most useful back saw is the tenon

saw, which is used to make small accurate cuts both with and across the grain—typically for making the tenon part of a mortise-and-tenon joint. Blade length is between 250 and 300mm, and there are usually 13 to 16ppi.

Smaller versions are also available, known as dovetail saws or gent's saws. These are intended for even finer work and the blades are thinner and shallower, and have 20ppi or more.

There's another saw which superficially resembles the tenon saw, but lacks 23

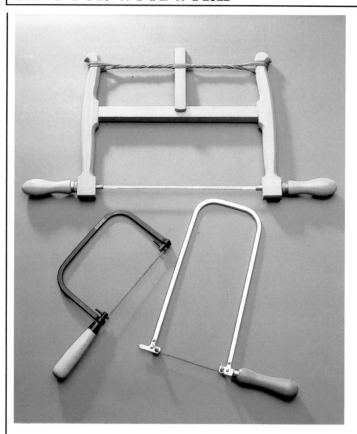

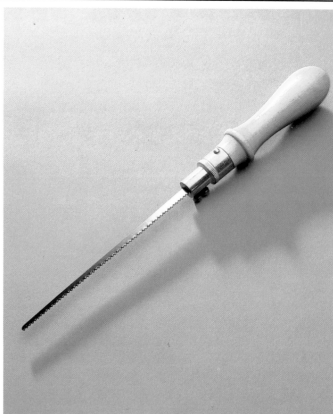

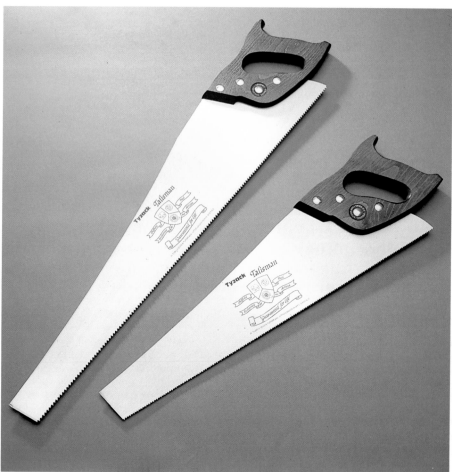

Above: *The frame saws—bow saw, coping saw and fret saw are for cutting curves* **Above right**: *The pad saw, ideal for keyholes and other internal cut-outs* **Right**: *The rip saw and panel saw*

the stiffener. This is the flooring saw, designed to cut across and between floorboards. It has a round nose which allows you to start the cut without damaging adjacent boards.

For cutting curves by hand, you need a frame saw—one with a thin, flexible blade that will follow the curve, fitted in a rigid frame that can be held clear of the work. The most useful is the coping saw, which holds a blade around 200mm long under tension in a C-shaped metal frame with a handle at one end. The blades are designed to be thrown away when blunt. They're usually fitted with the teeth pointing towards the handle, but this can be reversed. Angled pins holding the blade in the frame can be twisted to allow the angle of cut to be varied. The fret saw is similar, but has a shorter, thinner blade and a deeper frame which allows cuts to be made further in from the edge of the work-piece in thin sheet materials.

The pad saw or keyhole saw is used for making cuts in the centre of a work-piece. The blade is fairly thick to keep it rigid. Cuts are best started at holes drilled within for the area to be cut out.

CHISELS AND GOUGES

Left: *Chisels come in many forms. Among the specialist varieties are paring chisels (left), firmer chisels (right) and gouges*

by striking a nail in the wood you're working on. Most chisels are supplied with small plastic blade guards; keep these on whenever you are not using the chisels, to protect the blades from knocks and chips in your tool bag.

Chisels come in a wide range of sizes, ranging from 3mm (⅛in) wide to 50mm (2in). Up to 25mm, sizes go up in 3mm steps; thereafter the usual increment is 6mm (¼in).

Bevel-edge chisels

The most versatile type of general-purpose wood chisel is the bevel-edge chisel, so called because the upper surface of the blade has two bevelled edges. This has a blade strong enough to cope with most joint-cutting work, and the shape of the blade allows it to get into awkward corners and to cut angled joints such as dovetails. For most purposes a maximum of six chisels ranging from 3mm up to 25mm (1in) wide will be quite adequate.

Firmer chisels

Firmer chisels are similar in size to bevel-edge chisels, but have a blade that is rectangular in cross-section. This makes them somewhat stronger than the bevel-edge type, and capable of withstanding heavy blows from a mallet (wood handles) or a hammer (plastic handles) as well as a fair degree of levering. The blade is slightly tapered in width from the handle to the tip, to prevent it from jamming in deep cuts.

Paring chisels

Bevel-edge and firmer chisels are ideal for most joint-cutting jobs. However, because they have relatively short blades (designed for strength) they are less than ideal for jobs such as paring (shaping the curved ends of workpieces, for example) and cutting the long grooves needed when making housing joints. For these tasks you need a special type of chisel known as a paring chisel. This has a much longer blade, often up to 175mm (7in.) long instead of the more usual 100-125mm (4-5in.), enabling you to grasp the blade itself during delicate paring jobs and to reach to the centre of housings from the edge of the wood. Both firmer and bevel-edge patterns are available; the latter are generally more versatile.

Chisels are essential tools for any woodworker who wants to progress beyond the most basic carpentry. Several types are available, each designed for a specific type of job.

Woodworking chisels come in a number of different patterns, but they are all similar in design and action. The working part of the tool is a steel blade, sharpened at one end into a cutting edge; the other end of the blade, known as the tang, is housed in a wood or plastic handle which can be guided by hand or struck with a hammer or mallet. The blade profile varies according to the use for which the tool is designed.

When you buy a chisel, its blade will have been ground during manufacture to

an angle of between 20 and 25° to form a slope called a cannel. To get it ready for use, you have to sharpen (hone) the edge of the cannel to a slightly steeper angle—usually 30 to 35°—on an oilstone. A small wheeled trolley known as a honing guide makes it easier to get this angle correct.

You will have to re-sharpen the blade regularly during use to keep a good cutting edge, but you will need to re-make the grinding bevel only if you seriously damage the edge—for example,

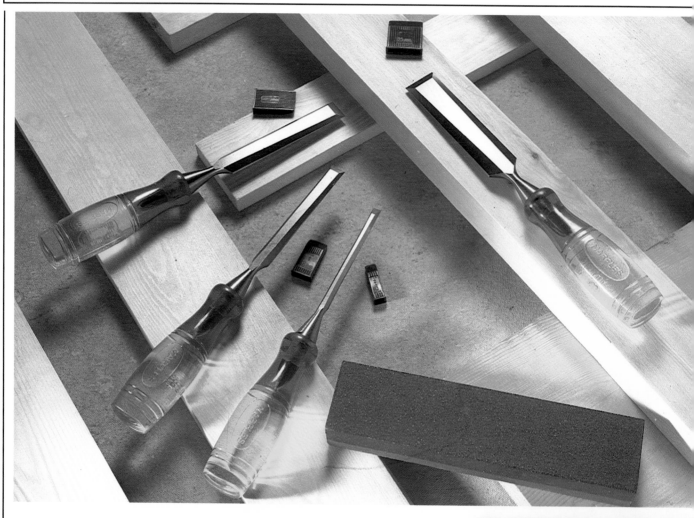

Above: *Bevel-edge chisels are the most versatile type to choose for general-purpose woodworking, because the bevelled blade will undercut awkward corners*

Mortise chisels

Cutting the mortise part of a mortise-and-tenon joint requires a chisel with a very strong blade, both to withstand the chopping action and to lever out the waste wood. An ordinary bevel-edge or firmer chisel may bend or break in these circumstances, but a mortise chisel with its thick, stiff blade is designed to stand up to this treatment. Common blade widths are 6, 9, 12, 15 and 18mm (¼, ⅜, ½, ⅝ and ¾in). Traditional types with wooden handles often have a leather washer between handle and blade to absorb the shock as the chisel is driven into the wood.

Gouges

Gouges are simply chisels with the blade curved across its width, and are invaluable for shaping wood in three dimensions, which an ordinary chisel cannot do—for cutting concave finger pulls in draw handles, for example, or shaping the shoulders of a tenon to meet a mortise in a round leg. The blade is generally of the firmer type (ie, without edge bevels), and may be sharpened on the inside (known as an in-cannel gouge) or on the outside (an out-cannel gouge). Bevel-edge versions of the in-cannel gouge are more commonly known as scribing or paring gouges, and have longer blades than the ordinary fimer type. Blade widths for both types range between 6 and 25mm (¼ to 1in).

Chisels for masonry and metal

There is a wide range of tools for cutting masonry, including bolsters for splitting bricks and chopping off plaster and render, and masonry chisels of various types for jobs like cutting chases in walls and hacking out old pointing in brickwork. Various sizes are available. Cold chisels are intended for cold cutting of metal, and not for masonry work, although they are commonly used for this purpose. Cold chisels have keen edges whereas masonry chisels and brick bolsters have dull edges that don't need sharpening.

Above: *Brick bolsters (top) cut bricks and strip plaster and render. Masonry chisels chop holes and chases in masonry*

WOOD PLANES

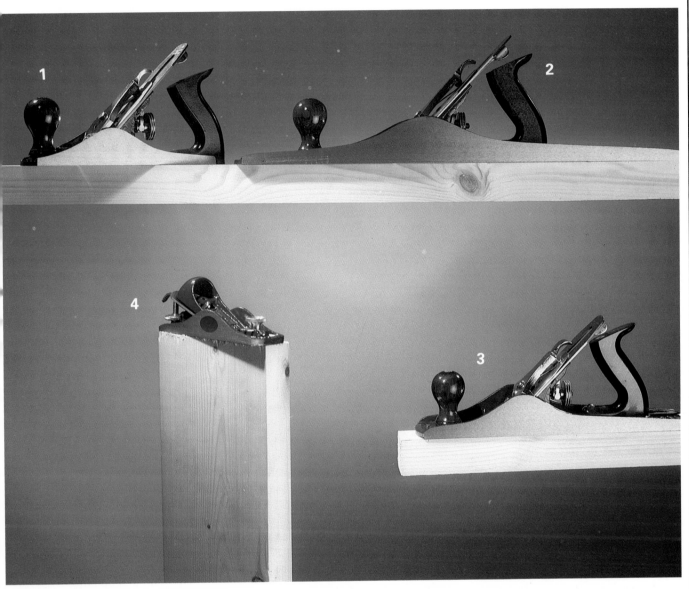

There are more varieties of wood plane than any other woodworking tool, but for general-purpose squaring and smoothing work you need look no further than the bench planes. Surforms handle other shaping jobs.

Bench planes look frighteningly complex at first glance, but really a plane is nothing more than a wide chisel set in an adjustable holder.

The difference between the various bench planes is essentially one of size; the longer the plane, the flatter and truer the edge it will produce. The main part of the plane is the cast iron body with a polished underside (the sole) and a slot through which the blade protrudes. The blade itself is mounted on a wedge-shaped component called the frog, which carries the mechanisms you use to adjust the cutting depth, and is held in place by the cap iron and lever cap. At the rear of the frog is a nut which you turn to move the blade up and down; this controls the thickness of shaving the plane produces. The lever above it allows you to adjust the blade so it's parallel with the sole plate. Adjustment screws move the whole frog backwards and forwards and alter the slot size.

1 The smoothing plane *is the smallest bench plane—usually between 235 and 260mm long, and with a blade 45, 51 or 60mm wide. It's used on all sorts of small-scale finishing jobs.*
2 The jointer plane *is the longest type, measuring about 560mm long with a 60mm blade. Its main use is for truing up long edges.*
3 The jack plane *is about 360mm long with a 51 or 60mm blade, and is used for reducing timber to size, squaring up and smoothing—a jack-of-all-trades plane, and the one to buy first of all.*
4 The block plane *is about 175mm long, with a 40mm wide blade, and is used mainly for planing end grain.*

27

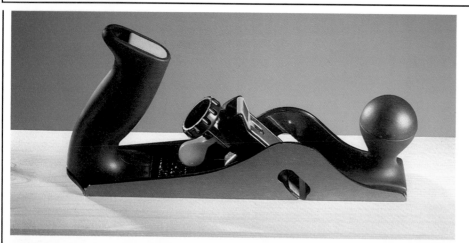

Replaceable blade planes *(left)* are similar in design to conventional bench planes, but the full-length blade is replaced by a holder into which small, pre-sharpened cutting blades are clamped. When the blade ceases to cut cleanly, it is simply replaced by a new one; re-sharpening on an oilstone is a thing of the past. A snap-in holder within the hollow rear handle holds a supply of spare blades.

  Another advantage of the replaceable blade plane is that the blade runs the full width of the sole, allowing rebates to be planed when the side fence is fitted.

Surforms are a cross between a plane and a rasp, and are used for a wide range of shaping jobs. The blade is made from sheet steel, punched with a regular pattern of protruding teeth which work rather like a cheese grater to remove wood as the tool is passed over the surface. When it no longer cuts efficiently, a new blade is fitted in its place. The Surform range includes block and bench plane equivalents, plus flat and round rasps that are ideal for intricate shaping once the larger tools have been used to create the basic outline of the workpiece.

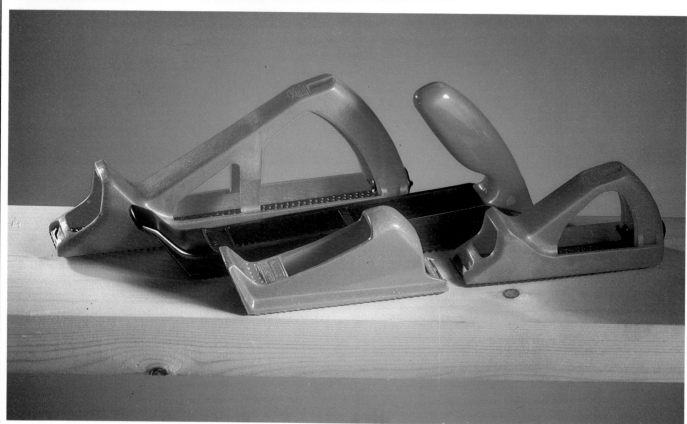

ELECTRIC DRILLS

The modern electric drill, once thought of as a luxury, is now an essential part of any toolkit. However, with so many models to choose from, picking the right one can be tricky.

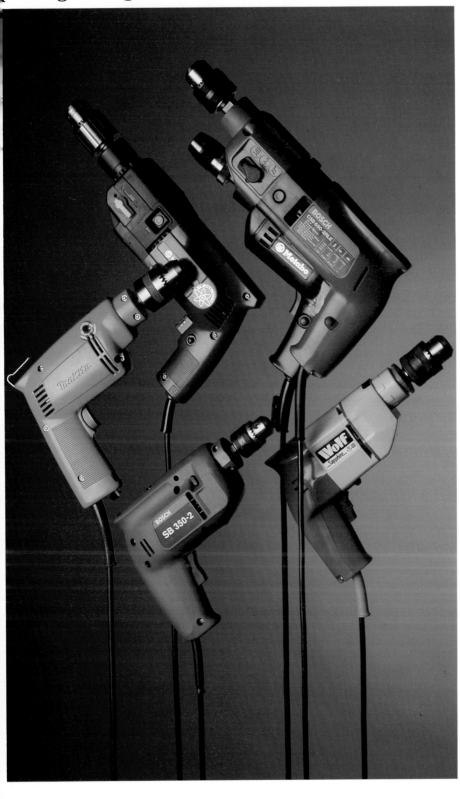

One of the most important factors to take into account when choosing a new drill is its power. Manufacturers usually quote the rated input power of their drills, but this is not a good guide to the amount of usable power you will get out of it. Usable output power is typically about 60 per cent of the rated input power, although expensive tools usually have better input/output ratios than cheaper ones.

Choose a model with a high input rating (over 600 watts) if you plan to do a lot of heavy drilling in concrete, or if you want to run a big saw attachment. One with a low input rating (around 250 watts) will cope with light work in wood and soft masonry. One with a rating of between 350 and 400 watts will handle most jobs, plus the occasional burst of hard work.

Speed control improves the drill's versatility, by allowing you to select low speeds for drilling things like metal or ceramic tiles, and high speeds for wood. Mechanical gearboxes allow the drill to deliver more torque than ones with electronic speed control.

Some drills offer reverse as well as forward speeds, which is useful if use your drill as a power screwdriver on repetitive work.

Hammer action is essential if you want to drill easily through concrete

Left: *There is an enormous range of electric drills available nowadays, from inexpensive single-speed models to semi-professional types*

Above: *Cordless drills are becoming increasingly popular, and are ideal for jobs remote from a power source*

and stone. The drill has an extra mechanism which vibrates the chuck backwards and forwards as well as rotating it, to help break up the material being drilled. Special drill bits must be used with hammer action.

Most do-it-yourself drills have a 10mm or 13mm chuck, which restricts the maximum diameter of hole which can be drilled in various materials. Drills with a 13mm chuck will cope with most normal diy drilling requirements.

There are several other points to watch out for when buying a new drill. The first is comfort; check that the drill sits comfortably in your hands, and that its weight is well distributed; it can be very tiring using an uncomfortable or heavy drill for long periods. Next, check what length of flex is provided. Short flexes are a nuisance, because you have to use an extension lead unless you are working close to a power point. Finally, if you want so use attachments with your drill, check that the ones you require can be fitted to the drill you choose.

Right: *The size of the drill chuck determines the maximum size of hole the drill can be expected to make in different materials*

Below: *Most drills can be used with a wide range of attachments. Check which are compatible before you buy*

Right: *Some drills are designed for one-handed operation (top), others have an extra front handle*

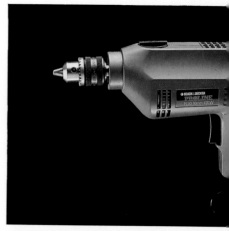

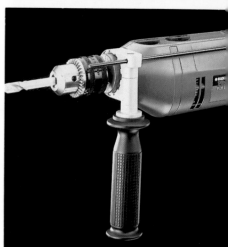

DRILL BITS

Drilling holes in things is the mainstay of every do-it-yourselfer's workload, and to get good results you need to have a selection of the right drill bits for every job in your toolkit.

By far the biggest range of drill bits available is for drilling holes in wood. **Twist drills** are the commonest and most widely used, for drilling small holes in wood up to about 13mm in diameter. Most are now produced in metric sizes, but imperial sizes are still available. Twist drills are made from either high-speed steel (HSS), which is tough but fairly expensive, or carbon steel which is cheaper but doesn't wear so well.

Wood bits are similar in appearance to twist drills, but have a central point which helps to locate the bit more accurately when starting drilling. They are available in larger diameters—up to 20mm; larger sizes have reduced shanks to fit standard 13mm drill chucks. Both twist drills and wood bits can be used in power or hand drills.

Auger bits have a deep-cut spiral shaft with a wide cutting edge and a tapered point for accurate positioning, and are used to drill large, deep holes accurately in sizes up to about 35mm across. They're used with a carpenter's brace.

Flat bits, sometimes called spade bits, have a different shape to other bits. Instead of a round spiralled shank, there is a single spade-like cutter which can be up to about 35mm across. They're designed for use only with power drills.

Expansive bits resemble spade bits, but have a movable outer cutter and can make holes up to around 75mm in diameter. They're designed for use in hand drills and braces, and are expensive.

Hole saws offer a cheaper way of cutting large holes in wood up to about 30mm thick. They consist of an arbor containing a twist drill and carrying a circular blade; the drill locates the hole centre and then draws the blade down into the wood. Various sizes are available, up to a maximum diameter of 150mm; nests of saws include several interchangeable blade sizes.

Countersink bits are used to form a neat conical recess in the wood surface, so allowing a countersunk screw head

Below: *Drill bits for wood include twist drills (top left), auger bits, flat spade bits (bottom left), expansive bits and hole saws*

Below: *Countersink bits cut countersinks, while screw sinks form pilot and clearance holes too.* **Bottom:** *A drill stand means accurate 90° holes*

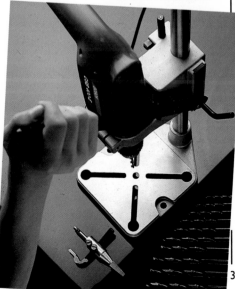

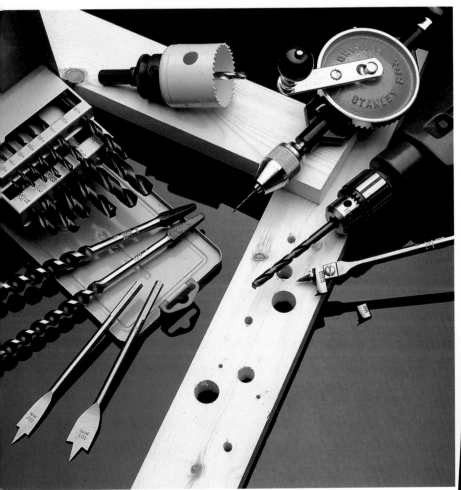

DRILL BITS

Right: *Use an ordinary masonry drill for making holes in ceramic tiles, and a special spear-point drill (right) for drilling glass and mirrors*

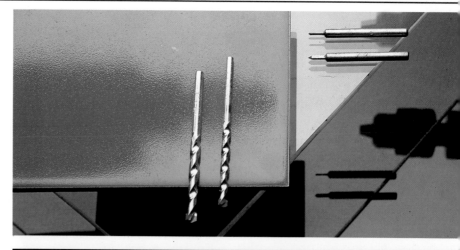

to lie flush. **Screw sinks** are a combined miniature flat bit and countersink bit, designed to drill pilot, clearance and countersink holes in one operation.

You can use high-speed steel twist drills for drilling metal too, and a hole saw with a special blade can cut holes in thin metal sheet. Alternatively, a **tank cutter** with its adjustable cutting blade can be used instead, fitted to a brace.

For drilling masonry, you need special **masonry drills** which have tungsten carbide cutting tips brazed onto the end of the drill shaft. Masonry drills may be sized in millimetres, or according to the gauge number of the screw that will fit the hole. Most are a standard length, but extra-long types are available for drilling holes right through walls to take things like pipes or electric cables. Special high-impact types are required for use with power drills featuring hammer action. **Core drills** are used for making larger holes than an ordinary masonry drill can manage.

Lastly, for drilling glass and mirrors you need a special **spear-point drill**, used with plenty of lubrication.

Right: *Tungsten carbide-tipped masonry drills are the basic tool for making holes in brick, blockwork and concrete. An impact tool with interchangeable bits can be used with a hammer instead on particularly stubborn materials*

Below: *Your tool kit should contain a basic selection of twist drills, flat (spade) bits and masonry drills*

CRAMPING TOOLS

If you have ever wished you had three hands, you will know how important the right type of clamp can be for holding your workpiece securely. There is a wide range available

It's next to impossible to saw or drill through a piece of wood that is skating around on your work surface, and if you don't hold a frame together while the adhesive dries the joints will be weak. For all these jobs, holding the work securely is almost as important to success as your skill in working on it.

Although there are dozens of different types of holding and cramping tools, all of them are designed for cramping two things together—either a workpiece to your bench, or two workpieces to each other. The commonest type is the G-clamp, which is available in a wide range of sizes or jaw capacities—commonly from 10mm to 200mm. You need a range of sizes for general woodworking use; the larger clamps can obviously cope with bigger workpieces, but are too heavy for use on delicate work.

Another useful type is the sliding screw clamp, a variation on the G-clamp which is often quicker and easier to position. There are also several patented proprietary variations on the basic clamp theme, combining instant setting and release with an ingenious pincer action and interchangeable jaw facings.

Special clamps are available for jobs like holding edging strips to shelves and table tops (edge clamps) and for making mitred assemblies such as picture frames. The latter sometimes incorporate saw guides, allowing you to cut and assemble the joint using the clamp as a jig.

For cramping large frame and panel assemblies during construction, you need sash clamps. As their name implies, these were originally used for cramping up window sashes and the like. They consist of a long bar with a series of holes in it and a fixed head at one end. A second head slides along the bar and can be locked to any one of the holes. The clamp can then be adjusted for span by screwing the fixed head in or out, as with a G-clamp. An alternative approach is to buy just the sash heads, and to use these with a wooden bar.

You can, of course, use many of these clamps to hold workpieces securely on your workbench as well as to clamp two

Below left: *G-clamps come in a wide range of sizes. Also shown are three self-grip clamps (right), two red and black sliding screw clamps and a small edging clamp (top)*

Below: *Sash clamps have one fixed and one sliding head on a metal bar. Clamp heads fit on a timber bar*

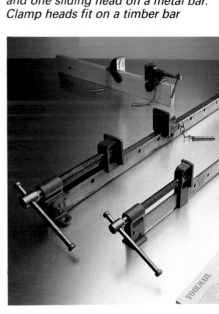

CRAMPING TOOLS

workpieces together. However, there are several other cramping tools designed solely to hold workpieces steady. The simplest is the bench hook, which allows you to steady the workpiece with firm hand pressure while sawing it. A holdfast is a bar with a clamp head at one end, designed to be dropped into a hole in your bench surface and tightened down onto the work. Then there is a wide range of bench vices, some designed for woodwork and others for metalwork; all can be attached to the bench temporarily or permanently.

For assembling things like chair frames, a webbing clamp is invaluable. This is a tough belt which is passed round the frame to be clamped, and is held tight by passing the ends of the belt through a screw-up tensioner. A small-scale version of this, consisting of four plastic corner blocks and a length of nylon string, is a useful alternative to the mitre clamp when assembling small picture frames.

Finally, one of the most useful cramping devices available is in fact the portable workbench, of which the Workmate is the best-known example. This not only functions as a work bench (with variable height on some models); it can also be used as a giant clamp for holding things vertically between the fixed and movable halves of the bench surface (allowing you to plane the edge of a door, for example) and horizontally (with the aid of bench dogs, for cramping large frames).

Above right: *Bench aids include the bench hook (top centre), the holdfast (left centre) and various vices*
Below: *String, corner and mitre clamps for mitred frameworks*
Right: *Portable workbenches can clamp large objects with ease*

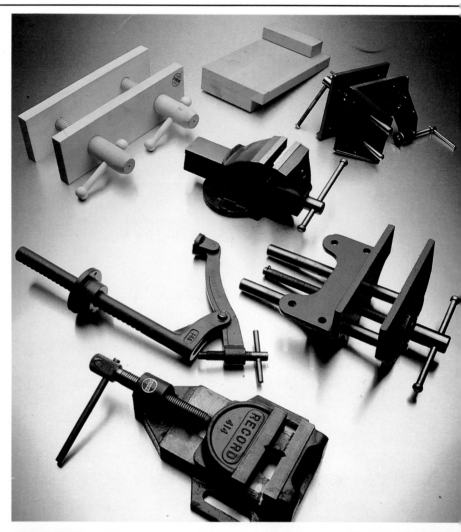

LADDERS & STEPS

It's almost impossible to carry out any but the most basic do-it-yourself jobs without some access equipment. At the very least you'll need steps for indoor work and an extending ladder for outside — or a combination ladder to do both jobs.

Stepladders are perhaps the most useful general-purpose pieces of access equipment in the home. Apart from being used for indoor jobs, you can also reach to about halfway up outside walls — helpful for many maintenance, repair and decorating jobs. The best type are made from light-weight aluminium, which needs no maintenance. They come in a wide range of sizes from a simple two-step hop-up to versions with seven or more treads and a top safety rail which is ideal for jobs like painting ceilings and cleaning windows.

Right: *Stepladders come in a wide range of sizes. Combination types can be converted into a short ladder*

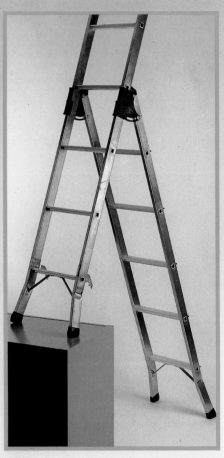

Extension ladders consist of two or three ladder sections which slide over one another — usually operated by hand, but occasionally by rope and pulley on larger ladders. The upper section(s) have two hooks attached to the stiles which hook over the rungs of the section beneath when the ladder is extended. There are also guides at the top of the lower sections through which the upper sections slide; these ensure that the sections cannot separate in use.

When choosing a ladder, pick a size which will reach the highest point of your house comfortably with a minimum of three rungs overlap between sections. Consider storage space for the ladder — you may need to go for a triple rather than a double if this is limited.

Most extension ladders are made from aluminium nowadays; this has the same advantages as for stepladders, of lightness combined with strength and freedom from maintenance. Timber ladders are still available, but they do need careful looking after to keep them in good condition. The one advantage is stiffness; aluminium ladders flex in use.

Combination ladders are cunningly-hinged stepladders which can be used as steps, with the two halves fixed in the standard A-frame configuration, or as ladders with the two halves brought into line and locked together. They can also be used with the halves set to unequal lengths, enabling them to be set up on stairs and other uneven surfaces.

Above: *Combination ladders can be adjusted to stand on stairs or uneven surfaces — ideal if you are decorating a stairwell*
Below: *The locking device on a combination ladder can hold the two halves in line with each other*

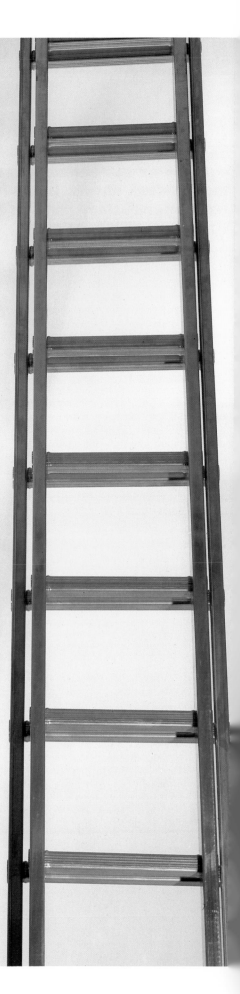

Right: *Extension ladders have two or three sections which slide over each other. The sections have guides so they cannot separate*
Above: *Hooks on the sliding sections clip onto the sections beneath and hold the ladder rigid*

SCREWS AND NAILS

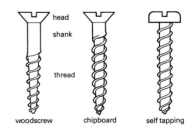

Above: *Screws come with three basic threads—ordinary woodworking, chipboard and self-tapping (for metal)*

Above: *Cross-headed screws may have recesses in one of three patterns— Phillips, Pozidriv or Supadriv*

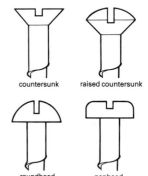

Above: *The commonest head profiles for ordinary slotted-head screws are countersunk, raised countersunk, round head and pan head*

Below: *Some common screw finishes: from left—stainless steel, dark bronze, plain steel, chrome plated, zinc plated, brass and black japanned*

Screws and nails are by far the most widely used fixing devices. There is a huge range of types and sizes, in several styles and materials; make sure you use the right one for the job.

Screws give a stronger fixing than nails, can be removed if you need to dismantle the join and, if you drill a pilot hole first, they are less likely to split the wood.

At one time the basic woodworking screw was the steel countersunk screw with a slotted head, but now alternatives are becoming increasingly common. New varieties of cross-head screw such as Pozidriv and Supadriv offer easier driving with less risk of the screwdriver slipping out; in particular they are easier to drive in awkward corners since the screw can be offered up to the hole on the end of the screwdriver blade.

Modern screw threads are designed to make driving easier and to give better grip. Chipboard screws have finer flanges and a shallower taper, and are threaded right up to the head to grip the material more securely than ordinary screws, which tend to pull out. Supafast screws have a steeper-than-usual pitch so you need fewer turns to drive them, and a twin double-helix thread to give improved grip in the wood. Their thinner shanks also help prevent the wood splitting.

When you are buying screws, you need to specify the screw **length** in mm, the **gauge** (its thickness—the higher the number the bigger the screw), the **head pattern** and **slot type**, the **thread pattern**, and the **material** or **finish**. Buy small quantities in pre-packs (or loose, if available), larger quantities in boxes of 50, 100 or 500 as required.

SCREWS AND NAILS

Nails are quicker to use than screws and also a lot cheaper. For general work the most widely used are the round and oval wire nails; the latter are preferred because their oval shank doesn't split the wood if its long axis is aligned with the grain direction. Both are available in 'lost head' versions which can be punched beneath the wood surface and concealed with stopper. For finer work, smaller wire nails called panel pins are used instead, and there is a special version designed for fixing hardboard to floors and timber frameworks. Cut floor nails are used to secure floorboards to the joists beneath, and are so-called because they are stamped out of sheet metal instead of being drawn as wire.

In addition to nails primarily for woodwork, there are also several nails used in other jobs and materials. The masonry nail is used to fix battens and the like to walls, while the plasterboard nail fixes plasterboard to wall and ceiling surfaces. Clout nails secure roofing felt to the roof decking, while tacks and upholstery nails fix carpet and fabric respectively. Annular nails have ringed shanks which grip the wood more securely than ordinary nails and are used where the fixing will be under stress. Lastly, cut sprigs are used to secure glass in window frames prior to the facing putty being applied, while staples

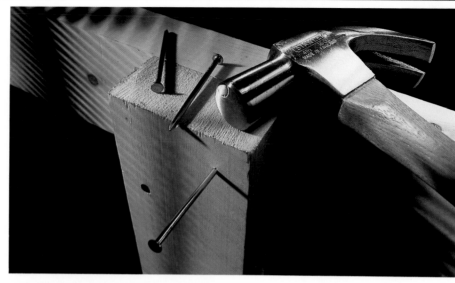

Above: *Round wire nails are generally used for rough carpentry work where their large heads can be on show*

are used for jobs like fixing netting and support wires in the garden.

When you are buying nails, you need to specify the nail **type**, its **length** in mm, and its **finish**—galvanized, coppercoated etc—if you want something other than plain steel. Nails are sold in pre-packs for small quantities, or by weight for larger quantities.

Below: *The only cut nail still in widespread use is the cut floor brad, used for fixing floorboards*

Right: *Some of the more common nail types. There's a wide range of sizes and finishes available for each*

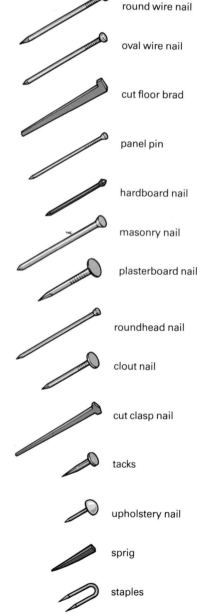

round wire nail

oval wire nail

cut floor brad

panel pin

hardboard nail

masonry nail

plasterboard nail

roundhead nail

clout nail

cut clasp nail

tacks

upholstery nail

sprig

staples

BRICKS AND BLOCKS

Alan Marsh

Left: *Bricks come in many different shapes and colours, the majority being made from fire-burnt clay. There are three categories: Facing bricks (for an attractive finish), 'Commons' (for general work) and engineering bricks*

You may think that bricks and blocks need no further definition, but although they typically conform to standard shapes and sizes, there's a bewildering selection that can make choosing a headache.

Whether you're constructing a new extension to your home, building a garden wall, or simply patching an area of damaged masonry, its important to choose the correct materials for the job. Don't assume that all bricks and blocks are alike, however; although they may conform to a set of standard formats, there's a vast array of different grades and qualities for use in all kinds of situations and conditions, indoors and outdoors—plus a huge selection of colours and textures.

Brick types
Nowadays bricks are made from fire-burnt clay, in a process which invests them with their strength and durability. Although you can still obtain hand-made bricks, most types are now machine-made.

Clay isn't the only material used in brickmaking: concrete and calcium sili-

cate types are also available.

Calcium silicate bricks (often called sand limes) are made by a reaction of a mixture of lime and silica sand with steam under pressure. They resemble clay bricks but tend to be smoother in appearance and have more uniform and unusual colours than clay types.

Bricks may be solid or perforated but even solid bricks often contain a depression (the frog) on one face or a few holes or perforations. Bricks classified as solid have perforations no more than 25 per cent of their total volume.

Most bricks are the same size, but you may find a few variations in some areas. The only real exception is with some hand-made bricks which, because of the way they are made, can never be strictly of a standard size.

The standard size is $225 \times 112.5 \times 65$mm (virtually the same as the old Imperial size of $9 \times 4\frac{1}{2} \times 3$in). This is

known as the format size and includes a 10mm allowance for the mortar joints. Actual sizes are 10mm smaller.

There are hundreds of names used to describe different types of bricks, but for most practical purposes they fall into three varieties.

Facing bricks are specially made to be used where appearance is important. They can be rough, smooth, hard or soft and come in a vast range of colours; facing bricks look good whichever way you look at them. There are also 'faced' bricks, with one or two sides that are presentable.

Common bricks are cheaper and without a deliberate attractive face, although some can be quite attractive and suitable as facings. They're typically used where appearance doesn't matter (say below ground level or the inner leaf of a cavity wall, which is to be plastered).

Engineering bricks are strong, dense and water resistant, making them more suitable for heavy construction work. For most domestic building jobs you won't need them, unless you're working on the house foundations or below DPC level. They come in two classes—A and B—which describe their strength and water resistance. A version, semi-engineering bricks, can also be used as facing bricks.

Brickwork is durable and generally requires little maintenance. However, all clay bricks, whether common, facing or engineering are specially graded.

● **Interior quality bricks** are only suitable for internal use.
● **Ordinary quality bricks** are suitable for general use but should be protected if used in exposed positions.
● **Special quality bricks** are durable even when used in severely exposed sites where the masonry could become saturated and frozen in winter.

Common and facing bricks come in all three qualities but because engineering bricks have to be frost-resistant, they are all special quality.

Calcium silicate bricks are classified in a different way to clay bricks, in six grades, the strongest being class seven, the weakest class two. Class two is for general walling above the DPC; class

Below: *Blocks are sold in a variety of sizes. Thick blocks are often used for cavity walls; thinner blocks for simple partition walls*

Above: *Blocks are used where appearances are not important. Types include solid dense and hollow dense, and facing blocks*

three for work below it.

The many names of bricks denote their colour and texture (frequently their place of origin). The term **Stocks** generally refers to the area: typically used as facings or commons, the colour relates to that of the local clay—Kentish stocks are usually yellow, Dorking stocks come in various shades of pink, and so on.

Flettons are named after the village in Cambridgeshire where they originated; Staffordshire blues and Leicester reds are both examples of where the brick comes from as well as its colour.

Block types

Concrete blocks are best used where appearance isn't important, or where the finish of the wall will be sand and cement rendering or plaster. They're basically large versions of bricks, typically cast from concrete. They're cheaper than bricks and, because they are larger, you save building time when using them. Made in sizes relating to whole numbers of brick sizes, they will bond with one another and can be used in conjunction with ordinary brickwork.

They're 150mm to 225mm high (two or three brick courses), 450mm, 600mm or 620mm long, and come in thicknesses ranging from 50mm to 305mm. The best size is 450mm × 225mm, as this is two bricks long and three courses high. The thickness you use depends on whether the wall is a simple partition (when a 50mm block will do) or whether it's the inner leaf of a cavity wall, (where you'd need a 100mm block).

You can buy Common or Facing blocks: walls built from commons should be rendered but those built with facing blocks don't need a surface finish. Common blocks include lightweight aggregate, aerated and dense concrete.

Lightweight aggregate blocks are easy to handle and the best choice for most jobs. You can nail, screw, and cut them and they are suitable for most walls. You can get loadbearing and non-loadbearing types.

Aerated blocks, more costly, are just as easy to work with and they have superior insulation qualities. They are not suitable in exposed positions but are fine for partition walls.

Dense concrete blocks are much heavier and don't really have any practical advantages over the other types, except if they are used below DPC level.

Facing blocks are used where you don't want to have to render or plaster the wall. They have a surface which resembles natural stone—essentially, they are large blocks which have been cast with crushed stone aggregate.

PAPERHANGING TOOLS

If you want to hang wallcoverings of any type successfully, it's worth investing in the proper tools for each stage of the job—they not only make life easier but the results are inevitably neater

The first step in paperhanging is to ensure that each length is hung to a true vertical; it's no good using the room corners as a guide. The first length on each wall should be hung to a line marked with a plumb bob—a shaped weight attached to a length of string.

Once you've cut the first drop to the length you need, you can apply the paste. For this you need a folding pasting table,

Above: *A folding paperhanging table makes pasting and handling easy. Powder paste can be mixed up in any clean bucket, and is applied to the back of each length with a pasting brush or a large, clean paint brush. For smoothing the length onto the wall, a paperhanger's brush is used for most types; a sponge is better on washables and vinyls.*
Top right: *A plumb bob and straight-edge are used to give a true vertical guide line on the wall*

PAPERHANGING TOOLS

a bucket in which to mix and store the paste, and a pasting brush to apply it. Most wallcoverings except washables and vinyls should be smoothed in place on the wall with a paperhanger's brush. This has a wide wooden handle and long, thick bristles which gently press the paper into angles and round obstacles without stretching or tearing it. With washables and vinyls, a sponge can be used instead.

Trimming is best done with a pair of paperhanger's shears; the long blades make straight cuts easier to achieve. On some papers a proprietary wallpaper trimmer or a sharp handyman's knife plus a straight-edge can be used instead.

A seam roller is a useful accessory for hanging smooth wallcoverings; it helps to ensure that butt-jointed seams are firmly stuck to the wall.

For removing old wallpaper, a stiff flat-bladed scraper is the best tool to use, in conjunction with a hired steam stripping machine on painted or washable surfaces.

Right: *A seam roller, plus two stiff-bladed wallpaper scrapers*
Below: *Paperhanger's shears, an edge trimmer and a sharp knife*

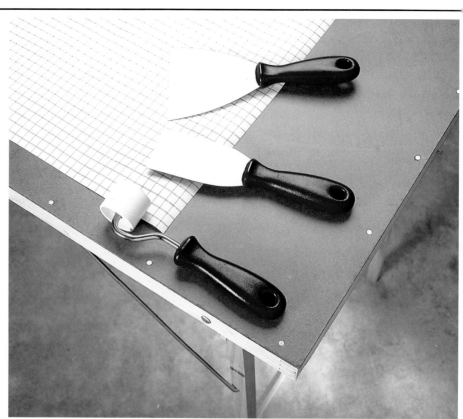

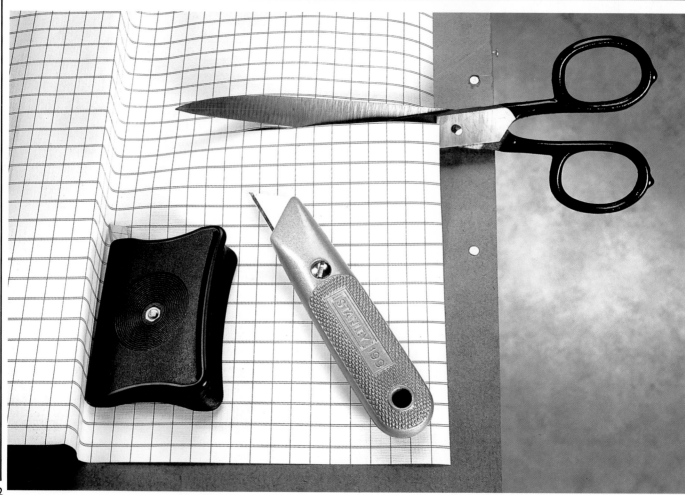

PLASTERING TOOLS

Plastering is a skill which many do-it-yourselfers regard with some awe, yet it is not difficult to master so long as you have the right tools.

Plastering, rendering and floor screeding are jobs with a common theme; the aim is to spread a layer of of material—plaster, mortar or self-smoothing compound—onto a wall, floor or ceiling surface to give it a hard, smooth finish ready for final decoration. The tools and equipment you need for this vary slightly according to the material being used, but fall into three broad groups:

Below: *Plastering tools include a spot board (A), hawk (B), laying-on trowel (C), skimming float (D), and angle trowels (E and F). The flooring trowel (G) is used for applying floor screeds. The mastic trowel (H), pointing trowel (I and K), gauging trowel (J) and spatula (L) are useful for small-scale repairs, and the bricklaying trowel (M) for mixing*

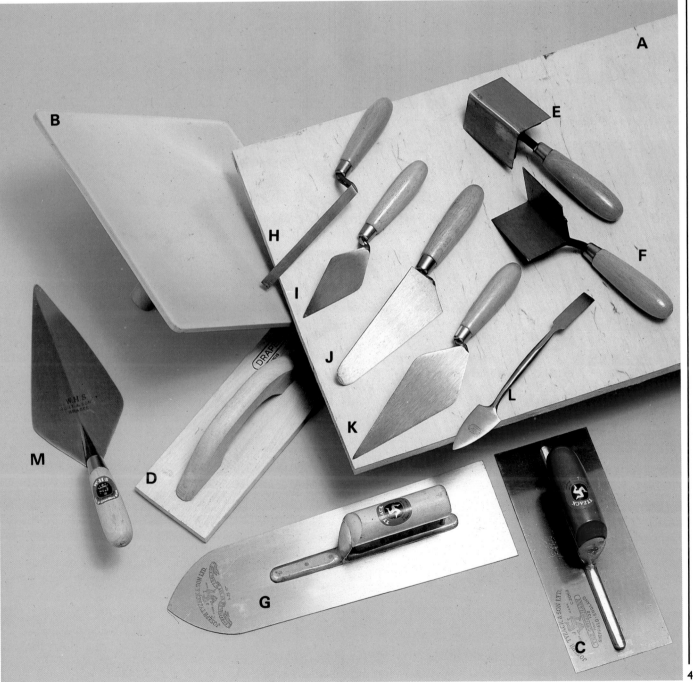

PLASTERING TOOLS

Right: *Plastering tools you can make yourself from timber offcuts include a square for ruling off rebates (top left), a scratching comb for keying surfaces (centre) and a hawk (bottom)*

something to hold the material being applied, a tool to spread it on the surface and a tool for finishing it off.

Once the material concerned has been mixed, it needs to be placed close to the work site, on what is known as a **spot board**—a piece of exterior-grade ply-wood is ideal. For plastering and rendering work, small quantities of plaster or mortar are then taken up on a **hawk** for transfer to the actual surface. Hawks can be bought (in metal or moulded plastic) or made from wood offcuts, and are about 300mm square.

The actual application of the material to the surface is carried out with a metal trowel—a **laying-on trowel** or plasterer's trowel for plaster and render, and a **flooring trowel** for floor screeds and self-smoothing compounds.

The surfaces of render coats are smoothed with a wooden **skimming float**, which can be converted to a devilling float (for keying the surface ready to receive the next coat) by driving some pins through it. Plaster coats are finished and polished with the plasterer's trowel.

Plastered corners can then be finished off neatly by using a special **angle trowel**; both internal and external types are available.

In addition to the tools mentioned, you can make a scratching comb (as an alternative to the devilling float for keying surfaces), and a simple square for ruling off plastered rebates, using softwood offcuts and nails.

Life gets much simpler if you are using one of the modern ready-mixed plasters. All you need to apply these successfully is a paintbrush for putting the mix on the wall and a plastic spreader (supplied with the mix) for smoothing it out. They stay workable for several hours.

Left: *If you are using a ready-mixed plastering system, the only tools you need are a brush to apply the material and a flexible spreader to smooth it out and fill any hollows*

PROTECTIVE CLOTHING

Lots of do-it-yourself jobs are dirty, messy and even potentially dangerous. If you value your health and want to avoid injury, it will pay you to invest in some simple protective clothing

Protective clothing of various types is an essential part of any do-it-yourselfer's tool kit. Sometimes it is worn as much for comfort as anything else, but generally it is chosen to provide specific protection against the hazards of the job in hand.

Overalls of some sort are a sensible choice when carrying out a wide range of dirty, dusty or otherwise messy jobs. They not only protect your clothes; they can also keep you warm and dry if you're working out of doors, and can provide useful carrying capacity for tools and materials as well. When choosing, make sure they are not so tight as to restrict your movements, nor so loose as to catch in moving machinery and the like.

Headgear is not just a matter of fashion when you're doing things like demolition work, or are working in confined spaces. In the first case, you need a hard hat to guard against the risk of things falling on your head. Look for one that's marked 'Made to BS5240' and carries the Kitemark. For low-level protection—against banging your head on scaffolding or rafters in the loft, for example—buy a padded bump cap instead.

Face masks help to prevent you breathing in clouds of dust when you're sanding floors, using angle grinders to cut roof tiles and similar jobs. They consist of a bendy metal plate which holds a disposable cotton filter over your nose and mouth.

Gloves are essential when handling coarse building materials such as bricks, paving slabs and roofing tiles, or sharp things like broken glass. Leather palms with cloth or plastic backs are best for jobs like this. If you want protection against chemicals, buy PVC or synthetic rubber types (ordinary household rubber gloves are no substitute).

Eye protection is vital for jobs involving the use of potentially dangerous liquids such as paint stripper and some other products such as wood preservatives and insecticides, especially if they are being applied near to or above eye

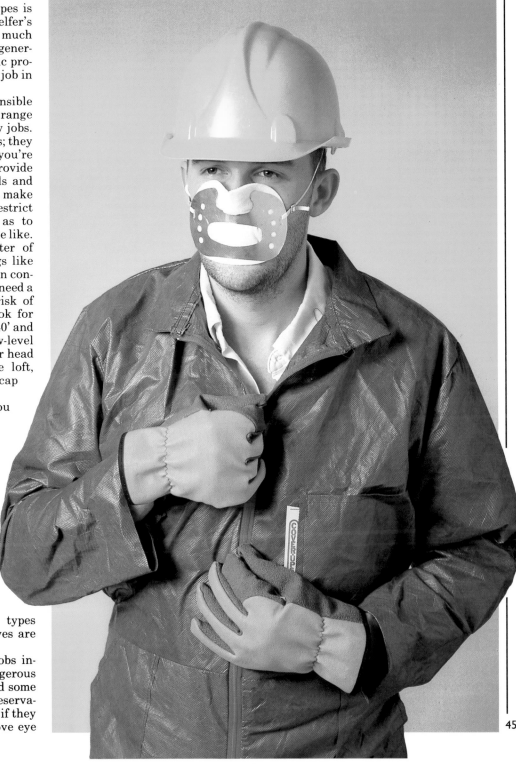

45

PROTECTIVE CLOTHING

Left: *A basic kit to provide protection to head, eyes, ears, breathing and hands. Hard hats should be a comfortable but not tight fit, as should ear defenders. Safety goggles may tend to mist up unless they have ventilation openings. Simple face masks have disposable cotton filters. Gloves come in a range of types*

Below: *Work boots with internal steel toecaps prevent the crushing injuries that can result if you drop heavy building materials on your feet. They should be Kitemarked and marked 'Made to BS1870'*

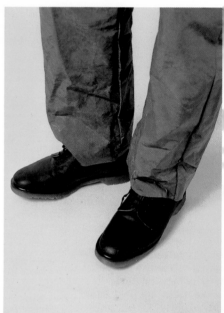

level. Goggles and safety spectacles should be marked 'Made to BS2092' and should carry the Kitemark symbol. An additional letter C means they are resistant to chemicals, while a numeral 1 or 2 means they are designed to be impact-resistant. Always use a special combined eye and face mask if you are doing DIY welding work.

Ear protection is also sensible if you are using noisy power tools such as a demolition hammer or an angle grinder, especially if you are working in a confined space. Simple ear plugs may suffice, but proper ear defenders (which resemble old-fashioned stereo headphones) are a better bet.

Shoes or boots with steel toecaps are worth wearing if you are carrying out building or demolition jobs.

Right: *Gloves come in a wide range of types, from simple fabric for light jobs to leather-palmed models for heavy work. PVC and rubber gloves give protection against chemicals*

BASIC PAPERHANGING

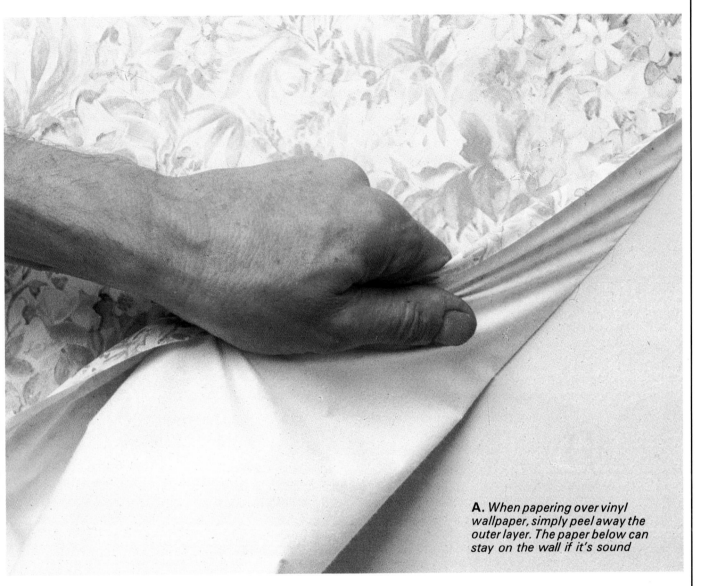

A. When papering over vinyl wallpaper, simply peel away the outer layer. The paper below can stay on the wall if it's sound

- **PREPARING WALLS**
- **STRIPPING PAPER**
- **MEASURING**
- **PASTING**
- **HANGING LENGTHS**
- **OBSTACLES**

Wallpapering may look simple, but it is all too easy to get into a mess unless you know the right way to do it. Most of the techniques involved are easily mastered and will help give your walls a professional touch.

Preparing the room
Start by removing as much furniture from the room as possible, then remove all wall hangings—such as pictures, mirrors and lamps—together with their fixings.

To mark the future positions of the fixings in a masonry wall, stick a steel pin into each wall-plug—later, you can hang wallpaper over the pins and leave the fixings clearly marked. Protect the floor with dust sheets: polythene sheets tend to be too slippery and paper will make a mess if it gets damp during stripping and other preparation.

Preparing the surface
Painted walls: Unless the paint is flaking or the surface is uneven, painted walls do not have to be stripped. However, make sure that the surfaces are completely free of grease and dirt. To give the new wallpaper something to grip on—especially if the surface is gloss—sand the surface and wipe clean.

Bare walls: Freshly plastered or rendered walls and walls that have been stripped to the plaster can be papered over with little trouble, providing they are free of damp. Your first task is to make good any chips or cracks in the surface with filler and to sand down bumps and bulges.

For the small blemishes normally 47

encountered when redecorating, use either a cellulose-based filler in powder form (such as Polyfilla), or a ready-mixed vinyl-based compound which comes in tubs.

Cellulose fillers are the cheaper of the two and are suitable for most internal uses, but the hard-drying qualities of vinyl-based fillers come in handy where the cracks result from expansion due to heat—around hot water pipes for instance.

The secret of using filler is to apply a little at a time, waiting for each layer to dry before you apply the next.

Sizing, or painting the wall with a suitable compound, evens out the absorbent qualities of the plaster or plasterboard surface and creates a smooth surface on which to wallpaper. If you are using a cellulose wallpaper paste (see below), use this as your sizing compound. For starch pastes a bone glue size is available. Vinyl wallpaper pastes require their own, special size. Leave the wall to dry thoroughly before you start hanging your paper.

Walls already papered: In most cases, it is inadvisable to lay fresh paper over an already papered wall—over-papering causes the paste between layers to interact, giving rise to additional problems such as peeling, staining and blistering.

However, with vinyl-laminated paper, it is sometimes possible to peel away the vinyl layer from its paper backing strip. If the backing paper remains firmly and evenly pasted to the wall, you can paper directly on to it.

Stripping wallpaper

There are two methods of stripping wallpaper in general use: soaking and scraping—with or without a proprietary stripping compound—and steam-stripping, using a special machine.

Soaking and scraping tends to be a messy job and if just water is used to soften the paper it can also be hard work. So where medium and heavy-weight papers are concerned, you can add either proprietary stripping compound or some vinegar or acetic acid —available from chemists—to the water.

Normally, the mix is simply painted on with a distemper brush. But if you are dealing with PVA-coated washable paper, you may need to score the surface with a wire brush so that the stripper can penetrate through to the wall. Leave the stripper to soak for a few minutes, then use a stripping knife to scrape it away from the wall. Make sure that your knife is kept ground sharp. Ideally, it should be of the type which has a stiff steel blade incorporated into the handle—the cheaper varieties bend and gouge plaster out of the wall.

If a piece of paper proves particularly stubborn, paint on some more water, leave it to soak, then try again—on no account attack a stubborn patch with the scraper as you may damage the plaster. Like washable paper, thick layers of old paper can be shifted more quickly if you carefully score the surface first with a wire brush.

Steam stripping is about as fast as using water but requires much less effort, creates less mess and minimizes the chances of damaging the wall. You can hire a steam stripper quite cheaply from hire shops and, if your old wallpaper is particularly heavy, it is worth the cost.

To use the tool, you simply press the steam-generating pad against the wall with one hand (fig 1) and scrape off the loosened paper with the other. These operations soon become continuous with practice, although thick

1 A steam stripping machine makes light work of stripping heavier papers. Easy to use, it can be obtained from most hire shops

2 Taking the trouble to fill cracks in the wall before you paper over it will improve the overall finish. Build up the filler in layers

3 Sizing a plastered wall before you paper over it will stop the paste from soaking in too quickly and causing the paper to peel later

4 To mark up the wall for the first strip, measure the width of your roll along the wall from your chosen starting point and make a mark

5 Next, to give some overlap at the starting point, measure back 25mm from the mark. Repeat this procedure at the base of the wall

6 Now hang a chalked plumbline over the mark nearer the corner. Secure the line at top and bottom, and 'snap' it to leave a line on the wall

ayers of paper may require more than ɔne application.

ɔreparing to paper

Ꭺ good working surface on which to ɔut and paste the wallpaper is essenɪial. Ideally, you should use a pasting ɔoard about 25mm narrower than the ɔaper you are hanging. Alternatively, ɪse a sheet of chipboard or a flushɪaced door—laid over a pair of trestles ɔr the kitchen table. To help you ɪeach the top of the walls, you will ɪlso need at least one pair of steps. Ⅳlake sure that these are safe.

Arrange the equipment so that you ɔan work on it comfortably and ɛafely, not forgetting that you will ɔften need both hands free to hang ɪhe wallpaper. At the same time, ɡather together all the other tools ɪecessary for the job—plumbline, ɛhears, tape measure, pasting brush, ɔencil and bucket. The shears are ɔarticularly important—try not to ɛconomize by using ordinary houseɪold scissors which are too small for ɑccurate cuts on this scale.

One final preparatory step is to ɔompare the shades of each separate ɪoll of wallpaper. Where the batch ɪumbers on the outer packing are ɪhe same, there should be no prob-

lem. But especially if the numbers differ, check the colour of each roll and arrange them so that similar shades run next to each other when you come to paste them up on the wall.

Where to start

Where you start papering depends to a large extent on whether your wallpaper is subdued, or bold and striking. In the former case, follow the general rule that you should paper away from the light so any unavoidable overlaps between strips will not cast shadows.

Start at the end of a wall, or against a window or door frame, where you will have a straight run before tackling the more intricate bits.

Where the wallpaper you have chosen has a bold pattern, start with a feature wall or chimney breast which immediately catches the eye. Centre up the pattern so it is symmetrical, then work on from either side.

If your wallpaper pattern consists of strong geometric shapes, plan for the final strip to be hung in an obscure corner of the room—well away from the light—where the break in pattern is not too noticeable.

Measuring and cutting

The simplest way of measuring and

cutting wallpaper is to offer each strip up to the wall as you go along. But use a plumbline to make sure that the first strip is straight or you will run into difficulties later on.

Having chosen your starting point, which should be in a corner or against a door frame, measure from this along the top of the wall 25mm less than the width of your roll and mark the spot with a pencil.

Secure a plumbline running from the top of the wall and through this point, rub it with chalk, then snap it against the wall as shown in fig 6. This leaves a vertical chalk line down the wall which in turn acts as a guide to help you position the side edge of the first strip.

Cut your first strip of paper about 50mm longer than the height from the ceiling to the edge of the skirting board. When measuring the next strip, use the edge of the first as a guide. Allow a 50mm overlap for trimming top and bottom, then mark and cut it as described above. If your wallpaper is patterned, make sure that you match the design from strip to strip—*before* you allow for your top overlap.

Wallpapers with patterns which match on each horizontal line can be matched in strips without difficulty.

7 *Align your first strip of wallpaper against the chalk mark. Do not forget to allow for an overlap top and bottom*

8 *When you are cutting strips of wallpaper, take the overlap on to match the pattern. Fold the paper back on itself to keep the cut square*

9 *When pasting a strip, paste the edges of the strip off the table. This will avoid accidentally getting paste on the other side of the paper*

10 *Folding strips 'paste to paste' as shown makes them far easier to handle. The end you paste last will go at the top of the wall*

11 *Cutting strips lengthways is easier if you paste and fold them first. Mark cutting lines in pencil and slice them with the shears*

12 *When you have positioned a strip correctly on the wall, crease the overlaps, peel away the paper around them and trim*

But if you find that you have to allow an overlap of about half a strip's length before the pattern matches, you have what is known as a 'half drop and repeat' pattern.

In this case, save on wallpaper by working with two rolls at a time. Take your first strip from the first roll, your second strip from the second roll, and so on.

At the end of the first wall, you will almost certainly have to cut a strip lengthways to get it to fit. Do this when the strip has been pasted and folded. Measure the width of the gap top and bottom, transfer these measurements to the whole strip, then mark the strip off with a timber straight edge. Cut down this line with the shears (fig 11).

Pasting and folding
When pasting wallpaper it is important to stop the paste from getting on the table (fig 9). Note that edges are only pasted when they overhang the table. Brush on the paste in a criss-cross 'herringbone' fashion, ensuring not only an even coverage but also that the edges receive plenty of paste. Work from the middle of the strip outwards.

When you have pasted about two-thirds of the strip, take the top edge in your fingers and thumbs and fold the strip down on itself. Make sure that the edges line up then slide the rest of the strip on to the table and paste it. Fold this back on itself as well, so that you are left with two folds—a large one at the top of the strip and a small one at the bottom of the strip (fig 10).

If your strips of wallpaper are particularly large, you may find that you will have to increase the size of the bottom fold. Short strips need be folded only once.

Ready-pasted paper must be soaked in water before hanging in order to activate the adhesive on the back. Having cut a strip to length and folded it to fit your water tray, immerse it for about a minute and move the tray to directly below the wall to be papered. You can then lift the strip straight out of the tray and on to the wall.

Hanging and trimming
Lift the folded strip off the pasting table, take the top edge in your fingers and thumbs and allow the top fold to drop. Lay the strip against the wall, in line with your chalk line at the side and with about 25mm of trimming overlap at the top. Brush

down the middle of the strip with the paperhanger's brush and unfurl the bottom fold.

Next, use the brush to form trimming creases at the top and bottom. Mark off the waste by running along the creases with the back of your shears, then pull the edges away from the wall again.

13 Where the paper goes over a switch or socket, crease an impression of the outline then make vee-shaped cuts to the corners

14 Trim away the flaps with a sharp knife. On circular switches, use the same procedure but make more cuts to the edges

15 When you are measuring thin strips before corners, do not forget to take measurements at both the top and bottom of the wall

16 Butt a strip before a corner up against the previous strip, then crease the overlap into the corner with the back of your shears

17 Always plumb a fresh line after turning a corner. As you hang the next strip, run the overlap into the corner, crease and trim it

18 On small sections of wall, there is no need to plumb a line. Align one side of the strip on the edge with the other overlapping

Cut along each crease mark in turn, pressing the finished edges down as you go. Run over the finished job with the brush to remove air bubbles —working from the centre of the strip out towards the edges and using short, light, strokes.

Butt subsequent strips up against each other so the side edges touch, but do not overlap. Make sure that the pattern matches at the top of the wall before you start trimming.

Switches and sockets
First offer up the pasted strip in the normal way, lining it up with your plumbed line or an adjacent strip. Brush the top part of the strip down against the wall to hold it in place, but leave the rest of the paper hanging freely over the obstruction.

Now press the strip lightly over the obstruction so that its outline is left indented on the paper. Pull the strip out from the wall again and pierce it with the shears, roughly in the middle of the indentations. Gently snip out to the four corners of the indented mark so you are left with four triangular flaps (fig 13).

Papering around corners
When you come to an internal corner, paper into the corner with one piece and out again with another. As you paper in, allow about 25mm overlap and crease the paper into the corner with the back of the shears.

Whenever you paper out, plumb a fresh line on the adjoining wall first. As you hang the paper, align it with the plumbed line and make sure it goes well into the corner to cover the overlap on the previous strip.

Folding paper around an external corner is possible only if the corner is vertical and cleanly finished.

If you have any doubts, treat the corner as you would an internal one. Paper up to it with your first piece, allow an overlap of 25mm and fold this around the corner. Having plumbed a fresh line, hang your second strip, again allowing about 25mm over the corner for trimming. Make sure that the second strip is firmly stuck to the overlap of the first, then trim it flush with the edge of the corner.

Ideas for wallpaper borders

Used on their own, wallpaper borders add a touch of style and elegance to a plain painted room. It is also an inexpensive way of brightening up a room and achieving an original effect.

Available from most wallpaper and decorating shops, they are normally employed to finish off a semi-papered wall which has no picture rail. But the borders can often be used to better effect to highlight windows and alcoves, pick out fixed wall mirrors or extend architraves and covings.

The borders are pasted up in the same way as ordinary wallpaper. It is a good idea though, to pencil in the positions of the strips so that you can make alterations before they are stuck down.

To make the mitred (angled) joints between strips, cut them overlength so that they overlap one another. When you paste them up, put a piece of paper between the flaps then cut through the strips at the desired angle. Peel away the off-cuts from each section and brush the strips back into place.

Papering round a window reveal

Top right: *When papering into a window reveal or bay window, cut your first strip so that you can fold part of it round as shown*
Below: *Continue laying strips across the wall around the reveal. Leave the ends of the shorter strips hanging at this stage*
Below right: *Paper the top of the reveal, leaving enough overlap to turn each strip up onto the wall. Finally, stick the hanging ends down and trim them to length. Paper the remaining parts in the normal way*

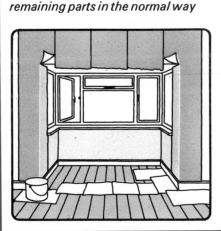

MORE PAPERHANGING

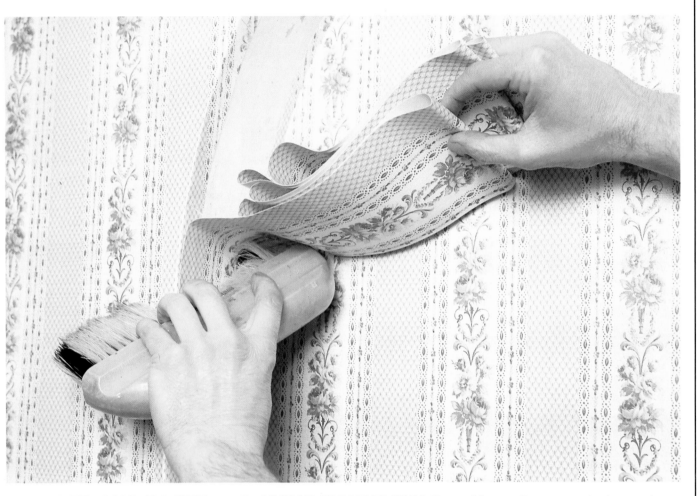

- ● **PAPER AND PASTE**
- ● **DOOR REVEALS**
- ● **CURVED CEILINGS**
- ● **WINDOW REVEALS**
- ● **ARCHES**
- ● **RADIATORS**

Above: *Paper an arched recess in three stages—the wall round it, the back wall and the curved surface*

Wallpapering on straight, uncluttered walls can be great fun and sometimes almost therapeutic. But papering walls which have many things fitted to them, or which are sloping, recessed or out of true, can have the opposite effect. They are always difficult and often very frustrating.

Even the person who is skilful at measuring, handling and cutting wallpaper can have great difficulties where walls are uneven. Angled walls are often slightly out of plumb and rarely straight. Curved surfaces wobble and plain surfaces undulate. To expect to apply materials to such surfaces to the accuracy of 1mm and to match a pattern at the same time is asking a lot and may sometimes be impossible.

Before you set about papering each and every angle you might consider alternative methods of decoration. Some areas will not be worth the extra bother of wallpaper and might look just as effective painted in a colour complementing the paper in the rest of the room. But where you have an area which definitely requires papering, there are certain methods and approaches that make the task more straightforward.

Types of paper
Your first job is to make a simple test on the walls to determine whether or not they are true. Hold a wooden straightedge against the wall and see whether it touches right along its

length. Providing the end of the straightedge is cut square, you can hold it also to the corner angles of window and door reveals and alcove recesses. If the angles are particularly out of true and the wall undulates, it is a good idea to use either a woodchip paper coated with emulsion or a good quality paper with a very tiny pattern. Avoid large patterns and stripes as they tend to show up poorly matching and out of plumb faces.

Use a good quality paper also in a room where there are a great many awkward features. A cheap, soft paper quickly absorbs the paste and in such a wet state easily tears or becomes marked. Cutting round reveals, arches or radiators means that you have to handle the paper more, and for longer periods, than on flat areas, and cheap paper cannot stand rough treatment.

1 When you come to a window, hang the wallpaper matching the previous piece so that the waste area overlaps the window soffit and reveal

2 Push the paper close against the line of the soffit, then cut along this line into the corner with a handyman's knife

3 Cut a small piece of wallpaper to fit at the end of the soffit overlapping on to the reveal in the corner and on to the main wall

4 Carefully brush the overlap of the main piece so that it fits snugly into the reveal, then cut off the excess paper at the edge

5 Match the next piece of paper above the window allowing for an overlap at the bottom, and brush the hanging piece into the soffit

6 When you come to an arched alcove, hang the first piece in line with the previous one so that it overhangs the edge of the arch

Paste

Paste is another important consideration: it must be a thick or stout solution which sticks readily to the surface without the need for continuous or heavy brushing. Thick pastes also stay wet longer—important when you need time to cut the paper carefully to fit an awkward shape. Nothing is more frustrating than finding that, after five minutes patient cutting around an arch, the paste has dried and you have to remove the paper and repaste it. Paper often tears if it is handled and pasted twice.

Quite often it is necessary to lap papers when you are trying to fit them into odd shapes. And though ordinary flat papers will stick to each other with paste, vinyl papers will not: they require special adhesives to bond the backing paper to the vinyl.

Check this with your retailer when you buy the paper, as there are several brands of highly efficient adhesive for the purpose. But remember these are used only for the overlapping areas —not instead of the paste.

Window and door reveals

There are several practical ways of papering reveals. The illustration on page 51 shows one method which is particularly good for deep recesses or bay window borders and ceilings. But where reveal and soffit (the top internal wall surface) are narrower than the width of wallpaper you are using, the method shown in figs 1 to 5 above may be more appropriate. The step-by-step photographs also show how to paper around pipes and cables and deal with the sloping kind of walls found in an attic bedroom.

7 Press the wallpaper to the edge of the arch and cut off the waste area about 25mm inside the edge of the arch using wallpaper scissors

54

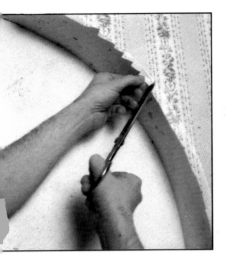

8 *Snip the wallpaper that overlaps the curved section of the arch at distances about 50mm apart and 25mm apart at the most curved part*

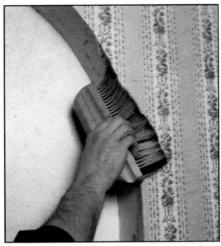

9 *Gently brush the overlapping paper on to the reveal and soffit of the arch and press the cut edges of the paper into place*

10 *Match up the adjoining piece above the arch and hang it in the same way making sure that the cut sections stick firmly to the soffit*

11 *Stand directly in front of the arch and match the piece for the back of the recess, then press the waste edges into the corner*

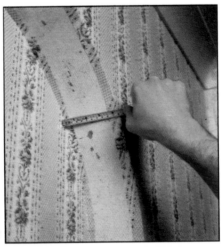

12 *When the waste is cut and you have folded the overlap on to the reveal, measure the width of the reveal and soffit*

13 *Cut the exact width for the reveal and, with the whole length concertina'd, unwind the paper in the reveal and brush it into place*

Study them carefully before tackling obstacles in your home, so you fully understand the stages involved.

Arches and alcoves

When you come up against the problem of papering arched openings, make sure you do not use heavily patterned paper. When you come to cut the strip to fit the reveal (fig. 12) the pattern will be upside down on one side of the arch if you use the wrong paper. If, at this stage, you need to cut the reveal filling strip, do so either where the arch soffit meets the strip or at the top of the arch. The choice is entirely yours and the pattern will often determine the most suitable place to join them.

An alcove in the form of an arched recess in the wall is another feature that is often difficult to paper. The problems of the arch and reveal are similar to those of papering arched openings, but papering the wall at the back of the recess often presents an added difficulty.

Start, as you would for an arched opening, by cutting around the shape, making small cuts in the overlap and smoothing down the lapping piece into the soffit and reveals to form a smooth line along the edge of the arch.

Next, match a length of paper to go on the wall inside the recess. Do this by holding the roll up against the wall and lining up the edge of it with the edge of the paper stuck to the wall

outside the recess. Move the paper up or down so that the pattern appears to match with the pattern on the outside. When it looks right, mark the crest of the arch on the paper in a soft pencil and also the position of the reveal.

Take the paper away and cut a piece out about 10-15mm bigger than your pencil marks. Paste this and carefully apply it to the wall, pushing the paper into the angle with the aid of a paperhanging brush.

It will be necessary to make a few cuts at the top of the piece to the shape of the arch in order to get it to fit the angle. To do this, mark the position of the internal angle with the back of the scissors, pull the paper a little way from the wall and cut it about 10mm bigger than the shape you have marked. Make a number of small cuts along the overlap on the arch section and brush it back into position. You might be lucky enough to fill the alcove with a single width of wallpaper but if not, you can fit a second or third piece in exactly the same way.

If you are using patterned paper and the alcove is a feature or focal point of the room, it may be better to start papering here. The pattern is unlikely to be centrally positioned in the alcove if you start from one end of the wall, and this may jar the eye.

If the alcove is wider than the width of the paper, hang to a centre line marked down the back wall of the recess with a plumbline.

A domed alcove cannot be papered. It is impossible to spread the paper to cover a spherical surface without severe creasing.

Curved ceilings

In some older properties the ceiling curves into the wall so that there is no line at which to stop the wallpaper. You must get round this by deciding on the line you want and marking it before you cut the paper.

The curves are very seldom true so it is probably best to select a line at a point where the wall starts to curve. Measure up the height you have decided upon at each end of the wall and stretch a piece of fine string, which you have thoroughly rubbed with coloured chalk, between these two points. When the string is pulled taut and snapped against the surface, you will have a chalked guide line to work from.

You need a very sharp craft knife —preferably with a curved blade—and a straightedge for this job in addition to the other wallpaper hanging tools. Your straightedge can be a piece of 50mm x 25mm timber, about 100mm longer than the width of the paper. Plane one edge straight and chamfer it so that it is easier to cut to.

Cut the paper so that it will overlap the chalked line by at least 30mm, then hang the paper. Place the straightedge carefully on the paper so that each end is touching the chalk line and cut along it with one sweeping cut. Remove the cut piece and wipe the curved area free of paste.

When you hang the next piece, cut from the edge of the first length to the chalk line on the other side of the paper. Continue in this fashion, hanging and cutting a piece at a time.

14 *When you wallpaper to a pipe in an awkward corner, fold back the paper and indent it with the scissors where it meets the brackets*

16 *When you have cut for each bracket, push the paper behind the pipe with closed scissors so that the paper slips over each bracket*

Wall-mounted radiators

You will get the neatest results if you can take radiators off a wall before trying to paper behind them. But this is difficult with radiators that are connected to a 'wet' central heating system; you will probably have to drain the system before moving them.

If the radiator cannot be moved, you need to make a simple tool to help get behind it and smooth the paper down flat.

A flat piece of wood about 500mm long is suitable for the job, though you should wrap a piece of rag around it to avoid tearing the paper. A wire coat hanger is another possibility: straighten the hook out to act as a handle and then wrap a piece of soft

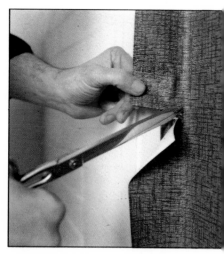

15 *Cut down to the mark, then make an upward and downward angle cut from a point about 15mm before the initial mark*

17 *Snip the paper behind the bracket so that it lies flat to the wall, then cut off the waste bits with a handyman's knife*

fabric around the cross bar.

To hang a length of wallpaper behind a radiator start by pasting half the length and hanging from the wall in the normal way. Take the free bottom half, fold it back on itself face side to face side, and slide it behind the radiator. Adjust the fold to coincide with the tops of any brackets, crease the paper then mark the bracket positions in pencil.

Make vertical cuts from the bottom of the length up to the marks, fold the paper back against the wall and paste.

Finally, slip the pasted length down behind the radiator so that the brackets run in the slits you have just made. Smooth the paper as thoroughly as you can with the special tool.

PAPERING CEILINGS

Left: *The ceiling paper must be supported and folded concertina-style for ease of handling*

The ceiling must be sized to make it less porous before you start hanging, or lined with lining paper. With cellulose wallpaper paste, you can use some of this, diluted, as your size. Cold-water starch pastes require a special glue size.

Lining paper
Lining a ceiling with lining paper is not essential but gives a more lasting finish—providing you hang it at right-angles to the direction which the top paper will eventually take. Also, it prevents the ceiling plaster from showing through if gaps should appear between the joints of the top paper— the embossed and anaglypta papers have a tendency to shrink as the paste slowly dries out.

A final plus for using lining paper is that it absorbs paste more evenly than plaster, thus making it easier to apply the top paper.

Preparing the ceiling
Whether or not you decide to apply lining paper, the ceiling must be thoroughly clean and free from loose or flaking paint. Gloss paint must be rubbed down with a glasspaper and any cracks filled with a cellulose-based filler. Any old paper must be completely stripped off so the ceiling is left as smooth as possible for the application of the new layer.

Where to start
Where possible, all papering should start and work away from the natural daylight source. This system prevents

- **HOW MUCH PAPER?**
- **ACCESS EQUIPMENT**
- **HANGING PAPER**
- **PREPARATION**
- **PASTING**
- **TRIMMING TO FIT**

Papering a ceiling is not as difficult as it looks. With a sensible scaffolding arrangement and the right technique, the job is no harder than papering an ordinary wall. Just make sure that all essential materials are to hand before you start hanging the paper.

How much paper?
First decide which way the paper is to be hung, as this determines how many lengths of paper can be obtained from one roll. A standard roll of wallpaper measures about 10m long, is between 500mm and 550mm wide and covers an area of around 5.3m². To estimate the number of rolls required for your ceiling measure the length of each wall (ignoring any protrusions such as chimney breasts) add the measurements together and match the total against the chart given right.

Other materials
All papers suitable for walls can also be used on ceilings. However, if you choose one of the popular embossed or anaglypta ceiling papers, remember that they turn yellow very quickly and must have at least one coat of emulsion paint applied after hanging. The heavily-embossed ones usually need two coats of paint for a good and even finish.

Different papers require different pastes for hanging and your wallpaper stockist can advise on which is the best for your chosen paper.

How many rolls?

Standard rolls 10.05m × 530mm

Distance around the room in metres	No of rolls required
10.0—12.0	2
12.5—14.5	3
15.0—17.5	4
18.0—20.0	5
20.5—21.5	6
21.5—22.5	7

PAPERING CEILINGS

shadows from obscuring the joints as you hang the paper. Obviously if there is a window in both ends of the room, either one may be used as the starting point. Where a bay window is involved, the first length should be hung across the opening of the bay and then work back towards the top of the window.

Before you start papering, get yourself properly prepared so all essential equipment and materials are to hand. As far as papering ceilings is concerned the erection of a proper scaffolding arrangement is the most important piece of preparation.

Scaffolding
Make-shift scaffolding is extremely dangerous. To be safe you need two pairs of sturdy stepladders and a wide scaffold plank. Obviously, you do not want to constantly be jumping up and down to move the steps and planks along, so try to get a length of plank approximately the same width of the room, allowing room for the supporting ladders.

Remember—the most important item of all is safety. A few minutes care can avoid unnecessary injury.

Experiment with the positioning of the plank so you have it at a height which does not make you stoop or stretch as you apply the paper (fig. 1). Check the height by standing on the plank and reaching up to the ceiling—you should be able to touch it comfortably with the palm of your hand.

Marking a guideline
The scaffold should be set up under a chalked guideline which marks the outside edge of the first strip. To work out where this line should run, measure the width of the paper and deduct 10mm. The deduction allows for bumps and other imperfections at the junction of the ceiling and the wall. Measuring out from the wall, mark off this measurement on the ceiling at either end of the first run of paper (fig. 2).

Next, fix a steel drawing pin into the ceiling at one of the measured points and tie a length of twine around it. Thoroughly rub the twine with coloured chalk then pull it taut across the ceiling to the other measured point and fix it securely. Pull the centre of the twine down from the ceiling, letting it snap back into place (fig. 3). This leaves an accurate guideline by which you can hang the first length of paper and just the right amount of overlap at the side wall.

Cutting all the lengths of paper you

A. *The most sensible scaffolding arrangement, shown here under the chalked guideline. Do not be tempted to use chairs or stools*

need at one time is useful as it cuts down on the number of interruptions in your work flow. Measure the length of the first strip carefully against the wall allowing at least 100mm excess for trimming. Subsequent strips can then be measured and cut against it. After cutting, the strips are laid face-down on your pasting board.

Pasting
To paste a length of paper evenly, slide it across the board so that it overhangs the edge furthest from you (the back edge) by about 10mm. This prevents the paste from being deposited on the board or on the other lengths of paper.

Apply a full brush of paste down the centre of the paper—the larger the brush the quicker the paste can be applied, thus avoiding the risk of drying before the paper is hung.

Brush the paste outwards over the back edge with an overlapping criss-cross action to avoid missing any patches of paper. Gradually draw the paper towards you, overhanging the front edge by about 10mm, as you apply the paste.

Folding
When you are sure that the length of paper has been completely coated in paste, fold it ready for hanging. Fold over the first 300mm paste to paste, lift the fold and place it on top of the next 300mm (fig. 4). Continue this pattern down the whole length to obtain a concertina-type series of folds. This enables you to release the paper in manageable lengths on the ceiling.

Before climbing up onto the scaffolding to hang the pasted paper,

make sure that you have a paper hanging brush and a pair of sharp scissors or shears within easy reach—in the pocket of your apron or over alls. A cleaner cut is obtained if you take the trouble to clean the paste from your scissors after each length of paper has been trimmed.

Hanging the paper
Place a part roll of paper or cardboard tube under the concertina-folds of the pasted length—this supports the paper and should be held parallel and close to the ceiling at all times (fig. 6). If you are right-handed, take the roll, with its folded, pasted paper on top, in your right hand and hold the paper in place with your thumb—leaving the top fold free.

Pull this top fold open and lay it onto the ceiling against one end of the chalk line. Taking the brush, smooth down the centre of the section then to the edges to expel any air bubbles under the surface (fig. 7).

Make sure this first fold is running true to the line and then release the next fold and smooth it out in the same way. Any adjustments which are needed should always be made with the flat of the hand—never use fingers as the concentration of pressure may tear the wet paper.

When you have applied a few folds of paper, you can move around so that you are facing the roller and the folded paper. Walk along the platform, slowly releasing the folds and brushing them into place (fig. 8).

Continue hanging the paper in this way until the whole length has been pasted up. The surplus paper can now be trimmed off allowing 5-10mm to

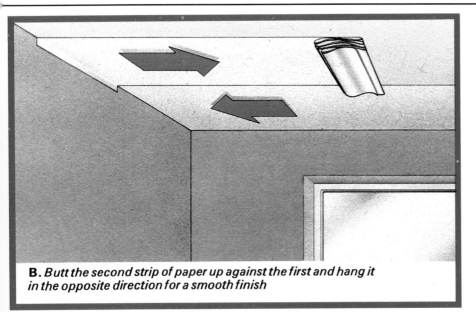

B. *Butt the second strip of paper up against the first and hang it in the opposite direction for a smooth finish*

remain hanging down the wall. This makes for a cleaner finish when the walls are papered. If you are papering up to a decorative coving, crease the paper against the edge to make a cutting guide, then trim off the excess.

Paste and fold subsequent strips in the same way as the first, applying them to the ceiling and using the edge of the previous strip as the guideline. Take care not to overlap the strips—they should only butt tightly up against each other.

To get a really neat finish and to ensure that the edges are well stuck down, use a seam or angle roller on the joints. The joints should be rolled after the paste has set—say every four lengths of paper.

The full face of the roller should not be used on embossed paper as the pressure will flatten out its design. In-

1 *When you can comfortably touch the ceiling with the palm of your hand, then the scaffolding is in the correct position*

2 *Deduct 10mm from the width of the paper to find the right measurement for marking off the position of the guideline*

3 *Securely fix the chalked line at one end of the room. Hold the line taut against the other mark and snap it against the ceiling*

4 *Turn in the first 300mm of paper, lift this fold and put it on top of the next 300mm to make a concertina of the whole sheet*

5 *Thread string through the handle loops of the paste bucket and rest the brush on it. This keeps it free of excess paste*

6 *Support the folded, pasted paper with a roll of paper, leaving the top fold free ready to lay on the ceiling*

stead, use the edge of the roller directly on the joints.

Lights and chimney breasts

The paper will need to be cut so that it fits round obstructions such as light fittings. If the fitting is near the edge of a strip, you can cut from the edge of the paper inwards to the centre of the fitting (fig. 9). Make a few cuts outward to form a star pattern and press the paper over the fitting (fig. 10). Thread the loose electrical flex through the hole and smooth down the rest of the strip. Trim off the excess paper with a sharp knife.

Where the fitting comes in the centre of a strip, poke a hole through the paper with your scissors. Make star-shaped cuts outward from this point and finish off as above.

How you paper around a chimney breast depends on whether it is parallel, or at right-angles, to the direction of the ceiling paper.

When the chimney breast is at right-angles, make a cut along the length of the strip—equal to the depth of the breast minus the usual 10-15mm overlap—and smooth the paper into the corner. Repeat on the other side of the chimney breast.

If the chimney breast is parallel to the direction of the ceiling paper, smooth the paper right into the corner (fig. 11). This makes a crease mark indicating the depth of the chimney breast on that strip of paper. Crease another mark at the point where the side wall of the chimney breast and the ceiling meet.

Next, gently peel the strip back from the ceiling and cut down a line connecting the two creases. Replace the strip, checking as you smooth it down that the other side is lined up with your chalk line or correctly butted against the adjacent strip further out in the room.

As you continue along the face of the chimney breast, leave the excess paper to hang down the wall (fig. 12). When you get to the other edge, make a cut upwards from the waste edge of the strip. You can now smooth out the rest of the strip over the ceiling and trim in the usual way.

The final strip

The final strip of paper will almost certainly be narrower than a standard width. If this is the case, you will find it easier to hang and trim if the piece is measured and cut to size. Allow about 50mm extra on the strip then paste, fold and hang it as above.

7 Lay the first fold of paper against the chalked line and smooth it out before applying the second and subsequent folds

8 Smooth the paper out as you go, expelling any air bubbles and always keeping the support parallel and close to the ceiling

9 Mark the position of the light fitting with your fingers and cut in from the edge of the paper towards the centre of the fitting

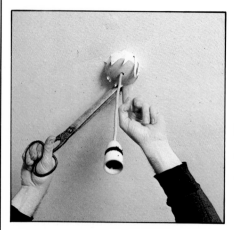

10 Make a few cuts outwards to form a star pattern which can be pressed round the fitting, and then trim off the excess paper

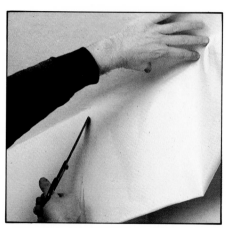

11 At the corner of the chimney breast, press the paper into place to make a mark and then peel it back so that it can be cut

12 The last cut should be a 'V' shape up as far as the mark to enable the rest of the paper to be pasted down the side of the chimney

PAPERING A STAIRWELL

- ● ESTIMATING
- ● THE HEAD WALL
- ● THE CEILING
- ● ACCESS METHODS
- ● THE WELL WALL
- ● HANDRAILS

Most homes in most countries include at least one stairwell. And because the side walls—called well walls—are usually the highest interior walls of a house, this area is usually hard to decorate.

Before you attempt to hang paper in a stairwell, it is advisable to gain some experience by papering a normal room (see pages 47 to 52 and 57 to 60). Once you have mastered the basic techniques involved, it should be possible to paper a stairwell without difficulty.

Choosing the right wallpaper goes a long way towards ·determining how good a finish you finally achieve.

Above: *By employing the correct wallpapering techniques and using a suitable type of paper, you can transform a dark and narrow staircase*

Because well walls are much higher than other walls in the home any irregularities in the surface, such as corners that are out of true, are likely to be highlighted by unsuitable types.

Steer clear of striped paper as this will show up an irregularly sloping wall particularly badly. You may also find it hard to match up strips of wallpaper at the edges if the pattern is too large. For best results choose plain wallpaper or one with a small pattern.

Estimating quantities

Due to the irregular shape of a well wall where it meets the stairs, it is harder to work out how many rolls of paper you need than it is for a normal rectangular wall.

To make the job easier, divide the wall into two halves by drawing a line along the wall, extending horizontally from the floor of the landing. On a single-flight staircase, the space above this line is usually rectangular so simply calculate the area to work out the amount of paper required.

To estimate the amount needed for the area beneath the line, draw a vertical line from the foot of the stairs up to the horizontal line. Depending on the slope of the stairs, the paper needed for this triangular section is between a half and two-thirds the amount you would need for a rectangle formed by the same horizontal and vertical measurements.

Access platforms

Due to the height of the stairwell it is essential to erect a safe and secure platform, giving you easy access to the walls, before you start work. The arrangement of ladders and boards depends on the type of staircase involved, but you will need at least two ladders and one scaffold board.

Make sure that all ladders to be used are sound and, with step ladders, take care to check that the hinges are secure and that the ropes which hold the legs together are not worn or frayed. Before erecting your working platform, take up the stair carpet, if it is fitted, and check for any weakness in the staircase—such as a loose tread—that could result in an accident.

Single-flight stairs

If you are working on a straight flight of stairs, place a ladder on one of the steps with its foot resting against the riser of the step and its top leaning against the head wall. Do not lean the ladder against the wall at an angle of less than 60°, or its stability will be seriously impaired. To give protection to the wall, you can tie pieces of cloth around each leg at the top of the ladder. Place a step ladder, with its legs fully extended on the landing at the top of the flight and run the scaffold board between the two (fig. A).

well wall

head wall

A

well wall

head wall

B

well wall

head wall

C

well wall

head wall →

D

wooden stop

A. *If you are working on a straight flight of stairs, place a ladder on one of the steps and run a scaffold board from it to a step ladder placed on the landing.* **B.** *If the staircase is enclosed with a well wall on each side, lean a ladder against either wall and run the scaffolding between them to gain access to the head wall.* **C.** *This more complicated arrangement allows easy access to both the well wall and the head wall.* **D.** *To prevent a ladder from slipping over the front of a step, nail or screw a batten to the tread of the step*

If the unsupported length of the scaffold board is more than 1.5m, it is advisable to place a further board on top of it to lend extra strength. In this case, be sure to lash the boards with some thin rope to the ladder at either end, to prevent the top board from slipping over the lower one. Tie the ropes behind the face of each ladder so that you will not trip over them as you move along the scaffold.

If you do not have a step ladder, you can place a packing case on the landing to support the board as long as its unsupported length does not exceed 1.5m.

Double-flight stairs

Where a staircase doubles back on itself at an angle of 180°, there is often a landing between the two flights and the scaffolding arrangement for single flight of stairs can be employed. But sometimes the bend in the stairs is formed by a series of triangular steps and there is nowhere to place a step ladder.

In this case, lean a ladder against the wall at the top of the first flight with its foot resting on one of the steps, again at an angle of not less than 60°. Then, to prevent the bottom of the ladder from slipping over the front of the step, firmly nail or screw a small wooden batten to the top of the step and prop the foot of the ladder against it (fig. D).

The head wall

When you come to paper the head wall, you will have to alter the scaffolding arrangement so that no ladders are leaning against it. If the staircase is enclosed with a well wall on either side, lean a ladder against each of these and run the scaffolding between the two (fig. B). Fix a batten into place to support the foot of the ladder that leans with the slope of the stairs. The other ladder rests against the riser and is thus prevented from slipping.

Where there are banisters on one side of the staircase and the handrail is sturdy enough, you can lash the scaffold board to the top of it. A safer method is to erect a scaffolding arrangement as shown in fig. C.

Papering the stairwell

When a suitable scaffolding arrangement has been erected, you can start to paper. Begin by dropping a plumbline where the edge of the longest length of paper will fall and mark a vertical line down the well wall. Cut a length of paper about 100mm longer

than required and, starting from one end of the length, paste it working from the centre outwards. Fold the paper over itself into a concertina-type series of folds, and align the edges of the paper (fig. 2).

Once the length of paper has been pasted and folded, carry it to the wall. Hold the top end of the paper to the wall, aligning its edge with the vertical line, and let the rest of the length drop down the wall. On particularly high walls get assistance at this stage as the paper may tear.

Place the paper onto the wall, leaving a 50mm overlap at the top, and smooth it in to place with the hanging brush. With the paper in place, trim it to length at the bottom then, holding the bottom edge away from the wall, wipe away any excess paste from the string (wooden side to the stairs), fig. 7. Repeat this process at the top of the length (fig. 8).

From the first strip, work in both directions to cover the wall. When you reach the point where the well wall meets the head wall, paper around the corner as described on pages 47 to 52.

When you have papered the well wall or walls, rearrange the scaffolding arrangement and begin work on the head wall. Leave the paper for an hour, then flatten the joints with a seam roller (fig. 10).

Paper the ceiling of a stairwell as described on pages 57 to 60, so that the strips lie in the same direction as the scaffold board you are using. Never hang the paper on the ceiling at right angles to the scaffold as this may result in a fall.

Wall handrails

Papering a well wall is sometimes complicated by a handrail attached to the wall. But as wall handrails do not form part of the main structure of a staircase and are screwed directly to the wall, they can usually be removed without difficulty.

As you paper over the screw holes of the removed handrail, press the paper firmly against them. With the paper in place, push a matchstick through into each screw hole so that you can locate the holes later and refit the handrail.

Papering around banisters

On a double-flight staircase, there is often a banister attached to the wall at the point where the stairs turn or at the top of the flight of stairs. In this case, as the post cannot be removed without affecting the struc-

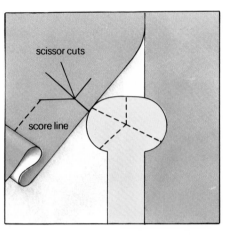

E. *Papering around a banister. Hang one sheet against the banister, make cuts in the next piece as shown, then lay the paper gently into place*

ture, you will have to paper around it.

The wall is usually highest at this point, but even if it is not, hang your first strip of paper here so that its edge is against the banister. If the banister widens at the top, cut a piece out of the paper to accept the shape of the wood.

Paste the adjacent strip of paper, again starting at the top of the wall, and when it reaches the top of the banister make a diagonal cut 40mm below the top as shown in fig. E. Make two further cuts as shown and lay the paper lightly around the edges of the banister.

Using the back of the shears, score the paper down the edge of the banister where it meets the wall. Lift the paper away from the wall, cut along the score line and brush it back into place around the banister.

1 *Drop a plumbline where the edge of the longest length of paper will fall. Draw a vertical line down the wall at this point*

2 Paste the paper, working from the centre outwards, then fold it over itself into a concertina-type series of folds

3 Once the length of paper has been pasted and folded, take it to the wall. Align its edge with the line on the wall

4 Let the remaining paper drop down the wall, keeping its edge to the vertical line, and press the top edge firmly into place

5 Use the hanging brush to smooth the paper downwards and outwards, making sure you are positioned safely on the platform

6 When the paper comes into contact with a corner or skirting, leave a guideline for trimming by scoring with the back of the shears

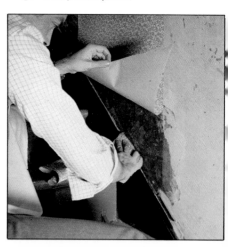

7 Pull the paper away from the wall and cut off the waste areas along the guideline. Wipe excess paste away from the string

8 To prevent paste from getting on to the ceiling, fold the top edge of the paper back, wipe off excess paste and trim

9 Where you meet obstacles such as mouldings on the ceiling, **again make a guideline with the shears**, then trim the waste

10 Leave the paper for about an hour to allow the paste to dry, then smooth and flatten the seams with a seam roller

PAINTING WALLS

- ● **PREPARATION**
- ● **USING BRUSHES**
- ● **CLEANING EQUIPMENT**

- ● **PAINT TYPES**
- ● **USING ROLLERS**
- ● **PAINTING MURALS**

When you are painting walls and ceilings, bear in mind the preparation of surfaces for paint is the most important part of the process. Without a smooth, clean and dry surface, no amount of care in applying the paint is going to give a professional finish.

New plaster
Make sure that new plaster is absolutely dry before applying paint to it: water trapped in the plaster weakens the adhesion of the paint and may cause blistering. Some plasters have an alkaline nature and when the plaster dries out, white, fluffy alkaline crystals may be deposited on the surface. Remove these deposits with a dry brush before painting.

The plaster should, in any case, be dry-brushed before painting to remove surface dirt, and scraped to remove any plaster splashes. Make good any cracks or holes with a plaster-based or general purpose cellulose filler.

After preparation, the plaster must be sealed. If you are using emulsion (latex) paint, a coat of emulsion thinned with water is sufficient. With oil-based (alkyd) paint use alkali-resisting primer.

Wallpapered surfaces
It is advisable to remove existing wallpaper before painting, as it is never possible to know how well the paper is adhering to the surface and the finished work can be spoiled later by unsightly blisters or lifting edges. Also, it is not normally possible to wash ceiling and wallpapers so nicotine and other deposits on the paper may be left which stain the paint coating. This is especially true of emulsion paints, which are particularly good for dissolving nicotine. Stripping the wallpaper can be quite a difficult and time-consuming job. If you have a large area, hiring a steam stripper will save a lot of time.

Old plaster walls
After stripping the old wallpaper, it is important to remove any trace of paste and size left on the surface as these can cause newly-applied paint to flake. Remove old paste by washing the wall with warm water and, when the surface is dry, sanding it with glasspaper. Afterwards, fill the surface in the same way as you would do for new plaster.

If the surface is a mixture of bare plaster and painted areas, you can achieve a more uniform surface by first covering the wall with a heavy-duty, 600 grade lining paper. Make sure that it is stuck well to the surface before you start painting.

1 Patch holes in walls and ceilings with plaster or filler. Moisten the surface first to cut suction, then fill the hole slightly proud

2 When the filler has hardened completely, use fine-grade abrasive wrapped round a sanding block to smooth the repair down flush

3 If you have a lot of repairs to sand down, you can speed the job up considerably by using an orbital sander

Existing painted surface

Painted surfaces must be washed down to remove dirt and grease. In bedrooms and halls, a mixture of washing powder and warm water should be sufficient to remove it. But in kitchens, where the grease is thick, stronger cleaning agents such as a washing soda solution may be required. The walls must be rinsed afterwards, as residues may attack and soften the paint.

Shiny gloss surfaces should be lightly abraded, then rinsed, to provide a good key for the new paint.

Paints

Emulsion paints are produced with varying degrees of sheen. Matt emulsions have no sheen at all and are best suited to bumpy and old walls

where any imperfections will not be so apparent. Emulsions with a small degree of sheen are often called silk finish (semigloss). With these, any imperfection in the surface may be more apparent.

Emulsion paints

Emulsion paints dry by the evaporation of their water content, so when you are applying emulsion, keep the windows closed to stop it from drying too quickly. Open the windows as soon as the work is completed to remove moisture from the atmosphere.

Oil paints

These are generally more durable than emulsion paints and are well suited to kitchens and bathrooms where there is a lot of moisture.

Oil paint is available in gloss or eggshell (semigloss finish). Although gloss requires an undercoat if used on an unpainted surface, most brands of eggshell specify that two coats of the finish paint gives sufficient coverage.

Some brands of oil paint are supplied in jelly-like *thixotropic* form. These are designed to produce thicker coatings and—if applied correctly—present fewer problems with drips and spashes. The jelly-like characteristic breaks down as the paint is applied so it should not be over brushed or over rolled.

When oil paint begins to dry, the thinners base evaporates into the atmosphere and oxygen then combines with the oil in the coating to form a hard film. Because of this, you must complete each coat as quickly as

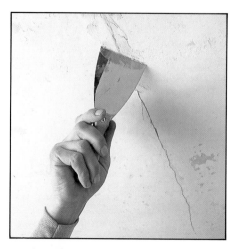

4 Where cracks have opened up between plasterboard sheets on a ceiling, rake out all the loose material using a bent nail or similar implement

5 Fill the cracks by drawing the filling knife first across the crack, then along it. Leave the filler standing slightly proud

6 As with repairs to walls, sand the filled area down smooth with fine grade abrasive wrapped round a sanding block

ossible and have adequate ventila-
on as you apply the paint. Lack of
entilation allows the solvent fumes
o be inhaled: this combined with a
ick of oxygen can result in headaches
nd nausea.

Painting ceilings

The most important considerations when
ainting ceilings are to have a suitable
caffold arrangement (see pages 57 to
0), to avoid the temptation to over-
each, and to ensure that there is
ufficient light to show up the wet edge
etween the applied paint and the
npainted surface.

Painting walls

As with ceilings, it is most important
hat the wet edge is not allowed to
et before more paint is applied. If
his happens, the paint does not flow
ogether and thick ridges appear.

Unless the walls are very high, a
pair of stepladders are sufficient to
each all points. Start painting in the
op corner, coating about one square
netre of wall at a time. When this is
omplete, paint a similar-size area
lirectly below it and continue in this
vay, down to the skirting board.

This method gives you a metre-wide
and the height of the room—which
hould be completed before the next
ection is started—and keeps the size
of the wet edge to a minimum.

Recommended equipment

Brushes should be as large as you can
nandle—130mm or 150mm are the
nost suitable sizes for emulsion
paints, while 75mm or 100mm brushes
are better for applying the more
viscous oil paints.

If you use a roller, mohair or short-
pile synthetic coverings are suitable
for smooth surfaces. For heavily-
textured surfaces such as plastic
texture paints or heavily-embossed
papers, lambswool or medium-pile
synthetic covers are more suitable.
Foam rollers are not suitable for
applying oil paints as the thinner in
them may soften or dissolve the foam.
Make sure that you have a proper
roller tray, to match the size of roller
you are using.

Applying the paint

Apply brushed-on emulsion in all
directions, using long sweeping
strokes to give a full, level coat of
the paint. Use a smaller brush of
about 25mm to apply the paint behind
pipes and in other awkward areas.

A similar method is used for applying emulsion paint with a roller. Coat

7 Pull off any loose wallpaper first, then brush water liberally on to the paper which cannot be taken off easily by hand

9 Old varnishes are sometimes difficult to remove so use a stiff wire brush to bite into the surface of the paper

the roller evenly with paint and roll
in all directions, making the final
strokes lighter to cut down the
texture imprint which is produced by
the roller pile.

Brush on oil paints with much
firmer strokes, making sure that there
is not too much paint on the brush.
Oil paints are more viscous and
without good, firm strokes they will
run or sag. Apply the thixotropic type
paints firmly in all directions and
leave them to flow out smoothly of
their own accord.

Oil-based undercoats and gloss must
be applied in three distinct phases:
● Spread the paint in all directions to
give an even distribution.
● Cross the paint with firm, horizontal
strokes.
● Lay off the paint with light, vertical
strokes.

8 Allow the water a few minutes to soak in, then use a paint scraper flat to the wall to remove the paper without damaging the plaster

10 When you have removed all you can with the scraper and scratched the surface, brush more water on the paper and repeat

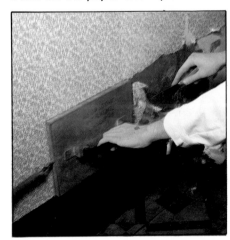

11 If you are using a steam stripper, work in straight lines from the bottom of the wall and let the steam rise up the wallpaper

67

These three phases must be carried out fully on each square metre at a time. The final laying off should be a vertical action which lightly leaves the surface as it extends into the finished area directly above it. This action is certainly worth practising.

Remember that paint can only be brushed while it is still wet—brushing after the thinners have evaporated results in an unsightly mess. It is for this reason that once a wall or ceiling has been started, you should complete it without a break. Having the correct scaffolding helps to maintain continuity and avoids wasting time moving furniture or short steps.

Drying

Most water-based paints can be given a further coat after approximately four hours, depending both on the temperature and humidity of the room and on the porosity of the surface.

Oil paints may appear dry after about three hours but if further coats are applied at this time, you will find that the existing coat starts to soften and pull off onto the brush. This is due to the action of the thinner in the paint which 'is being applied. If you are not certain that the coating is sufficiently hard to paint over, leave it until the next day.

If the paint is not dry after 24 hours, it is probably due to poor preparation of the surfaces—grease, in particular, retards the drying of emulsion paints. If an emulsion paint has been applied to a shiny surface, the coating may break up and expose the surface underneath. This is called 'cissing' and can only be remedied by washing off the emulsion while it is still wet and further abrading the surface to remove its gloss.

Joining colours

Attractive decoration schemes can be ruined when the divisions between colours are not precise—such as the meeting of the ceiling and wall, or the wall and skirting board.

To achieve a straight line between ceilings and walls, paint the ceiling colour a little way down the walls. When the paint is dry, measure down from the ceiling about 10mm at both ends of the wall and snap a chalked line between the marks (see pages 57 to 60) to produce a straight line. Carefully paint the wall colour up level with this. The same technique can be used if the walls are of different colours.

Though it is difficult to produce a long, straight line freehand with a brush, and even harder with a roller, the problem can sometimes be overcome.

Masking tape can be applied above and along the chalk line, but must be removed as soon as you have painted up to it. As well as being expensive and time consuming, this method only really works well on smooth surfaces: on textured surfaces, the paint tends to 'creep' underneath. Tape should never be used on walls which have paper underneath the paint as the adhesion of the tape to the surface will pull off the paint when it is removed.

A more successful method of painting a straight line is to run a small paint pad along a wooden straight edge. This method is suitable for both oil and emulsion paints.

Cleaning equipment

Remember that paint dries on roller and brushes just as easily as on wall or ceilings, and is difficult to remov once it has dried. So, if you have t pause while painting it is impor tant not to let the equipment dry out

Stand brushes and rollers which have been used for oil paints in enoug water to cover the bristles and preven air from getting to them. Shake thi water from the brushes before usin them again.

Brushes and rollers which are bein used for emulsion paint should neve be soaked in water, as this will thi the paint contained in them. Instead you must wash them out and dry then after every session of work, thoug for very short breaks, you can wra them in plastic or a damp cloth.

12 *When using a roller to paint the wall, use a small paint brush to cut in at the corners before painting the main area*

13 *When you have cut in the line at the edges, paint the first strip. Make sure the handle join of the roller is not against the corner*

14 *It is best to paint an area of 1m² at a time, working from the corners where you have cut in and overlapping the strips*

15 *Extend the strokes of the roller out from each completed area and get a smooth, even coat by criss-crossing each strip of paint*

How to paint a mural

A mural in a child's bedroom gives the room an atmosphere of fun and enlivens the decoration—often making a small square room more interesting.

Painting murals may at first appear an awesome project, but is often surprisingly simple. The most important rule is to ensure that the image you want to portray has very straightforward lines, so that the process of painting the detail is not too complicated. The method illustrated here is almost as simple as painting by numbers except that you have to map out the paint areas yourself:

The size of the mural depends on the scale of enlargement you employ. This in turn depends on the size of the wall space available and how much of it you wish the design to cover.

First, site the mural where it will have the most effect. It is best to allow a border area of bare wall so the picture has some background relief. When you have decided on the location, mark out the grid with a soft pencil making sure that the point does not score into the surface of the plaster.

Mark the vertical line at the edge of the square using a plumbline or spirit level and a straightedge such as a metre rule. Lightly pencil in this reference line for the grid. For the mural shown here, the line must be broken up into 13 equal points for the horizontal lines. Make the vertical line, therefore, about a sixth longer than you wish the height of the mural to be, allowing for the area within the grid

at the top and bottom which is not painted. Divide the length of the line by 13 and mark the points for the horizontals. Then mark the top horizontal in the same way—with a spirit level and straightedge—and set the points for the vertical lines at the same distance apart (this time only 11 are needed). Draw in the grid from these points, taking great care to get them level.

When this is done, mark in the image lightly in pencil, following the pattern grid and working methodically from left to right along each row of squares. Use emulsion paint to fill in a large image and poster paints for a smaller one.

This process can be applied to enlarge any illustration to mural size.

PAINTING WOODWORK

- **SURFACE PREPARATION**
- **USING A BLOWLAMP**
- **MAKING GOOD**

- **PAINTING DOORS**
- **SKIRTINGS & ARCHITRAVES**
- **PAINTING WINDOWS**

Repainting the woodwork around the house will give your decoration a facelift for very little cost. And if you set about it the right way, you can be sure of a really professional finish.

Preparing the surface

Whether painting over new woodwork or a surface that has been painted previously, it is vital to make sure that the surface is sound, clean and dry.

With new woodwork, smooth the surface down with glasspaper, slightly rounding off any sharp edges. Treat knots or resinous patches with a knotting compound to prevent them from leaking sap through to the new paint. You can either buy this or make up your own from 70 parts of methylated spirit mixed with 30 parts shellac. Apply the knotting as accurately as possible, using a small brush or a pad of cloth wrapped round one finger. Fill cracks and open joints with a cellulose filler such as Polyfilla.

Above: *A light upward stroke of the brush will ensure that your painted surface is free from unsightly streaks and ridges*

To ensure that the paint adheres to the surface, new wood should be given a coat of primer. Primer also partially seals the wood surfaces, preventing leaking sap from spoiling the final coat of paint.

Check that the primer you use is suitable for the particular type of wood to be painted. Highly resinous wood should be treated with aluminium wood primer which has very effective sealing qualities. If in doubt about which primer to use for a particular job, consult your paint dealer.

In most cases, previously painted woodwork needs no more than cleaning and lightly rubbing down to prepare it. Remove all dirt and grease by washing the surface with warm water and detergent or sugar soap, paying

particular attention to areas on doors which are handled often and to wax polished surfaces.

If the paintwork has been particularly exposed to grease, in a kitchen for example, use a proprietary paint cleaner. Rinse off with plenty of clean water and allow the surface to dry.

To key the surface for the new paint, old gloss must be abraded to remove its shine. Although glasspaper can be used for this, better results are obtained with wet and dry paper, used wet.

Dealing with damaged surfaces

Unless a damaged surface is thoroughly prepared beforehand, flaws such as blisters and bubbles will be accen-

1 When treating woodwork that has been previously painted, abrade the old gloss to remove its shine and provide a key for the new paint

2 When the old paintwork has been sanded, wipe over it with a cloth dampened in white spirit to remove any traces of dust and grease

PAINTING WOODWORK

tuated and may spoil the finish.

Blisters and bubbles are usually caused by pockets of moisture or resin which become trapped beneath the surface of the original paint coat. Use a sharp knife to cut out the blistered paint, smooth off the hard paint edges with glasspaper then treat the area with multi-purpose primer.

Large or resinous knots and small resinous patches in woodwork should be treated with a knotting compound.

Flaking paint is most likely to be found on window frames which have been affected by the weather and by condensation. Remove as much of the loose paint as possible with a paint scraper or sharp knife (fig.3). Smooth down the area with glasspaper until all the remaining paint is quite sound. Any knots that have been exposed in this process should be dealt with as described above.

Cracks occur when wood joints have dried out or split. The most common problem areas are window frames, architraves—the mouldings around doors and windows—and the corner joints between skirting boards. Start by widening the cracks with a sharp knife, raking out any dust and dirt as you go. Prime the enlarged cracks and plug them with cellulose filler (fig.6). When dry, smooth with glasspaper (fig.7) and prime with a multi-purpose primer.

Particularly large or deep cracks should be filled in layers. Allow each layer of filler to dry before you start to apply the next.

Chips and dents develop through general wear and tear. Correct them as you would blisters and bubbles, using cellulose filler to level up the areas with the outer paint coat. When dry, sand smooth and prime.

Stripping paint

If a painted surface is particularly badly damaged, strip the paint off completely. Although paint can be stripped using just a paint scraper this can become tiring over large areas. More efficient methods are chemical stripping or heat stripping with a blowlamp or electric hot air gun and scraper. However, use a low flame—and extra caution—when stripping window frames with a blowlamp as the heat may crack the glass.

If you decide to use a blowlamp, buy a special paint-stripping head which spreads the flame over a wider area (fig.8). Use a waste tin to catch the pieces of hot paint, making sure none falls on the floor.

Begin stripping at the bottom of an area and work upwards, covering only a small area at a time. Play the flame from side to side to avoid burning the paint and charring the wood. As the paint melts, scrape it off holding the scraper at an angle so that shreds of hot paint do not fall on to your hand. For stripping mouldings, use a shave

3 Remove any flaws on the surface of old paintwork, such as flaking paint around removed door fittings, with a paint scraper

4 Paint on the areas around window frames and glass panels in doors often flakes. Scrape off as much of the old paint as possible

5 Use a paint brush to apply primer to any areas that are chipped or dented, or where old paint has been stripped altogether

6 Use cellulose filler to fill in any chips and dents in the wood, so that the damaged areas are brought up level with the existing paintwork

7 When the cellulose filler is dry, smooth the area with glasspaper wrapped around a wood or cork block, then prime the area again

8 Use a paint-stripping head when stripping paint with a blowlamp. Play the flame from side to side to avoid charring the wood

72

---

ook (fig.9). When all the paint has een stripped off, prime the bare wood.

ndercoats
you are painting new wood that has ly been primed, or over paintwork f a different colour, it is advisable to pply an undercoat to provide a good ey for the final coat of gloss. Check e paint charts when buying the gloss nd undercoat to make sure they are ompatible. Leave the undercoat until ry—the manufacturer's recommended rying time will be given on the tin— efore applying the gloss top coat.

loss paint
terior woodwork is traditionally ainted with gloss or semi-gloss paint. oors, skirtings and window frames ll take quite a few knocks and gloss aint stands up to hard wear better han flat paints—as well as being asier to clean with a damp cloth.

Traditional gloss paint is oil-based and includes resin to give it hard wearing qualities. Modern solvent-based gloss paint is often jelly-like in consistency, and does not drip. It should never be stirred, however, as this will reduce its non-drip qualities. If applied incorrectly, gloss shows up blemishes and brush marks more than any other type of paint. It is therefore vital to use proper brush strokes.

Apply ordinary gloss quickly, evenly and in as full a coat as possible. Using non-drip paint, apply a little at a time and take care not to overbrush or runs will occur. For small areas of woodwork, your brush strokes should always run the same way as the grain of the wood.

In large areas, brushing in three different directions will help you obtain a smoother finish. Start by applying the paint in a random way, criss-crossing the brush: when a section has been covered, draw the brush over the paint horizontally.

Finally, 'lay off' the paint by running the brush upwards over the paint very lightly so that no mark is left (fig.10).

Painting doors
Doors are not as easy to paint as you might think. To make the job easier, start by wedging the door base against the floor with a wedge or screwdriver. This will stop it from swinging shut, and perhaps ruining a wet edge. Remove as much metalwork as you can including handles, knobs and key escutcheons.

When painting flush doors, start at the top and work down in rectangular sections using a 75mm brush. Work quickly so that the paint does not harden before you have completed an adjoining section. Blend the sections carefully as you go, to eliminate any overlap marks.

Apply the paint by making two or three separate down strokes. Without reloading the brush, fill in any gaps by

9 Use a shave hook when stripping mouldings. To prevent shreds of melting paint from falling onto your hand, hold the tool at an angle

10 To ensure that no brush mark is left on finished paintwork, 'lay off' the paint by running the brush upwards with a very light stroke

Above: Hang used brushes in solvent. Remove excess during painting on string across tin

pencil (or wire)

string

11 För mouldings on panel doors, use a 12mm brush. Apply the paint sparingly so that it does not accumulate in ugly ridges

12 When painting panels, start brush strokes from the edges and work towards the middle. Blend the edges to eliminate overlap marks

13 To keep paint off glass, protect it with a paint shield. If paint does get onto the glass, wait for it to dry, then scrape it off

PAINTING WOODWORK

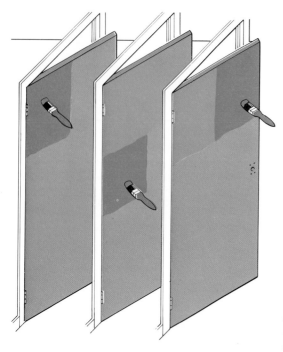

A. Paint flush doors in a series of overlapping panels, working quickly so you can blend in the wet edges (left). With panel doors (below), start from the centre and work outwards. First paint each of the inner panels, starting with the mouldings round their edges and then filling in the rest of the panel surface. Next tackle the horizontal rails, working from the top downwards. Finish off by painting all the vertical rails; tackle the centre rail first and then do the two outer rails (the stiles). Don't forget to paint the leading edge (nearest the handle) to match the inward opening face.

B. To 'cut in' where a skirting board or an architrave meets the wall, use a shaped cutting-in brush

into the paint. Cut in with one, continuous stroke, supporting your 'painting' hand with the other hand to steady it.

If walls are to be papered, extend the paintwork about 10mm up the wall above the skirting.

Paint the remaining parts of skirtings and architraves with a wide brush—50mm or 75mm—following the grain of the wood.

Windows

The paintwork on wooden windows must be kept in good condition if the frames are to be prevented from rotting. You should therefore take the opportunity of painting the top and under edges of any opening frame at the same time as the visible ones.

Remove any window fittings such as sash fasteners and make sure that the surface is clean and sound. Clean the glass, to prevent any dust or dirt on it from falling on to the wet paint.

To keep paint off the glass, you can if you wish mask up each pane. This is best done with an aluminium or plastic paint shield (fig.13)—obtainable from do-it-yourself shops— or masking tape. If paint still penetrates on to the glass, wait until it is dry then scrape it off with a paint scraper or a knife. If you are using masking tape peel it off when the paint is touch-dry.

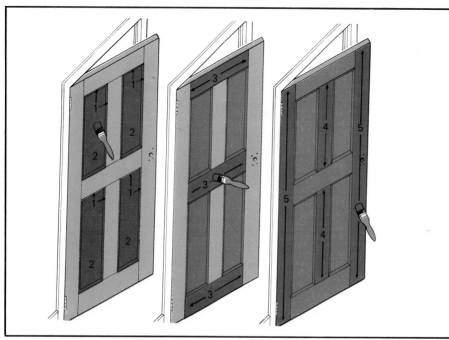

cross brushing then gently lay off the paintwork. When you are painting the edge of the door, use a brush slightly narrower than the width of the edge. If you use a wider brush, paint is likely to run down the front and back surfaces of the door.

Panel doors should be painted in a strict sequence (fig.A) and as quickly as possible—any pauses will result in the formation of a hard edge which is almost impossible to remove.

When painting mouldings in a contrasting colour to the rest of the door,

use a 12mm brush to work the paint well in to each corner (fig. 11). Do not overload the brush or paint will accumulate in ugly ridges.

Skirting and architraves

Start painting skirtings (baseboards) at the top edge and architraves at the edge where they meet the wall.

To brush up, or 'cut in' to the wall at this point, use a cutting-in tool—a specially angled brush—or a 25mm brush on its side. Avoid overloading the brush, dipping it only about 13mm

TIP FROM THE TRADE

Q I have just enamelled an interior door red, and the colour is very patchy. Can I remedy this?

A Only by sanding back and starting again. This time, make your undercoat a colour which is a close match to the desired top coat—either by squeezing a tube of red tint into the undercoat, or by asking the paint merchant to colour it for you. Red, unfortunately, is a very 'tricky' colour for showing patches and blemishes; it is even worse than white.

Casement windows, like panel doors, should be painted in a strict sequence (fig.C). Paint in the direction of the grain and use a cutting-in tool, or narrow brush on its side, to cut in where the paint meets the wall and the window pane.

To paint a double-hung window, begin by pulling the bottom sash up and the top sash down to expose the meeting rail. When the bottom parts of the top sash have been painted, almost close the window then paint the remaining areas (fig.D). Finish off in the order shown for casement windows.

For safety at each stage of painting, fix the sashes in position with a small wooden wedge. Wait until the paint is quite dry before closing the window or it may stick fast.

Painting the channels within which the sashes slide can be rather more difficult. When all the other paint has dried, slide the top sash down as far as it will go and paint the channels carefully, avoiding build-up of paint on corners and beads. Let it dry hard, then push both sashes up as far as they will go and repeat the operation. The important thing to remember is that the paint *must* be absolutely dry.

If you want to paint the edges of the sliding sashes themselves, the only option is to remove the sash and parting beads and lift each sash out of the frame so you can paint it in the comfort of your workshop. If you do this, take the opportunity to replace the sash cords, and carry out other maintenance needed to the sashes or the window frame.

14 Use a small paint brush to paint glazing bars. Wrap an elastic band round the bristles to stop them splaying out

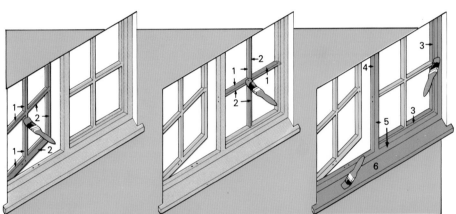

Above: *Paint a casement window in three main stages. Begin with the glazing bars, then the casement frame itself. Move on to paint areas of fixed glazing, then finish off with the window frame and ledge*

15 Use masking tape as an alternative to a paint guard. Overlap the tape at corners, and trim the ends neatly with a knife

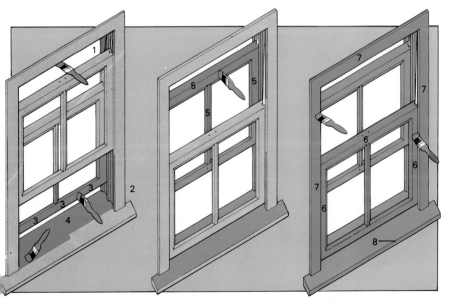

Above: *With sash windows, pull the top sash down and paint its lower half, then push it up and paint the top half. Paint the channels at the same time if you wish. Then tackle the lower sash and the main frame*

TIP FROM THE TRADE

Q How can I ensure that when I take the paint film up onto the surface of window glass it will stick?

A The paint film shoud extend onto the surface of the glass by about 3mm (⅛in) to seal the join between glass and putty. Clean the glass first with a rag soaked in white spirit to help the paint to adhere properly.

Dress up your doors

Most people paint their doors in single plain colours. But, with a little imagination and the use of different colours and designs, a dull door can be made to enhance the appearance of a room. On panel doors you can paint the panels and mouldings in different colours or, if preferred in differing shades of the same colour. Stripes and designs can be painted onto flush and panel doors, with the use of masking tape, and extended across the adjacent walls. For a really modern look, try painting a design onto a door that matches, and draws attention to, a nearby picture on the wall.

Even more adventurously, a children's room can be transformed by a cartoon character on the door or, as in the picture below right, occupying a whole wall. Either way, you enlarge the cartoon by dividing it into a grid pattern of tiny squares and the wall into corresponding, larger squares.

Skirting boards can also be painted imaginatively to liven up the look of a room. For instance, if you decide to paint a coloured stripe across or around a door, try painting the skirting board in the same colour or a matching shade. Here are just a few ideas you can try out to brighten up your home.

Left: *'Door with a difference' uses strips of the green wallpaper in the middles of the panels, with a border painted to match the bedspread*

Below: *A subtler scheme using dark blue, light blue and white to echo the colours of the wallpaper, carpet and furniture*

Above: *Bold, colourful stripes enliven a children's room. Each stripe must be masked off with masking tape and painted separately*

Below: *Adding adventure to a boys' room, a striking cowboy cartoon panel occupies not just the door, but the whole wall*

OUTDOOR WOODWORK

● WHEN TO PAINT
● SEQUENCES
● PAINTING METAL

● WHERE TO START
● PREPARATION
● PAINTING WOOD

Painting the outside of your house is by far the most demanding and time-consuming type of decoration you can do. It is obviously not work you want to repeat often so careful planning, the right tools and materials, and an extremely methodical approach are important. This way, you can be sure of an attractive and durable finish.

When to paint
Although spring is the traditional time to paint the outside, it is not necessarily the best time. If the exterior wood and metal need painting in the spring, no doubt they needed it in the autumn; and the ravages of winter can worsen the condition of the paintwork and make your job far harder.

Early autumn is a good time for painting, providing you can be sure of finishing before winter sets in. Should the work be delayed by bad weather, conditions can only get worse and you will probably have to leave it until the following spring. Days are also shorter at this time of the year and evening painting is rarely possible as the light fails.

If you intend to paint in the spring, it is worth a weekend's work in the autumn scraping back peeling paint from the timber and metalwork. Coat the patches with an oil-based primer to protect the surfaces during the winter months.

Ideal conditions for exterior painting are rare. If you try to paint when it is raining, the water will prevent the paint getting a good grip on the substrate—the bare surface—and after a short period it will flake or peel off. Rain falling on a recently painted surface forms small craters which reduce the gloss and spoils the appearance very rapidly.

Even a heavy dew forming on a paint film before it is dry can cause the gloss to disappear completely. And if varnish is used in these conditions, it may turn milky.

In late summer or autumn, it is best to finish painting about two hours before sunset to reduce the risk of condensation.

Extreme heat causes the paint to set very quickly and reduces its flow as you apply it—resulting in severe brushmarks or a textured, 'feathered' finish. High temperatures also thin the paint film, reducing its effectiveness and covering power.

Painting in high winds should be avoided as they carry dust which is deposited on the wet paint and spoils the finish. And winds make any ladder work very precarious.

Cold weather makes the paint thick and hard to mix, so runs are more likely to occur. It can also delay the drying time of the paint and you may have to wait up to two days before applying a second coat.

The worst areas
Exterior paintwork rarely deteriorates to the same degree throughout a building. You will probably find that the paintwork on the wall of the house which faces the sun breaks down quicker than on other aspects. It is here that you should concentrate your renovation work—a complete repaint is not always necessary.

The first sign that a paint film is coming to the end of its effective life is when the gloss disappears. The paint becomes porous, and severe winter frost and rain will quickly penetrate it. If you prefer to do the whole house at one time, try to make up for the relative levels of deterioration by putting an extra coat on the most exposed or sun-facing surfaces and on any other face which shows signs of rapid breakdown.

Checking for damage
Check all surfaces very carefully before starting preparations: the paint film which appears firm can often hide a decaying substrate. Usually, flaking paint indicates that the surface is wet, rotting or rusting.

Scrape the paintwork and prod the timber surfaces to ensure that there is good adhesion and sound material underneath. If the timber is rotten, it must be removed and replaced with sound, seasoned wood. Paint does not halt corrosion or wood rot and to

Above: *Before painting plastic gutters clean them with a piece of steel wool and a bucket of water*

ignore such defects will result in very expensive repairs in later years.

Investigate the sources of damp around affected timber and put them right before starting to paint. Damp may be entering through porous brickwork, a broken downpipe or a perforated damp proof course (see pages 165 to 168). Replace any broken windows or damaged putty and check all mastic or caulking seals.

Where to start
Always start work at the top of the house so that at no time are you painting, or preparing, above finished work. Your main objective is to avoid having to move the ladder or scaffold tower more often than is absolutely necessary. Plan your sitings carefully before starting so that you can safely reach as large an area as possible and carry out as many processes as you can in that position.

It is not a good idea to apply two coats of oil-based paint in one day, but you can leave the scaffold in position and apply the second coat the next day. Afterwards, move the scaffold in reverse order back along the house.

Priming or undercoating can usually be carried out as soon as the surface has been prepared, so avoiding a scaffold move between preparation and painting.

Metal gutters and pipes

Cast-iron or mild steel gutters and cast-iron drainpipes rust if they are not properly protected. Always take the opportunity to clean out and paint the inside of gutters when you paint the outside.

Scour the surfaces of both sides of the gutters with a wire brush. If rust is left on the surface it will continue to form under the paint film and eventually cause flaking. Continue brushing until there is a dull shine on the metal surface (fig. 2). Use rust remover on the pitted areas.

When you have cleaned the surfaces, dry them thoroughly with rags or *carefully* pass a blowlamp over them. The bare metal areas are then ready for immediate priming before any moisture can settle and restart the rusting process. The primer should overlap the sound paint around the derusted areas by about 5mm.

Calcium plumbate is an excellent primer for both iron and timber but if there is any possibility of animals or young children coming into con-

1 *Clean out all the accumulated dirt from the inside of the gutter. Make sure that the downpipes are free of any blockages*

2 *Use a wire brush to ensure that all rust is removed from the inside of the guttering. Try to clean down to bare metal*

tact with the paintwork, use a non-toxic metal primer with a zinc chromate base for protection.

When the primer on the bare area is dry—after 24 to 48 hours—wash all the surfaces with a detergent solution to remove accumulated grime and dry them with a rag or chamois leather. You can then apply an oil-based undercoat to the primed areas.

After the patches of undercoat are dry—at least eight hours later—apply undercoat to the entire surface. When

this is dry, follow it with a coat of gloss paint. For gutters, 25mm is the handiest size of brush.

Although you can paint the insides of gutters in the same way as the outsides, it is cheaper to use either black bitumastic paint or a thick coat of any gloss paint left over from previous jobs (fig. 4). Be sure to prime all bare areas before applying either paints. If you use bitumastic paint, keep a tough brush solely for this purpose; traces left in the bristles can

Sequence for Exterior Painting

Start all preparation and painting work on a house exterior at the top and work downwards. Following the correct sequence ensures that the whole exterior is completed and no painting interferes with or spoils any other part.
1 Gutters: *Start at one end of the roof and work around the house*
2 Eaves: *Prepare and paint the eaves working from one end*

3 Barge boards: *Begin at the ridge and work down the board towards the eaves*
4 Downpipes: *Prepare and paint these working from top to bottom*
5 Brickwork: *This should be cleaned and pointed before painting*

6 Rendering: *Fill in any cracks and render walls where necessary*
7 Doors and windows: *Complete the sequence by painting any wooden walls, front and garage doors and windows as well as wooden railings*

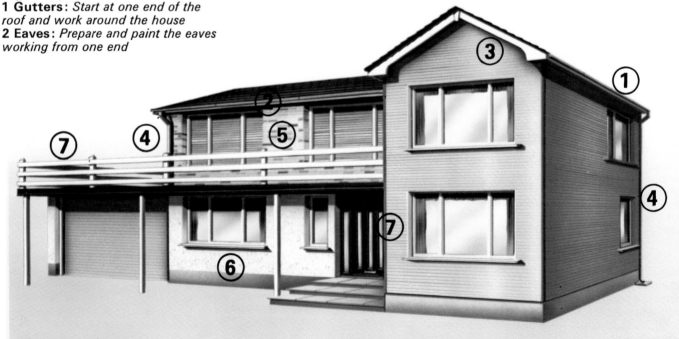

3 *Wash out the inside of the gutter and dry it thoroughly with a cloth or with the flame from a blowlamp*

4 *Prime the bare metal. After 24 hours apply undercoat and finish off eight hours later with a top coat of gloss or black bitumastic paint*

5 *Downpipes and fittings should first be cleaned with a wire brush. This is a good opportunity to check fixings*

6 *Make sure that any areas of bare metal around fixings are liberally painted with primer as these areas are more likely to rust*

seriously affect the colour and drying of oil paints.

Treat all downpipes the same way as gutters. If the pipes are black, check first if they are painted with bitumastic either by rubbing with white spirit, which will quickly dissolve bitumastic, or by applying a white undercoat to a small section to see if it becomes stained.

Pipes painted with bitumastic will not take an oil-based finish unless you seal them first with stop-tar knotting or aluminium sealer. Do this after the surface has been derusted, primed and washed with detergent. Apply undercoats direct to the sealer when it is thoroughly dry.

You can also paint plastic gutters and downpipes. These need to be cleaned thoroughly with strong detergent solution, scoured with fine steel wool, dried, and painted with two coats of gloss paint. Gutters painted in this way then match metal ones.

Windows
Metal windows are usually made from galvanized steel and do not rust. But if they are very old and badly maintained, the zinc coating may fracture allowing the metal underneath to rust. In such cases remove the rust with medium grade steel wool or a flap-wheel drill attachment and prime immediately with a calcium plumbate or a proprietary zinc chromate metal primer.

Make sure that you remove all traces of steel wool before you prime, or they will rust under the paint and stain the gloss finish. If you use an electric drill with a flap wheel, wear safety goggles and a disposable face mask to protect you from the dust.

If paint is flaking but the galvanized metal underneath is in good condition, this indicates that there is poor adhesion and all the paint should be removed. You can do this easily by dry scraping with a 25mm stripping

knife or the flat side of a shave hook.

Use a liquid paint remover (any can be used on painted metal), on the more stubborn areas. Most paint removers are rinsable, so a final wash with a detergent solution will remove all traces of the solvent and leave the metal clean for priming.

If there are no signs of rusting or flaking, sand the old paint film with grade 240 wet-and-dry paper, used wet. Put detergent in the water to make the rubbing down easier. When the surface is rinsed and dried, it is ready for undercoating.

Primed or washed and abraded surfaces need only one coat of undercoat and one coat of gloss. You can get a good straight line along the edge of the glass by using a well worn brush which 'cuts in' easily at the edges. Bring the paint about 1mm on to the pane to make a seal between the putty and the glass. Wash and clean the glass before you start painting.

Aluminium garage doors
If flaking is considerable—about 20 percent of the total area—strip off all the paint and start from scratch. Use a liquid paint remover as described above then, after washing and drying, prime the aluminium with zinc chromate—calcium plumbate is not suitable for aluminium.

If the paint is in good condition, use grade 240 wet-and-dry paper with detergent in the water to prepare the surface. On a large surface, such as a garage door, keep wiping the surface with a sponge so that the abrading paper does not become clogged.

On large, flat surfaces it is advisable to use a rubber or cork sanding block. Keep rubbing until the gloss of the old paint has all gone: the new paint will then key well.

One coat of undercoat and one of gloss is quite sufficient over primed or wet-abraded aluminium. If you are painting a large door, use a 50 or 75mm brush to get the best results, with a 25mm brush for getting into edges and grooves.

Timber surfaces
Exterior timber surfaces may be small in area—eg windows—or large—eg weatherboard or clapboard siding. Preparation is much the same, however. The existing paintwork will be in one of three conditions:
Severe flaking: This usually leaves large areas of the substrate exposed so you need to remove the old coatings completely. You will get rid of most of the paint by dry scraping it with a 79

75mm stripping knife. Remove the tricky areas with liquid paint remover, protecting the areas which are not being treated with plastic sheets or paper. Wash off the paint remover with medium grade steel wool and detergent, rubbing in the direction of the grain.

When the surface is dry, sand it with fine grade glasspaper to smooth the grain which will have raised slightly by the action of spirit and water on the surface.

Coat any knots in the timber with shellac knotting, or they may later release resin which would stain the paint. You can apply knotting with a piece of rag. Make sure that the whole area of the knot is covered and overlap it about 3mm on to the surrounding surface of the wood. The surface can then be primed.

Isolated areas of flaking: These are to be found most often around edges and joints. Scrape away the flaking paint with a stripping knife, shave hook or paint scraper until a hard, firmly-adhered edge of paint is left. Then use glasspaper (or wet-and-dry paper used wet) to feather the edges of the area. Dust off and prime the wood, pushing the paint as deep as possible into the joints and overlapping the old paint by about 5mm all round.

Good condition: Paint in this state needs only to be wet abraded.

When the priming paint is dry, fill any holes or open joints so that no moisture can penetrate the wood and cause rotting. You could use linseed oil putty (mixed with a little undercoat to make it dry faster and be more flexible), mastic or caulking compound, or a proprietary filler, depending on the nature and size of the gap that you are filling.

Press the filler (or whatever) well into the gaps, and aim to leave a smooth surface as you work. With fillers, rub down smooth when hard.

Give timber surfaces which have been stripped at least three coats of paint over the primer to ensure good protection. This can be one undercoat and two coats of gloss or two undercoats and one coat of gloss.

Surfaces which have a covering of old paint in good condition need only one coat of undercoat and one of gloss.

All undercoats and glosses used on the outside of the house must have an oil base. The same undercoat and gloss paints can be applied to all primed or painted timber, metal or plastic surfaces; only the primer varies from material to material so that a good base is provided for painting.

Doors

Unless you require a special finish, you can treat and paint front and rear doors in the same way as timber windows. Doors, being larger areas, show up surface and painting defects more clearly, so you should take great care when preparing and painting them.

Because they are less exposed, doors rarely get into such a bad state that they need stripping. In any case, the extra thickness of old paint coats in good condition provides better protection for the timber and a smooth, hard foundation for high quality finishes. When the paint is completely stripped off a door it takes some time to build up a good enough finish with several coats.

You may have to strip your door completely if it is severely blistering or flaking, or if the paint coats already on it are too thick, making the door difficult to shut.

7 *Begin work on windows by cleaning old putty out of the rebate using a chisel. Dig out any areas of flaking paint*

9 *Metal window frames should be cleaned with a wire brush. By opening the window you can clean the underneath of the frame*

Whatever method of preparation you use, always remove the door furniture—handle, letterbox, key escutcheon—before starting work. This saves time 'cutting in' around them and produces a better finish.

The easiest, quickest and cheapest method of stripping the door is to burn off the paint with a blowlamp. Start on the mouldings, using a combination head shave hook to scrape away the peeling debris. Strip the flat areas with a 50 or 75mm stripping knife, working behind the flame torch and always pushing the knife in the direction of the grain. When the paint is completely stripped, prepare and paint the wood in the same way as you would timber window frames.

If the paint is not to be stripped you should still sand the door. For paint coatings with very coarse brush marks and deep chippings use a grade 180 wet-and-dry paper. If the paint has

8 *A blowlamp and scraper can be used to clean off areas of paint but use these with care near glass to avoid cracking it*

10 *Primer should be applied to areas of the frame which are later to be covered with filler or filled with putty*

reasonable finish, a 240 grade paper will be sufficient.

Keep the surface wet and clean with a sponge dipped in the detergent water, rubbing the paintwork until all the gloss is removed and all the hard edges are erased. This may take a long time with regular changes of water and paper, but the effort is worthwhile. Keep a dust sheet or pad of newspapers under the door during the entire preparation and painting process: these absorb water and debris, and prevent dust being picked up during painting.

Apply the undercoat, laying off very lightly with the tip of the brush in the direction of the grain to avoid brush-marks (see pages 71 to 77). When the undercoat is dry, sand with a grade glasspaper to remove any unevenness.

For a really smooth finish, fill the whole surface at this stage with either oil-based paste filler or vinyl-based fine surface filler.

If you cannot get the filler smooth with the knife, sand it with fine glasspaper. Use this method also between primer and undercoat for a door which has been stripped. A second coat of undercoat will seal the absorbency of the filler and provide a surface of even colour, but take great care when laying off the brush strokes. Two coats of undercoat will also ensure that any old colour will not show through.

Before applying the gloss paint, wipe over the surface with a tacky duster and lay clean newspapers under the door.

Remember to include the top edge of the door and, if possible, the bottom edge. If the door opens into the hall, paint the hinge end in the same colour as the outside. To achieve a glass-like finish, apply a second coat of gloss as soon as the first is hard. When the entire job is finished, you can replace any fittings.

Illuminated house signs

Brighten up the outside of your house with a number or a name which is as easy to read at night as it is in daylight.

All you need is an inexpensive exterior light fitting and some paint. It is important to use a light which is designed for outdoor use, and that all electrical work is done safely. Then, following the ideas below, you can simply add the numbers or letters.

11 Press the putty into the rebate first using your fingers and then a putty knife. Flatten the putty into a smooth bevelled edge

12 All cracks in the surface should be covered with filler. Press it hard into the crack and smooth off with a knife

13 When the filler has hardened smooth down the whole frame with sandpaper which should be mounted on a block

14 When the putty has hardened apply undercoat and topcoat. Paint onto the glass for a few millimetres to prevent leaks

Choose a light fitting with an opal cover of glass or plastic. You must use a waterproof fitting designed for exterior use, and fitted with a low power lamp such as a 25 watt pygmy bulb or a 8 watt fluorescent tube. There are many different types on the market

Choose shapes like these for numbers
Choose long shapes like these for names

You can use several methods to put your house name or number onto the light. In methods 1-4, the characters stand out against an illuminated background. Method 5 illuminates the characters themselves

① If you have a good eye, paint onto the lamp cover by hand. Draw up guidelines on the cover to help you position the characters. You will need several coats

② It is much easier to paint the characters using stencils and a stencil brush or paint spray. Use a guideline to help you get the letters straight

③ You can use self-adhesive P.V.C. lettering which is available in many different sizes, and styles

④ Stick on moulded plastic lettering. Use plastic cement if the lamp cover is plastic or epoxy cement if it is glass

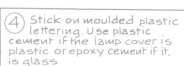

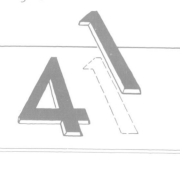

⑤ To leave the letters illuminated, stick on P.V.C. lettering as in method ③. Spray or paint the whole cover until it is opaque, then peel the letters off carefully to leave a clear shape behind

N.B. <u>To paint on glass or plastic</u>

① Make sure the surface is clean
② Use a gloss enamel paint, whether spray or brush applied
③ Use several coats, and check for opacity by holding up to the light

<u>Connecting</u>

Follow the lamp manufacturer's instructions for fitting the lamp to the wall. Outside wiring must be done using waterproof fittings. If in doubt, consult a qualified electrician.
In Canada, electrical work may have to be carried out by an electrician

PAINTING OUTSIDE WALLS

- **PREPARATION**
- **PAINTED WALLS**
- **DAMP SURFACES**
- **SAFE ACCESS**
- **BRICKWORK**
- **EXTERIOR CLADDING**
- **KILLING MOULD**
- **APPLYING PAINT**

As with all painting, the quality and integrity of the finish depends to a large extent on the preparation of the surface before you even open a tin of paint. And the preparation differs according to the surface to be painted.

New brick
Concrete, cement rendering and pebbledash should be treated in the same way as new brick.

To start with, remove any dust or loose material using a stiff brush, and scrape off any splashes of cement or concrete. Look out for any patches of white fluffy crystals; these are a result of efflorescence, and indicate that moisture is coming to the surface of the wall. If you paint over the patches the moisture will tend to lift the paint off. Clean the efflorescent debris off the walls with a stiff brush and wait about two weeks to make sure that no more patches emerge. Wash any mould growth or lichens with a proprietary mould inhibitor or bleach. Then scrape off these growths, and apply a further coat of inhibiter or bleach to the bare surface. Finally, make good deep cracks or holes in the surface with sand and cement.

Where new, shuttered concrete is to be painted it is important to degrease the surface because it may still bear traces of the release oil used on the inside faces of the shuttering.

An extension pole gives a paint roller a new dimension in versatility, allowing you to cover exterior surfaces without the encumbrance of a ladder

PAINTING OUTSIDE WALLS

1 To start with you must remove all wall decorations such as shutters and tie trellis-trained plants well out of harm's way

2 Next brush away any heavy deposits of dirt with a stiff brush. Do not use a wire brush, however, because stray strands will cause rust marks

tion to the cleaned walls. This will soak into the existing material, binding it into a solid film not soluble in water and resistant to it.

Wood
Preparing large areas of wood—eg weatherboard or clapboard siding—for painting is dealt with on pages 79 to 80. The amount of work needed depends mainly on the condition of the existing paintwork.

Damp surfaces
Walls which display signs of either damp or mould growth must be treated before you can paint.

Where surfaces are prone to damp, such as basement walls or garden walls, you must apply a coat of bituminous emulsion sealer and allow it to dry thoroughly.

Previously painted masonry
It is always advisable to prepare painted surfaces before repainting, and in the case of exterior work it is essential if the new coatings are to protect the building in the way they are designed to.

Oil (alkyd) paints: Wash with a strong cleaning agent such as washing soda, then rinse with clean water. Scrape off any loose or flaking paint, make good any deep cracks and holes with sand and cement, and fill shallow cracks with an exterior filler. Note that interior filler must not be used for exterior work because it will rapidly deteriorate and cause the new coating to blister and flake off.

Emulsion (latex) paints: Wash with a detergent, then rinse with clean water. Anything stronger, such as washing soda, will damage emulsioned surfaces. Where water penetrates the surface, allow it to dry completely before you start painting. Again scrape off loose and flaking paint and then repair cracks.

Cement-based paints: These and other non-washable types of paint have been used extensively in the past on large areas of exterior masonry, mainly because they are fairly cheap. However, most cement paints tend to become very powdery with age, and washing, which only softens them further, must be avoided. Moreover, the water content of the new coating can cause these paints to soften, and this will prevent proper adhesion of the new paint. You must, therefore, thoroughly brush, and if necessary scrape, the walls until you have a firm surface. Finally, you must apply

84 a masonry sealer or stabilizing solu-

3 Make up a strong bleach solution and apply it to all mould and plant growth in order to destroy it—wash off the bleach with water

4 The finished work can only be as good as the ground surface. You must go over the surface carefully and repair any defects like bad pointing

5 It Is wise in most cases to apply a coat of stabilizing solution to the brickwork. Brush it on liberally, allowing it to soak into the bricks

6 Before painting cover all nearby plants, grass and tile steps or thresholds so that you avoid spoiling them with splashes of paint

Mould infected surfaces

Mould growths are common on exterior surfaces where moisture is present as a result simply of the atmosphere, structural faults or defective plumbing. To remove them first brush a coat of proprietary mould inhibitor on to the infected areas, and then strip all the mould back with a stiff brush and scraper. Do not use a wire brush, however, because any metal particles left behind can cause rust stains. Then apply a second coat of mould inhibitor to the surface and allow it to dry. These solutions contain strong fungicides and you must wear rubber gloves and goggles to guard against splashes.

This process must be carried out before any sealer is applied to the surface of the wall.

Masonry paints

Masonry paint is a water-based paint similar to emulsion (latex) but with the addition of other materials such as granulated quartz, mica, and in some instances fine strands of glass fibre. These additives render it highly durable, moisture resistant and give it the ability to resist cracks in the surface, while providing a very attractive fine texture. The coverage is usually about half that of emulsion; approximately 6m² per litre depending on the absorbent quality of the material. One or two coats will be needed depending on the existing colour and nature of the surface.

Applying masonry paint

Masonry paint may be applied by brush or roller. A roller is much faster than a brush, but for inaccessible corners a brush is unbeatable. On smooth surfaces the texture of the roller is more suitable than a brush. On heavily textured surfaces such as pebbledash or rough brickwork a long pile roller, which can penetrate into all the crevices is most suitable.

However, a conventional roller tray is not practical for use on ladders. It is necessary when painting from a ladder to use a roller bucket or scuttle, designed to hang on the underside of the ladder or scaffolding around you.

Brushes, if you decide to use them, must be as large as possible—100-150mm wide. Nylon or bristle and fibre brushes will stand up to the abrasive nature of exterior surfaces much better than pure bristle. Furthermore, the close pack of bristle will only hold small quantities of the rather thick masonry paint.

Access for application

In most cases exterior surfaces are larger and higher than interior surfaces. Consequently some form of scaffolding may be required, and a method of working which will result in even coverage after a number of sessions (see below).

Do make sure, when erecting the scaffolding, that there is adequate space between the tower and the wall to enable you to prepare the surface and apply the material. If you erect the tower too close to the wall you will inevitably be left with small areas which will need touching in afterwards; and they will invariably show.

A. Below: *You must approach house painting in a methodical way—starting at the top, then working down. Try to end each session at a natural break*

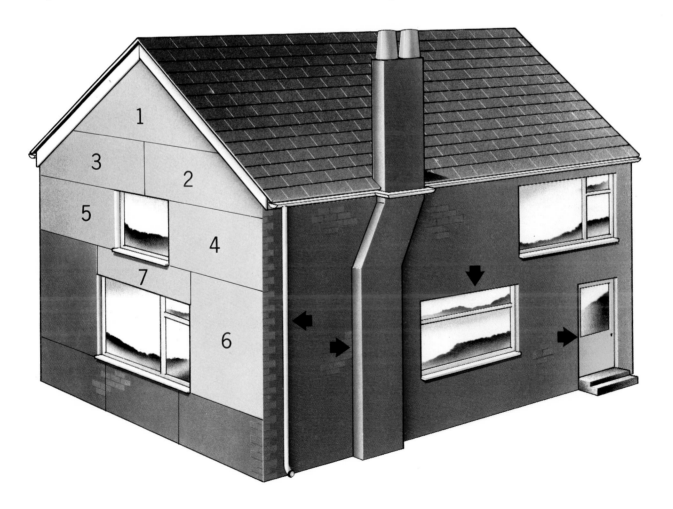

Unless you have to contend with a large expanse of wall, a ladder will probably suffice. Use a ladder stay when working at heights; it will make the ladder more stable and make it easier to hang a bucket or roller scuttle on the underside with easy access for the brush or roller. Extend the ladder so that you can reach the top of the wall. But remember that it is unsafe to leave less than four rungs above your feet; this will allow you a safe hand hold. Position the ladder so that you can reach the extreme right hand side—or left hand side if you are left-handed—of the wall.

However, assuming that you are right-handed complete the panel to the right of the ladder, then move the ladder to the left, and work on the adjacent panel as shown in fig. A.

Continue horizontally across the

B. Above: *When you stop in the middle of a painting session put the brush or roller in a polythene bag to keep it moist*

7 *In order to avoid changes in colour, mix a sufficient quantity of paint to complete the job then fill a paint bucket with the mixture*

8 *A ladder stay is a very useful accessory which makes the ladder more stable. A paint bucket can be hung from it.*

9 *It is not possible to use the roller when painting inaccessible areas. In these cases you must resort to a small distemper brush*

10 *Always work from one side of the ladder only. Trying to cover both sides will result in difficulties because the ladder is in the way*

wall until you reach the left hand side of the wall, then adjust the ladder to allow access to the area below, and so on. If the light or weather forces you to abandon work before it is complete, you must try and break off at a point where the joining of the dry and wet film will show least; at a pipe running down the wall, a window, moulding or similar.

Painting

Try to plan exterior painting for warm, dry days. Extreme cold or frost can affect the water content of the paint, causing a complete breakdown in the film. Rain on the surface before the paint is dry can thin it disastrously.

The first coat on porous surfaces can be thinned—but follow manufacturers instructions carefully.

Charge the brush or roller with plenty of paint, and lay it or roll it in all directions. Do not apply the material too far, however, because correct covering and protection requires that it be twice as thick as ordinary liquid paints. Any spots and splashes must be washed off immediately with water because exterior grade paint sets rapidly. During short breaks, wrap the brush or roller tightly in a plastic bag to prevent the air curing the material. Do not be tempted to leave it in water because the initial application will be patchy.

When you have completed a session of work immediately clean all the equipment in detergent and water. But take care not to block sink wastes with the fine granulated quartz, or scratch enamel or stainless steel sinks.

Painting wood surfaces

For painting outside woodwork, you have the choice of using ordinary gloss paint, or of stripping existing paintwork and then applying one of the new microporous paints which allow the wood to breathe and do not suffer from cracking and peeling. They can be used on any exterior woodwork. On horizontal, overlapping cladding, paint the underneath projections before painting the vertical surfaces, making sure they are completely covered—areas that you miss will be very obvious from ground level. Try not to break a painting session in the middle of a length of cladding—make your breaks between adjacent boards.

Exterior wood stains and coloured wood preservatives can also be used, especially on shingles and shakes. But check manufacturer's instructions first: most products have to be applied to new, bare wood.

SPECIAL PAINT EFFECTS

- ● BASIC TECHNIQUES
- ● CHOOSING COLOURS
- ● BRUSH GRAINING
- ● MARBLING
- ● PREPARATION
- ● MIXING COLOURS
- ● GRAINING A DOOR
- ● FINISHING

Good timber is not cheap—and the cheaper materials often used in wall cladding or to make wooden doors do not always bear close inspection. For this reason many decorators, rather than using a single flat colour to paint bare and inferior timber doors and panels, prefer to brighten them visually by using two time-honoured techniques: marbling and brush graining.

Both rely on the skilful use of a paint-brush to suggest the finishes their names imply, and neither are particularly difficult. There is usually no pretence at imitating real timber or marble; the aim is rather to create a pleasant finish with a subtle texture.

Brush graining

This is where a woody grain is produced in the paintwork by applying a fairly light ground coat followed by a slightly darker topcoat. Before this topcoat dries, a brush is drawn across it to produce lines or streaks which reveal the lighter ground colour. You can create different effects by varying the colour of the ground coat and by the way you draw the brush through the topcoat.

Surface preparation: If the finished work is to last, the existing timber surface must be prepared properly. Sand down rough paintwork then fill chips and indentations in the same way as for ordinary paintwork, priming bare surfaces before applying filler.

Apply the ground colour when the filler and primer is hard, and try to achieve the smoothest possible finish. The best paints to use as a ground are oil-based eggshell paints that dry hard with a slight sheen.

Ground coat colours: These must be chosen carefully as they can clash with the topcoat to create an unpleasant effect. For example, a white ground with a black topcoat creates a pleasant grey effect, while red on white looks pink. Where you want to create a more traditional timber effect, paint the ground the same colour as the lightest shade of wood you are trying to imitate. This can vary from off-white for pine through cream or tan for oak to pink for mahogany. You can obtain most of these colours from a specialist builder's merchant, but certain colours or shades you may have to mix yourself from proprietary oil-based paints.

A. Marbling and graining are interesting alternatives to flat colours, and are comparatively cheap ways of suggesting a more expensive wall finish

1 When graining wood assemble all the brushes, white spirit, and scumble colours before you apply the top coat. Mix the scumble carefully

2 Apply the scumble coat to the door panel using an ordinary paintbrush. Spread it evenly over the surface and paint the beading at the same time

3 Now draw an open-bristled brush through the scumble coat to create the grain effect. Make sure all the brush strokes are parallel

4 Grain the muntin (or central stile) next. Wipe excess paint off the rails with a cloth, using a straightedge to protect the new grain pattern

5 Next, paint and grain the three rails, still using the straightedge to prevent grain patterns overlapping, and then grain the stiles

Applying the topcoat

The topcoat (often called the *scumble* or *graining coat*) can be either an oil or a water-based paint. As water-based paints tend to dry too quickly to allow you to work at a leisurely pace, however, it is best to choose oil-based paints.

The scumble should be thinner and more transparent than ordinary paint as its purpose is not to obliterate but to complement the ground coat. A fairly wide range of scumble colours is available from specialist suppliers, and they require only the addition of thinners to bring them to the correct consistency.

If no scumble is available in the colour you want you can make it up yourself from equal amounts of linseed oil, white spirit, and varnish. To prevent the grain pattern from blurring while the scumble dries, add a little body to the mixture in the form of fine whiting (which is actually transparent), or clear oil scumble glaze.

Finally, to give it the correct colour, add the required amount of liquid oil stainer or artist's oil colour and stir the entire mixture thoroughly. If you use artist's oil paint mix it with a little scumble on a piece of board using a palette knife and then mix this into the rest of the scumble. When using oil stainer, stir this into the mixture and remove hard particles by straining the scumble through a fine nylon stocking.

Applying the scumble: The golden rule here is to paint one complete section at a time so that the grain effect along a single panel is continuous. Apply it evenly with an ordinary paintbrush and make sure the brush marks run in one direction only. Do not attempt to obliterate the ground coat: where lighter areas are required in the final effect draw the edge of the brush through the scumble in a scrubbing action; where you want to darken the effect simply apply more.

To produce the finished grain effect, draw an open-bristled brush through the scumble before it dries, keeping the grain nearly parallel to the edge of the panel. Do not use an ordinary paintbrush as this will tend to remove too much of the top coat; instead use something like a dusting or wallpapering brush. Alternatively you can cut combs of varying fineness from strips of leather, rubber, or plastic, and experiment with these.

Where you must use two or three strokes to grain a wide panel, make sure that they all run parallel to each other, and that you keep the pressure on the brush or comb constant at all times. You can also soften the grain slightly by very gently brushing across it with a soft brush. Professionals use a hog's hair softener for this but you can achieve good results simply by experimenting with various soft paintbrushes.

Specific techniques: As stated above, the grain pattern should imitate that of natural wood. In the case of a skirting board (baseboard) this means that the grain would run horizontally. On doors, however, the direction of the grain depends on the type of construction and also on the positions of the individual panels, styles and rails.

In a panelled door, for example, the grain in the panels, muntins (central stiles) and stiles runs vertically (fig. 5), while the grain runs horizontally in the rails. Grain the mutins and panels first, followed by the rails. It does not matter if you overlap into the rails while doing this—wipe the rails clean and then apply and grain more scumble. Use a straight-

6 *You can use a similar technique on larger areas as well. Apply the scumble to the ground coat making sure the brush marks are roughly parallel*

7 *Now use the same brush to create a rough imitation of the grain in a large timber panel. Run the grain pattern to the edges of the piece*

8 *Use a small piece of lint-free rag to highlight the grain pattern and create the effect of 'rings' in the timber by removing more scumble*

9 *Finally, before the scumble dries, soften the grain effect slightly by flicking a soft brush across it, working from the centre of the pattern outwards*

edge to prevent the scumble overlapping on to a grained panel (fig. 4).

If you make a mistake while graining the scumble do not try to touch it up – the damage will show all too clearly once the scumble has dried. Instead you must brush out the grain and re-do the entire panel starting from scratch.

Protection: Lacquer the timber once the scumble has dried to protect it. Use two coats of gloss for outside work and matt, eggshell, or gloss for internal work. Rub the lacquer down between coats with 500 grade wet and dry paper to give a smooth and attractive surface.

B. Below: *Typical applications of brush graining and marbling. The door has been grained and the architrave and ceiling coving marbled in dark colours to complement the graining*

Marbling

Marbling, as its name implies, is the imitation of smooth polished marble or timber, and for best results a completely smooth ground coat surface is required. Accurate imitation of specific types of marble requires practice, but a basic and quite effective finish can be achieved very simply. For most types of marbling work a black or white ground coat is used but you can experiment—with quite spectacular results—on other finishes.

Preparation of the timber surface is done in the same way as for ordinary painting, but it must be done properly for the best results. The same applies to the

C. Left: *A simple marbling project for beginners: a detachable timber table top finished in warm colours and polished to resemble old marble*

10 *The basic requirements of marbling: liquid oil stainer; white spirit; linseed oil; a drying agent; and brushes, rags, and natural sponges*

11 *Prepare for marbling by applying a smooth groundcoat to the panel, and then run a lint-free rag soaked in clear gilp across the surface*

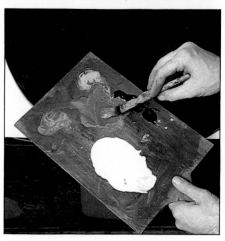

12 *Mix an artist's oil paint or liquid oil stainer into the gilp. Use an artist's palette and a palette knife to mix the colour and gilp completely*

13 *Brush the colour in to the panel using an ordinary artist's paintbrush. Do not cover the entire surface and vary the depth of colour slightly*

pplication of the ground coat.

The scumble (or, as it is more usually nown in marbling, the *gilp*) differs in a umber of respects from that used in rush graining. For a start it must be hinner than a graining topcoat so that olours can be merged more easily into ach other and subtly softened. It must lso include a small amount of a drying gent such as Terebine or it would never ry properly.

The Terebine is added to three parts vhite spirit, one part linseed oil and as nuch oil stainer or artist's oil paint as the ob requires, to make up the coloured vorking mixture.

To apply the gilp you need no pecialized equipment—a range of small rushes, some lint-free rag, small pieces f natural sponge, and a few goose eathers will be quite adequate.

Before starting work it is important to carry in your mind's eye a picture of what a piece of polished marble looks like. This is virtually impossible to describe in words, so consult art and masonry reference books to get an idea of the colours, patterns, and differences between types.

As a basic guide, polished marble is a flat colour dotted with patches of a contrasting colour and very often lined with a network of fine, spidery veins. Sometimes the ground colour is slightly tinted by the contrasting colour so that the marble looks rather like a tied and dyed cotton T-shirt.

Technique: Start by mixing the gilp and, before adding the colour, soaking a lint-free rag in it. Wipe the ground coat with this so that the colour coats applied later flow more easily.

Next mix the colour with the gilp in the same way as for graining scumble, and keep the mixture handy on a non-absorbent surface such as an artist's palette. If you like you can mix up two or three lots of gilp in different colours or in shades of the same colour to create interesting effects but you must let each colour dry before applying the next.

Now apply the colours using a brush or rag, depending on the effect you require. Rag gives a shallower colour of uniform consistency over a given area, while brushes apply the colour more thickly to obliterate the ground coat. You can work the gilp once it is applied by dabbing it with a sponge soaked in white spirit to soften the colour slightly, or else flick white spirit off a brush on to the colour to expose the ground coat in random patterns and interesting shapes.

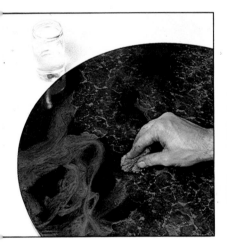

14 Soak a small piece of sponge or rag in white spirit and dab this on o the coloured areas to soften the colour nd to create a mottled marble effect

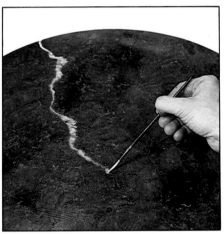

15 You can paint veins in to the panel once the gilp has dried. Use a small brush and twist and turn it to get the correct spidery effect

16 Create a white marble effect by brushing a light grey gilp on to an off-white ground coat. You can also use rag or sponge to apply the gilp

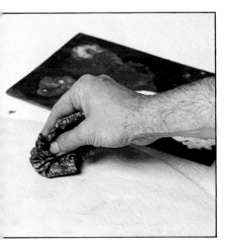

17 Work the gilp in the same way as for dark marble. If you cannot get the effect you want wipe all the gilp off and start again from the beginning

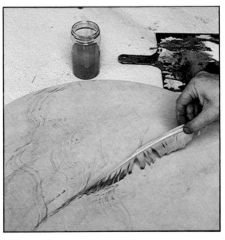

18 For a really fine veined effect rub a large goose feather in the gilp and draw this across the panel, twisting and turning it and varying the pressure

19 You can get some spectacular effects by applying gilp to a metallic foil groundcoat. Either brush or dab the paint on with a rag or sponge

To reproduce a veined effect rub one of the goose feathers into the gilp so that it forms a series of fine, brush-like tips, and draw this across the ground coat. To create a more natural effect vary the pressure on the feather and twist and turn it to form a spidery pattern of approximately parallel lines. You can achieve a similar effect by using a small brush, or by soaking the feather or brush in white spirit and drawing this across patches of colour to make a 'negative'.

For a more subtle effect many professionals apply several coats, allowing each one to dry and then lacquering it before applying the next. All finish the job off in the same way, however, by applying several coats of lacquer in the same way as for a grained surface, rubbing each coat down to end up with a smooth, polished finish.

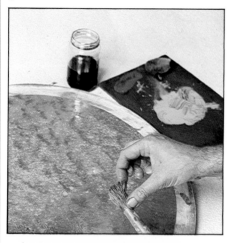

20 *To vary the effect slightly use an artist's paintbrush to flick a different coloured gilp – or even clear white spirit – in to the marbled surface*

D. *Once you have got the hang of the marbling technique, you can expand your horizons and try it out as a wall decoration – the effect can be quite*

stunning on small areas such as the back of alcoves. You can work on emulsioned plaster, or line the walls with extra white lining paper first

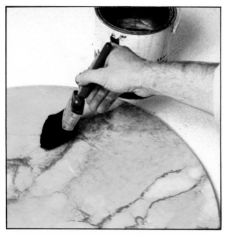

21 *Protect the grained or marbled panel by painting it with several coats of clear lacquer. Rub down each coat to get the best possible finish*

22 *Work on walls as you did on the table top, applying a thin glaze, breaking it up with your sponge and adding colour*

23 *When you're satisfied with the overall depth and variation of the background colour, use the feather again to add light veining*

A marbled column

Practice marbling techniques by making this elegant pedestal. It will make an attractive stand for a potted plant—or even a treasured antique.

The base of the structure is the central column which is made from four pieces of a fluted wooden moulding. The elaborate mouldings at top and bottom are built up on softwood frames pinned and glued to the main column.

Assemble the main column, then attach plywood plates to top and bottom. Build up the softwood sub-frames on these. The joint is covered by birdsmouth mouldings, mitred at the corners. Frame around the subframes using architrave mouldings as specified. Note that no measurements are given for the individual parts as you will need to take cutting tolerances into account when making the mitre joints.

Finish the top with a plywood panel and weight the base. Fill any gaps and sand the entire surface ready for painting.

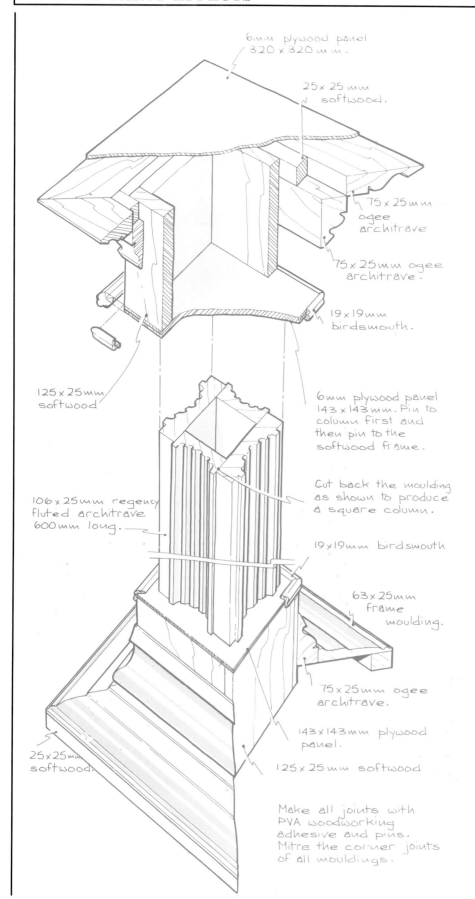

6mm plywood panel
320 x 320 mm.

25 x 25 mm
softwood.

75 x 25 mm
ogee
architrave

75 x 25mm ogee
architrave.

19 x 19mm
birdsmouth.

125 x 25mm
softwood

6mm plywood panel
143 x 143mm. Pin to
column first and
then pin to the
softwood frame.

Cut back the moulding
as shown to produce
a square column.

106 x 25mm regency
fluted architrave
600mm long.

19 x 19mm birdsmouth

63 x 25mm
frame
moulding.

75 x 25mm ogee
architrave.

25 x 25mm
softwood.

143 x 143mm plywood
panel.

125 x 25mm softwood

Make all joints with
PVA woodworking
adhesive and pins.
Mitre the corner joints
of all mouldings.

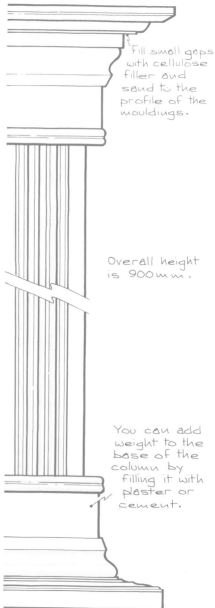

Fill small gaps
with cellulose
filler and
sand to the
profile of the
mouldings.

Overall height
is 900mm.

You can add
weight to the
base of the
column by
filling it with
plaster or
cement.

This diagram shows the
finished profile of the column.
Note that no dimensions
are given for cutting the
mouldings to length. Instead,
you should make the centre
column and upper and lower
softwood subframes first.
Then build up the mouldings
in stages, taking your
measurements directly from
the timber and framing
around it.

DECORATING WITH TILES

- ● **TYPES OF TILES**
- ● **SQUARING UP**
- ● **CUTTING & SHAPING**
- ● **DIFFICULT AREAS**
- ● **MAKING GOOD**

As coverings for walls, tables and working surfaces, ceramic tiles have several distinct advantages over other materials. As well as offering a superb range of colours, patterns and glaze finishes, they make a hard-wearing, easy to clean, practical surface.

They also have a high resistance to both acids and alkalis and a permanent colouring, unaffected by prolonged exposure to sunlight or steam.

The one drawback to ceramic tiles is that they are brittle, making them slightly more difficult to work with than vinyl or cork.

Types of tile
Ceramic tiles come in a wide variety of plain colours, patterns and shapes. The three most common sizes are 108mm square by 4mm thick, 152mm square × 6mm, and 203mm × 102mm × 6mm. Mosaic tiles—group arrangements of tiny tiles on a backing sheet—are also available. Always take a ruler and actually measure a sample tile before you buy, particularly if you are buying contrasting tiles from different shops.

Universal tiles are the commonest type—they have slightly bevelled edges so that when they are butted up against each other, there is an even gap all round.

When tiling food preparation surfaces in the kitchen, you should always check with the manufacturer or retailer that the tiles are suitable for the purpose—some have a potentially toxic heavy lead glaze. Tiles used near heat sources such as cookers and fireplaces should be heat resistant or at least 9.5mm thick.

The basic tool kit
Cutting tools, adhesive and grout are readily available from any do-it-yourself shop.

You will need a simple wheel cutter or a scriber with a tungsten-carbide tip. A wheel cutter with breaker wings, for scoring and breaking in one action, costs a little more. A carborundum file is useful for smoothing down the edges of cut tiles.

Materials
Tile adhesive is available either in powder form, to which water is added, or else ready-prepared in cans: five litres will cover about 6m² on a good surface.

However, use a water resistant adhesive for areas around sinks, baths and showers and one which is heat resistant where temperatures are likely to be high, such as around cookers and fires.

Grout is a cement-based paste which is rubbed into the gaps between tiles to provide a neat finish. As a rough guide 500g of the powder, mixed with water to a fairly stiff consistency, will grout about 2m² of small tiles or 4m² of larger ones.

How many tiles?

To estimate how many tiles you will need for a wall or worksurface, measure the length and height in metres then use our formula

108mm square tiles: Length x Height x 86 = No. of tiles
152mm square tiles: Length x Height x 43 = No. of tiles
203mm x 102mm tiles: Length x Height x 49 = No. of tiles

If necessary, add on the required number of special border tiles or subtract tiles to allow for fittings. Add on an extra 5 or 6 tiles to cover breakages.

Cutting tiles is not as hard as it seems. To make a straight cut, simply score a line with a tile cutter, then snap the tile over a matchstick

A non-toxic grout should always be used on tiled food preparation surfaces and a water resistant grout around sinks, baths and showers.

Preparing the surface

The quality of any tiling job is largely dependent on the surface to which the tiles are fixed. This should be firm, level, clean and dry.

Most surfaces require only a little preparation before they are tiled. A few, though, need more extensive treatment.

Plaster: Minor bumps and cracks can be filled with a proprietary plaster filler. The entire surface should then be given a coat of plaster primer, to

1 Make a pencil mark a tile's height from the top edge of the skirting board. This will show you where to draw the baseline

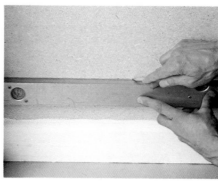

2 Drawing the baseline. The spirit level ensures that the baseline is level and acts as a straight edge for marking the line

3 Pin the batten along the bottom of the line to provide a level base for tiling. The bottom row will be filled in later

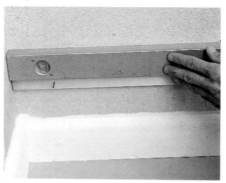

4 Check the batten with the spirit level to make sure it is horizontal. If it is not, it will have to be unpinned and re-adjusted

5 Mark tile widths along the batten to give an even cut at each end of the wall. This ensures the symmetry of the tiled wall

6 Use the spirit level to draw the vertical line at the last tile mark. The line acts as a guide to keep the tiling square

provide a non-porous base for the adhesive. If the surface is very uneven, it should be replastered and left for a month before being sealed and tiled.

However, rough surfaces can often be relined with plywood, chipboard or plasterboard (wallboard). To do this on a brick wall, you will need to plug and screw wood battens—50mm × 25mm will do—to the wall at regular intervals. Make sure that each batten is vertical, using wood chips to pack any gaps between the wood and the old wall surface. Space the battens to suit the width of the lining material.

Before screwing your panelling material to the battens, give each strip a thorough coat of wood sealant. As you secure the panels, plan your work so that adjacent ones butt up against each other over the centre of a batten.

Wallpaper: On no account should tiles be laid on to wallpaper. Strip the wall back to the bare plaster or wallboard, then fill and level as described above.

Painted walls: Providing these are smooth and firm, tiles may be applied direct. But flaking or rough paint should be partially stripped with medium glasspaper and brushed clean.

Timber walls: These must be sanded or planed level and treated with wood primer before the tiles are applied.

Existing ceramic tiles: The ideal tiling surface, providing the tiles are clean, firmly fixed and not chipped.

Constructing a baseline

Before you start tiling you will need a horizontal baseline from which to work—floors and skirting boards are not suitable, as they are seldom completely level and can throw the tiling out of true.

7 With adhesive spread over about 1m², fix the first tile at the intersection of the batten and the vertical line. Press the tile home

8 When fitting cut tiles into corners and other awkward areas it is easier to apply the adhesive to the backs of the tiles

9 Once you have tiled the rest of the wall you can remove the batten and fix the bottom row, carefully scribing each tile to fit

10 Use a tile cutter to score through the glazed surface of tile. The try square ensures that the score mark is straight and even

11 Place a matchstick under the score mark on the tile. Exert downward pressure and the tile should snap cleanly along the mark

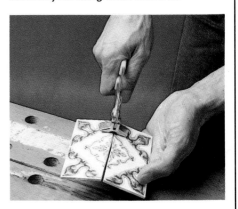

12 An alternative method of cutting tiles is with the angle-jaw cutter. The tile is snapped by breaker wings

To draw a baseline, measure the height of a tile from the floor or skirting board and make a mark (fig. 1). Using the spirit level as a straight edge, check for level and draw a line through this mark (fig. 2).

Pin the top edge of a batten along the line so it forms a level base, right along the length of the surface to be tiled (fig. 3). Check that you do not have more than one tile's depth at any point below this line. If you do, lower the batten slightly.

Later, when you have tiled above it, you can remove the batten and fill in the space below (fig. 9). The tiles here may have to be cut or trimmed.

Marking a side line
To keep the tiles exactly square to the baseline, you will also need a vertical line at one side of the surface. Find the centre point of the batten and mark out the tile widths along either side of it. Draw your line where the last full tile ends on the lefthand side, using the spirit level—or a plumb

line—to give you an accurate vertical line (fig. 6).

Fixing the tiles
Begin tiling at the intersection of the horizontal batten and the vertical line (fig. 7), filling in the bottom row and working upwards.

Adhesive should be applied thinly to the wall over an area of not more than 1m² at a time. If applied to the backs of the tiles themselves, the finished surface could be uneven. If adhesive is applied over a greater area, some may dry before it has been tiled over. Drive the serrated edge of the spreader over the adhesive, forming ridges to provide good suction and adhesion.

Press the tiles firmly into place without sliding them, wiping away any adhesive which squeezes onto the surface of the tiles with a damp cloth. The alignment of the tiles should be checked with the spirit level on completion of every three or four rows.

When the tiles have set, the corner tiles may be fixed and the batten re-

moved before filling in the bottom row —butter their backs with adhesive and fit them firmly home. Always fit cut tiles so that the spacer lugs—that is the uncut sides—face those of the adjacent tile (fig. 9).

Butt the spacer lugs of the tiles on the adjacent wall against the surface of the cut corner tile at right angles to it—thus allowing a grout line to run down the junction of the two walls.

Cutting and shaping tiles
Straight cuts in ceramic tiles can be made either by scoring and snapping with a standard tile cutter (figs. 10 and 11) or by scoring and breaking with an angle-jaw tile cutter (fig. 12).

Notches and curved cuts must be 'nibbled' by hand with a pair of pincers (fig. 13). In the case of curved cuts, make a straight cut first as near to the curve as possible—the tile will snap if you attempt to pincer out larger areas.

The guidelines for curved cuts can

13 *For a shaped cut, score the area that is to be removed then nibble out small pieces of the tile with a pair of pincers*

14 *When the shape has been nibbled out of the tile, smooth off any unevenness on the cut edges with a carborundum file*

15 *Once the tiling has been completed and the adhesive has set, rub grout firmly into the joints with a sponge or piece of rag*

16 *When the grout is almost dry, draw a stick with a round point along the joints to give a neat appearance to the finished tiling*

with tiles cut to fit.

Where the fitment is in the middle o a wall—such as a basin or wc—til around it as closely as you can wit whole tiles, then fill in the space with cut tiles when the rest of the wa is completed.

Grouting

When the tiling is finished, leave i to set for 12 to 24 hours, then ru grout firmly into the tile joint with an old sponge, squeegee or clot (fig. 15). Remove excess grout with damp sponge: when it has almost set run a blunt stick across the joints t leave a neat finish (fig. 16). Allow th grout to dry and then give the tiles final polish with a soft, dry cloth.

TIP FROM THE TRADE

Q The tile grouting on my coffee table is badly discoloured, and the edges of the tiles have started to stain. What can I do about this?

A Surfaces on which liquids are likely to be spilled, or on which food is prepared, need a special waterproof grout such as Evo-Stik Hi-White. Otherwise stains will penetrate the grout and the unglazed edges of the tiles. If the tiles are **not** too badly stained you can scrape out the grout and re-do it; otherwise, unfortunately, you may have to re-tile the whole surface

be drawn in either by eye, or—more satisfactorily—with a cardboard template. Trim the template to shape in situ then transfer it to the tile and draw around it in felt-tip pen.

Pipes present some of the trickiest tiling problems. The safest way to tile around them is to cut the relevant tile in two and to cut a semi-circle out of each half.

All cuts in ceramic tiles look neater and more professional if they are smoothed afterwards with a carborundum file or block (fig. 14).

Tiling around fitments

Where the fitment runs the length of a wall—a bath or kitchen unit for example—treat the top edge as you would a floor or skirting board. Fix a horizontal batten along this edge and leave it in place while you tile the wall above. When the tiles are dry, remove the batten and tile down to the edge

Tiling around windows

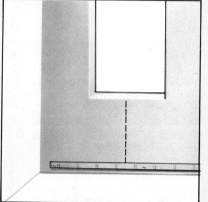

A. *When tiling around a widow, work from a line down the centre of the reveal—not from the edge of the wall on either side*

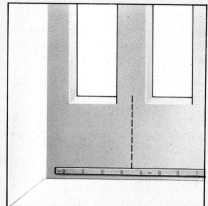

B. *On a wall with two windows, work from a line midway between the two. This will give your tiling a neat visual balance*

BASIC FLOOR TILING

Left: *Dry laying of tiles to check the fit at room edges. These vinyl-coated cork flooring tiles are being laid on floorboarding that has been covered with sheets of suitable hardboard. Chalked lines ensure accurate tiling*

- ● **PREPARATION**
- ● **USING HARDBOARD**
- ● **CENTRING TILES**
- ● **LEVELLING**
- ● **SETTING OUT**
- ● **BORDERS**

A tiled floor can transform the appearance of any room, and for the most part the job is straightforward and quick. Badly-laid tiled floors can be an eyesore, but you can prevent this by taking a little extra care at the planning and preparation stages.

Vinyl floor coverings are by far the most popular choice, especially for kitchens and bathrooms, and it is not difficult to see why. Vinyl tiling is available in various forms and a seemingly infinite range of colours and designs. And although various types of fixing methods may be used, none presents a problem. The techniques of laying vinyl tiles are covered in the next part of this course.

Cork has some splendid characteristics which make it well-suited for

use as a flooring material, and is almost as easy to lay and finish. And of course there is nothing to match the quality and durability of quarry or ceramic tiles. Laying these tiles is covered in a later part of the decorating course.

You can tile a floor only if the surface is sound, firm and level. Loose floorboards, damp or uneven concrete, old linoleum and pitted asphalt are typical floor conditions that need to be checked and corrected before laying vinyl or any other form of tiling. Bumps and high points quickly cause wear or cracks in floor coverings.

Preparing wood floors
Nail or screw down any loose boards and drive in or remove insecure nails

and screws. Wood floors should be covered with plywood or hardboard.

Vinyl flooring may be laid directly on chipboard used in place of floorboarding provided the chipboard is of flooring grade and has a minimum thickness of 18mm. Be sure to remove any existing floor covering first.

Suspended wooden floors at ground level must always remain well-ventilated if damp and rot are to be avoided. A vinyl or tile floor covering will not allow timbers beneath to 'breathe' and this can only aggravate any borderline condition that may be present. Check that air bricks in the outside walls are not blocked and take the additional precaution with old, damp properties of raising a floorboard here and there to check for both dry and wet rot. Add extra airbricks if underfloor ventilation is poor, and call in an expert to advise on professional treatment if any traces of dry rot are found beneath the floor.

Preparing concrete floors
Provided concrete floors are dry, clean, level and free from anything which could conceivably react with the overlay (particularly grease and solvents which can have a marked affect on vinyl), they form an ideal base for flooring whether in tile or sheet form.

The most common problem is dampness, particularly on concrete floors laid directly on top of earth that have not been provided with a permanent damp-proof membrane. Even if a concrete floor looks dry, try a simple test to check whether or not it is so. Place a rubber mat, piece of cooking foil or plastic sheet on the concrete and tape the edges down as best as possible. Turn on the heating at a setting a little higher than normal, then, after 24 hours, peel off the test sheet. The presence of any moisture on the underside indicates a damp floor.

If the floor is damp, it must be treated with waterproofer before being overlaid with flooring of timber, cork or any other material that could be affected by moisture. A wet floor may have to have its surface relaid and a waterproof membrane inserted (regardless of the floor covering used).

A damp floor can be treated with waterproofing compound—usually an epoxy coating or a rubberized bitumen material. You cannot, however, lay sheet material over some damp-proofing compounds—so check this point with your floor covering dealer.

Pitting and general unevenness can be rectified using what is known as a self-smoothing compound. Pour this over the floor area to a minimum depth of about 4mm, following the maker's instructions closely as these may vary. Spread the compound with a trowel.

To fill larger holes, make up a mortar mix of three parts soft sand to one of Portland cement. Add just enough water to make the mix workable and a little plasticizer to minimize shrinkage during drying.

Damp the holes with water and apply the mortar with a bricklayer's trowel. Tamp it down with the end of a piece of timber and slice off any surplus with a timber straightedge.

Floors with a surface which is powdery but otherwise sound can be coated with a latex-based sealer before being overlaid by tiling.

Other floors

It is possible to lay vinyl and cork flooring over existing quarry or ceramic tiling provided that the gaps between the original tiles are filled with self-smoothing compound. This is to prevent the old tile pattern from working through—a particular problem near doorways and other areas subject to continuous wear.

Also, take particular care to remove grease, dirt and grit: perhaps harmless to the original tiling but often damaging to vinyl and cork. A good wash with household detergent and hot water is normally sufficient.

You can also lay some types of vinyl and cork tile over existing linoleum and vinyl flooring where removal poses problems. Again, make sure the surface is clean and that all edges on the old tiling are stuck down properly. Where possible, do remove all old tiling as this helps avoid problems both in laying the new tiling and later. Old tiling must be removed if quarry or ceramic tiles are being used.

Laying hardboard

On an old, rough wooden floor, laying hardboard or plywood over the entire

1 Measure up the room and decide how best to use standard hardboard sheet sizes. Allow for cuts around obstacles

3 Measure back the corner depth and use a straightedge to mark the cutting line, allowing a slanted cut if this is necessary

2 When cutting hardboard to fit a corner, pull the sheet as close as possible to this so that direct measurements can be made

4 You will find it easier to cut the hardboard at floor level, propping up the edges as best as possible to enable sawing

5 When the board has been cut to shape, push it home and then use hardboard pins or screw-thread nails for permanent fixing

surface is often the only way of easily achieving a smooth surface on which to lay tiles. Concrete floors sometimes require the same treatment but usually this is not essential, although you may prefer the additional insulation this underlay provides.

Standard hardboard comes in sheets measuring 2440mm × 1220mm; use oil-tempered boards in bathrooms.

Hardboard sheets have to be conditioned prior to use otherwise buckling may occur through localized shrinkage or expansion after they have been laid. Temper the boards by brushing the rough side with water and lay the sheets flat, smooth sides together, overnight or longer so the moisture is fully absorbed. The idea is that the sheets will dry out after being laid, in the process shrinking slightly to form a very tight, level surface.

The hardboard is laid rough side upwards as this gives a better key for any tile adhesive used. Stagger the joints to reduce the likelihood of strain at any particular point—which could lead to cracks or wear in flooring placed above—and avoid coinciding the hardboard joins with those of floorboarding below for the same reasons.

On a wooden floor, use 25mm hardboard pins to nail the board at 150mm spacings over the entire surface and at 100mm spacings along the edges. On a concrete or cement floor you have to glue the board in place using a suitable adhesive such as synthetic rubber. When sticking anything to concrete, check whether or not an initial coat of primer is required as concrete can very easily absorb some types of adhesive, and this can result in a weak (or even a failed) bond.

Few rooms are truly square and you will need to use wedges and strips to fill the small gaps left after trimming the boards as they are laid. If these gaps are very small, it is worth using non-setting mastic which can cope with any future movement of the boards.

When you have laid the boards, allow them to dry out before overlaying vinyl tiles or sheet—a day or so is normally long enough. Spend the time correcting any tight-fitting doors which open into the room. Normally the gap between the base of the door and the floor surface will be large enough to accommodate a layer of thick floor covering or, in this instance, a layer of plywood or hardboard—but only rarely both together. So check the gap beneath the door both before and after laying covering boards.

If necessary, lift the door off its hinges and trim (by planing or sawing) 6mm or so from the base. You may find it easier to replace the existing hinges with rising butt hinges.

Where board laying continues through a doorway into an accompanying room, ensure that draughtproofing aids such as a threshold bar are removed. Sheet edges should be tightly butted here—and then covered with the threshold bar again if further draughtproofing measures are necessary, which seems likely.

Laying plan

Once the floor preparations have been completed, some idea of the lie of the room is necessary for planning a design and for choosing tiles or sheet floorcoverings.

In theory, all designs should radiate or progress from the centre of the room. Find this by measuring off the centre line of two opposing walls. Stretch a chalked string between the two and snap this against the boards on the floor. Repeat this for the two remaining walls so that another chalk mark is made: where they cross is the centre point of the room. This is a simple enough job for a normally-shaped room. Figure A shows the procedure for awkward rooms and you can adapt the method to suit your needs.

Border walls

Although any design is based on the centre of the room, border walls must be considered if an even pattern is to be achieved. Also, the tile direction should be square, or perfectly symmetrical, to the main doorway of the room. So in figure A you would base

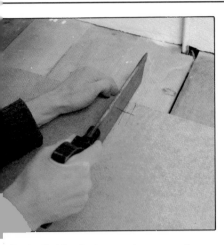

6 Individual obstructions can be dealt with as they are encountered but remove only as much of the board as necessary for a tight fit. Use a coping saw for a perfect fit

7 Nail boards at 100mm spacings at the board edges, and at 150mm centres over the whole surface area of the sheet

8 Use a measure to find the midpoint of each wall. By joining the opposing mid-points you can find the centre of the room

9 To produce a chalked mark for accurate tiling, stretch a chalked string between opposing walls and snap this against the floor

10 The crossed chalk lines at the centre of the room are used as the starting point for a trial, 'dry run' and later permanent fixing

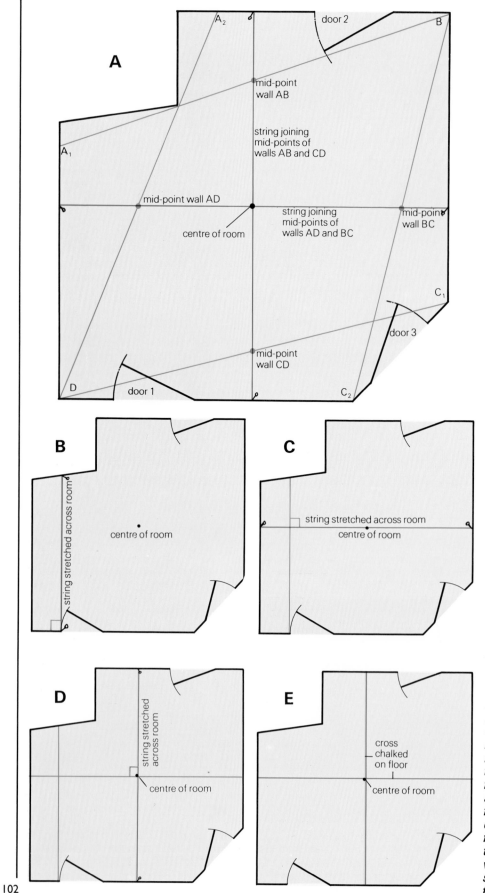

the tile pattern on either door 1 or door 2 in preference to door 3 even though the tile pattern falls at 45° to this, which is visually acceptable.

To mark out guide lines for laying produce a chalked mark at right angles to the doorway (fig. B), far enough for another chalked mark to be made across the room and coinciding with the centre point (fig. C).

Make another chalked line at right angles to the second line, again passing through the centre point (fig. D). This line is of course parallel with the first. The resulting cross you have chalked on the floor is now used for the exact planning of a pattern, and also provides a guide for the tile-laying sequence which follows.

When, later, you have chosen your tiles and have designed a pattern for these, follow the cross-lines in a 'dry laying' sequence to check how the tiles finish off at the edges. Ideally the border round the room should be even and although this is not always possible as far as the pattern is concerned, it is certainly possible to rearrange the position of the chalked cross so that tile widths are even on each pair of opposing walls.

Left: *To find the centre point of a perfectly square or rectangular room presents no problems, but awkwardly shaped floors need a different approach (A). Instead of totting up individual parts of each wall, measure across the room to take in the obstruction (shown by red line A_1B) and find the mid-point of this. Repeat the procedure for each of the three remaining sides of the room (red lines A_2D, DC_1, C_2B) and find the mid-point of each.*

Mark the floor at these points. Now stretch strings across the room in such a way as to join up each pair of opposing mid-points (green lines). Where the two strings cross is the mid-point of your room.

Your laying plan must be based both on the centre point and on the main doorway (taken here to be door 1) if the tile pattern is to look regular and symmetrical. To do this, first stretch a string at right-angles to the doorway to a point on the facing wall (B). Follow this with another string, at right-angles to the first and coinciding with the room centre point (C). A third string line, fixed parallel to the first, completes the cross (D). By rubbing the strings with chalk, a chalked cross can be snapped on the floor to act as your final tiling guide (E)

LAYING FLOOR TILES

- ● DRY LAYING
- ● SEALING TILES
- ● SCRIBING TRICKS

- ● CUTTING TO FIT
- ● FITTING VINYL
- ● TRIMMING TIPS

Above: *Cutting flooring to fit around complicated shapes like this is easier if you use a shape tracer to get an accurate pattern of the moulding*

Laying vinyl or cork floor tiles is one of the best ways of providing a room with a good-looking and tough floor covering. And provided that the floor preparation and design stages have not been skimped, the job is quick and uncomplicated. Laying hardboard on a wood, cement or concrete floor to provide a smooth and level base for all forms of tiling is covered fully in pages 99 to 102.

Finding the centre of the room is the first stage of planning a design and for calculating the number of tiles of any one type that may be required. The tile direction, and hence design, is also influenced by positions of the main doorways.

The centre of the room is also used as the starting point for tile laying. This ensures that the tiles are laid evenly and squarely in what is the most conspicuous part of the room and means that you end up by trimming and cutting tiles to fit. Even in small rooms or hallways, always start tiling in the middle.

Before tiling, do a 'dry run' to

check for problems in laying and also that your design works. Tile fit can be checked across the length and the breadth of a room, in alcoves, and anywhere else where the basic shape of the room alters.

This is a particularly important job if a large, unusually shaped room is being tiled. Figures A to D show how to deal with a seven-sided room which, if hardly typical, highlights most of the problems you may encounter with a room of more normal shape.

Arrange two lengths of string to cross the centre of the room and to act as guides for tile laying. Fixed carefully to the skirting and stretched taut a little above the floor, these can then be chalked and snapped against the floor to produce the final laying marks (fig. C).

Before you go further, consider if moving the strings a little away from the middle actually reduces the amount of fiddly cutting needed at the edges: in the featured room (fig. A), there is too much of this so the line was moved. You could, of course, take

up this border width by using feature strips incorporated into the overall design, so that the borders are highlighted, but this will still probably involve you in a lot of fiddly cutting. So, shifting the whole lot one way or the other so that at least a third or half a tile is left at the borders makes accurate cutting and shaping much easier.

In the featured room (fig. B), moving the tiles to the right a little avoids fiddly cutting at the 'window wall' border and leaves half-tiles on the 'inner wall' border. Only door 3 and the opposite corner present anything of a problem.

You may prefer, however, to shift the whole tile pattern to the left (fig. C). This time the half-tiles occur at the 'window wall' border, and less fiddly cutting is involved both at door 3 and the corner opposite to this.

Too much fiddly cutting means wasted tiles, particularly where a directional pattern has to be matched. Spending time on a dry laying run keeps this wastage to a minimum, reduces the work-load and makes for a better-looking job.

Having finally established the laying guides, chalk these on the support flooring. Remove the strings but leave the skirting pins in place so that chalked marks can be remade if necessary.

Tile preparation

With vinyl tiles, by and large you get what you pay for. The more expensive forms contain a greater proportion of vinyl, are better wearing as a result, and are usually less of a problem to lay. All benefit from being left a day or so in a warm room or airing cupboard, after which time they become more pliable and easier to handle. Sheet vinyl, in particular, ought to undergo this acclimatization procedure. There is no need to do the same for cork tiling.

Laying individual tiles

Individual tiles are laid from the centre of the room and outwards. If tile adhesive is required, spread a little of this along the chalked cross lines. Always use the adhesive recommended by the tile manufacturer, and follow the specified instructions for applying this. With cork tiles, for example, you may have to apply adhesive to the underside of the tile as well as to the floor, perhaps leaving an interval for drying before bringing both together.

The important rule for tiling is to cover only a small part of the floor at a time. Lay the centre four tiles against each other to coincide with the crossed chalked marks at the centre of the room.

Take care not to push the tiles together if adhesive is used: this may force the excess up between the tiles. Wipe off surplus adhesive with a damp cloth before it has a chance to dry. Smears can be removed with soap and a brush—never use solvents.

Work outwards from the centre four tiles once these have set, applying only as much adhesive as is necessary for each small area before you tile. Deal with one quarter of the floor before moving on to the next.

The physical finish of some tiles is directional and if this is not immediately obvious, check to see if there is a laying direction arrow printed on the underside. If light catches the surface of an improperly-laid directional tile it can considerably affect the overall appearance. To avoid slight shade differences from box to box, shuffle and mix the tiles.

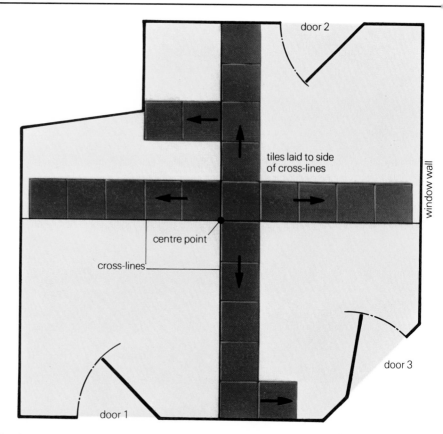

A. *Starting from the centre 'dry lay' outwards to check how the tiles fit. You can then see what cutting is required at window and interior walls*

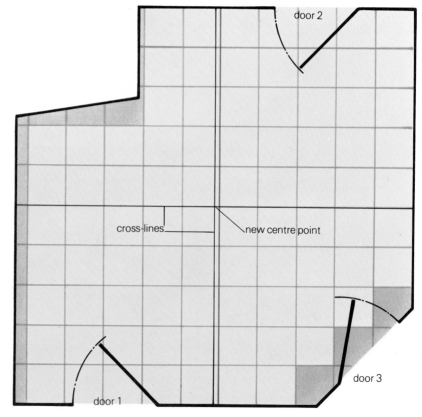

B. *By moving the string guide lines to the right, cutting (dark areas) is avoided at the window wall, with better widths on the inner wall*

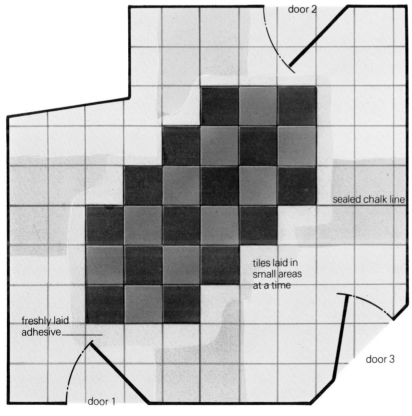

C. *The best arrangement for this room means laying against a string cross where the 'vertical' is slightly to the left of the true centre*

(labels on diagram C: door 2, cross-lines, new centre point, door 3, door 1)

(labels on diagram D: door 2, sealed chalk line, tiles laid in small areas at a time, freshly laid adhesive, door 3, door 1)

D. *Fix and let dry the centre four tiles, working to the chalked, crossed, lines. Work outwards from these tiles, doing a few squares at a time*

Cutting tiles to fit

Eventually you will come to the border where, unless the fit is arranged to be perfect, the tiles need cutting to shape and width. This is an easy enough job if you are familiar with scribing techniques, but if these are new to you it may be worthwhile sacrificing a few spare tiles to practise on.

Place a tile squarely on top of the last one before the border. Take another and place this partly on top but firmly butted against the wall. The inner edge is then used to mark a cutting line on the middle tile—you can score this using a cutting knife and then complete the cut elsewhere using a cutting board, steel rule and safety blade. Make sure the middle tile is of the correct type and in the right direction before cutting.

1 *You can lay tiles on a level and smooth concrete floor if an underlay is not required. Use a bolster to remove surface flaws*

2 *In a small room there is no need to mark the floor for tile laying but do go through a dry lay routine to check the tiles for fit*

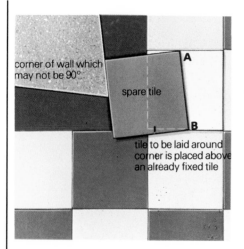

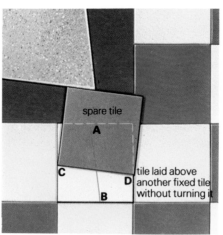

E. The procedure for scribing a tile. Use a matching tile as the transfer ruler, and pencil the cutting mark

F. Without twisting the tile, scribe the second mark and then remove the waste corner

G. The finished tile fixed into place. The procedure for internal corners and edges is identical

3 Use the recommended adhesive and fix a small area of tiles at a time. Remove adhesive squeezed up between tiles before this sets

4 Use a steel rule, heavy-duty handyman's knife and—just as important—a cutting board when you trim sheet or individual tiling

When you are laying into and around a corner, tiles need to be cut both widthways and lengthways. Use the same procedure as for a straight border but repeat this for the two sides of the corner without turning the middle tile (figs E to G).

Even on what looks to be a straight and even border, mark up tiles for cutting individually so that you take care of any irregularities. For odd shapes—such as mouldings, radiator pipes, and beam uprights—carefully nibble away the tile freehand until you can slide it into place (fig. 5). A template cut from card saves wasting too many tiles.

You can also use a shape-tracing tool or template former with metal teeth similar to a comb. These teeth take the form of any firm object against which they are pushed and once tightened in place, the outer ends can be used as a cutting guide. The tool is particularly useful for dealing with the often intricate shapes of door architrave mouldings and other fixed obstacles.

Sealing the tiles

Vinyl tiles do not require any surface treatment after laying. Some cork tiles are pre-finished with a vinyl coating and also need no further work. Untreated tiles can be treated with oleo-resinous and polyurethane varnishes which are available in eggshell, matt or gloss finishes.

Of these, polyurethane has the advantage of being extremely hard wearing as well as being resistant to both heat and most chemicals. At least two coats are required for cork tiles as a single coat will tend to soak into the cork, leaving a patchy appearance.

5 Take special care in cutting tiles to fit door frames and other awkward obstacles. A card template or shape tracer is useful

6 By mixing your packets of tiling, slight differences in colouring become less noticeable when tiles are laid on the floor

H. *A scribing tool made from a square-ended piece of battening. Cover the end with cloth or felt. Start the sequence for cutting sheet vinyl by measuring back from the wall, marking a point on the edge of the sheet (I). Pull the sheet back enough to back-mark the edge by the same distance and place the scribing nail on this (J). Scribe the cutting line and remove the waste. Slide the sheet into the corner, and repeat for next length*

It is not a good idea to wax cork tiles as they then require frequent re-waxing—at least twice each year.

If cork-tiling a bathroom, it is advisable to lay uncoated tiles in preference to coated ones. The sealer, when applied, will then cover the cracks at the joins as well.

Avoid walking on unsealed tiles as these damage easily and marks can be very difficult to remove and disguise. If a high-gloss varnish is used, make sure dust is not allowed to spoil the appearance by thoroughly sweeping the floor beforehand.

Fitting sheet vinyl

Sheet vinyl has taken the place of the once popular linoleum flooring and is warmer, if not quite so hard wearing. It provides a simple solution to those who require a good-looking floor covering—possibly highly patterned—but cannot be bothered with the planning that laying individual tiles involves.

Sheet vinyl comes in rolls from 2m wide, so have a clear idea of the way it is to unroll and be laid before choosing a particular pattern. As with individual vinyl tiles, allow the roll to acclimatize before laying—about two days loose rolled is enough.

Vinyl sheet flooring can sometimes shrink, so the makers usually advise cutting oversize when the material is first laid: follow these cutting instructions closely. After about two or three weeks of use, final trimming can take place at join overlaps and edges.

The possibility of shrinkage must always be considered when planning and laying down cuts and joins. Where possible you should keep these well clear of doorways, so if you are

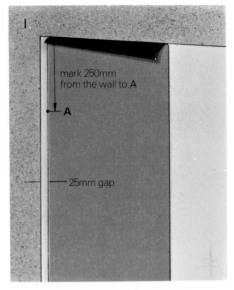

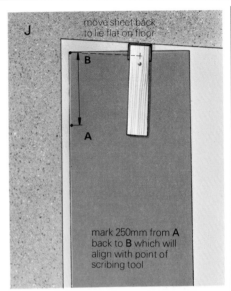

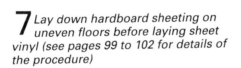

7 *Lay down hardboard sheeting on uneven floors before laying sheet vinyl (see pages 99 to 102 for details of the procedure)*

laying sheet in two adjacent rooms, arrange to have the sheet straddling the doorway threshold

You will need a scribing tool for marking cutting lines at the sheet edges and ends. Make this by driving a nail partly through a wooden batten, 50mm from the end, so that the point protrudes about 3mm (fig. H).

Allowing a little extra for shrinkage and trimming, cut a length of sheet from your supply roll. Lay the sheet to allow an overlap of up to 150mm at sides and ends. Follow the scribing techniques outlined (figs. I and J) for final trimming. Use the same procedure for trimming sheet edges as you lay. To do this, make a pencil mark on the edge of the vinyl sheet 250mm from the wall (fig. I) and draw the sheet back from the wall so that it lays flat.

8 *Cut sheeting to fit into every nook and cranny as the whole sheet is laid down. Use a cutting board and handyman's knife for safety*

9 *Slit the sheet edges so that a good fit, but a coarse trim, is obtained at the base of all obstacles and fittings—trim no further yet*

LAYING FLOOR TILES

10 *After settling and shrinkage the vinyl sheet can be properly trimmed. Use a float or other metal straightedge as a cutting guide*

11 *Use suitable adhesive to fix edge joins and elsewhere that may cause problems if curling occurs—particularly at doorways*

Now measure back 250mm towards the wall and make another mark (fig. J). By carefully sliding the sheet, arrange it so that the point of your scribing tool coincides with the second mark when the batten end is held against the skirting board (fig. J). Take care not to twist the sheet out of alignment in the process. Finally, scribe along the sheet as described above, cut off the waste and push the sheet tight against the skirting.

This method of scribing should also be used where a narrow strip is being fitted, such as in a hall or small kitchen.

Where two sheets meet at the middle, the overlap can be trimmed quickly and easily by running a handyman's knife along the double thickness. If possible coincide the cut with a pattern line in order to conceal

it. Raise both edges and lay double-sided tape beneath if this is thought necessary

The pattern direction should be laid square to the room or doorway, however, if this wall is in any way angled.

Lay the end of your scribing tool at right-angles against the skirting and mark the sheet along the length of the wall. Take your time over doing the job, and try not to scrape the skirting board paintwork in the process.

The mark left on the sheet should mirror the shape of the wall and skirting. Individual obstructions are best dealt with as they are encountered. Slit the sheeting (fig. 9) but do not nibble away any more of the sheet than is necessary for fitting—trimming is best left to much later (fig. 10).

Cut the sheet edge to shape using a handyman's knife, steel rule and cut-

ting board, then push it against the wall. The surplus at the ends can be turned up against the adjoining walls.

The sequence is repeated for the other sheet and rough cuts made again where fittings and protrusions occur, such as at a corner, chimney breast or radiator.

The alignment of the second sheet should of course match that of the first. Also check that trimming to fit the wall still leaves an overlap of at least 30mm with the first sheet. This may mean a little bit of calculating before the second sheet is laid down and coarsely trimmed.

Trimming sheet vinyl
After the two-week settling period, final trimming can take place. Use a metal straightedge to force the sheet firmly against skirting boards and fittings before making the trimming cuts (fig. 10).

To trim the surplus at the roll ends, you can again use the straightedge to force the sheet flat as you cut. But as you can only do sections at a time, the appearance may suffer as a result.

A better method—especially if the wall is angled or uneven—is to duplicate the scribing technique used for the edges.

After the final trimming. vinyl sheet that needs to be glued in place can be raised and the adhesive applied. Use the products and techniques suggested by the manufacturers if you have to do this (fig. 11).

With modern, 'lay flat' vinyl sheet, gluing is not normally necessary. Specially designed double-sided tape can be used in areas where a raised edge may cause problems, such as at doorways and joins.

12 *To cut vinyl accurately round a WC pedestal, lay a rough paper template and scribe round it with compasses or a block and pencil*

13 *Then lay the template over the vinyl floorcovering, and scribe the outline back onto its surface*

14 *Finally, cut carefully along the line on the vinyl sheet with a sharp knife, make a release cut back towards the wall and fit the covering*

FURNITURE FACELIFT

That shabby old chest of drawers can be transformed simply and cheaply by stripping off the old paint and refinishing the wood in an up-to-date, eye catching style

By stripping old furniture down to the natural wood you can ensure a smooth surface—free of bumps and blemishes—which can then be polished, varnished or even stencilled for a completely new look.

Make sure, though, that you know what finish you are stripping. It could be one of several—paint, polish, lacquer or varnish—and they all need different treatments.

Stripping paint
Paint on furniture can be removed either by immersion in a caustic bath—a job for a specialist—or by hand, using a chemical paint stripper. Hand stripping usually gives the best results, as it adds an extra lustre to the bare wood.

Equipment
To strip paint by hand, you need a supply of proprietary paint stripper. Available in either jelly or liquid form, it is more economical to buy it by the gallon than to opt for one of the smaller cans. The back of the can should tell you what to wash the stripper off with once it has soaked in—either water, methylated spirits or turps substitute.

To apply the stripper, you need rubber gloves and an old 25mm or 50mm paintbrush. For peeling away the softened paint, use a stripping knife and a moulding scraper or coarse wire wool. Put the shreds—which will be caustic, and therefore dangerous—in a jam jar or an empty paint tin.

Above: *An old chest, covered with flaky paintwork, can easily be stripped and refinished with polish (left)*

Method

If you are working indoors, ensure the room is well ventilated before you start—paint stripper gives off unpleasant fumes. Put down some newspaper or an old dust sheet to protect your floor and furnishings.

On a chest of drawers start with the drawer faces themselves, removing handles and key escutcheons where possible. A dab of paint stripper, left to soak for a few minutes, will help loosen stubborn screws.

Wearing rubber gloves, pour some of the stripper into a jar and start brushing it on to the paint. Work the stripper into all the cracks and crevices with a brush making sure none of the paint is missed.

Having covered a drawer or the equivalent area, leave the stripper to act for several minutes. When the paint starts to bubble, remove the top layer with a stripping knife or a shavehook and scrape the shreds straight into a container.

Continue this process with each layer of paint—sometimes there are as many as five or six on an old chest of drawers—until you reach the wood. You will need several applications of stripper. If you find any corners difficult to reach with a stripping knife, use the shavehook instead.

When all the paint has been stripped off, the next step is to wash down the wood. This will help to remove any remaining debris and also neutralizes the stripper.

Follow the manufacturer's recommendation on what neutralizer to use with your particular stripper. Soak it into a hand-sized wad of wire wool and thoroughly rub over the stripped surfaces. If water is the recommended neutralizer, use copious quantities.

Finally, when the wood is dry, **sand it down to create a smooth finish.** Use medium grade paper to work out the deeper scratches, then go over the whole surface with a fine grade. Rub in the direction of the wood grain when using wire wool or glasspaper.

Stripping polish

If the chest of drawers is polished you need to know which type of polish has been used before you can remove it successfully.

French polish gives a fine, mirror-like surface which is very delicate and easily marked by heat or liquid. The surface shine is the result of the polishing techniques rather than the ingredients of the polish.

French polish can easily be removed with methylated spirits. Wipe it on

1 Remove the handles from drawers if possible. Pour some stripper into a jar and apply it to the wood. Work it well into any cracks

3 *Use a shavehook to get* the paint out of difficult corners and continue applying stripper until all the paint has been removed

generously and then leave it for a few minutes. When the polish has softened scrape it off, first with a scraper, then with fine wire wool soaked in methylated spirits. When the wood is dry, glasspaper it down to a smooth finish.
Wax polish and oily surfaces can be removed by rubbing with fine steel-wool soaked in turpentine or turps substitute. Dry with an absorbent rag and repeat the process until you reach bare wood.

If you are not sure what sort of polish is on your furniture, choose a small, unobtrusive part of the surface and rub real turpentine on the spot with a soft cloth. This will remove dirt and wax or oil finishes and quickly reveal bare wood. If there is polish left after applying the turpentine, rub on a little methylated spirit—if the surface has been French polished it will go soft and sticky.

2 Leave it until the paint starts to bubble then, with a stripping knife, remove the top layer of paint. Scrape the paint shreds into a tin

4 Rub the bare wood with coarse wire wool dampened in turps substitute or water. When dry, rub with glasspaper to smooth it

Varnished and lacquered finishes

If your chest of drawers is more than 30 years old and is varnished, you are dealing with oil-based varnish. This is made from resins dissolved in oils and solvents and is quite different from modern cellulose and polyurethane varnishes.

The cleanest way to remove oil-based varnish is with a carpenter's cabinet scraper—a cheap tool consisting of a rectangle of metal with one sharp edge. Tilt the scraper away from you and push it along the grain of the wood, working away from your body. Never use it across the grain.

To remove polyurethane varnishes use paint stripper. Cellulose-based varnishes can be removed with paint-stripper, acetone, cellulose thinners, ammonia, caustic soda or turpentine. You may need to test small areas first to see which works best.

Doing repairs

Once you have stripped off all the old paint, you may find that various faults show up and that repairs are necessary before the new finish can be applied.

If the back of the chest of drawers is weak, nail some new battening on.

Any weak joints should be glued, pinned, then held in place for several hours—either with string or in a clamp. Make sure that the corners of the chest of drawers are protected from the cutting action of the string with some paper or a piece of wood.

Cracks and holes must be filled with plastic wood or a commercial non-shrinking stopper—both are available from do-it-yourself shops. You can also buy coloured fillers and stains to match the natural colour of the wood. Level filled holes with fine glasspaper.

Large holes, greater than the size of a keyhole, should be plugged with a piece of similar wood cut to shape. Make sure that the grain of the plug goes the same way as the rest of the surface, then glue it in place with a suitable adhesive.

Finishing—with polyurethane

Polyurethane varnish gives bare wood a lustrous, hard-wearing finish which is easy to clean and maintain. As well as clear varnish, a wide variety of colours and natural wood shades are available. The clear varieties come in matt, gloss and coloured varieties.

Polyurethane can withstand heat without marking, though intense heat may eventually damage the wood underneath. It is important to let the polyurethane set: with some varieties it can take up to two weeks to achieve maximum hardness.

Apply the varnish directly to the sanded wood with a paintbrush. Because the varnish must be applied in coats, it is a good idea to dilute the first with white spirit so it soaks in and seals the wood. When the first coat is dry, lightly rub it down with fine glasspaper before applying the next. Subsequent coats can be diluted in the proportion of one part white spirit to three parts polyurethane to give thinner coats which will brush on more easily.

If you want a matt finish, start with one or two coats of gloss and make only the top coat matt. This gives a harder-wearing finish.

Before applying the coloured variety apply one coat of clear polyurethane to seal the wood or you may get a patchy effect. For a matt finish, apply a final coat of clear, matt polyurethane after the coloured coats.

Finishing—with wax polish

Wax polish can either be used in conjunction with polyurethane, or by itself as an alternative finish. Although wax gives a warm, mellow look to the wood, it has hardly any resistance to heat and marks easily—so its use should be confined to more decorative furniture.

With polyurethane, use a proprietary, white wax polish. After the final coat of varnish has dried, rub over it lightly with a very fine (0000) grade of wire wool. Having brushed away the dust, rub in the polish with a coarse rag to give an even, matt sheen.

Finally, buff up the surface with a fine cloth. Successive layers of polish, built up at the rate of one every two days, will deepen and harden the finish.

For a pure wax finish, you can make up your own beeswax polish. For this you need pure beeswax—available from hardware shops—turps substitute and a glass jar.

Grate the beeswax with a cheese grater and put it in a jam jar. Pour in just enough turps to cover the wax.

Stand the jar in a pan of very hot water and stir until the mixture melts and forms a thick paste—on no account expose the jar to a naked flame as the turps substitute is highly inflammable.

Dip a clean rag in the wax and rub the mixture into the clean wood surface, taking care to spread the wax evenly. Apply enough wax to soak in to the grain but avoid leaving any proud of the surface.

When the wax has hardened completely—in about an hour—buff up the surface with a fine cloth to give a mirror finish.

5 Grate the beeswax, using a cheese grater, to help it melt. Then put the wax in a jam jar and add enough turpentine to cover it

6 Stand the jam jar in a saucepan of very hot water and then stir the mixture until it all melts and forms a thick paste

7 Put some of the beeswax polish on a rag and rub it into the surface of the wood. Finish it off with a dry, clean cloth

8 If using a polyurethane finish, this can be applied directly on to the stripped wood. For the first coat, dilute the varnish with white spirit

Stencil magic

Above: *Stencil kits, containing sheets of designs and a sharp knife for cutting them, are available from art and craft shops or stationers. Apart from the stencil kit, you need newspaper to protect the floor, sticky tape or drawing pins, chalk, a palette knife or blunt kitchen knife, cardboard, a stencil brush (available from art and craft shops), small cans of gloss or enamel paints and white spirit. Make sure you gather all these materials together before you start*

Cut out the stencils on a flat surface such as a board, securing them with tape or drawing pins before you begin cutting out the patterns.

If you want to stencil a group of designs, arrange the stencils in patterns until you find an arrangement that you like. Lightly chalk in the pattern to get an idea of how the finished design will look.

Mix your chosen colours with a knife, using a sheet of cardboard as a palette. Fasten the stencil to the wood with clear tape, rub off the chalk and use the stencil brush to daub paint through. Hold the brush square to the surface to avoid the paint creeping. If the area of the stencil is fairly large use a spray can (of enamel, not car paint).

With practice, you can grade colours by lightly applying a contrasting colour over the first colour at the edges of the stencil. Wait until the paint is almost dry before painting adjacent designs or you may smudge the first ones. If you make a mistake, the paint can be removed with white spirit while it is still wet.

When you have finished, clean each stencil with white spirit.

Above: *A dark background shows off brightly coloured stencils to the full in a design imprinted across the entire face of the chest*

Below: *More subdued designs add a touch of prettiness to this cupboard in which the individual door panels serve as frames for the motifs*

FIXING FLOORBOARDS

Floorboard repairs are straightforward and require few special tools. But repairs are essential for safety and for preserving the good condition of the joists beneath, and the floor covering above the boards

Above: *Replace cracked or split boards with new lengths of timber, cut to length and planed down in width to match the available space. Screw them down to prevent creaks.*

Although solid and hardwearing, floorboard timbers are prone to all sorts of minor faults and irritations. For instance, creaks under the carpet are annoying but not dangerous; rotten boards which collapse underfoot can be dangerous as well as annoying. Even if your floorboarding is in perfect condition, it may still need work to improve draughtproofing—or to get to wiring underneath.

Types of floorboard

Most floorboards are made of softwood—usually pine. In a single-skin floor as used in Britain, the boards are fixed at right angles to the joists that support them, and may be nailed or screwed in place. The cut ends of the boards are arranged to coincide with the joists, so that they are well supported and can be secured to them to prevent warping and lifting. Floorboards are traditionally fitted before skirtings are fixed, so that any uneven cut ends round the perimeter of the room are concealed.

Floorboards fall into two basic types: square-edged, and tongue-and-grooved (fig. D). Tongued-and-grooved (T&G) boards and their derivatives are designed to eliminate draughty gaps but are more difficult to take up than their square-edged counterparts.

If you are in any doubt which of the two types is used for your flooring, choose two boards with a slight gap between them and slide a knife blade in as far as possible—compacted grime or draughtproofing in the gap may have to be scratched out first. If the blade is stopped, the boards are either tongued or rebated.

Lifting square-edged boards

For your starting point, choose the most convenient free end of the board you wish to lift. If the board extends right across the room and under the skirting (baseboard) on both sides, you have to start lifting it in the middle and work gradually towards the ends. When all the nails are loose, you spring the board free by pulling it upwards into a bow shape.

To lift the board, insert a bolster into the joint gap between it and the board

Joists and floorboards

A. *Joists of a suspended floor are supported on small sleeper walls or piers on a concrete base*

B. *Metal joist hangers built into the inner wall are one method of supporting an upstairs floor*

C. *Flooring joists can also be built into the inner of two masonry walls*

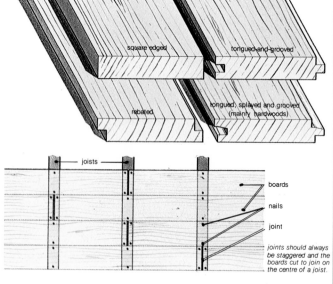

D. *Types of floorboard. Square-edged boards are found in older British houses, tongued boards elsewhere*

on one side, in line with the nails at the free end. Use a club hammer to drive it home. Then stamp on the bolster to push it down towards the floor (fig E). Do the same on the other side of the board.

As the board is levered up, insert the claw of a hammer under the end and continue levering up from here until the board comes completely free of the joist.

To help lift the rest of the board, insert a metal bar, length of stout timber or piping underneath the free end. Use the bolster and hammer to loosen the board at each line of nails, then lever it clear with the metal bar. For safety, immediately remove any exposed nails—particularly those left upright in the joists. A crowbar is much easier than a claw hammer for this job.

If a board proves particularly stub-

born, try to free one end and insert a metal bar under it. Using the bar as a levering support, stamp on the free end. After each stamp there should be some 'give', so move the support along the board towards the next joist until the nails give way here.

Lifting T&G board
Start by choosing a suitable free end and section of board, well clear of the

skirting. To break the tongue, insert a bolster into the join between two adjacent boards at the end of the board you wish to lift (fig. E). Give the bolster a few sharp taps with a hammer, until you feel or hear the tongue below start to split. Continue until the split extends at least 75mm from the nails, or until you otherwise judge it to be clear of the joist. You can then replace the bolster with a saw, knowing that its blade will escape damage from floorboard nails.

You can use almost any type of saw but a compromise between the awkward length of a panel saw and the short length of usable blade on a tenon saw is a purpose-made *flooring saw* (fig. E).

If a power saw is used, set the sawing blade depth to about the thickness of the board to avoid any damage to the sub-floor (if any), or to pipes or wires suspended below the flooring.

Continue cutting between the two boards until you are about 75mm from the next line of nails, and once again use the bolster to break the tongue along the stretch over the joists.

When the tongue is fully severed, use the bolster, claw hammer and

metal bar to lever up the board as you would do to lift a square-edged one. In this case, though, concentrate your levering activities at the end and along the severed side of the board at each joist. You should be able to lift the nails and tilt the board enough for the interlocked side to slide free of the adjacent board.

Well-fitted tongued-and-grooved boards may be so tightly cramped together that splitting them apart with a bolster and hammer may not be possible without causing extensive damage to both boards. In this case, the board you wish to remove must be split lengthways at the middle. A power saw is best for this job.

Cutting across floorboards
In a single-skin floor of the sort used in Britain, it is best to cut across a floorboard either over a joist or to the side of one, so that support for the new board ends is readily available. Cutting over a joist is a little more difficult than cutting beside one, but enables you to nail the cut section straight back in place. A double-skin floor can be cut anywhere, but try to avoid having two cut ends side-by-side on the floor.

1 To remove a damaged section, first locate a joist position. Mark a cutting line either over the middle of the joist or to one side of it

Cutting on a joist: It is important to make the cut along the centre of the joist, otherwise one or other of the two freshly-made board ends is not going to be supported properly.

The centre line of the joist can be pin-pointed by following on the line of nails of adjacent boards and board ends. Use a try square to pencil a cutting mark on a line joining the farthest possible reference points on each side of the board you are cutting. You can do this by eye or, better, by stretching a piece of string over the distance between the two points. If you are cutting alongside a board with a clearly indicated joist, just continue the line of the board end (or fixings) when marking the cutting line. If the nails are staggered, take a common centre-line from as many boards as possible.

To make the cut, you can leave the board in place and use a padsaw, compass saw or power jig saw. But if the board is long enough, it is easier to lift it up into a 'hump' and cut with a tenon saw or flooring saw. To do this, you lever the board upwards with the bolster and then support it with two offcuts of timber wedged beneath it.

Cutting beside a joist: First locate the side of the joist. You may be able to do this by inserting a knife or metal rule into the gap between the floorboards, sliding it along until it hits the joist. Mark the board at this point, and use a try square to complete the cutting line. Alternatively, and if there is a gap between the floorboards on the other side, repeat probing and simply join up the two points marked on the board (fig. 1).

Drill an 8mm hole up against and at

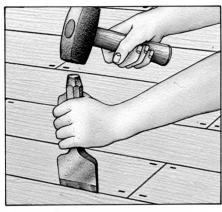

E. A bolster (top pictures) is used both to break the tongues of T&G boards and to loosen the edges of

boards. A claw hammer is useful for lifting boards, and a flooring saw for cutting out shorter lengths

2 Using a piece of wood as a guide, scratch and then tease a cut with the first few teeth if you are using a tenon saw to cut on the joist

3 If you are using a padsaw or power jig saw to make a cut beside a joist, drill a small hole the width of the blade

4 Use a padsaw or compass to cut right across the board or, if you prefer, just to give you a slot in which to start off your handsaw.

5 A padsaw can be used to sever the tongue of a tongued-and-grooved board if other forms of sawing are impracticable

6 Remove nails from the joist using a claw hammer. Protect the board alongside with an offcut. Do not hammer old nails into the joists

7 When making an extra support, start by cutting a generous length of stout timber. The extra width ensures that the board is firmly fixed

8 Mark the floorboard gap on the upper surface of the bearer. As you can see the bearer straddles the gap and acts just like the joist

9 Partly face-nail the support, to the point when the nails are just about to break through on the other side of the timber

10 Complete the nailing while pushing the bearer against the joist and upwards against the fixed boards on both sides

one end of the cutting line (fig. 3) then use a padsaw or power jig saw to cut next to, and along, the cutting line. The padsaw can be replaced with a handsaw or circular-blade power saw when convenient, and re-used if necessary at the end of the cut.

Fitting an extra bearer (cleat)
If you have removed a section of floorboard by cutting along the side of a joist, you must fit an extra bearer (cleat) of timber to the joist, in order to provide support for the new board end.

Make this bearer from an offcut of softwood, whose minimum dimensions ought to be no less than 38mm by 50mm. Cut it to length, slightly longer than the width of floorboarding removed and use either nails or screws for fixing it in place (fig. 9). If you choose nails, use two or three about 75mm long for each floorboard width, and hammer these partially into the broader side before positioning the bearer. If you use screws, two for each board width are enough, but drill pilot holes before fitting them.

Position the bearer against the joist and make sure that the top edges of both pieces of timber are exactly flush. Pull the bearer upwards, tightly against the floorboards on either side, while you hammer or screw it securely in place (fig. 10).

Replacing square-edged boards
There are few problems in replacing square-edged boards. New ones of the same thickness are cut to length and—in the case of non-standard sizes—to width. If part of the board has to be tapered or otherwise shaped to fit, use the discarded board as a template when

you saw to shape the new one.

If a single board is to be replaced simply slot it into place and nail down. A number of boards covering a large area are best fitted individually—if possible in the same flooring 'pattern' as originally. No two board ends should lie side by side on the same joist.

When fitting a number of boards, do a 'dry run' first to check the width fit, and whether tight butting of the boards is possible. Where the boards are to remain visible, keep to the original spacings for the sake of appearance.

If a complete floor area is being replaced, make a point of butting all boards as tightly as possible before fixing. This is done with a floor cramp —available from hire shops—and substantially improves underfloor draught-proofing (fig. 18).

11 If fitting a thicker board than the rest, a cut-out has to be made where the board crosses a joist. First mark the joist's position

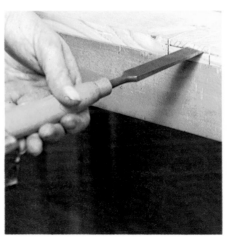

13 Carefully cut the board in order not to exceed the required rebate depth—this can be gauged by sight or by direct measurement

If part of the original floorboarding is to be replaced, cut off any wood which is badly split where nails were removed. Do not re-use old nail holes. These, and new holes along the length of the board, should be made good with a filler paste.

Replacing T&G boards
Replacing tongued-and-grooved boards is not quite so straightforward. If you are re-using the old board, this can be replaced by fitting the remaining tongued or grooved side into the adjacent board. A small gap will remain on the other side—this must be plugged for complete draught-proofing.

To fit a new tongued and grooved board, you may have to plane off its tongue to get it to fit, but leave its grooved side intact.

12 Transfer the marks from the underside of the replacement floorboard to its edges. Repeat this step at every joist position

15 Check that the rebate fits snugly and is of the required depth. Continue chiselling if the board is proud of those alongside

14 Use a chisel to remove wood between the cutting lines. The chisel face should be down. Work in stages to end with a level cut

If a number of adjacent boards have been removed, any necessary combination of used and new boards may be used when reflooring. The technique is to loosely fit these together over the floor area to be covered, in the process forming a low arch by making the boards slightly over-sized. Lay a spare plank over this, and press or stamp the boards down: the tongues and grooves knit together in the process. The flattened boards can then be fixed in place. Alternatively, you can use an off-cut and mallet as in fig. 17.

Replacing short sections
If you are cutting out and replacing a short section of floorboard you may want to use up a spare piece of timber lying about the house. Alternatively, you may have difficulty getting a re-

placement board which exactly matches the thickness of your existing ones. Either way, the new board will be better too thick than too thin.

Having cut your new section to length, lay it beside the gap in the floor and mark off on the underside where it is to pass over a joist. Chisel out rough rebates between the marks, to the same depth as the board is oversize (fig. 14).

When you lay the board, the rebates should fit over the joists and allow it to rest flush with the others.

Dealing with creaking boards
Loose and creaking floorboards may be caused by incorrect nailing, by the joists below them settling, or by warping and shrinkage. It is usually possible to cure a loose board simply by re-nailing or screwing it back in place.

But before you do this, check that the loose joint coincides with the centre of the joist below, taking the board up if necessary. If it does not, widen the joist with a new bearer (figs. 7-10), or replace the whole board.

To nail floorboards, use 50mm lost-head nails or flooring nails. Position them next to, and about 12mm away from, the existing nails. When you have finished, drive all the nail heads well below the surface of the board with a nail punch (nail set).

To secure floorboards with screws, use 40mm countersunk steel screws. Drill pilot holes for them 12mm from each existing nail, taking care that the holes go no deeper than the thickness of the board. When all the screws are in place, make sure that none of them protrudes above the surface.

16 *If the replacement board is too thin, use sheet wood to make up the difference. Do not use newspaper folds for this job*

17 *When replacing tongued boards the last two will need force before slipping into fit—use a mallet and protective wood offcut*

18 *Nailing boards into place. A pencil line ensures accuracy. A floor cramp—worth hiring for big jobs—keeps the boards tightly packed*

19 *If you decide to use nails for fixing a floorboard in place, hammer in the heads using a punch. Use filler and stain to conceal the hole*

20 *If you choose to screw down a board, drill a hole to accept the screw body only. This minimizes the effort needed in fixing boards*

21 *Use a countersink bit to drill a recess for the screw head and— if necessary—fill the hole once the board has been screwed to the joist*

DOOR REPAIRS

Hinging and rehanging a door successfully is easy if you follow a few simple rules. And even more complicated jobs, such as changing the direction in which a door opens, are not as hard as they seem

There is nothing more annoying than a door which is difficult to open and close. And although the trouble can usually be put right quite easily, neglecting such a door may cause more extensive damage which is costly and difficult to repair at a later date.

Before attempting any repairs, it is worth considering what hinges are available and how you hang a door properly. Indeed, when a door hangs badly, the hinges are often at fault: either they are fitted badly or the wrong ones have been used.

Choosing hinges
Plastic, nylon, or—better still—pressed steel hinges are suitable for light internal doors, but if you are fitting hinges to a heavy, outside door, use the strong type made of cast steel. If you want a finish which is rust free, jam free and decorative, brass hinges look good but are more expensive and less durable.

By finding out the thickness, weight and height of your door, you can estimate what size of hinge you require. For example, a lightweight door, 32mm thick, would need a 75mm × 25mm hinge whereas a heavier door, 45mm thick, might require a 100mm × 38mm hinge. Be careful not to buy a hinge which is too wide for the door as this will result in a weak, narrow strip of wood where the hinge is fitted. To find the size of a hinge, first measure its length and then the width of one of its leaves to the middle of the knuckle where it swivels.

Most doors are fitted with butt hinges and you can buy either the fixed or the rising variety. The rising butt hinge allows the door to rise as it is opened but shut down closely on to a carpet or threshold as it closes. This means that though the door does not scrape against floor coverings, it will stop draughts and reduce fire hazards once it is shut.

Rising butt hinges are either right or left handed, so decide which way you want your door to open before you buy a set. Avoid confusion by getting the difference clear in your own mind.

Marking and fitting
Before you fit the hinge decide which side you want the door to open. Panelled doors can be hinged on either edge but most modern flush doors can only be fitted with hinges on one edge.

On some doors the hinge positions are marked on the edge of the door and these areas are usually reinforced, so it is advisable not to try to fix hinges to any other spots.

Once you have decided which edge of the door is to be hinged, arrange it so that it is resting on the opposite edge. Support the door by wedging it into a corner, cramping it to the leg of a table, or by holding it in a vice (fig. 1).

The best positions for the hinges are 215mm from the top of the door and 225mm from the bottom, but make sure that this does not leave them over any joints or the door may be weakened.

Use a marking knife and try square to mark the hinge positions on the door edge, starting from the knuckle edge where the hinge will swivel. Mark across all but 6mm of the edge then continue on to the face of the door, marking the thickness of one hinge leaf (fig. 2).

Next, open one of the hinges and lay it in position on the door edge to check that the lines you have drawn are accurate. Hold the hinge in position and use a marking knife to mark each end (fig. 3). Then scribe the width and depth of a hinge leaf on to the door edge and frame (figs. 4 and 5).

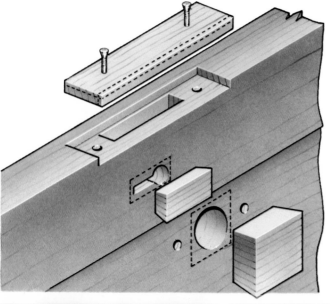
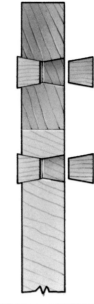

A. Left: *Holes left in the frame by relocating the lock, keyhole and handle need to be filled with wood*

Cutting out

The hinge recesses are now ready to be cut out. Use a bevel-edged chisel and start by chopping downwards across the grain in a series of cuts 5–6mm apart (fig. 6). Leave a thin uncut border of about 2–3mm around the three edges (fig. 6). Hold the chisel flat, bevel side up, and pare away the chipped-up timber. Finally, with the flat side of the chisel parallel to the door edge, clean out the recess.

The hinge should now press firmly into place flush with the surrounding timber. You may have trouble with some types of hinges which are bent due to pressure in their manufacture. If

1 Before fixing hinges, stand the door on edge and support it securely with a vice firmly clamped to one end of the door

2 Position the hinges 215mm from the top of the door and 225mm from the base, keeping them well clear of any joints

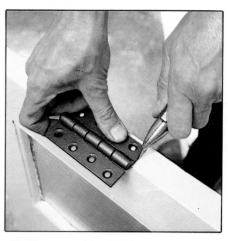

3 Use a marking knife to mark the hinge position on the door edge. Make sure that the hinge knuckle is facing the right way.

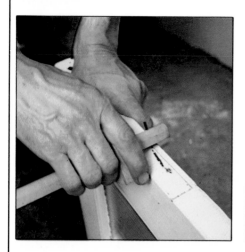

4 Then set a marking gauge to the width of a hinge leaf and scribe this on the door edge between the two lines previously marked

5 Reset your marking gauge to the depth of one hinge leaf and mark this on to the face of the door frame between the two knife cuts

6 Use a bevel-edged chisel to cut out the hinge recesses. Make a number of cuts 5-6mm apart, to leave an uncut border around the edge

this is the case, pare away a further 1-2mm from the recess.

Fixing hinges

Once the hinge is comfortably in position, carefully mark the screw holes with a sharp pencil then remove the hinge and remark the screw centres with a centre punch. Try to mark these a little off centre—towards inside of the recess—so that once the screws are inserted, the hinge will be pulled snugly into position (fig. 8).

Drill pilot holes to the depth of the screws and then clearance holes deep enough for the screw shanks. For heavy butt hinges use No. 7 or No. 8 × 38mm screws. Insert the screws so that they finish level with or slightly below the hinge plate (fig. 9).

If you are using brass screws, put in a steel screw first. This will cut a thread in the wood and avoid the possibility of shearing off or damaging the soft brass screw heads.

Fitting the door

Position the door in its frame by supporting the base with wooden wedges made from offcuts (fig. 10). Both door and hinges should be in the fully open position unless you are using rising butt hinges, in which case they should be closed.

With all types of hinge, make an allowance at the base of the door for any proposed floor covering and adjust the gap as necessary by altering the positions of the wedges. When you are satisfied that the door is in the right place, mark the position of the top and bottom of each hinge on the door frame with a pencil.

With the door removed from the frame, mark out the hinge recesses—

their length, width and depth—accurately with a marking knife and adjustable try square. Use the same technique to cut the recesses as you used for those on the door.

Replace the door and position it exactly using the wooden wedges, then tap the hinge leaves into place in the waiting recesses. Finally, mark and pre-drill each screw hole, then insert one screw in each hinge so that you can check that the door opens and closes properly. If it sticks at any point, make minor adjustments by chiselling away more of the rebates before you drive home the remaining screws.

Sticking doors

If a door sticks and you can find nothing wrong with the hinges, it may be that part of the door frame has swollen. Where the swelling is slight and there is plenty of clearance between door and frame, investigate the possibility of bringing the swollen part away from the frame by either packing or deepening one of the hinge recesses. Be sure to make only the slightest adjustments in one go, or the door may stick elsewhere around the frame.

Where the swelling is more severe, you have no choice but to plane off the excess and redecorate the door. The planing can be done with the door in situ providing you first wedge the base to take the weight off the hinges.

Older doors and those particularly exposed to damp may warp or become loose at the joints, causing them to fit badly in their frames. In the case of

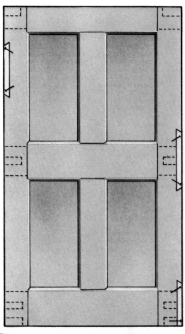

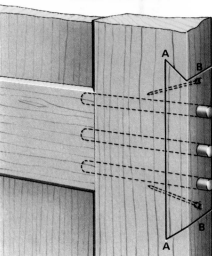

B. Right: *Badly weakened areas need to be cut out and replaced with dowelled sections. Start by cutting along line A-A, then B-A*

7 *Cut out the chipped-out timber in the hinge recesses with a chisel —held bevel side up—until the recess is clean and smooth*

8 *Mark the screw holes slightly off centre towards the inside of the recesses. This allows the hinge to bed securely once it is fixed*

9 *Once you have drilled pilot and clearance holes, insert the screws so that they are slightly below the level of the hinge plates*

10 *Wooden wedges made from offcuts can be placed under the foot of the door so that it can be positioned to fit the frame exactly*

11 *Broken or damaged joints can be strengthened by first drilling out the old wedges to a depth of 75mm using a 15mm twist drill*

slight warping, one answer is to make a small adjustment to one of the hinge positions so that you take up the twist. Do this on the frame—not on the door.

However, a more satisfactory solution is to remove the door so that you can cramp and strengthen the frame. Take off all the door furniture—the hinges, knob, lock, key escutcheon—place it flat on a workbench, then cramp the frame square using a sash cramp with a long bar.

Where gaps appear in the joints, scrape out any dust, accumulated grime and old glue with a chisel or knife. Then bring the joints together by cramping across the frame in two or more places. Use softwood offcuts to protect the door from being bruised by the cramps.

Next, drill out the old wedges holding the tenons at each frame joint to a depth of 75mm (fig. 11); use a 15mm twist drill bit. Make up some 85mm lengths of 15mm dowel with longitudinal cuts in them to allow for compressing (fig. 12) and chamfers at one end to give a snug fit.

Liberally smear each piece of dowel with external grade waterproof woodworking adhesive then drive them home into the drill holes with a mallet. Check that the cramps are still holding the frame square by measuring across the diagonals—which should be equal—and leave the adhesive to set. When it is dry, cut off the excess dowel with a tenon saw and finish the edges in the normal way.

Repairing a damaged stile or rail

If a stile or rail is split, it is usually possible to open this up, force in some adhesive then cramp it closed again. In this case, where necessary, place some

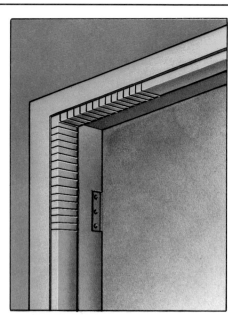

C. Above: *Remove a rebated door stop by first making a series of cuts around the corner of the frame*

newspaper between the split and the cramp protective offcuts to stop the latter from sticking to the frame. When the adhesive has set, fill any remaining cracks with wood filler and finish with a block and glasspaper.

Very badly damaged or rotten areas must be cut out completely and replaced with new timber. Using an adjustable bevel and marking gauge, determine and mark out the extent of the damage along the frame. Mark the width of the damaged area with a marking gauge on the face of the door.

You must now cut out the timber. In the example shown in fig. B, you would make the internal cuts A-A by drilling through the wood, then finishing with a

12 *The holes can be filled with glued 15mm thick dowels, chamfered at one end and with longitudinal cuts*

13 *When removing a planted door stop, first use a blunt, wide chisel and a mallet to prise the stop away from the door frame*

14 *By inserting the claws of a hammer into the gap, the door stop can then be worked loose and away from the frame*

padsaw or powered jig saw. Make the cuts B-A with a tenon saw, remove the damaged section, and smooth the cut edges with a wide, bevel-edged chisel.

Mark out and cut a replacement section, making it slightly wider than the frame so that it can be planed flush after fixing. Secure the section with woodworking adhesive and oval nails, the latter punched well below the surface level.

If the replacement section is over a joint, the tenon in that joint will have been seriously weakened by the repair. The remedy is to drive two or three dowels through the new timber into what is left of the tenon (fig. B). Drill and glue the dowels as described above.

Changing direction

It is often useful to change the direction in which a door swings—to make more space in a small room for example —or to hang it from the opposite side of the frame.

Making a door open in the opposite direction involves removing and resiting the door stop, altering the hinge rebates and possibly changing the door furniture. You may or may not have to change the hinges, depending on what type you have. Ordinary butt hinges can simply be used the other way up.

How you go about the job depends on whether your door stop is simply planted—nailed to the frame—or rebated into it.

Removing a planted stop: Remove the door from the frame and clear the space around you. Then use a blunt, wide chisel and mallet to cut into the joint between stop and frame and lever the latter away (fig. 13). The stop is bound to be securely fixed and you may have to use considerable force.

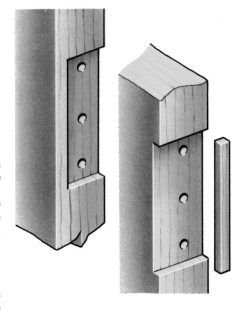

The job becomes easier when you can insert the claws of a claw hammer and ease the stop away, working upwards from the base of the door (fig. 14).

Once the door stop has given way, remove any old glue or chipped wood with a chisel, plane and glasspaper.

Removing a rebated stop: Start by measuring by how much the stop protrudes, then mark this amount down and around the outside face of the frame with a marking gauge.

Next, take a tenon saw and make a series of cuts 12-18mm apart in the top corners of the door frame (fig. C). Remove the waste between these with a wide chisel as you would that in a halving joint (see pages 237 to 242). This done, you can insert a rip saw or power saw and cut downwards through the remainder of the door stop. Afterwards, plane the cut timber flush with

D. Left: *When changing the direction of opening, the hinge recess has to be moved to the opposite edge*

the rest of the frame and use a chisel to clean up the corners (fig. 15).

Rehanging

When you come to rehang the door, the hinge recesses may well have to be moved. Do this by chiselling them across to the other side of the frame. Then make up wood blocks to fill the now unused parts of the recesses and pin and glue them in place (fig. D).

Refit the door stops—or make up new planted ones in the case of rebated stops—in accordance with the new door position. Make sure that the stops are firmly pinned and glued (fig. 17).

If the door lock or latch is handed, you must exchange it for a new one and fit it according to the manufacturer's instructions. Alter the position of the striker plate and make good the old recess as you did the hinge recesses. Finally, re-hang the door.

Changing sides

If you decide to change the side on which the door hangs, all the above operations will be necessary and you will have to swop over the door furniture to the other side.

As this is often handed, make sure that it is still suitable for the new door opening. Indeed, this is a good time to exchange the furniture for a new set.

Make good the holes left in the door by driving in tapered and glued wood blocks, cut oversize so that you can plane them flush with the surface. When you have done this, fill any remaining gaps with wood filler and repaint the door (fig. A).

15 To remove a rebated stop, make a series of cuts around the corners. Chop out the waste and cut away the remainder of the stop

16 When rehanging a door which was hinged on the other side, pin pieces of wood block to fill the gaps and plane smooth

17 If the door is rehinged to swing in a different direction, a new door stop must be added so that the door will close properly

DOOR REPAIRS

Dealing with rattling doors

A rattling door is usually an indication that the timber has shrunk and the door no longer butts tightly up against the door stop. You may be able to cure the rattle with self-adhesive draughtproofing foam, but a better remedy is to reposition the striker plate on the door frame so it is a little nearer the door stop. This involves unscrewing the striker plate, enlarging it slightly and fixing it, using new screw holes.

If the door has also warped slightly along its opening edge and cramping is not effective in pulling it back square, the best solution is to mark the profile of the warped door edge on the door stop and then prise it off so you can plane it down to the line. Replace it so its planed edge meets the door surface snugly, then fill the nail heads and repaint the bare wood to complete the repair.

18 *Close the door and measure the gap between the door and stop. Then mark this distance on the frame, measured from the edge of the striker*

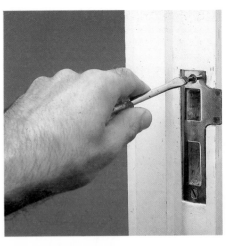

19 *Unscrew the countersunk screws holding the striker plate in place along the door frame. Set the striker plate and screws aside*

20 *Use a straightedge (or the striker plate itself if you prefer) and a marking knife to indicate the edge of the new striker plate rebate*

21 *Next use a sharp bevel-edged chisel to enlarge the rebate up to the marked line. You may have to enlarge the latch and lock recesses*

22 *Test the fit of the striker plate, then screw it into position and test the operation of the door. Finally, fill the exposed edge of the old rebate*

23 *If the door is warped and cannot be cramped square, reshape the door stop. Scribe the profile of the door edge onto the stop*

24 *Lever the bottom edge of the stop away from the frame, starting at the bottom and working upwards. Pull out all old nails*

25 *Cramp the stop in a vice and plane the edge down to the marked line. Then nail it back to the door frame so the door fits against it*

124

WINDOW FRAME REPAIRS

It is essential to keep timber-framed windows in prime condition—if neglected, the wood will quickly deteriorate. And if signs of decay are left uncorrected, rot may set in

Below: *Sash cords are fitted into grooves in the side of the sash and held in place by four or five clout nails. Sash cords inevitably fray through constant use and age and eventually need replacing*

A neglected window spoils the appearance of a home, causes draughts and damp, and can tempt intruders. If the signs of decay are not detected and dealt with at an early stage, further deterioration will make repair more difficult.

Types of window

The two basic types of timber-framed window are the casement sash (fig. C) and the double-hung sliding sash window (fig. B).

The sliding sash window operates by means of cords, pulleys and weights which counterbalance the sashes—the opening parts of the window—as they slide up and down. Two sets of beadings —thin lengths of wood—hold the

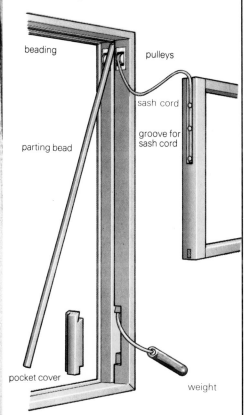

A. *Components of a sash window. The sash cord is nailed to the edge of the sash and tied to a weight*

WINDOW FRAME REPAIRS

sashes straight in the frame. Covers or caps in the lower part of the inner edge of the frame are usually provided to allow access to the compartments containing the weights. Where this is not so you will have to remove the inside frame cover. Modern sash windows usually have spring-operated mechanisms instead of cords, and these are simply replaced if they fail.

A casement window is attached to the frame by hinges and is held open by means of a stay which is designed to allow progressive adjustment. It is the most common style of window.

Working considerations
The most common problems affecting timber-framed windows are decay from wet rot, loose joints in the sashes and —in the case of sash windows—fraying or broken sash cords. To repair these faults you have to remove the sash so that you can get at the individual components of the window or work on the sash itself—difficult or impossible if it were left standing in the frame.

Where a section of a sash is decayed, you can strengthen it by cutting out

and renewing the affected part of the wood. If the joints which hold the sash together are working loose, you can reinforce these by knocking them apart and re-assembling them with fresh adhesive. But if the decay is particularly widespread, rot may have irreparably damaged the whole sash and the only solution is to discard it and fit a new one.

If you have modern casement windows, replacing a decayed section of the casement may be difficult because there is insufficient wood to work with. In this case, it may be quicker and probably more effective to replace the faulty casement altogether.

If you are dealing with a window affected by rot, it is best to carry out the work during dry weather as the timber remains swollen in damp conditions, making any repairs less than perfect after eventual shrinkage in dry, warm conditions.

Before starting work, identify the type of rot. Wet rot is more common in window frames but you may find dry rot in which case treatment must be more drastic .

Removing a casement window
Older types of casement windows are constructed from thick timber and are therefore heavy. So, if you have to remove the casement for replacement or repair, the work must be tackled with great care.

Begin by passing a strong cord around the window, under the top hinge, and tie this to the upper part of a step ladder to prevent the casement from falling to the ground.

Before you attempt to remove the screws holding the hinges in place, use an old paintbrush to dab a small amount of proprietary paint stripper on any paint around the screw heads.

If the screws prove particularly obstinate and difficult to turn, try to tighten them slightly first to help loosen the threads, or give the end of the screwdriver a few sharp taps with a mallet. If all else fails, try heating the head of the screw with a soldering iron to loosen the thread's grip.

Remove the screws which fix the hinges to the frame first—those in the casement are easier and safer to remove once you have taken the window

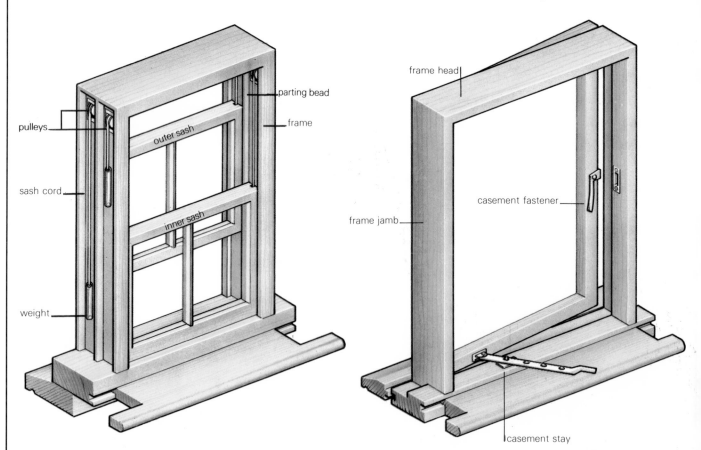

B. *The weights counterbalance the sashes, allowing them to slide up and down. The sashes are held in*
place by lengths of beading pinned into grooves

C. *A casement window. The casement is attached to the frame by hinges. A casement stay holds it open and a fastener allows it to be shut tight*

1 To replace a sash cord, take the sash and parting bead from the frame, then remove the pocket cover to gain access to the weight compartment

2 Lay the cover aside, then remove the weight from the compartment and pull the old, decayed sash cord away from the frame

3 Tie some string to a small weight such as a nail, then thread this over the pulley wheel and out through the pocket opening

4 Tie the new cord to the string, pull this down through the pocket, then tie the end of the cord securely to the original weight

5 Pull the free end of the cord so that the weight is raised—25mm for the outer sash or almost to the pulley for the inner one

6 To hold the weight temporarily in position, half-drive a nail through the cord, securing it to the edge of the frame

7 Fit the new sash cord into the groove in the edge of the sash and fix it into place with four or five clout nails

out of the frame. Loosen each of the screws by one full turn and then unscrew two from each hinge, leaving one screw in each.

Now, starting with the upper hinge, remove the remaining screws. Give the casement extra support with one hand under the outer corner and then swing it sideways into the room or, if you are working on the ground floor, lower it to the ground.

Removing a sash window

If a sash window is neglected, it becomes difficult to open and close properly and eventually its cords may fray and snap. To cure these problems, it is usually necessary to remove both sashes from the frame.

Start by removing the fixing beads around the inside edge of the frame. Beginning with a long piece, use an old chisel to prise it away starting from the middle of its length. Bring it out to a distance of about 25mm from the frame and then tap it smartly back into place. This should cause the bead's fixing pins to rise up through the surface so that you can remove them with a pair of pincers.

Repeat this procedure for the remaining pieces of beading, then take out the inner, or lower, sash and rest it temporarily on the window sill. Ease the parting bead which runs between the two sashes from its housings then slide out the outer sash.

Sashcords are usually nailed into grooves in the sides of the sashes. To detach the cords of the inner sash, make pencil marks on the front of each sash to show where the ends of the cords reach to, then make corresponding marks on the outer frame. 127

Afterwards, remove the clout nails which hold the cords in place and—unless you intend to replace the cords —immediately tap the uppermost nails into the edges of the frame to prevent the weights on the other end of the cords from falling down behind the stile boards (fig. 6).

With both cords removed from the inner sash, you can take it from the frame and repeat the procedure for the outer one.

Replacing sash cords

If the frame of a sash window needs attention, it is likely that the sash cords are also in a poor condition and need to be replaced. And if one of the cords has already snapped, it is possible that the others are frayed and about to break, so it is best to replace all four at the same time.

For renewing the cords, buy a slightly longer length of pre-stretched wax cord than you need to allow for waste. You will also need a lump of lead or a large nail to act as a weight for dropping the new cords down into the pockets.

Remove the sashes from the frame, as described above, and begin work on the cords of the outer sash. To get to the weights to which they are attached, unscrew the pocket covers—or lever them out if they are simply nailed or wedged into place—then pull the weights through the pocket openings and remove the cords.

Check the pulleys to make sure that they run smoothly and, if not, apply a little oil to the pivots. If the window is in particularly bad condition, the pulleys may have rusted and you will have to replace them altogether.

To fix the first new cord, tie your nail or lead weight to a piece of string about 1.5m long and feed it over the groove of the outer pulley wheel until it falls down behind the stile. Tie the new sash cord to the other end of the string and pull it over the pulley and out through the pocket opening. Now untie the string, secure the cord to the original weight and replace this inside its compartment.

Pull the weight up about 25mm and half drive a nail through the cord, into the edge of the frame to hold the weight temporarily in position. Cut the cord so that it is level with the pencil mark on the frame, made when you first removed the sashes.

Next position the outer sash so that you can fit the cord into its groove, align the end of the cord with the pencil mark on the front of the sash, then fix the cord in place with four or five clout nails. Repeat the procedure for

8 *If the mortise and tenon joints of a sash become loose, remove the sash from the frame so that you can re-assemble the joints*

10 *Knock the loose mortise and tenon joints apart, making sure that you protect the frame with a piece of waste timber*

the other cord, remove the temporary nails and lift the sash back into place within the frame.

The procedure for renewing the cords of the inner sash is almost the same but in this case pull the weights up further, almost to the pulley, before fixing the temporary nails (fig. 5).

Then replace the pocket covers, parting bead, the inner sash and then the outer beading. Grease the channels with a little candle wax to aid smooth running.

In some windows, the cord may be knotted into a hole in the side of the sash. The method of replacing is much the same, but tying the knot in exactly the right place might require some trial and error.

Strengthening a sash

If the mortise and tenon joints of a

9 *With the glass removed from the sash frame, use a shave hook to scrape away all traces of putty from the timber.*

11 *Clean all the old glue from the tenons with wire wool, then clean the area in and around the mortises with an old, blunt chisel*

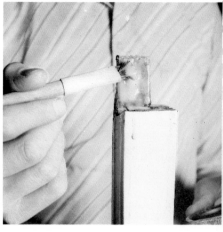

12 *Having made sure that the pin and socket of each joint are clean and dry, coat the tenons with waterproof woodworking adhesive*

13 *Slide the tenons into position, then glue replacement wedges and fit them into place. Drive them home until the joint is secure*

15 *When all the joints have been re-assembled, check that the sash is square, then cramp it using an improvized web cramp*

sash become loose, water will eventually penetrate the gaps causing decay in the sash and possibly the surrounding timber as well. Extensive and costly repairs could then be the result of an initially minor fault.

Do not be tempted to strengthen a loose-jointed sash simply by filling the gaps. To do the job properly, remove the sash from the frame and chip away the putty holding the glass in place. Remove the glazing pins and the glass, then use a shave hook to scrape away all the remaining putty from the edges of the timber (fig. 9).

Now knock the joints apart, using a mallet with a timber offcut to protect the sash, and clean all the old glue from the tenons with wire wool. The joints in sashes are usually reinforced with two small wedges in each mortise to ensure a firm fit. Remove these and clean the inside of the mortises with an old, blunt chisel.

14 *When the wedges have been fitted firmly into position, trim off their ends with a chisel so that they are flush*

Using the removed wedges as a guide, mark up and cut replacements slightly longer than the originals to allow for trimming. When you have cut all the replacement wedges, coat the tenons with a waterproof woodworking adhesive and slide them into position in the mortises (fig. 12).

Tap them home with a mallet, again protecting the timber with a piece of waste wood, then apply some glue to two of your new wedges. With the angled edge of each wedge facing inwards, tap them into place with the mallet then trim off the ends with a chisel (fig. 14).

Fit the remaining wedges, and check that the sash frame is square by measuring the diagonals—which should be equal. Cramp the sash as described in pages 229 to 232. Once the glue has set, you can reglaze the window and rehang the sash.

Renewing decayed timber

If part of a sash is affected by wet rot, make a probe into the wood with a bradawl to check the extent of the damage. Providing the decayed section is small and is spread over no more than half the thickness of the rail, you can cut out the affected wood and replace it with new timber.

Knock apart the joints as described above to remove the rail which needs repair from the rest of the sash frame. Use a combination square to mark a 45° angle at each end of the decayed area (fig. 16). Then mark horizontal lines slightly below the depth of the decayed section. Make these lines on both sides of the rail.

Next, secure the timber in a vice and saw down the angled lines to the depth line with a tenon saw. Use a

keyhole saw or a jigsaw to cut along the depth line and, with the waste wood removed, smooth down the sawn edges with a bevel-edged chisel.

Use the cut piece of wood as a pattern to measure up the replacement timber, then mark the cutting lines with the combination square.

Angles of 45° are easiest cut using a mitre box to guide the saw blade, but if you do not have one, continue the cutting lines around all the faces of the timber, then secure it in a vice and cut the replacement section. Plane down the sawn edges of the new wood and check its fit in the sash rail. If it is slightly oversize on any of its faces, sand down the unevenness.

The replacement wood is fixed into place by two or three screws, countersunk below the surface. Drill holes in the new section for these, staggering them slightly, then apply some glue to the underside and angled faces and cramp the section into place. Extend the screw holes into the sash rail to a depth of at least 12mm, drive in the screws and sink their heads well below the surface of the wood.

When the glue has set, remove the cramp and plane down the surfaces of the new wood until it is flush with the surrounding timber. Then reassemble the sash as described above.

Sticking windows

Apart from the faults already described, casements and sashes can stick because of a build-up of old paint or because the timber in the frame swells slightly.

The former problem is easily solved by removing the offending frame, stripping off all the old paint and then repainting. But swelling is a problem which can come and go with the weather. On casement windows, where it occurs most often, swelling can usually be allowed for by adjusting the casement hinges—a far less drastic solution than planing off the excess.

Mark the swollen part of the casement and judge whether increasing or decreasing the depth of one of the hinge recesses will bring it away from the window frame.

To increase the depth, pare away 2mm or so of wood from the recess with a sharp chisel. Try the casement for fit again before you start to remove any more.

To decrease the depth, cut a shim of cardboard or thin hardboard to the shape of the recess and fix it in place with a dab of glue. Punch or drill screw holes through the shim then replace the casement. Do this with great care to ensure a proper fit.

16 To replace a small section of decayed timber, mark a 45° angle at each end of the area of rot using a combination square

17 Mark horizontal lines slightly below the depth of the decayed section, then use a tenon saw to cut down the angled lines

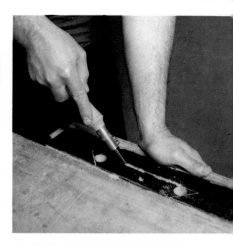

18 Take care not to extend the cuts beyond the depth line, then saw along the horizontal line with a pad-saw or a jigsaw

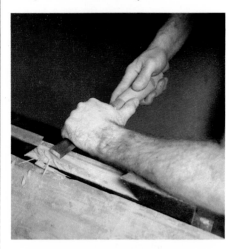

19 With the waste wood removed, use a bevel-edged chisel to smooth down the cut edges and sever any remaining fibres

20 Use the waste wood as a pattern to measure up replacement timber, then mark the cutting lines with the combination square

21 Cut out the replacement piece of timber, then drill holes for its fixing screws, down through the face of the new timber

22 Apply some glue to the new wood and lay it in place. Extend the screw holes into the sash rail, then drive the screws home

23 When the screws are in place and the glue set, plane down the faces of the new timber until it is flush with the surrounding wood

24 Now fill in the screw holes with wood filler, leave this to dry, then reglaze the sash and rehang it in the frame

FIXING FUSE FAULTS

A repeatedly blowing fuse points to a fault in the relevant electrical circuit. A repair is essential if the possibility of a fire is to be avoided and this means making a logical search through the system to locate the fault

Left: When more than one appliance or light suddenly stops working, your first move should be to inspect each of the main fuses. But before touching the fuse box or removing any fuses, make absolutely sure that the main switch is turned off

A circuit fuse is relatively simple to mend (see the illustrations) but when a fuse continues to blow each time you replace it, either the circuit is overloaded—in which case you should switch off some appliances—or there is a serious fault somewhere along it which must be located and rectified before the circuit will function again. On no account must you replace the blown fuse with a length of wire or any other bridge, such as a nail. To do so could ultimately kill someone.

Having a thorough understanding of the theory of fuses and the faults which cause them to blow will help you to maintain the electrical circuits around the home. And even if you do not intend to carry out the repair work yourself, being able to locate the area of a fault will help to save on the cost of repair.

Why fuses blow

A fuse is a deliberately weak link included in the wiring of a circuit. If a surge of current occurs in the circuit, caused by a wiring fault of some kind or by overloading, the thin fuse wire is melted by the resulting extra heat generated by the current surge.

Fuses often blow because two wires in the circuit are in contact with one another. If the live ('hot') and neutral wires make contact, this is called a short circuit; when the live wire touches the earth (ground) it is called a line/earth fault or a short to earth. Or the live wire may be in contact with earthed metalwork—such as the mounting box of a flush-mounted light switch—to which the earthing core is attached via the earth terminal.

Although a fuse is a 'weak' link in the wiring, it requires quite a large amount of current before it blows. For example, a cartridge fuse requires a current of one and a half times its current rating before it melts, and a wire fuse may take a current of twice its rating. This means that under certain conditions, a 5 amp wire fuse (used in UK lighting circuits) may take a current surge of up to 9 amps for some time before it blows.

But when a short circuit occurs, the resulting current surge is enormous. This is also the case with a line/earth fault—if the earthing is in good condition. If the earthing is faulty, there may be insufficient current to blow the the fuse in which case the fault will remain undetected and a potential fire hazard—the earth return will heat up due to the high resistance it meets.

A fault in an electrical appliance is unlikely to keep blowing the circuit fuse, if the circuit is protected by a cartridge fuse in the appliance's plug as in UK 13 amp ring-main circuits. But a circuit fuse may blow if the circuit is heavily overloaded—drawing far too much current.

Miniature circuit breakers

All the faults and checks described below apply equally whether your consumer unit (service panel) is fitted with

1 *On this type of protected wire fuse holder the window lets you see if the wire is broken. First take out the remnants*

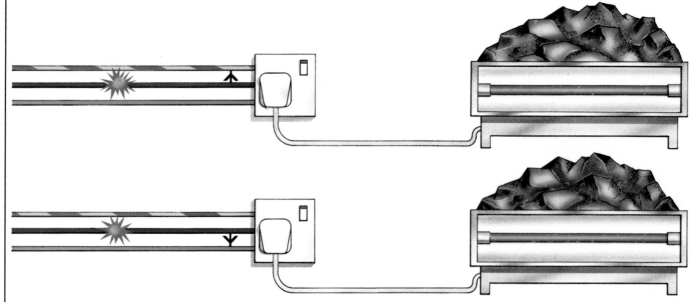

A. *What makes a fuse blow. A line/earth fault may remain dangerously undetected if the earth is poor (A). A short circuit between live and neutral (B) will always result in a blown fuse*

wire or cartridge fuses, or with miniature circuit breakers. A miniature circuit breaker (MCB) is a single-pole switch which cuts off automatically when excessive current caused by a fault flows through the circuit.

The principal differences between MCBs and normal fuses are that they require less current to shut them off than is needed to blow a fuse of the same current rating, and they operate more quickly. When a fault in the circuit persists, the circuit breaker trips off again if an attempt is made to switch it on. However, it is advisable not to switch on the MCB more than twice under fault conditions or you may blow the overload unit.

Cable faults
If a circuit fuse continues to blow each time it is replaced, a possible cause is

that two wires are in contact with each other somewhere along the cable of the circuit.

If the wiring in your home is old, persistent fuse blowing may just be an indication that the wiring needs replacing altogether. For instance, older UK houses may still be wired with rubber-insulated or even lead-sheathed cable which has a life of only about 25 years. After this time it may begin to break up, causing short circuits all along the wiring.

Trying to locate a specific fault on a relatively recent cable is a tedious job which is best left to an expert using special test equipment, especially where the cables run under floors and are recessed into the walls. But it is still worthwhile knowing the possible cause of cable failure if only to narrow down the area of investigation.

Cables are often damaged in the course of alterations to a home, so begin by checking the wiring around the site of any recent work. For instance, if you have been fixing floorboards a nail may have penetrated a cable causing a short circuit or line/earth fault. And cables which are chased into masonry walls without a proper conduit are sometimes damaged by nails or screws.

Also check any recently installed wiring: you may have disturbed the old when running additional cable to new lights or socket outlets, or you may have failed to make proper connections to the new wiring.

If there is no reason to believe that the cable has been damaged when working on the house, you can investigate other, more accessible parts of the specific circuit as described below.

Lighting circuits
If the main fuse of a lighting circuit (one supplying only lighting outlets) keeps blowing, turn off all the light switches fed by that circuit, shut off the electricity supply at the mains then replace the fuse.

Turn on the mains again, then switch on each light in turn. When the fuse blows, you will have found the part of the circuit in which the fault lies. Now you must track it down.

The first thing to check is the flexible wiring which connects the lampholder to the ceiling rose. This

2 *Snip off a slightly generous length of the correct amperage rated wire—the holder is marked with the value—and fix it in place.*

WARNING
The descriptions of fault location and fuse repair on these pages refer primarily to the wiring systems used in the UK. Wiring practice in many other countries is different, and cable colour coding and types also differ from those in the UK.

Electrical work in other countries is often required by building regulations and supply authority rules to be carried out only by a licensed tradesperson. Unlicensed people must not undertake any work involving light switches and power points.

Whatever country you live in, treat electricity with respect. **Never** work on a circuit until you are certain that it is not live.

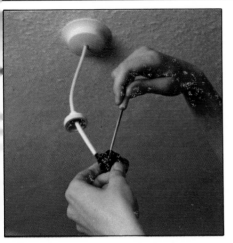

3 In the case of a blowing fuse in a lighting circuit, replace the fuse then test each light. Start your checks at the lampholder

4 Next check that the wires in the ceiling rose are intact and that there is no contact between a naked earth wire and a live terminal

5 If necessary—and possible— inspect the underfloor junction boxes for clues such as a smoky discoloration or melted insulation

may be worn or damaged, particularly if it is of the obsolete, twisted twin type. Once more, turn off the electricity supply and remove the relevant fuse holder. At the light, unscrew the lampholder to check the condition of the flex and make sure that the cores are securely connected to the terminals. If necessary, renew the faulty flex.

Now check the wiring in the ceiling rose by unscrewing the cover from the base which is fixed to the ceiling. A common problem here is that the earth wires are left unsheathed and make contact with one of the live terminals in the rose. If you find that this is the case, disconnect the wires from the earthing terminal, slip lengths of green and yellow PVC sleeving over them—leaving about 6mm of bare wire protruding—then reconnect them to the terminal.

Where a bare earth wire is not the problem, check the condition of the remaining wires. If the insulation of these is all intact and they are connected tightly to the correct terminals, replace the rose cover and turn your attention to the light switch itself.

Remove the cover plate of the switch and check the wiring. The most likely fault is, again, that the earth wire is bare and in contact with the live terminal. But it may be that the fixing screws of the cover plate have penetrated the insulation of one of the wires and that, with a flush-mounted switch, a section of live wire is in contact with the earthed metal box.

If it is the live return wire that is damaged in this way, the fuse will blow only when the switch is turned on; but if it is the live feed wire which is damaged, the fuse will blow whether it is on or off. The latter fault is easily

recognized by the burnt insulation and smoke marks around the damaged area.

Where the area of damage is slight, you can make do by firmly wrapping some insulating tape around the bare section, then laying the wires carefully back into the box so that the screws will not interfere with them. But if the damage is particularly bad—such as where a wire has almost been severed— the length of cable must be replaced.

If, after examining the lampholder, ceiling rose, switch and any accessible cable you are still unable to find the fault, call in expert help. On no account be tempted to make a temporary 'repair' by fitting a fuse of a higher amp rating in the fuseholder.

Power circuits

When the circuit fuse of a ring mains circuit continues to blow, the fault is unlikely to be in one of the portable appliances plugged into the circuit: when these are faulty, the cartridge fuse in the plug will blow leaving the circuit fuse intact. However, before you start work on locating the fault, unplug all appliances and check that the fuse in each plug is of the correct amp rating for its wattage. Also switch off any fixed appliances at their fused connection units.

On a ring mains, the next step is to check the 30 amp main fuse. Very occasionally, when the circuit is already loaded to near its capacity, a fault on a small appliance may cause it to blow.

Other than an overload or a damaged circuit cable, the most likely fault in a ring mains circuit is in the mounting box behind one of the socket outlets. Turn off the electricity supply at the mains and examine each socket on the circuit in turn.

6 A typical source of trouble is an unsheathed earth wire coming into contact with a live terminal behind the switch plate

Unscrew the cover plate of the first socket and examine the wiring attached to the terminals on the back: the likely faults are similar to those found in lighting switches.

Earth wires are often left uninsulated and therefore can easily make contact with the live terminal. This is particularly likely on a socket outlet as the earthing core is connected to a terminal on the back of the socket plate, rather than to one on the box, and can therefore be bent into a dangerous position while the socket is being screwed into place.

Sleeve any bare earth wires, then carefully check the insulation of the live and neutral wires. These sometimes perish if the terminals are not tightened properly or where a cheap— or faulty—plug or adaptor has been used in the socket and has overheated. 133

FIXING FUSE FAULTS

Alternatively, the insulation may have been pierced by the socket's fixing screws. Deal with this problem as described above and, if necessary, use shorter screws to fix the socket plate into place.

When you have checked the first socket, replace the cover plate and move onto the next. Even if you think you have found and rectified the fault, it is worthwhile checking the remaining socket outlets: if the fault was caused by a bare earth wire, it is likely that the other earth wires are unsleeved and this is the perfect opportunity to sleeve them to conform with the wiring regulations.

If you do not find anything wrong with any of the sockets, the fault probably lies somewhere along the cable of the circuit, so it is best to call in expert assistance.

Cooker circuits

Because of the large amount of electricity it consumes, a free-standing electric cooker is always connected on a separate circuit protected by its own fuse in the main fuse box. The appliance is connected to its circuit by a special cooker control unit which contains a switch and sometimes includes a separately controlled socket outlet. Neither the cooker or its control unit contain a fuse, so a persistently blowing circuit fuse usually indicates a fault in either the control unit or in the appliance itself. Unless it has been damaged during renovations as described above, the circuit cable is unlikely to be at fault as it is protected by hard wearing insulation.

To find out whether the fault is in the unit or in the cooker itself, turn off the control switch, replace the circuit fuse with the relevant size of fuse wire or cartridge and turn on the power. If the fuse immediately blows again, the fault lies in the control unit or in the cable from the fuse board; with the power turned off, remove the unit's faceplate and inspect the wiring for damage as described above. If the fuse only blows when the cooker control switch is in the 'on' position, the fault is in the cooker itself and you should call in expert assistance to locate the fault.

Immersion heaters

An immersion heater is usually supplied directly from its own circuit fuse with no other fuse intervening. When this circuit fuse blows, the fault is most likely to be in the immersion heater itself and therefore requires expert attention.

When the heater is supplied from the ring circuit—nowadays considered bad practice—it is connected either by a fused plug and a socket outlet, or to a fused spur outlet. So a fault in the heater itself should blow the local fuse, not the circuit fuse. If your heater is wired up in this way, it's best to have it transferred to its own circuit.

Residual current devices

If you have a modern wiring system that incorporates a residual current device (formerly known as an earth leakage circuit breaker) in the consumer unit, you may well find that it trips off occasionally for no apparent reason. Older types of RCD were subject to nuisance tripping, and should be replaced with more modern versions. Tripping on newer types suggests that current is leaking to earth, and you should call in a qualified electrician to investigate.

7 *The best way to insulate the bare insulation wire is to disconnect it then slip on a length of green and yellow PVC*

8 *In the case of slight damage to the neutral or live wires, bind the affected portion tightly with insulating tape and then refit the switch*

9 *In the case of a ring main circuit it is necessary to check each socket in turn. A common fault is a bare earth touching a live wire*

10 *First disconnect the unsheathed earth wire and refit the loose live wire to the live terminal in the socket housing*

11 *Then sheath the earth wire with a length of green and yellow PVC sleeving and secure it to the socket before refitting the assembly*

WC REPAIRS

Problems with the WC, or toilet, may be just plain annoying—such as a slow-filling cistern—or more serious—such as a cracked outlet joint. But none requires much more than basic plumbing skills and common sense to put right

The WC (also called water closet, toilet, or lavatory) is a particularly hardworking, and fairly complex, piece of plumbing apparatus. So it is prone to a number of faults. Though these are rarely difficult to put right, the various jobs are made a lot easier if you know something of how a WC works.

The WC pan

There are two basic types of pan. The *washdown* type uses the force of the descending flushing water alone to push the contents into the soil pipe. In the more modern *siphonic* system, the impulse of the water flush creates a vacuum in the pan so that atmospheric pressure will force the contents out of the pan. The flushing water merely serves to refill the bowl. The siphonic suite is more complex, and therefore more costly, but it is quieter in use.

All pans have a built-in trap to prevent unpleasant gases coming back up the soil pipe from the sewer or cesspit. The shape of this varies according to the type of pan, but it always includes at least one 'U' bend which remains filled with water.

Traditional UK pans have their outlet either vertically downwards (called an S-trap) or nearly horizontal (a P-trap). Modern UK pans often have a short horizontal outlet at the back to which you can fix a number of patterns of connector pipe—this makes it possible to accommodate the vagaries

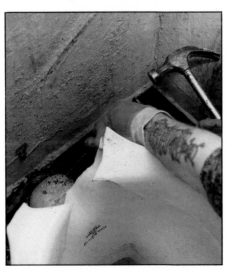

1 A crack in the rim of a washdown WC prevents the flushing action from working efficiently. The only solution is to replace the pan

2 Where the pan outlet is cemented to the soil pipe, you must break the S-trap at the joint. Take care not to damage the soil pipe

3 If the pan is set in concrete on a solid floor, you must break the pan with a hammer and cold chisel using purposeful blows

Three types of WC

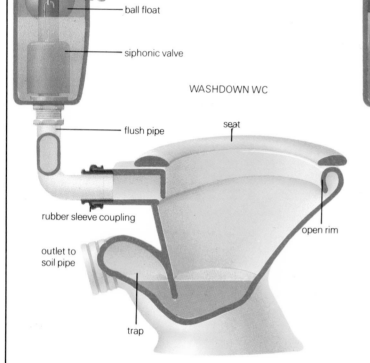

- inverted U tube
- ball float
- siphonic valve

WASHDOWN WC

- flush pipe
- seat
- rubber sleeve coupling
- open rim
- outlet to soil pipe
- trap

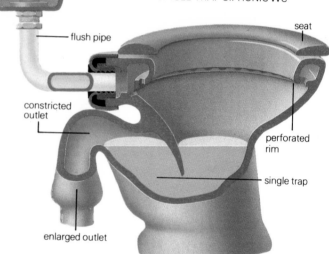

SINGLE-TRAP SIPHONIC WC

- flush pipe
- seat
- constricted outlet
- perforated rim
- single trap
- enlarged outlet

of most existing waste systems when fitting a new pan. Whatever the type of outlet, it is always at the back of the pan.

Australian toilet pans also have their outlet either vertically down (called an S-trap) or nearly horizontal (a P-trap). Modern pans often have outlets to which you can fix a number of patterns of connector pipe.

The WC cistern

The purpose of the WC cistern is to hold just enough water to clean out the bowl.

Modern cisterns are usually either *low-level*, with the cistern just above the pan and connected to it by a short flushing pipe, or *close coupled*, in which the cistern and pan form a single unit. Old-fashioned suites may be *high-level*, with the cistern as much as 2m above floor level.

UK cisterns usually have a siphonic-type flushing valve—pressing the lever jerks up a diaphragm within a U-shaped tube, pushing water over the top of the U (which is normally above water level) and down into the pan. Siphonic action keeps the flap up and water flowing until the cistern is empty; then the inlet valve opens and

A.: *In the washdown system, the force of the water descending from the cistern flushes the pan. In the single-trap siphonic system, the pan fills completely and its contents are emptied by atmospheric pressure as the movement of the water into the second section induces a partial vacuum. In the double-trap siphonic system a vacuum is created in the air space as the cistern empties*

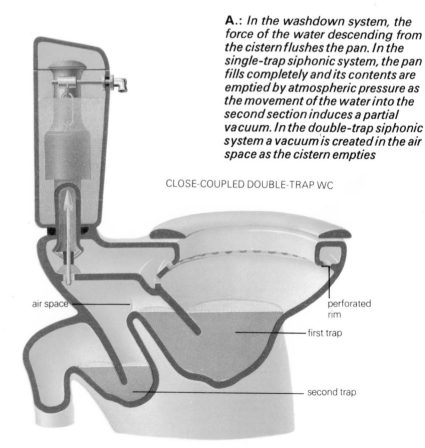

CLOSE-COUPLED DOUBLE-TRAP WC

- air space
- perforated rim
- first trap
- second trap

refills the cistern.

Australian flushing systems look less complex. The lever lifts a simple valve cover—a flapper or ball—at the base of the cistern. The rush of outflowing water prevents the valve cover from closing again until the cistern is nearly empty. Then the inlet valve opens and refills the cistern; some of the incoming water is diverted through an overflow tube to replenish the trap-sealing water in the pan. Alternatively, there may be no cistern at all; just an automatic valve (called a *flush valve*) connected direct to the water supply. This lets through a metered amount of water, then closes.

There are several types of inlet valve. They are strictly called 'float valves', because they all have a member which floats on the surface of the water and is connected to the actual valve mechanism. As the cistern empties, the movement of the float opens the valve to allow the cistern to refill. In most cases, the floating part is a ball, connected to the valve by a long arm—so these valves are usually known as ball cocks, or ball valves.

Cisterns need an overflow warning pipe, in case the ball valve fails to shut off when the cistern is full. In the UK, the overflow pipe usually discharges outside the house. In Australian cisterns, the overflow tube discharges direct into the WC pan.

Faults with a WC can be divided into plumbing faults (such as flushing problems, and usually the result of wear and tear) and accidental damage (such as a cracked pan).

Failure to flush

First check the water level in the cistern; if this is very low, the fault lies with the ball valve. Try pushing the float below the water level. If water rushes in then the valve is working correctly, but the float is closing it at too low a water level. You can correct this by gently bending the ball arm upwards (or with some patterns, altering the position of the float on the arm or guide).

If no water enters the cistern when you push down the float, then the inlet valve is blocked: for repair, see *Overflowing cisterns*, below.

If the water level in the cistern is not low, then you have a fault with the outlet flushing valve. Before you dismantle it, though, check that the various levers and wires are intact, and that moving the handle actually does move the valve flap. Broken or stretched linkages are usually easily replaced.

To replace a worn diaphragm, first tie up the ball valve arm to stem the water supply. Then empty the cistern—first by flushing it, then by mopping up any remaining water with a sponge.

On a close-coupled suite you must next remove the cistern from the pan. In all cases, undo the nut under the cistern securing the flush pipe to the siphon unit, and also the nut securing the siphon to the cistern body, then remove the whole siphon unit. Note the position of the parts as you continue disassembly.

Replace the diaphragm with one of the correct size and reassemble the siphon unit. You can obtain a new diaphragm from hardware shops or builders' merchants, or cut one from a piece of heavy PVC sheet using the old one as a template.

Check that the plunger moves freely in the siphon unit, then replace the unit in the cistern.

Flush fails to clean pan

In the case of the flush not efficiently clearing the pan, either the pan is not level or the flush pipe is blocked.

The washdown system is more sensitive to the pan not being level because of its dependence on the momentum of the flushing water. This should flow around each side of the flushing rim and meet centrally at the front of the pan. But if the pan is tilted slightly, the flush will be stronger on one side than the other and the result will be a 'whirlpool' effect which is inefficient.

Use a spirit level to check that the pan rim is level. If it is not, loosen the pan base retaining screws, and pack pieces of wood or linoleum under the lower side. Also, check the channel under the flushing rim for obstructions and clean it if necessary.

If the pan is level, check that the flush pipe enters the pan squarely and that there is no obstruction at this point.

Overflowing cistern

If water pours out of the cistern overflow pipe, it is likely that the float is perforated and waterlogged. In this case you must replace a faulty float with a new one, though as a temporary cure you could shake out the water and tie a plastic bag around it.

If on the other hand water is only trickling from the overflow pipe, it is more likely that the ball valve washer needs replacing—although sometimes the trouble is due to a speck of grit preventing the washer from seating properly on the valve nozzle. In both

cases, it is necessary to dismantle the valve.

There are several different types of ball valve, but the most common UK ones are the Portsmouth, Croydon, Garston, Equilibrium and Torbeck (fig. B). To dismantle any valve, the first step is always to isolate the water supply to the WC cistern.

In the case of a Portsmouth or Croydon valve, remove the split pin on which the float arm pivots and place the float and arm on one side. With a Croydon valve the plug will simply drop out of the valve body. To extract the plug from a Portsmouth valve, insert the blade of a screwdriver into the float arm slot and push the plug out of the end of the valve body, taking care not to let it fall.

At this stage, if possible, get an assistant to turn the water supply briefly on and off to your command so that the pressure ejects any grit that may be blocking the valve nozzle. Reassemble the valve and attach the ball arm and float, then turn on the water supply and see if the valve seals off the supply effectively. If it does not, the washer is defective and you must replace it.

The plugs of both types of valve are in two parts, but the cap that retains the valve washer is often difficult to remove. You can try applying some penetrating oil and warming the end of the plug gently, but you must not damage it by rough handling. If the cap refuses to budge, pick out the old washer with the point of a penknife and force the new one under the flange of the cap, making sure that it rests flat on its seating.

Clean the plug with fine emery paper, then wrap the paper around a pencil and clean the inside of the valve body. Smear a thin coat of petroleum jelly inside the valve before you reassemble it.

Some modern cisterns are fitted with a Garston ball valve. In this case, shut off the water, remove the split pin and the ball arm as before, then unscrew the cap and pull out the rubber diaphragm. Check that there is no grit or foreign matter in the nozzle as described above. Otherwise, replace the diaphragm and reassemble the valve in the reverse order.

If a plastic Torbeck valve sticks, the most likely cause is dirt on the valve seat. Slowly raise and lower the ball arm a few times. If this fails to remedy the fault, shut off the water, unscrew the front cap, and wash the diaphragm in clean water. When you reassemble the valve, make sure that the dia-

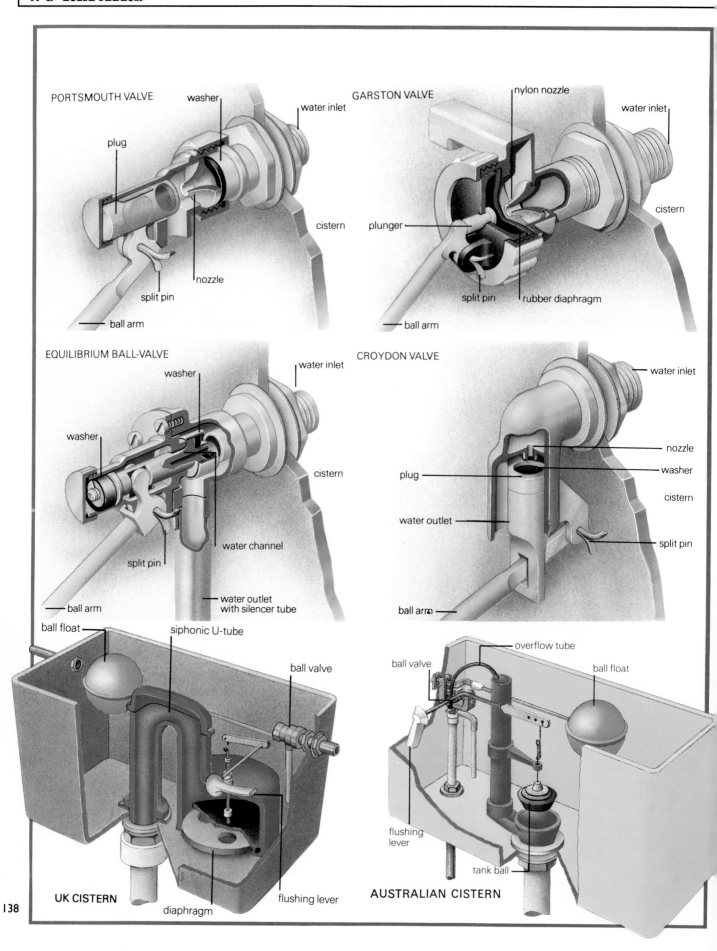

PORTSMOUTH VALVE

washer

plug

water inlet

cistern

nozzle

split pin

ball arm

GARSTON VALVE

nylon nozzle

water inlet

cistern

plunger

split pin

rubber diaphragm

ball arm

EQUILIBRIUM BALL-VALVE

washer

washer

water inlet

cistern

water channel

split pin

ball arm

water outlet
with silencer tube

CROYDON VALVE

water inlet

nozzle

washer

cistern

plug

water outlet

split pin

ball arm

ball float

siphonic U-tube

ball valve

UK CISTERN

diaphragm

flushing lever

ball valve

overflow tube

ball float

flushing
lever

tank ball

AUSTRALIAN CISTERN

4 *Stuff some crumpled newspaper or rags into the top of the soil pipe socket to stop debris entering and causing a blockage*

5 *Use a hammer to carefully break away the concrete surrounding the soil pipe socket and the remains of the old spigot*

6 *Liberally smear waterproof jointing sealant around the inside flange of the soil pipe to prevent water leaking from the joint*

phragm is the right way round.

The main type of Australian valve operates vertically, like a Croydon valve, at the end of a vertical water inlet which enters the cistern through its base—this makes the plumbing look neater. To dismantle, remove the two pins holding the rather complicated linkages which connect the valve piston to the float arm, and pull the piston upwards. There are two washers to replace—one in the bottom of the plunger and another one held in a groove around the circumference.

There is also a diaphragm type of valve, which also sits on the top of a vertical inlet tube. The cover is usually held in place with four screws; otherwise repair is much the same as for a UK Garston valve.

Australian flush-valves are either of the diaphragm or piston type. Though the mechanism is usually a little more complex than for their float valve counterparts, disassembly, cleaning and repair is much the same. You can usually get kits of replacement parts.

Slow filling
The cistern should refill within two minutes of flushing. If it fails to do so, there is almost certainly something wrong with the ball valve. In this case dismantle the ball valve as described above and clean it.

One problem in the UK is that a high

B. Opposite: *The four inlet valves are all float valves, controlled by the level of the water in the cistern. The outlet valves are specifically designed so that they open while the cistern is emptying, then close once it has been refilled*

pressure valve might have been fitted—this is not needed unless the cistern is fed direct from the mains. Normally, a low-pressure valve should be fitted, but in the event of the storage cistern being less than a metre or so above the WC cistern, then a *full-way* valve should be used.

Excessive noise
A WC can create excessive noise during refilling or flushing. Noisy refilling may be due to ball bounce and vibration, and this can often be reduced by tying a plastic flower pot to the float arm so that it is suspended, right way up, in the water a few centimetres below the float itself. The pot serves as a kind of 'sea anchor', and prevents the float rising and falling with every ripple.

The best solution, however, is to change the ball valve for either an Equilibrium or a Torbeck valve.

With the Australian valve, check that water from the refill tube goes squarely into the overflow pipe.

The best solution to noisy flushing is to replace the suite with a double-trap siphonic type.

Leaking outlet joint
In the case of a leak here, use a hammer and plugging chisel to rake out the existing jointing material. Bind two or three turns of proprietary waterproof tape around the outlet pipe and caulk this down hard into the soil pipe socket. Then fill the space between the outlet pipe and the socket with a non-setting mastic, and complete the joint with two or three turns of waterproof tape over the mastic filling.

Cracked pan
To fit a new WC pan, you must first empty the cistern by tying up the ball arm and operating the flush. Follow by scooping out the rest of the water in the pan, and mop it as dry as possible.

If the pan is screwed to a wooden floor, simply undo the fixing screws. But if it is set in cement on a solid floor, you must first disconnect the flush pipe. Where this has a rubber cone connector, peel back the rubber to free it; where it is lead or copper, cut it with a hacksaw as close as possible to the pan. Next break the pan with a hammer, and chisel the floor flat. Where there is a plastic connector between the pan and the soil pipe, simply pull the pan away from the pipe. Where the pan outlet is cemented to the soil pipe, break the S-trap of the pan just above the joint—taking care not to damage the soil pipe.

Stuff some crumpled newspaper or rags into the top of the soil pipe socket to keep out debris, then, with a cold-steel chisel and hammer, chip out the jagged pieces of the trap from inside the socket. Finally, remove the paper or rags and clean out any old sealant left inside the socket.

Fitting the new pan differs according to whether you are fixing it to a wooden or a solid floor.

Wooden floor: Start by positioning the pan outlet over the soil pipe and checking that they fit. If they do not, you can adjust the position of the pan with a wooden packing piece.

There are three methods of fixing the pan outlet to the soil pipe; with a rigid plastic connector and rubber insert; with a flexible plastic connector of the 'Multikwik' type; or with

7 The flexible plastic 'Multikwik' connector is easy to use. Simply position it inside the soil pipe socket and snap it into place

8 Make up a mix of one part cement to three of sharp sand and trowel this over the keyed floor in an area larger than the base of the pan

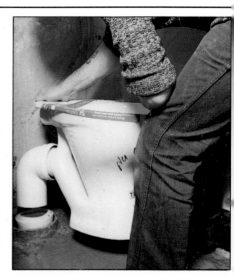

9 Where a P-trap pan is being fixed to a floor soil pipe, you must use an appropriate adaptor. Locate this in the 'Multikwik' connector

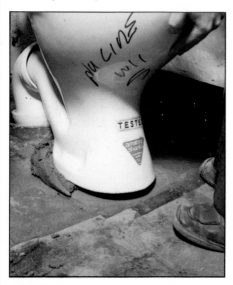

10 Manoeuvre the pan into the correct position, then press it down on to the still-wet mortar mix on the floor, rocking it gently as you do so

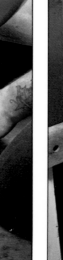

11 Use a damp cloth to clean away the excess mortar around the pan then scrape the floor clean with a trowel and wash it with water

12 Finally check that the pan is level—both sideways and back to front—and make any necessary adjustments before the mortar sets

a traditional cement and gaskin joint.

The plastic connectors simply push over both ends. If you are fixing the outlet directly to the soil pipe with a traditional joint, first lay two or three turns of gaskin (hemp rope) around the joint socket to stop cement running down the soil pipe. Tap this purposefully into place. Then make up a small quantity of plumbers' quick-setting cement and trowel this firmly into the collar until it protrudes just above the collar rim. Trim the cement until the angle rises about 30° from the collar rim to the pan outlet.

Screw the pan to the floor, using brass screws and making sure it is level with a spirit level. Take great care not to overtighten them. Reconnect the flush pipe, then flush the lavatory and check for an efficient flushing action and the absence of leaks.

Solid floor: Locate the pan against the soil pipe and mark its correct position on the floor. Having put the pan to one side, make a key in the floor for the cement pad—either by cutting grooves in it with a bolster or by driving in masonry nails and leaving about 25mm of the heads protruding.

The pan connects to the soil pipe in the same way as for a wooden floor;

but if you use a plastic connector, fit this to the soil pipe before you fix the pan in place.

To bed the pan, make up a mix of one part cement to three of sharp sand and trowel this over the key. Then lower the pan over it, making sure that the pan outlet enters the collar of the soil pipe or connector. Rock the pan slightly to settle it, and make sure that it is level with a spirit level. Allow the mortar to set for 24 hours, make the joint with the soil pipe if necessary, then check that the flush works efficiently and that there are no leaks or signs of moisture coming from any of the joints.

CURING DRIPPING TAPS

Dripping taps are a source of constant irritation for any household. But for a repair as small as mending a leaking tap, calling in a plumber is an expensive proposition

Since the leak is usually caused by a worn-out or perished washer, one way of solving the problem is to replace the whole tap with a new one of the non-drip, washer-less type. A far cheaper way is to learn to mend the tap yourself. Replacement parts cost only pennies and can usually be fitted in a few minutes, once you know how to take the tap apart.

How taps work

Most taps which have washers work in the same basic way: turning the handle raises or lowers a spindle with the rubber or nylon washer on the end in its seating. When the spindle is raised water flows through the seating and out of the spout; when it is lowered, the flow is cut off. But when the washer becomes worn and disintegrates, water can still creep through, irrespective of the position of the spindle. This is what usually causes the tap to drip. If the seals around the moving spindle are worn as well, leaks will also appear around the handle and the outer cover. Because you will have to dismantle the tap to replace either the washer or the seals, it is usually worth doing both jobs at the same time. If fitting new ones fails to cure the drips, the washer seating itself is probably worn. This is a common problem with older taps, and the cure is to regrind the tap seat or fit a plastic seat on top.

The most common type of household tap is the upright *pillar tap* (fig. A). The *bib-tap* (fig. B) is similar in operation, but fits into the wall above an appliance or on an outside wall. The patented Supatap is a British type of bib-tap incorporating a valve which enables you to complete repairs without having to turn off the water supply. Modern baths and sink units often have a mixer tap with a fixed or a swivelling nozzle. This is really two pillar taps combined and they are repaired in the same way.

Replacing a washer

To replace the washer on a conventional type of tap, start by turning off the water supply—either at the main stoptap for mains-fed pipes, or at the gatevalve for taps supplied from a cold cistern or hot tank. See pages 281 to 284 for more details. Then turn the tap you are repairing on fully to drain away any water left in the pipe. Put the plug in to prevent any of the tap com-

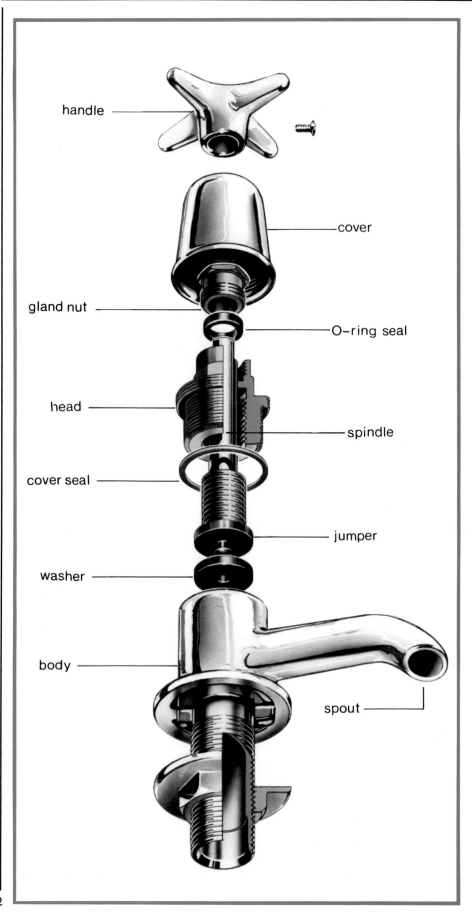

handle

cover

gland nut

O-ring seal

head

spindle

cover seal

jumper

washer

body

spout

ponents slipping down the plug-hole.

The assembly which holds the tap washer and the spindle is known as the head. On older taps, it is covered by an outer shield which screws into the tap body. Newer taps have a combined shield and handle which must be removed as one unit.

To remove a conventional shield make sure that the tap is turned fully on. Loosen the shield with a spanner or a wrench, unscrew it and leave it loose. You can avoid damaging the chrome plating by covering the jaws of whichever tool you are using with a piece of rag.

Modern shield handles are either simply a push-fit on to the spindle or else are secured in place by a screw through the top. Check the former first by gently pulling the handle upwards.

If it stays fast, dig out the plastic cover in the top to expose the securing screw. With this removed, the handle can be pulled off (fig. 1 on page 144).

The next stage is to remove the head. Locate the hexagon nut at the bottom of the assembly and loosen it again using the wrench or spanner. Unscrew the head from the body of the tap and remove it. At the base, you can see the washer (or what remains of it) seated on its *jumper*.

On older taps the head assembly will be made of brass and the washer will be held on the jumper by a small nut. Loosen this with the pliers, remove the old pieces of washer and put on the new one, maker's name against the jumper.

On newer taps, the entire head is made of nylon and the washer and jumper are combined in one replaceable unit which slots into the bottom of the assembly. To replace the washer, you simply pull out the old jumper and push in the new one.

Once you have fitted the new washer, you can re-assemble the tap and turn the water supply back on. If the new washer is seated correctly, there will be no drips from the nozzle and you should be able to turn the tap on and off with little effort.

Supataps

When replacing a washer in a Supatap, there is no need to turn off the water supply—this is done automatically by the check-valve inside the tap. To gain access to the washer, hold the

A. Exploded view of a typical pillar tap showing its components. On older types the washer may be bolted to the jumper plate

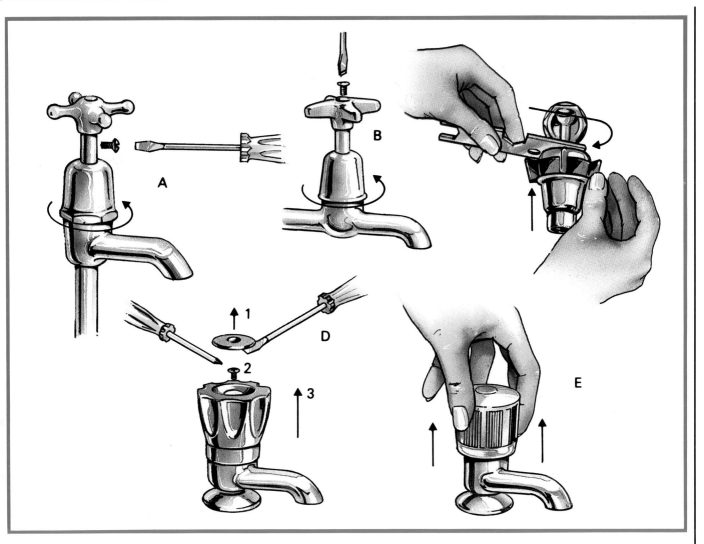

handle in one hand while you loosen the gland nut above it with the other. Holding the gland nut and turning in an anticlockwise direction, unscrew the handle from the tap. As you do this, there will be a slight rush of water which will stop as soon as the handle is removed and the check-valve drops down.

Protruding from the dismantled handle, you will see the tip of the flow straightener. Push or knock this out on to a table and identify the push-in washer/jumper assembly at one end. Pull off the old washer/jumper and replace it with a new one. Before you re-assemble the tap it is a good idea to clean the flow straightener with a nail brush.

Stop-valve taps
There is normally little difference between a crutch-type stop-valve tap and the more conventional type of pillar tap. However, you should remember, in addition to turning off the main supply 'to the valve, to

also turn on any outlets controlled by it. This will drain any water left in the pipe to which the valve has been fitted and minimize the risk of creating an airlock.

Normally, stop-valve taps have no outer shield and the head is exposed. Loosen the nut securing it with a spanner or wrench and then unscrew the head to expose the washer assembly. Stop-valve washers are usually held in their jumpers with a small retaining nut like the older type of pillar tap described above.

Leaking spindles
If the leak is coming from around the spindle of the tap rather than the nozzle there are two possible causes. Either the O-ring seal around the spindle has worn out or else the gland nut which holds it is in need of adjustment. Both problems tend to be more common on older taps with brass heads: the newer sort with nylon heads have a better record for remaining watertight.

B. *Designs of washer-type taps vary widely, but dismantling procedures will follow one of these: a) old pillar tap, b) old bib tap, c) Supatap, d) and e) new-style pillar taps*

To service the spindle, you have to remove the tap handle. On newer types of tap, this may have been done already in order to replace the washer, but on older cross-head taps the handle will still be in place.

The cross-head will be held on either by a grub screw in the side or by a screw through the top, possibly obscured by a plastic cover. Having undone the screw, you should be able to pull off the handle. If it will not move, turn the tap fully off and unscrew the shield below to force the handle loose.

Once you have done this, mark the position of the gland nut at the top of the tap head against the head itself with a screwdriver. Next loosen the nut and unscrew it completely. Check the condition of the O-ring 143

1 On this type of tap, remove the cover to expose the securing screw. Undo this and pull the loosened handle upwards to expose the spindle

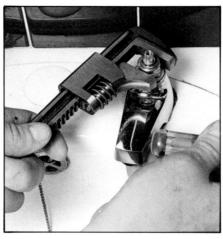

2 When you undo the locking nut, try to wedge the body of the tap against the nearest firm support to avoid undue strain on the pipe

3 Unscrew the head assembly to get at the washer. Check the seating in the tap body for corrosion while the tap is dismantled

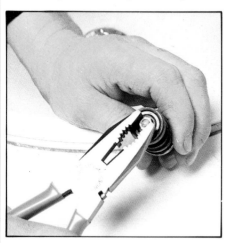

4 On some types of tap, the washer is held to its jumper by a small securing nut on the base of the head—undo this with pliers

5 You can then dig out the old washer and replace it. For a temporary repair you can reverse the old washer

6 To replace the spindle O-ring seals, dig out the circlip holding the spindle to the tap head. Take care not to damage the circlip

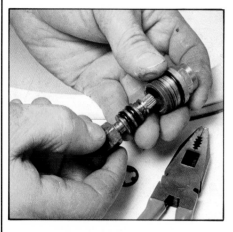

7 Once the circlip is loosened, you can slide the spindle out. You can see the various O-rings used on this particular design

8 If the seals are worn, prise them off with a pin. Slide on new ones and make sure these are properly seated before re-assembling the tap

9 To replace a Supatap washer, start by loosening the locknut above the nozzle assembly. There is no need to turn off the water supply

or packing around the seating below and, where necessary, replace it. If an O-ring is not available, use string smeared with petroleum jelly.

If the seal around the spindle appears to be in good condition, the leak is probably due to the gland nut above working loose. Replace the nut and tighten it gently so that it just passes the mark that you made against the head. Temporarily replace the handle and check that the tap can be easily turned. If it is too tight, slacken the gland nut. But if, with the water supply turned on, the tap instead continues to leak, then the gland nut will require further tightening to solve the problem.

Taps without gland nuts
Some taps do not have conventional gland nut assemblies, even though

their heads are made of brass. Instead, the spindle is held in the head by means of a circlip (snap ring). The seal between them is provided by two or more O-rings around the spindle body, and if these are worn they must be replaced. Follow the procedures above for removing the tap handle and unscrewing the head. Dig out the circlip around the top of the spindle as shown in fig. 6 and you will find that the spindle drops out. The O-rings around it can then be rolled off and replaced.

Leaking swivel nozzles
Mixer taps with swivelling spouts are often prone to leaks around the base of the spout itself, caused by the seals in the base wearing out. Providing you are working on the spout alone, it will not be necessary to turn off the

water. Start by loosening the shroud around the base, which will either screw on or else be secured by a small grub screw at the back.

Around the spout, inside the base, you will find a large circlip (snap ring). Pinch this together with the pliers and remove it, then pull out the spout.

Dig the worn seals out of the exposed base and discard them. Fit the new ones around the spout: if you fit them into the base, you will have great difficulty in getting the spout to go back in the correct position. With the seals around the spout it should slot in easily and you can then replace the circlip and the shroud.

If you have to make a temporary repair to a tap seating—necessary if dripping continues even when the washer has been replaced—use a new plastic washer and seating kit.

10 The flow straightener can be knocked out using light taps from a hammer. The washer and its jumper are on the other end

11 The combined washer and jumper is prised from the flow straightener and a new one of the same size slotted in its place

12 To cure a leaking nozzle, undo the shroud at the base. This either unscrews or may be released by a grub screw at the back

13 Pinch together the large circlip at the base. Use pliers for this and take care not to scratch the chromed finish of the nozzle

14 Pull the spout from its seat and then dig out the worn seal in the exposed base. Remove all bits before fitting new ones

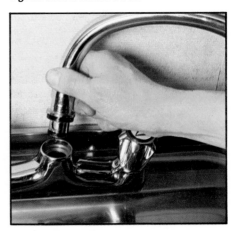

15 Place the replacement seal on the spout before refitting this. Replace the circlip and then screw on the shroud

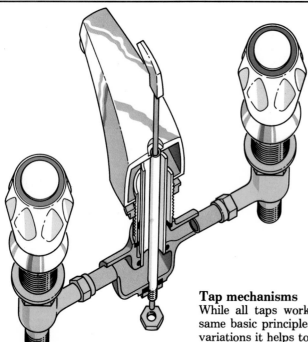

Above: *Three-hole mixer taps for basins and bidets have the body of the tap concealed below the surface of the appliance*

Below: *Kitchen mixers take their cold water supplies direct from the rising main; mixing takes place as water leaves the spout*

Tap mechanisms

While all taps work on essentially the same basic principles, there are internal variations it helps to know about.

Mixer taps come in two types. With bath and basin mixers (above left), the hot and cold water are mixed within the body of the tap before passing up the spout.

Pillar taps operate by screwing the washer down onto the tap seating; with Supataps, opening the tap allows the washer to drop away from the seating.

Above: *Modern pillar taps usually have O-rings instead of old-fashioned hemp packing. Ceramic discs are beginning to replace the washer mechanism on some taps; these need little maintenance*

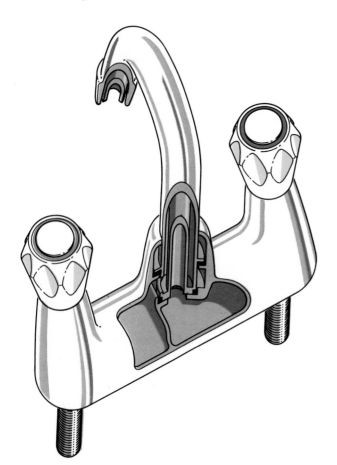

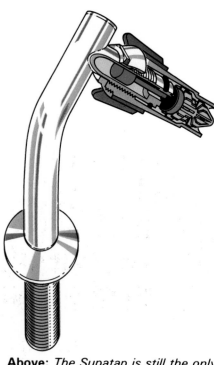

Above: *The Supatap is still the only type of tap that can be rewashered without the need to turn off the water supply first. They are available with different pillar heights for sink and basin use*

REPAIRING GUTTERS

Gutters and downpipes play a vital role in protecting your house from the effects of rain. But unless guttering is regularly maintained it will deteriorate, causing leaks or overflows. The damp in turn causes structural damage which often costs a fortune to repair

All guttering systems should be inspected twice a year, in late autumn and again in the spring. It will almost certainly be necessary to sweep out any accumulation of leaves and dirt with a hand brush and trowel or, in the case of plastic guttering, with a shaped piece of hardboard.

Keep the debris well away from the outlet leading to the down pipe. If the outlet does not have a cage or grille fixed to prevent debris from entering and blocking the downpipe, roll a piece of galvanized wire netting into a ball and insert it in the neck of the pipe. Do make sure that the wire ball is sufficiently large not to fall down the pipe.

With cast-iron or galvanized iron guttering, check carefully for any rust. Use a wire brush to remove loose flakes of paint and rust and treat the surface with a rust inhibitor. The surface should then be given one or two coats of bituminous paint to form a strong protective layer.

On Ogee-section guttering (fig. A), or galvanized guttering fixed on with through spikes, rust may well be found around the fixings to the fascia—in which case the damaged section may have to be removed for treatment on the ground.

Basic safety

In order to reach the gutters for a close inspection, you will have to rig up some form of access and in most cases this means using a ladder. If you haven't already got a ladder, you shouldn't have any trouble in hiring one from your local tool hire shop.

When using a ladder, it's as well to be aware of a few basic safety rules. First, don't lean the ladder against the guttering itself or the fascia which may not be able to take the weight. If you can, hire a ladder stand-off which clips to the rungs and holds the ladder away from the wall. Secondly, make sure that the foot of the ladder stands square and firm on the ground—the base should be placed out from the wall by a quarter of its height. And thirdly, never work from the very top of a ladder—you'll have nothing to hold on to and it's easy to lose balance.

Left: *Clearing a downpipe. A blockage in a downpipe can cause the system to overflow with damaging results*

1 *Leaves and debris soon accumulate in gutters, especially during the autumn. Clean them out with a trowel or stiff brush*

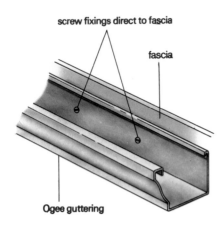

screw fixings direct to fascia

fascia

Ogee guttering

A. *Guttering of Ogee-section is often screwed directly to the fascia boards*

Sagging gutters

If a gutter sags, water may overflow or the joints may crack and leak. A bucket of water poured in at the highest point of the system reveals any such defects.

The commonest causes of sagging are broken or bent brackets, or loose fixing screws or spikes. Most guttering is supported on brackets screwed either to the fascia boards underneath the eaves of the roof (fig. C) or to the ends of the roof rafters.

To rectify a sagging gutter, remove the defective sections and examine the brackets to see if they are firmly fixed. If they are not, use longer screws to secure them. Where brackets are bent or corroded, replace them with matching new ones.

Replacing a rafter bracket (fig. D) normally involves removing the roof covering directly above it, though this problem can often be overcome by fixing a fascia bracket adjacent to the faulty rafter bracket to give the necessary extra support.

Ogee section guttering differs from other types in that it is screwed or spiked directly on to the fascia. Sagging here is usually caused by the fixing devices rusting and then pulling away from the fascia. In this case, plug the holes and re-fasten with new screws or spikes.

A common fault with guttering occurs where the slope or fall towards the downpipe outlet becomes distorted —because of faulty installation or settlement of the house itself. Too steep a fall causes water to overflow at the downpipe outlet. Too shallow a fall results in a build up of water and sediment along the run.

To determine the correct fall for an incorrectly aligned section, tie a length of twine along the top of the gutter—from the high end to the outflow point—and use it as a guide to reposition the intervening supports. The gutter should fall 25mm for every 3m of its length.

Leaking joints in cast-iron

The joints in cast-iron gutter systems are held together by nuts and bolts which are usually screw-headed. A proprietary sealing compound—often a mixture of putty and red lead or a mastic sealer—is sandwiched between the two ends to make the joint watertight (fig. D).

A leaking joint may be patched up by cleaning the area with a wire brush and applying one or two coats of bituminous paint. However, for a more permanent repair the section on one side of the leaking joint must be removed, cleaned and replaced. If the removed piece is in the middle of a run, two new joints have to be made—one at each end of the section.

Start by removing the bolts which hold the joints together. These may well have rusted and seized—in which case apply penetrating oil to loosen them. If this fails, saw through the bolts with a junior hacksaw. With Ogee-section guttering, remove the screws holding the section to the fascia as well.

Lift out the loosened section— making sure as you do so that its weight does not catch you off balance —and take it to the ground (fig. 3). Returning to the guttering, chip off all traces of old sealing compound from the hanging end (fig. 4) and scour it thoroughly with a wire brush. Repeat the cleaning operation on the removed section (figs. 5 and 6).

Apply fresh sealing compound to the socket section of the joint, spreading it in an even layer about 6mm

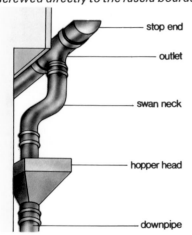

stop end

outlet

swan neck

hopper head

downpipe

B. *This downpipe connects to the gutter run via a swan neck*

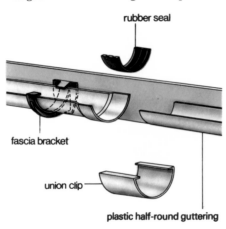

rubber seal

fascia bracket

union clip

plastic half-round guttering

C. *A section held by a fascia bracket. This joint type is sealed in the socket*

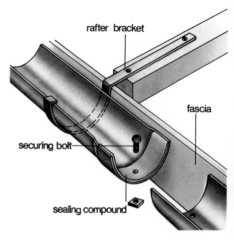

rafter bracket

fascia

securing bolt

sealing compound

D. *A joint in cast-iron guttering. The gutter is supported by rafter brackets*

2 This leaking section of cast-iron guttering is on the end of a run. The guttering is secured by screws in the fascia rather than by brackets

3 When the bolt in the joint at the other end of the section has been loosened and removed, you can pull the section away from the wall

4 The leak is at the joint with the adjoining section. Using hammer and screwdriver, gently chip off traces of old sealing compound

5 Repeat the cleaning operation for the section that has been removed. Scrape off old sealing compound from the joint end

6 When the old sealing compound has been removed, scour clean the two ends of the joint thoroughly with a wire brush

7 Apply new sealing compound to the socket section of the joint, spread in an even layer about 6mm thick over the socket area

8 Having replaced the removed section and fitted the joint together, take a new bolt and insert it in the hole in the joint from above

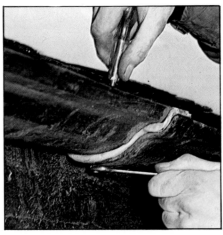

9 Screw the securing nut onto the end of the bolt and tighten with screwdriver and spanner so that joint closes and squeezes out compound

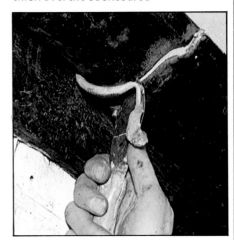

10 Use a putty knife to trim away all excess sealing compound squeezed onto the surface above and below the gutter

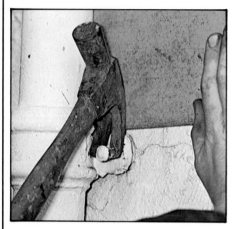

11 *This cast-iron downpipe is fixed to the wall by pipe nails driven into wooden plugs which have loosened. Remove the nails with a claw hammer*

12 *With the pipe nails removed, pull away the lower section. Joints sealed with compound will have to be loosened first*

13 *Having dug the loose plugs out of the masonry, extend the holes with a 12mm masonry drill to make sure replacement plugs fit*

14 *Using a hammer, firmly drive your replacement wooden plugs into the holes until they are flush. Make sure the plugs are firm*

15 *When both plugs have been fitted, replace the lower section so that the bracket holes are level with the plugs. Hammer in two new nails*

16 *To prevent the downpipe cracking, force some fresh jointing compound into the joint, then wipe it smooth with a rag*

thick (fig. 7). Relocate the removed gutter section, screwing it to the fascia or laying it on its brackets and fitting the joints together.

Insert a new galvanized bolt into the joint from above (fig. 8). Screw on its securing nut, tightening gently so that the joint closes up and squeezes out any excess compound (fig. 9). Trim away the excess with a putty or filling knife (fig. 10), wipe over the area with a damp rag, then repeat the operation for the other joint. Finally, repaint the joints with one or two coats of bituminous paint.

Replacing a cast-iron section
If the whole system has eroded, it may be advisable to replace it with plastics guttering.

However, if the rest of the run is still in good condition, replacing a corroded cast-iron section is well worthwhile.

Where possible, take the old section to a builder's merchant and obtain a matching replacement. As well as the shape and diameter, check that the new section matches the existing joints. If not, buy the appropriate union at the same time.

Cast-iron guttering is normally sold in 1.8m lengths, so the new sections may have to be cut to fit. When measuring it up, take into account any overlap for the joints or new joint unions.

To cut it, lay the old section over the top of the new and use it as a guide. Mark the new section in pencil and lay a strip of masking tape along the mark, towards the waste side, to give a clearer guide. Cut the section with a large hacksaw.

Mark the positions of the joint bolt holes and punch and drill them to a diameter of 8mm before you fit the new section into place.

Leaking joints in plastics
Leaks from plastics guttering can be just as damaging as those from cast-iron and should be attended to as soon as possible.

In most plastics guttering systems, the sections are connected by union clips, lined with replaceable rubber seals (fig. E). In some cases, the seal is positioned in the end of one section of gutter with a separate clip used to secure the joint (fig. C). When the clips are sprung home, the gutter ends compress against the pad to form a watertight joint—but this can leak if silt finds its way in.

To replace a seal, undo the clip holding the ends together, lift out the

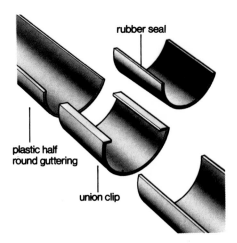

E. *This section of plastics guttering is connected by a sealed union clip*

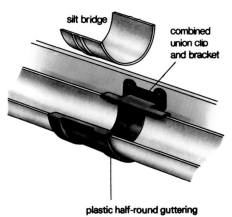

F. *The joint in this gutter is sealed by a silt bridge clipped into the union*

old seal and thoroughly clean the surfaces which come into contact with it. Fit a new seal of the same type and clip the joint back together by squeezing the ends of the gutter slightly and snapping the union clip over each edge of the section.

On systems which use combined union brackets, silt bridged joints are used (fig. F). The silt bridge clips into the union to prevent debris working its way into the joint and causing leaks. Leaks in such joints will be due to cracks—either in the bridge or in the union bracket itself—and can be remedied by replacing the defective part with a matching new one.

To fit a new silt bridge, hook one end under the front of the union clip and snap the other end under the lip at the back of the gutter.

Cast-iron downpipe repairs

Cast-iron downpipes are usually attached to walls by pipe nails driven into metal, lead or wooden plugs. The nails run through cast metal brackets (fig. 11) some of which have spacers behind to prevent contact between the pipe and the wall. Brackets often come loose, making the pipe dangerous.

To secure a loose bracket, start by removing the bracket nearest to the ground and repeat the operation up to and including the bracket that is loose. To remove a bracket, lever out the nails with a claw hammer (fig. 11). check that they are firm, then refit the downpipe (fig. 15).

In many houses, downpipe joints are unsealed. If dirt collects in an unsealed joint, water may gather and freeze and crack the pipe. Avoid this by filling any unsealed joints with a mixture of red lead and putty or a proprietary mastic. Wipe it smooth with a rag (fig. 16) then seal the joint with a coat of bituminous paint. Do the same with sealed joints that have become loose, having first chipped off the old compound.

Use an offcut of timber held against the wall to obtain the necessary leverage. Withdraw the section of corroded downpipe. Where the joints have been sealed and do not fall away easily, heat them with a blow lamp to loosen the sealing compound or chip the compound away by hand.

Remove the loose plugs by digging them out of the masonry, and make up replacements—slightly larger all round than the holes—from pieces of 12mm dowel. If necessary, extend the holes with a 12mm masonry drill (fig. 13). Drive the replacement plugs into the wall until they are flush (fig. 14).

Plastic downpipe repairs

Plastic downpipes are comparatively light and are less likely to work loose. However, if they do, they can be secured following the same procedure as for cast-iron downpipes. Sections of plastic downpipe are joined by socket and spigot connectors.

G. *Snap-together metal gutters come in several patterns, and in plain or enamelled aluminium or galvanized iron. Take an old section with you when you buy a replacement length to ensure the pattern matches. If there are no rubber seals where sections join, use plenty of caulking compound*

17 *Hopper heads are notorious for collecting leaves and rubbish. Lift out as much loose debris as possible—try not to push it down*

18 *Force out a blockage in a straight downpipe with a stout rod. If there is a bend in the pipe, try pulling out the blockage with wire*

19 *Wash out any residue with a strong jet of water from a garden hose. To prevent further blockages, cover with mesh*

Replacing an enamelled section

Gutters made from thin-section aluminium or galvanized steel, finished with white baked-on enamel, are less subject to rust than cast-iron gutters. But they are apt to dent sometimes just by your leaning a ladder against them.

The procedure for replacing a damaged section is much the same as for plastics. First, jam a block of wood inside the gutter while you draw the fixing spikes with a claw hammer, and disconnect the damaged section at the nearest joints. Cut the new section with a hacksaw, using the old one to measure the correct length, and file off the burrs on the cut edges. If you are using spike supports, drill holes through the new section to receive them.

Next, clean off the old sealing compound from the undamaged sections, as described above. Fill the joint connectors with sealing compound, slip them into place, and fit the new gutter section, spiking it into place. Finally, bend over into the gutter the top ends of the connectors if these are designed with fold-over tabs.

At external corners, as with other types of gutter, you need two fixing spikes—one into each length of fascia.

Clearing blocked downpipes

Before unblocking a downpipe, put a plastic bowl or large tin under the base of the pipe at the discharge into the drain to prevent any debris entering the drainage system.

When cleaning hopper heads (fig. B), use rubber gloves to protect your hands against sharp edges.

To clear a blockage in a straight downpipe, tie a rag firmly to one end of a long pole and poke it down the pipe. Once the blockage has been dislodged, flush the pipe thoroughly with a hose.

If the downpipe is fitted with a hopper head carefully clear by hand any debris which has collected. Try not to compress the debris, or it may cause further blockage in the downpipe.

With plastic hopper heads, wipe the inside with a cloth and soapy water once the debris has been cleared.

With some systems, the guttering is positioned some way out from the wall and water is directed into the downpipe through an angled section known as a *swan neck* (fig. B). To clear a blockage here, use a length of fairly stiff wire in place of the pole so that the bends may be negotiated. With wire it's best to pull out debris.

If a blockage is beyond reach, the lower part of the downpipe will have to be dismantled.

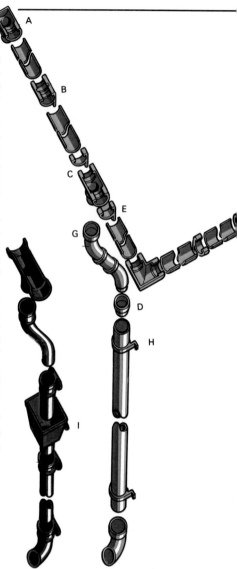

H. *Modern rainwater systems are nearly always made from plastic which doesn't rot and last virtually indefinitely. The weak points in a plastic system are the joints but in most cases it is possible to buy and install replacements. The sections that you are most likely to have to replace include the following.* **A.** *Stop-end outlet.* **B.** *Coupling clip.* **C.** *Running outlet.* **D.** *Angle piece.* **E.** *Support bracket.* **F.** *Stop-end.* **G.** *Three-piece swan neck.* **H.** *Downpipe bracket. When buying replacement parts, check that they are compatible with the existing system.*

Old cast-iron rainwater systems (inset) usually follow a different plan in that they have hopper heads to collect the water that drains from the gutter. Because cast iron is heavy and corrodes easily, the weak points are often to be found around the support brackets **(I)** *which have pulled away from the wall*

CARPET REPAIRS

You can make sure your carpets have a long life by careful and thorough maintenance. Repairing them before it is too late will always save you a lot of trouble and expense

Above: *There are various ways of replacing a worn patch of carpet depending on the type of the carpet. Here, a latex adhesive is being applied to the edges of a new piece of tufted carpet*

A carpet usually covers such a wide area of a room that it is painfully obvious when any part of it becomes damaged, stained or worn. But this everyday, minor damage need not be the disaster you might at first imagine. Most of it can, with care and patience, be repaired to a highly professional standard. Repairing carpets is a fast dying art and there are very few professional craftsmen who will undertake such a job as re-tufting a carpet. So if you have good carpets, you are even more duty bound to repair them yourself—or buy new ones.

Re-tufting

Tufts clawed out by pets, burned out by cigarettes or torn out by carelessly-used knee kickers when laying are among the most common forms of surface damage to a carpet.

To make a repair, your first requirement is some matching pile yarn. If the carpet is still in production, you can get this through the retailer from the manufacturers, who will need to know the range name and pattern number—sometimes a small cutting of waste suffices to verify the colours. Most manufacturers are very helpful

about supplying matching yarn and often do so free of charge.

If you cannot obtain the correct match, something fairly close is usually available in a knitting wool of a similar gauge. The only equipment needed for re-tufting is a medium-sized pair of very sharp scissors and a small quantity of latex or general-purpose household adhesive.

Start by isolating the damaged tufts and snip them off level with the backing, taking care not to cut the backing in the process.

Now put a dab of adhesive on the end 153

CARPET REPAIRS

of the replacement tuft and set it aside to dry. Use the end of an artist's paint-brush or similar implement to put a spot of the adhesive in the hole in the carpet. When this has dried, press the tuft into place firmly and trim off excess with a pair of scissors (see figs 14 to 22).

Continue in this way until the whole patch is filled in. With a patterned carpet, different coloured yarns should be used and the tufts correctly located in accordance with the design. Having stuck in all the tufts, smooth them out in the direction of the pile and snip them off level with the rest of the pile.

Complete repairs

If damage to a carpet extends below the level of the pile into the backing structure, a new piece of carpet has to be set in. For this you need a sharp handyman's trimming knife with a few heavy-duty blades, a thin, metal straightedge and a curved needle. The method of repair varies for each type of carpet.

Axminsters and Wiltons: Mark out the extremities of the damage with pins, pushing them right through the backing. With the carpet folded over, the pins enable you to locate the area of damage from the reverse side.

Use your handyman's knife to cut out the damaged portion in a square or rectangular shape, following the line of the weave. The cut must be deep enough to cut and separate the backing without damaging the over-hanging pile, which will be needed later to cover the join.

Next place the damaged cut-out on the replacement piece, with the pattern matching, and mark the position with pins pushed right through. Turn it over and cut out the piece required for the repair, following the weave and cutting only just through the backing as before.

1 Cut a square section from a piece of spare carpet as a replacement piece making sure that the pile direction is the same

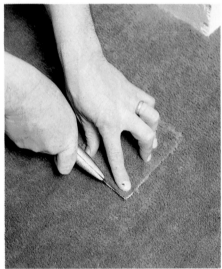

2 Place the section squarely over the damaged area and cut round the template piece with the knife blade angled inwards

3 When the damaged piece has been removed, apply a latex-based adhesive liberally along each of the edges of the replacement piece

4 Stick a piece of one-sided self-adhesive carpet tape under each side of the square and press the carpet down to make the tape stick

5 Position the replacement piece down at one end making sure that the pile runs in the right direction and push it into place at the seams

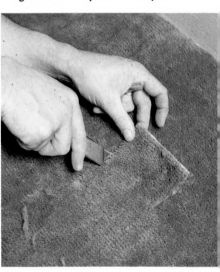

6 To get the foam rubber seams to stick firmly together push down into the join with the back of the blade of a handyman's knife

154

Before securing the new piece of carpet in position, seal all raw edges with a proprietary latex compound and allow this to dry. Then place the new piece of carpet into the prepared cut-out, making sure it is the right way round, with the pattern matching and pile direction corresponding.

The edges must be sewn firmly together on the backing section with an over and over stitch using a curved needle and stout thread. Most carpet suppliers sell carpet thread specially for this purpose.

Finally, apply a 35mm wide coat of latex compound to the back of the seam and cover this with a fabric tape. Apply gentle pressure on the area and allow it to dry.

Tufted carpets with non - foam backing: The repair method for these is similar to that for Axminsters and Wiltons except that there is no weave structure to follow when cutting out the damaged and replacement sections. Some tufted carpets appear to have a weave structure but this is only a layer of woven material which is stuck on the back and should be disregarded.

The best way to repair this type of carpet is to cut a generous amount of new material into a square or rectangle and place it directly over the worn section. This becomes a template around which you cut into the carpet with the handyman's knife angled inwards. Follow figs 7 to 13.

Foam-backed (cushion-backed) carpets: These are just tufted carpets with a foam backing and can be repaired as above—but do not use sewing or fabric tape. Instead, having cut out the replacement piece and placed it in the squared-off damaged area, bond the edges of the foam together with a fine bead of contact adhesive. Then complete the joints with a 50mm-wide self-adhesive carpet tape and allow this to set for about two hours before turning the carpet back into position (see figs 1 to 6).

Vacuuming and maintenance

Regular vacuuming is an essential part of carpet maintenance and is the only effective way to remove damaging grit which becomes embedded in the pile. If you leave this grit for a long time rapid deterioration occurs at the base of the pile.

It is worth having your vacuum cleaner regularly serviced, as it performs a very important job. Upright vacuum cleaners, for instance, need a new drive belt and brush inserts in the beater about every six to 12 months but this you can do yourself.

7 For a larger area of damage knock nails through the corners of the replacement piece and underlay to hold it in place

Carpets fall into two categories according to the type of vacuum which best suits them. Shag-pile carpets are a special case.

Wool carpets: Vacuum cylinder-type cleaners can be used on this type of carpet as and when required at any time during the carpet's life. However, the upright type of cleaner with revolving beater bar and brushes should not be used on a new wool carpet for about six months. Prior to this, the fibres in the yarn will not have had a chance to interlock sufficiently and may be pulled out.

Upright vacuum cleaners are easier to use and often more efficient but they are a little harsher on the pile than cylinder types and so should not be used more than once a week during the initial period.

Man-made fibre carpets: These can have an upright vacuum cleaner used on them from the day they are laid but limit this if possible to once a week. A cylinder-type vacuum cleaner can be used as often as required without risk of damage.

Shag-pile carpets: This type of carpet requires special care as the pile becomes tangled and flat if it is not regularly combed out with a special shag rake. You can buy one of these from any good carpet shop and it takes only a few moments to rake an average room. Shag-pile carpets are not designed for heavy use, but if they are subject to a lot of wear they should be raked every day. For vacuuming, use a suction-only cleaner or a heavy-duty upright with a high pile adjustment.

8 Cut round the template in the manner shown in fig. 2. This is made much easier by the nails that are holding the template in place

Lifting crush marks

Crush marks from heavy furniture can sometimes be removed by gentle brushing with a small, stiff brush but if this fails, the controlled application of steam can work wonders.

First vacuum the area to make sure it is quite clean, then cover the crush mark with a wet, white cotton cloth. Set a steam iron to suit the material of the carpet and hold it over the cloth so that it just touches. The resulting steam will then start to lift the pile—an action which you can assist by gently brushing against the pile after each application.

Steam only for a few minutes at a time, checking the effect as you go—oversteaming causes the yarn to untwist. Never allow the iron to be in direct contact with the pile and re-wet the cloth at frequent intervals. Leave the pile sloping in the right direction and allow it to dry. The carpet will soon look new again (see fig. B).

High tufts and loose ends

These are sometimes present in new carpets, but are more likely to be caused by snagging with a sharp object. Never pull out a loose end or tuft standing above the level of the pile: this only causes more damage. Instead, simply snip them off level with the other tufts using a sharp pair of scissors.

Carpet cleaning

Before embarking on cleaning a whole carpet, clear the room of furniture and vacuum away all loose dirt and grit. Two methods of cleaning are

9 *For this non foam-backed tufted carpet you need to cut four lengths of hessian carpet tape to stick under each side*

10 *Spread the latex adhesive solution liberally on one side of the hessian carpet tape and let it dry for a few minutes*

11 *In order to get a really firm bind, spread more of the latex adhesive along the underside edges of the carpet*

easily possible at home: shampooing which can either be done by hand or special machine, and hot water extraction (steam cleaning).

Though simple, shampooing is not particularly satisfactory as it tends to leave a sticky residue in the pile which is very difficult to remove. The residue in turn attracts more dirt and the carpet soon becomes dirty again.

By comparison, the hot water extraction method leaves no residue at all. The system works by forcing a jet of partly vapourized hot water into the pile of the carpet via a hand-held nozzle. This will loosen and break down the particles of dirt, which are then drawn out of the pile by a powerful vacuum in another section of the same nozzle.

Hot water extraction machines can be hired by the day from carpet shops. They are fairly simple to use, though overwetting of the carpet must be avoided as it causes shrinkage.

Treatment for spillages

Never start by rubbing the affected area, as this only drives the stain further into the carpet. Deal with the spillage immediately and gently—scoop up as much as possible with a spoon and then mop with white tissues.

With fairly fluid stains, remarkable results can be obtained by placing a thick wad of tissues over the affected area, weighted down with, say, a heavy book. During a period of 20 minutes or so, natural capillary action draws much of the stain into the tissues. For heavy stains, change the wad of tissues several times. When you are dealing with old or stubborn stains it is probably wisest to call in professional assistance.

A. *To soak up spillages a blotting device is often the most efficient method. Blot the spill two or three times using clean tissues under a heavy book*

B. *To lift crushed pile iron very lightly over a damp piece of cotton cloth, then remove the cloth and comb the pile in the same direction as the rest*

12 *Place the adhesive also on underside edges of the replacement piece and, with the hessian tape in position, join together*

13 *Push the seams into place in the same way as in fig. 6, then knock along each join lightly with a hammer to bed the edges to the tape*

Particularly important points to remember when attempting to remove the various types of carpet stains are:
- Always work with a clean, white cotton rag or white tissues
- Gently dab or wipe the stain, working inwards
- Never use excessive pressure as this only rubs the stain further in
- Change the tissue or rag as soon as it becomes soiled
- Avoid over-wetting and keep stain removers out of the backing
- Leave the pile sloping in the right direction
- Allow carpets to dry before walking on them
- Always test stain removal treatments on a spare piece of carpet.

Dealing with stains

STAIN	TREATMENT	STAIN	TREATMENT
Beer	A squirt from the soda syphon; sponge, rinse and blot dry	Milk	A squirt from the soda syphon; sponge, rinse and blot dry. Follow with mild carpet shampoo solution; sponge, rinse and blot dry. Finish with dry cleaning fluid
Blood	A squirt from the soda syphon; sponge, rinse with cold water and blot dry		
Candle wax	Scrape off as much as possible. Melt and absorb the remainder by covering with blotting paper and applying the toe of a warm iron. Do not let the iron come into direct contact with the carpet or use this method with polypropylene or nylon carpets. Dab with methylated spirit to remove any remaining colour	Soft drinks	Sponge with mild carpet shampoo solution; rinse with warm water and blot dry
		Soot	Vacuum up as much as possible and treat with dry cleaning fluid
		Tar	Gently scrape up the deposit. Soften with a solution of 50 per cent glycerine and 50 per cent water. Leave for up to an hour, gently wipe, rinse and blot dry. Obstinate marks can sometimes respond to treatment with dry cleaning fluid or eucalyptus oil
Chewing gum	Treat with any proprietary chewing gum remover or dry cleaning fluid		
Coffee	As for beer, but remove final traces with a dry cleaning solvent	Tea	A squirt from the soda syphon; sponge, rinse and blot dry. Finish with peroxide, 250mls to 250mls water
Egg	Remove with salt water and blotting paper		
Ice cream	Mild carpet shampoo solution; sponge, rinse with warm water and blot dry. Finish with a dry cleaning solvent	Urine	A squirt from the soda syphon; sponge and rinse. Sponge with mild carpet shampoo solution, rinse and blot. Then rinse several times using cold water with a few drops of antiseptic added. Blot dry
Ink	A squirt from the soda syphon; sponge, rinse with warm water and blot dry. Finish with dry cleaning fluid if mark persists		
Lipstick	Gently wipe away with paint remover, rinse with warm water and blot dry	Wine	Remove with glycerine or peroxide diluted in an equal proportion of water

14 If you cannot obtain matching tufts of fibre from the manufacturer, tease a few fibres carefully out of a part of the carpet

15 Use an artist's paintbrush or a similar implement to put a dab of adhesive in the hole you're patching, and let the adhesive dry

16 Apply some adhesive to one end of the tuft, and let this dry too. Then press the coated end of the tuft into the hole in the carpet

17 To ensure a really good bond, it's a good idea to hammer the tufts down. Brush them to match the pile direction, snipping off the excess

18 There are several ways of stopping a rug from slipping on a polished floor. The simplest is to brush latex adhesive onto the back

19 To stop rugs from creeping when laid over a carpet, stick thin latex foam to the back of the rug with double-sided adhesive tape

20 Stair carpet often wears unevenly; this can be minimized by moving it up or down slightly. Start by lifting the whole length

21 To move the carpet up, double over the top of the length and then tack it back at the top of the flight—usually below the first riser

22 Re-fit the carpet to the gripper strips, working down the flight. Then turn the carpet under the bottom tread and tack it to the riser

KEEPING HEAT IN

Heat loss around the house ● Jobs you can do yourself ● Insulating the roof ● Choosing the right insulating materials ● How to calculate quantities ● Filling in awkward corners

About three-quarters of all heating in an uninsulated house is lost to the atmosphere, much of it through the roof (fig. A). Insulating your roof space is a cheap way of counteracting this loss and will noticeably cut your heating bills. Insulation also helps keep the house cool in summer.

Regardless of the exact type of material used by the house builder, there is nearly always room for improvement. And because of fast-rising fuel costs, in the long run you will save money whatever the actual cost and quantity of your insulation.

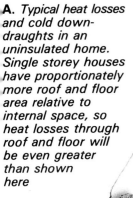

A. *Typical heat losses and cold down-draughts in an uninsulated home. Single storey houses have proportionately more roof and floor area relative to internal space, so heat losses through roof and floor will be even greater than shown here*

Insulating materials

The cheapest and simplest way of insulating the roof space is to place insulating material between, or over, the ceiling joists. Various types of natural and man-made material are available, either in rolled blankets or in granulated form. But as there is little to choose between them in terms of effectiveness you should base your choice on the cost and selection of what is available locally.

Mineral-fibre or glassfibre matting and blanket comes in roll form, cut to fit the average space between floor joists. On its own, this is normally adequate for insulating a roof; awkward nooks and crannies can be filled with off-cuts from the rolls once the main insulation is laid.

However, in older houses, where the ceiling joists are likely to be more narrowly spaced than is usual today, laying a standard-width roll material is a wasteful business—every bit has to be turned up at the edges. In this case, loose-fill insulation is much easier.

TIP FROM THE TRADE

Q My newly-insulated loft is starting to smell damp and a bit musty. Have I done something wrong?

A The loft insulation in an unheated loft will start retaining moisture if the loft is inadequately ventilated. Check that your insulation has not blocked the natural flow of air into the loft from around the eaves. If you have installed batts between the rafters, they must have a vapour barrier—sheets of battened-on polythene will do—below the rafters to prevent moisture penetration from above.

Loose fill comes in bags, either in granule form or as pieces of loose fibre. Among the materials used are polystyrene, vermiculite—an expandable mica—and mineral wool (rock wool).

Besides being handy where the space between floor joists is narrow, loose-fill insulates inaccessible corners more effectively than offcuts of rolled material. In draughty lofts however, the granules blow about unless the floor joists are covered over.

Whichever type of material is chosen and however this is laid, depth of insulation is the crucial factor. About 150mm is considered a satisfactory compromise between cost and effectiveness. Roll materials are available in thicknesses of about 80mm or 100mm for topping up existing insulation, and of about 150mm for dealing with a loft which has no insulation.

Calculating quantities

Inspecting the loft gives you a chance to estimate both the quantity of material required and the extent of work involved. To help you move around, and to avoid accidentally damaging the ceiling below, place stout planks across the joists.

If you are considering adding to existing insulation, think in terms of bringing it up to the 150mm depth of loose-fill or blanket insulation recommended for uninsulated roofs.

In Britain, a typical roll of blanket material of 150mm depth measures about 5.3m in length. 'Topping up' rolls, with depths of about 80mm or 100mm, are slightly longer at about 8m —and slightly more expensive. The easiest way of working out your needs is to add together the total length of the strips of ceiling to be covered, and divide this by the length of the roll material you are using to do the job.

Add to this number of rolls a generous surplus to take care of trimming and overlap. Remember to allow for the turn up at the eaves (see below), and add extra to wrap around the water tank and its piping, and to cover the trapdoor.

If you are using loose-fill material, your requirements are best based on the manufacturer's own tables and recommendations—on the assumption you will be adding insulation up to the depth of 150mm.

While you are in the loft, inspect the areas below the flashings which exclude water at the junction of the roof and other surfaces, such as around the chimney.

On no account should you proceed with insulation if there is any evidence of roof leakage or wet rot, as loft insulation can aggravate both these problems considerably.

At the same time, take a look at the electrics. Wiring perishes in time —especially the older cloth-covered rubber-insulated type—and in any

1 Take blanket insulation right up to the wall plate at the eaves, but make sure you leave a path for air from outside to enter the loft

2 Where possible, tuck the insulation under obstructions. Note the use of a stout plank as a working platform

case may not take kindly to repeated knocks while you are laying the insulating material.

Planning the work

When laying blanket insulation, it is infuriating to find that every roll ends short of the mark or repeatedly needs cutting at, say, a particularly large roof member—leaving an almost useless offcut.

The most convenient place for rolls to end is away from the eaves—it is difficult enough having to stretch into these inaccessible areas just to push the insulation home. You should therefore plan on working away from the eaves wherever possible. Any offcuts can be used up later to insulate a more accessible strip in the middle of the loft area.

The area underneath the cold water storage cistern should not be insulated—a certain amount of warmth must be allowed to rise up from below to prevent the water from freezing during very cold spells.

Insulation grants

Grants to help with the cost of installing loft insulation in domestic premises are still available from local authorities, but the general grant of 66 per cent of the cost has now been withdrawn and funds are currently being concentrated on helping disabled people and families with low incomes. They can apply to their local authority for a grant covering 90 per cent of the cost of installing loft, tank and pipe insulation if they are in receipt of housing benefit or supplementary benefit.

Vapour barriers and the condensation risk

During winter weather, warm moisture-laden air from inside the house tends to 'migrate' towards the colder, drier air outside. To prevent insulation materials from becoming wet as a result, a vapour barrier is essential. This can be of foil, asphalted paper or sheet plastic, and is always laid on the 'warm' side of the insulation—that is, the side nearest the inside of the house. Some insulation comes ready-wrapped in vapour-proof blankets.

Roll material can be cut to length and shape with large scissors or slashed, carefully, with a handyman's knife. Awkward shapes are more conveniently torn from a supply length. Be generous in the cutting length so that you can tuck in the surplus at the end. Where two lengths join, either tightly butt the two ends or leave the excess to overlap by about 100mm. Offcuts can be used to fill small gaps between lengths.

Around the edges of the loft, while strong draughts can be prevented, gaps must be left at the eaves to enhance ventilation. Inadequate ventilation results in damp conditions. But in most cases you need insulate only as far as the wall-plate—the barrier between the joists and eaves (fig. 1).

The loft area is finished off by insulating the access trap or door with spare lengths of rolled insulation, glued, tied or tacked in place. Allow the material to overspill when the trap or door is closed, so that any draughts are excluded.

3 Blanket material can be easily cut to shape with large scissors or garden shears. Offcuts can be used for pipe lagging and elsewhere

4 Loose-fill material is a quick and effective way of dealing with awkward spots such as around the chimney stack and wiring boards

5 Level off the loose-fill to the top of the joists. If these are very deep, use a 'T'-shaped board cut to give the required depth of material

6 Allow plenty of overlap when covering the loft door—this prevents draughts—but do not insulate beneath the water tank

7 Pipes in an insulated loft must be lagged. One way of doing this is to wrap hessian-backed felt around them, ensuring a good overlap

8 Flexible foam tubing is an alternative material for lagging pipes. Just cut the tubing to length with a trimming knife and slip it on

Laying materials
When you come to lay your insulation, simply follow the set pattern of joists across the roof. Loose-fill material can be levelled to the correct depth using a template made from thick card or wood off-cut. Shape this to fit the space between joists (fig.5). Like roll materials, loose-fill should be laid working inwards from the eaves. Level the filling towards a clear space in the middle of the loft where addition and removal will present far less of a problem.

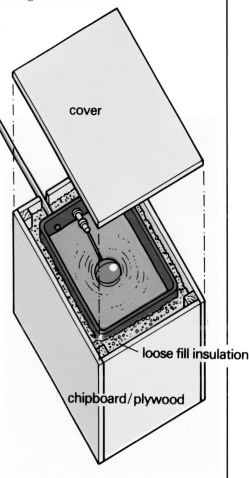

B. Cold water storage cisterns must be protected from the cold, but don't insulate underneath the tank. Loose fill insulation is perfectly adequate

161

TIP FROM THE TRADE

Q I have heard that glassfibre insulation can be damaging to health. Is there any truth in this and is it safe to handle?

A Glassfibre insulation can cause severe irritation so it is as well to protect yourself when handling it, especially if you have sensitive skin. Wear sturdy gloves, preferably a pair with wrist bands which will prevent any fibres and dust from reaching your hands. It's also a wise precaution to cover your arms with long sleeves tucked into the gloves. If there is a lot of dust in the insulation, which is often the case, wear a face mask to filter out particles that could harm your lungs.

Partial loft conversions

Boarding over the joists after you have insulated the loft will reduce heat loss still further. But if you may want to carry out a full-scale loft conversion later, as described later on in the course, do not lay a permanent floor; your ceiling joists (probably only 100mm × 50mm, in UK houses) will have to be strengthened for a permanent habitable room. Instead, lay a temporary chipboard floor, screwing down the chipboard so you can lift and re-lay it later.

If the loft already has a floor, lift about one board in five and force loose-fill material between the joists.

Insulating cold water cisterns

Water cisterns are particularly vulnerable in cold lofts and they must be protected. There are several ways of doing this—the method you choose will probably depend on how you have insulated your loft. You can use loose fill insulation if you first surround the cistern in a simple box-like structure (fig. B). Alternatively, you can wrap glassfibre blanket around the cistern and hold it in place with straps or string —don't forget to cover the top of the cistern. A third option is to panel in the cistern with blocks of polystyrene. Shape the blocks to fit around pipes and obstacles with a sharp trimming knife and hold them in place with strong tape or string.

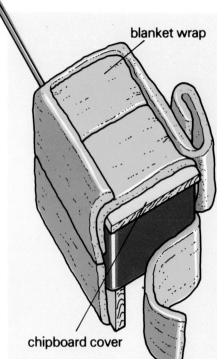

blanket wrap

chipboard cover

C. *Two alternative methods for insulating cold water cisterns. Polystyrene blocks are easily shaped with a sharp knife*

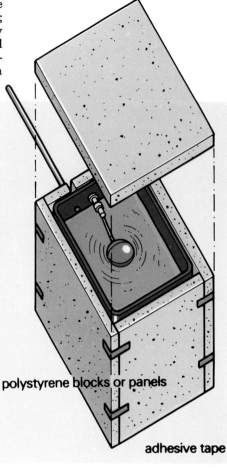

polystyrene blocks or panels

adhesive tape

Insulate your roof space

The illustration (opposite page) shows the various ways of insulating (left) an unused loft and (right) another in the process of being converted into a living space. Although the basic insulation materials are identical for each, they are used in slightly different ways.

Blanket insulation such as glassfibre rolls or batts is inexpensive and effective. In most instances the roll ends need only be taken up to the joist end or wall-plate (1) they should not block the eaves since this will prevent natural ventilation. Roll the blanket inwards from the eaves, allowing a generous overlap where a new length meets an old (2).

Other uses for blanket material include lining and draughtproofing of the loft door (3) and insulating between rafters (4). A double thickness further improves insulation, being particularly effective for sound-proofing a noisy floor (5) that forms part of a loft conversion. It is important that no insulation is laid directly beneath the water tank (6). If the loft area is used as a living room, the water tank itself need not be insulated.

Loose-fill 'rock wool' or vermiculite is much more convenient for insulating a 'bitty' ceiling, in areas well clear of draughts (8). Again, increasing the depth improves both heat and sound insulation (9). For insulating within a water-tank box loose-fill insulation is much more satisfactory than a delicate blanket lagging, but you will have to construct a softboard box (10) around the tank.

Lagging pipework

In an open loft remember that any pipework has to be lagged also. You can use blanket insulation offcuts, hessian wrapping, preformed neoprene (11) or polystyrene tubing for the job.

A draughty roof can be insulated with a special lined blanket material placed between the rafters (12). This is attached either to the tile battens, or to the rafter sides by battening (13). The material must be led clear of the wall ends to prevent any condensation from seeping into a wall cavity. Always start laying at the ridge and work downwards, overlapping the ends so that any moisture seeping through the roof

runs away at the eaves—not into the roof.

The rafters can then be covered with insulating softboard (14), and finished off with tempered hardboard if desired.

Living area conversion
In a loft conversion for a living area, insulation can be provided by blanket material, or by solid and easily worked slabs of polystyrene, rockwool or fibreboard.

The same types of 'solid' insulation can be used on the party wall between your loft and your neighbour's, particularly where his loft remains uninsulated. If appearance is important and rising sound from next door is a problem, box in the insulation behind a false wall.

The floor in a loft room can take a variety of forms, but chipboard is best (16). Fix it with screws, not nails, to avoid the possibility that hammering will crack or loosen the ceiling below.

In planning the conversion consider installing a professionally double-glazed window, or install a sealed-unit yourself (17). The roof is, after all, usually the most exposed part of the house and the additional cost of double-glazing—if kept simple—is unlikely to have much effect on the overall cost of the conversion.

If efficient underfloor insulation is installed (in part to act as sound insulation), rising heat from the house will not reach the loft area and additional heating must be provided there.

So if providing it would be too expensive or inconvenient, you would be better to omit the sub-floor insulation altogether.

Converting a loft into a living area is no small undertaking: quite apart from the work involved, there are Building Regulations to consider and you may need planning permission as well if you are going to alter the appearance of the roof (by installing a dormer window for example). So, before you go headlong into laying new flooring, contact your local building inspector who will be able to advise you on what you can and can't do—contrary to popular belief, building inspectors are there to help and their experience is usually both genuine and valuable.

A dozen ways to reduce heat losses

Jobs for the specialist

1. If the fireplace is no longer used, have the chimney stopped and vented to prevent an upwards draught

2. Some types of board or blanket insulation need to be fitted with care to prevent roof damage and excessive condensation

3. Spray-blown loft and cavity wall insulation are both extremely effective, but involve considerable expense

4. Insulation can be fitted above a false ceiling—useful when access to the roof space is not possible

5. Sealed-unit double glazing has to be installed by a professional as some structural work is involved

6. Floor cavity insulation involves considerable turmoil unless laid at the time of building or when flooring repairs are made

Jobs you can do yourself

7. Some forms of blanket insulation can be tacked to the rafters and covered by hardboard or softboard

8. Insulation placed between the joists, a covering for this, and lagging of tanks and pipes are jobs easily done

9. Another inexpensive and effective insulation job is cutting out draughts around doors, windows and unused chimneys and fireplaces

10. A bigger job, cheaper than cavity insulation and almost as effective, is to panel insulate the inside of the inner leaf of a cavity wall

11. Secondary sash double glazing, provided in kit form, is usually easily fitted to conventional windows

12. Thicker carpets help greatly to prevent heat loss through floors with gaps between the boards

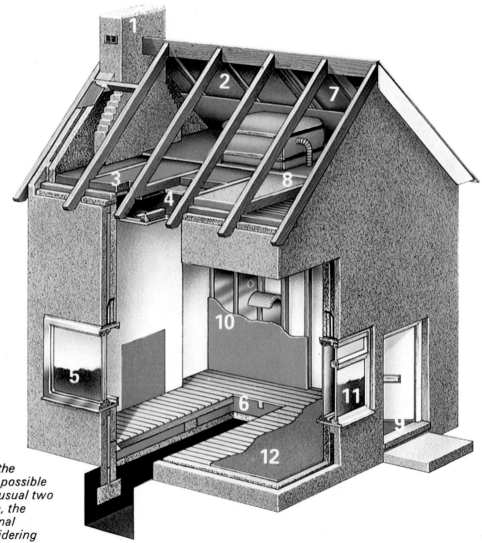

D. *Insulating your home—the possibilities. Although it is possible to combine more than the usual two or three forms of insulation, the cost-effectiveness of the final combination is worth considering*

DEALING WITH DAMP

Damp should never be ignored. If it is, the whole house is put at risk from structural damage. The longer damp is left unchecked, the greater is the risk and the expense

Above: *The injection of silicone under pressure into pre-drilled holes is the most common form of damp-proofing—usually carried out by experts. An impervious membrane is created around the house*

Damp is a danger sign for which you should always be on the lookout. If not controlled at an early stage, the damp can cause structural damage to the whole house. And by penetrating the porous brickwork and internal plaster, it puts even the furnishings and fittings inside the house at risk.

The causes and treatment of each kind of damp are different, so it is important to check exactly what type of damp you have before deciding on a course of action. Get professional advice if you are unsure.

Recognizing the signs
Condensation is by far the most common type of damp and it is fairly obvious when this is affecting a room. The windows tend to steam up easily and water runs down the walls—badly staining the paint and wall coverings. The more steam there is in a room, the

more likely it is to be affected by condensation damage. Bathrooms and kitchens, therefore, are particularly vulnerable but so too are bedrooms. Here, the warm, damp air which causes condensation comes from those sleeping in the room.

Continuous moisture on a wall could soon result in the whole surface becoming damp.

Superficially, condensation quickly provides the ideal breeding ground for unsightly moulds—a sure sign that the internal plaster has become saturated (see over).

If a room is not troubled by condensation but you still suspect damp is present, it is likely to be either rising or penetrating damp.

Penetrating damp is usually caused by something as simple as a leaking or blocked gutter. When penetrating damp is present in a room, therefore,

the affected wall is usually stained fairly high up.

Rising damp is found in houses with solid masonry walls, or with cavity walls whose inner leaf is of bricks or blocks. Its symptoms are similar to those of penetrating damp, except that the damp areas are likely to be near floor level. Affected rooms may also have an unpleasant smell.

Treatment of condensation
Condensation occurs when insulation and ventilation are both inadequate. There is always a certain amount of water vapour in the air, and the warmer a house gets, the more water vapour the air can hold. However, as soon as the air reaches saturation point, or the temperature drops—such as on cold, poorly insulated walls—the excess water vapour reverts to its liquid state. This is condensation. 165

Above: *Uncontrolled condensation has provided the ideal conditions for this wall to be penetrated with damp and for the growth of moulds*

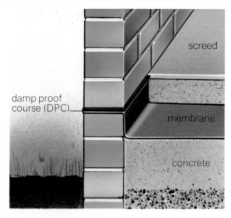

A. *Porous concrete floors must be covered with a waterproof film which joins up with the DPC so that damp does not rise up to the walls*

One of the worst causes of condensation is from the vapour given off by portable paraffin (kerosene) heaters.

Good ventilation—in the form of ventilation bricks, window vents and extractor fans—eases the problem to a certain extent by introducing drier air to the room and removing the moist air. Bear in mind that extractor fans work best when positioned high up. In bathrooms and kitchens, the fan should be as near to the source of the steam as possible but well away from windows which are usually left open.

The best way of controlling condensation is to insulate the external walls so that they retain heat. Walls at a temperature close to that of the room do not so readily produce condensation. An ideal situation is to have a constant air temperature, though there is not much point in having the heating system on 24 hours a day if the house is not properly insulated.

Humid conditions—high temperature, damp atmosphere—increase the amount of condensation on cooler surfaces such as walls and windows. But if the walls are properly insulated and there is an extractor fan in the window, this too can be controlled.

Take simple steps such as opening the window—in the summer at least—before running the bath water, or cooking, to reduce the amount of harmful moisture on the walls. When running a bath during the colder months, cold water run for a minute before adding the hot water will considerably reduce the amount of steam—and therefore condensation.

Rising damp

The most common cause of rising damp is the absence, or breaking down, of the damp proof course (DPC). The DPC is a layer of impervious material

inserted between courses of brickwork on all the walls of a structure at a minimum of 150mm above ground level.

Without a DPC, or where one has broken down, water rises up from the ground and is absorbed by the porous brickwork. A porous concrete floor within the building also allows moisture to pass through it and up the walls. In this case a damp-proof membrane should be placed over the complete surface of the concrete and below the final screed so that a continuous, waterproof film is formed up to the DPC in the walls (fig. A).

Any house built in the UK after 1920 should already have a DPC. However, the bitumen impregnated felt material that was often used can break down. This material becomes brittle with age and may have cracked due to thermal movement. Houses built before 1920 sometimes had a course of slate as a DPC in a brick wall—this, too, can break down with age and delaminates or cracks. To repair either of these

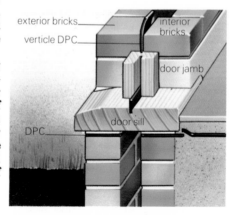

B. *To prevent penetrating damp around doors and windows in cavity walls, a vertical DPC must be fitted so that the cavity cannot be bridged*

problems, a new DPC must be created—by cutting out the brickwork so a new physical barrier can be inserted, or by impregnating the masonry with a waterproof chemical.

Earth or debris piled up against the side of a house which covers the DPC is a common cause of rising damp because it allows moisture to bridge across the DPC.

Removing the offending materials will usually cure the problem if caught early enough. But where the damp has been allowed to spread, some of the bricks and mortar above the DPC may have to be replaced together with the internal plasterwork.

'Bridging' can also occur when excess mortar has been carelessly dropped between the leaves of a cavity wall during building. The deposits often build up to the point where they rise above the DPC. In this case, the cure is to remove bricks from the outer leaf of the affected wall and chip away the deposits taking care not to damage the existing DPC.

Where external rendering extends down to ground level and has become porous or hollow ('blown') through old age, damp can bypass the DPC completely. Here, the affected rendering must be removed to at least one course of brickwork above the DPC.

A common cause of damp and rot in older houses with suspended (ie, timber, not concrete) floors is the blocking up of air bricks. These should be kept clear of debris at all times so that moisture-laden air beneath the floor has a chance to escape.

An adjoining wall—such as that on a lean-to—which either has a DPC at a higher level or none at all, will allow moisture to rise above the DPC in the main structure. This problem can be corrected by inserting a vertical DPC to bridge the gap.

Types of DPC

Inserting a DPC is a costly and difficult procedure which is usually best left to a professional contractor. Also, the professionals give a 20 year guarantee—a plus point when you come to sell the house. Unfortunately, the job is now considered essential in houses where no DPC is fitted or where the existing one has broken down beyond repair. There are several methods from which to choose but only one of these is within the scope of the handyman.

Silicone injection: This method is popular with both professionals and do-it-yourselfers alike because it involves no cutting of brickwork and

Right: *With pumped installations the silicone is injected through several nozzles at a time*

can be done from either inside or outside the house—the latter approach being more commonly used.

The first stage is to drill holes in all the walls, about 220mm apart and at least 150mm above ground level. Next, a silicone water-repellent liquid is forced into the holes and allowed to soak through the brickwork (fig. C).

Professional contractors introduce the silicone under high pressure, using sophisticated injection equipment. For the amateur, the silicone can be fed in from bottles by gravity flow; alternatively, the injection equipment can be hired from plant hire firms, who will also provide the chemicals.

Cutting out: Removing brickwork to insert a layer of damp-proof material is a lengthy, highly-skilled job which even the professionals are often reluctant to tackle. In any case, it is only feasible on houses where the brickwork is in good condition. If the overall structure is shaky, inserting a DPC in this way may literally bring the house down.

The brickwork is cut away in alternate 900mm sections with the aid of a hand masonry saw, power saw or grinding disc, using wood battens to counteract any crumbling of the structure above.

Afterwards, the chosen DPC material is inserted, set in mortar and the brickwork replaced. The intervening sections can then be completed in the same way to form a continuous DPC along the wall.

Slate is the traditional DPC material used in this way. The slate sections—which must be at least 230mm long—are set into the mortar in overlapping layers to form a continuous seal.

More recently, easier-to-handle sheet materials have come in to use. These include lead-cored bitumen felt, fibrous asphalt felt, sheet copper, sheet lead, sheet zinc and bituminized polythene. These are all laid in 675mm or 900mm strips, then set in to mortar (specifically lime mortar in the case of lead sheet).

Adjoining strips are either overlapped—by at least 100mm—or welded by folding the ends over each other.

Bear in mind that inserting a DPC does not get rid of rising damp problems immediately. The brickwork should be left to dry out for several months before you redecorate or make any internal repairs.

Penetrating damp
This kind of damp is usually caused by a fault higher up in the house than a defective DPC. Leaking roofs, gutters and downpipes, which allow a large amount of water to flow down a small section of wall, are common causes of penetrating damp. They should be quickly repaired, together with any damage to brickwork or pointing which may have occured.

A heavy growth of lichen, moss or clinging plants such as ivy can also provide an ideal inlet for moisture. These should be scraped from the wall and the wall then sprayed with a chemical fungicide.

Bad pointing and *spalled*—broken down and flaky—brickwork are common causes of penetrating damp. Check all exterior mortar joints and bricks for crumbling, holes and gaps before you decide on any further course of action against the damp.

If care was not taken during the building of a cavity wall to keep it free of obstructions—such as lumps of porous mortar on wall ties—moisture can bridge the DPC and cause damp to penetrate the inner wall. Some brickwork will have to be removed from the damp area to clean off the encrusted wall tie.

Treating penetrating damp
If you are certain that the penetrating damp is not caused by any of the above faults it may be that moisture is simply seeping through the walls. Where this is the case, there are several ways of making the exterior walls more impervious.

Cladding the walls with tiles or slates and rendering or painting the outside of the house are methods which are not always popular or practical because they alter the exterior look.

Spraying the outside of the house with a chemical water repellent is a less drastic and often just as effective solution. The liquid should be sprayed on with a pressurized pneumatic sprayer.

Before spraying, the walls should be as clean and dry as possible. All mortar joints must be in good condition and any structural cracks filled in. Fresh mortar should be allowed to dry for at least six weeks first.

Although the liquid is easily wiped off most other surfaces, it is advisable to mask windows and doors. Bitumen materials used for DPC's, roofing and so on should also be covered as the chemicals may react with it and cause staining on the brickwork below.

Two other key points where damp can penetrate are round door and window frames, and where flashings are used to seal the junction between a roof and a vertical surface, such as a parapet wall or chimney stack. The best way of sealing joints round frames is to use a non-setting mastic, which can be piped into any gaps between the frames and the masonry from a cartridge (see overleaf); because it remains flexible it can cope with any movement that takes place.

The simplest way of repairing defective flashings is to use a self-adhesive flashing repair tape (see overleaf again). To use this, brush away any loose material from the area, then apply a liberal coat of flashing primer to the surfaces. Allow this to become tacky, then bed in the flashing tape and rub down.

Damp: the trouble spots

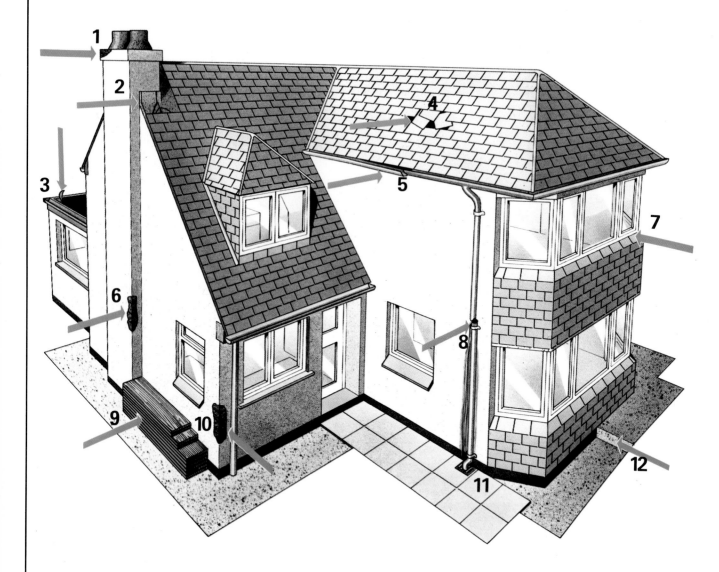

1 If the sloped covering around a chimney stack cracks, water can penetrate the brickwork

2 The join between the roof and the chimney is vulnerable—check the flashing regularly

3 Damaged roofing felt on a flat roof allows damp in and causes the roof timbers to rot

4 The ceiling beneath loose or missing roof tiles quickly becomes saturated with water

5 Broken guttering is the most common cause of penetrating damp at the top of internal walls

6 Rendering should not be allowed to decay, or damp will penetrate and spread through the walls

7 Check that the window frames have not cracked, leaving a gap between the brickwork for damp to get in

8 A broken downpipe allows a lot of water to pour down onto the wall, quickly breaking it down

9 Timber and other objects should not be piled up against the house as they bridge the DPC

10 Water can break down the mortar joints of brickwork, making the inside walls damp

11 A blocked downpipe or drain can cause the gutters to overflow and pour water onto porous walls

12 Make sure that paths are not built higher than the DPC or they will act as a bridge for damp

DRAUGHTPROOFING

● **The causes of draughts** ● **How to check for draughts using a lighted candle or smoking taper** ● **Sealing doors and windows** ● **Using ready-made and improvised door strips for problem draughts** ● **Curing other draughts**

Heat losses caused by draughts are effectively, easily and cheaply eliminated with efficient draughtproofing. Of all the forms of home insulation, draughtproofing brings with it the most quickly noticed improvement in personal comfort—and immediate savings in fuel costs.

Research has shown that up to 15% of all household heat losses are attributable to this persistent and niggling fault. Many other forms of heat insulation—and therefore heating—are largely wasted if draughts are present nearby. The most noticeable problems occur in the main living areas of the home.

In any room, a badly fitting door or window is likely to be the main offender—but less obvious sources of draughts can be significant. A weakly-sprung letter-box flap, cracks in brickwork, and gaps caused by collapsed mortar around door and window frames, or gaps in the exterior weather board of a timber clad house, all contribute to heat loss.

In a centrally-heated home these draughts may not be as noticeable as those in a house with single-room spot heating where draughts combine to produce cold spots. For reasons of economy it makes sense to try and eliminate the problem. In most cases, the job is not too difficult.

A. *A flickering flame indicates the presence of a draught and an unnecessary loss of heat which is easily and cheaply remedied. Use a candle for draught detection only where it is safe to do so. A smoking taper—such as a smouldering shoe lace—ought to be used otherwise*

The causes of draughts

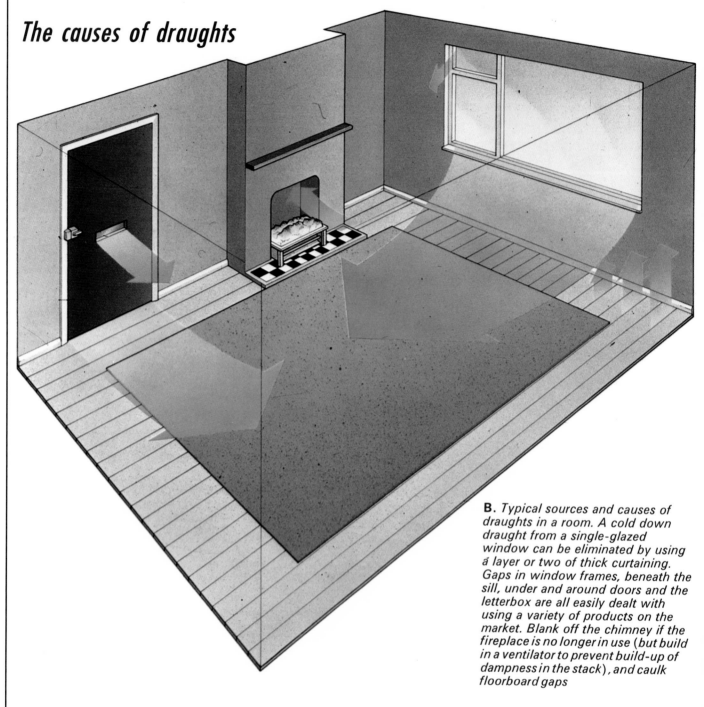

B. *Typical sources and causes of draughts in a room. A cold down draught from a single-glazed window can be eliminated by using a layer or two of thick curtaining. Gaps in window frames, beneath the sill, under and around doors and the letterbox are all easily dealt with using a variety of products on the market. Blank off the chimney if the fireplace is no longer in use (but build in a ventilator to prevent build-up of dampness in the stack), and caulk floorboard gaps*

The causes of draughts
Draughts are mostly the result of air pressure differences within a house but they will also occur wherever there is a large gap to the outside, or between a cold and a heated room such as hall and sitting room.

Convection currents are the main cause of air pressure changes, however slight, and the effect can extend from a single room to a whole house. In a single room a large expanse of cold single-glazed window often gives rise to cold down-draughts (fig. B), even if the whole room is sealed off as a unit. More usually, this cold window down-draught combines with seepage around doors and cracks to make living conditions very uncomfortable.

A greater problem is caused by an open-grate fireplace or, indeed, any fuel-burning appliance with a single chimney flue to the outside. Room air is required for the combustion process. This—and the fact that additional heated air rises up the chimney along with the fumes—creates a partial vacuum in the room which encourages incoming air seepage through gaps around ill-fitting door and window frames.

Locating draughts
If there is any doubt about their whereabouts, the job of locating draughts is best done on a cold and windy day. Use a bare candle flame (away from curtains and other inflammable fittings) to detect the slightest movement of air. If you have one, a smoking taper will give better visual indication and is safer.

C. *A badly-hung or warped door may need extensive work or, in some cases, replacement*

D. *Strip material—here ribbed rubber —is easily fitted and an inexpensive draughtproofing aid*

Hold the candle flame or taper close to suspect areas around windows and door frames, watching carefully to see which way the smoke is drawn. Also, check through-wall fittings and pipework where filling looks to be in need of repair.

If possible, seal each area as you proceed. Work from room to room, taking in the hall and other connecting areas as you go.

When draughtproofing each room do not forget to allow enough ventilation for any fuel-burning appliance that may be in use there. Even if a ventilator grille is provided, this may be positioned badly in relation to the appliance. Consider repositioning the grille closer to the appliance to reduce cold draughts across a room. A ventilator grille can be let into suspended flooring or into a nearby external wall.

Building and safety regulations insist on suitable arrangements for ventilation of fuel-burning appliances and this point must be considered in any project that involves extensive draughtproofing.

Sealing doors and windows
Sealing doors and windows accounts for most of the draughtproofing that is likely to be needed. Though in each case the job can be simple and inexpensive, better looking fittings are available at greater cost.

At the cheapest end of the scale of proprietary draught-excluding products is strip-plastics sponge, attached to a self-adhesive backing and cut to length off a supply reel. With the backing peeled off, the sponge strip can be stuck in place on the cleaned contact surface between a door or window and its frame (fig. D).

Strip-plastics sponge is an effective draughtproofer—providing it is used around the whole frame. However, it does tend to get dirty and tattered, and may disintegrate if exposed to damp and sunshine for any length of time. The wipe-clean surfaced type should last longer but is more expensive.

Perhaps as cheap—and certainly more effective when used in old, warped or rustic frames—is one of the new-generation of mastic-like sealants such as silicone rubber. Squeezed from a tube in a continuous, even length along the contact area between window and frame (fig. E), it acts as a rotproof barrier against moisture and draughts.

Though the sealant is flexible enough to take up the irregularities of the frame and window, it can be removed when required. Allow up to a day for

it to dry completely, although windows can be shut after just a few hours.

Rigid strips of polypropylene, vinyl, phosphor-bronze or aluminium can be used in place of foam strip. Though no more efficient, these sprung, hinge-like strips do last indefinitely and are a better proposition on sash windows (see overleaf) and outside doors.

Cut to length and tacked in place round the door or window rebate the strips are easily fitted. As the door or window is closed the two halves of the 'hinge' close together— one side fixed to the frame, the other sprung against the sash or door.

The plastics types should last as long as their equivalents in metal and are easier to fit, though special aluminium strip is necessary for metal-framed windows. The metal ones have ready-punched fixing holes. All types of hinged strip can cause jamming if fitted to an already tight door and frame, in which case foam strip would be better.

Secondary-sash double-glazing also acts as a fairly efficient draughtproofing aid for windows but ought to be used in conjunction with excluding strip in order to prevent undue condensation build-up when it is fitted.

Mastic can again be used for making good small gaps between a door or window frame and the accompanying brickwork where the filler mortar has crumbled. Cellulose or plaster-based filler is cheaper and usually easier to apply but tends to crack.

Take a particularly close look at the underside of window sills—especially large ones such as those found in some types of bay window—and check for draughty gaps there. Use mastic or filler to seal these (fig. F).

E. *Sealant can be squeezed into the most inaccessible parts of a door or window frame*

F. *Take a close look at the underside of window sills, and use filler to make good any gaps*

G. *To draughtproof sash windows, prise off the staff bead so you can gain access to the vertical channels in which the sashes slide*

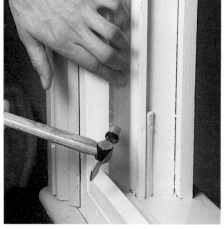

H. *Cut lengths of the draughtproofing material—here sprung bronze strip—to fit the channels, and pin them in place*

I. *You can draughtproof the meeting rail junction by nailing a length of the sprung strip to the inner face of the outer sash meeting rail*

Insulating floors

Bare floorboards may look great, but they can also be a source of strong draughts which you cannot afford to neglect. The tongued-and-grooved types (see pages 113 to 118) are designed to get round the problem but even so, some joins—especially those near the skirting—may need attention. The worst offender is the old, square-edge boarding. Here, even fitted carpet is not always completely successful at excluding draughts.

The best solution is to fill the gaps between the boards with wedge-shaped strips of wood if they are large, or to cover the boards with hardboard or underlay.

To fill large gaps, use a circular saw to cut a number of wedge-shaped strips of softwood from the edge of a new floorboard. Then coat the edges of the

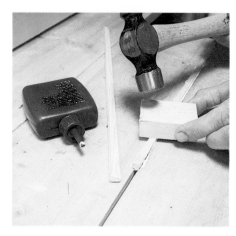

J. *To draughtproof large gaps in floorboards, cut wedge-shaped strips of wood. Coat their edges with woodworking adhesive*

K. *When the adhesive has dried, plane or sand down the strips so they're level with the surface of the surrounding boards*

L. *Draughts can penetrate gaps between skirting boards and the floor. Block these by pinning lengths of slim quadrant beading*

M. *Alternatively, cover the entire floor surface with sheets of hardboard, pinned at regular intervals*

N. *If you're laying carpet, glass fibre underlay helps cut out underfloor draughts. Secure edges and joins with lengths of double-sided tape*

strip with wood-working adhesive and hammer them down into the gaps (fig. J). When the adhesive has set, plane or sand down the strips to leave them flush with the surrounding boards.

Lay hardboard directly over the floorboards and pin it at regular intervals. Secure glass fibre underlay at the edges and any joins with double-sided tape beneath carpets.

If suspended timber flooring is being installed or repaired, or if you have crawl space under the house, you can prevent quite heavy heat losses by insulating between the joists. There are two kinds of insulation you can use for this particular job. Paper-faced glassfibre batts (fig. O) have flanged edges for easy stapling to the joists. Foil-backed batts are rammed between the joists and held in place by wire mesh stapled to the bottoms of the joists. The foil vapour-check barrier must always face upwards.

Timber clad houses
One source of draughts in timber clad houses is the inevitable gaps between the individual planks forming the cladding, and between these materials and door and window frames. These gaps should be filled with a flexible filler—anything rigid will be cracked by movement of the timber. Clean out the old mastic, and wipe the area with a rag soaked in white spirit, turpentine, or other solvent. Mastic is available in disposable cartridges, and is forced into the gap using a cartridge gun (fig. P). Make sure the bead of mastic adheres to both sides of the joint. Very deep or wide gaps may need some packing out first with slivers or offcuts of timber to prevent slumping.

Door strips
There are many types of draught excluder for the gaps under a door.

Strips of inexpensive rubber or plastics draught-excluder about 30mm wide can be screwed or tacked to the lower edge of the door on one or both sides (fig. R). But these tend to wear quickly, especially if positioned too low and hard against floor covering. Position each strip so that the edge just indents, or is bent by, the floor covering against which it rests.

A better long-term proposition is a metal door sill and door seal arrangement (fig. S) fixed to the outside of the door. A weatherproofing shield can be fitted instead of this to protect a sill fixed to the floor (fig. T).

Better for inside the house—and well-suited to sliding doors—is the brushpile type of strip, the bristles of

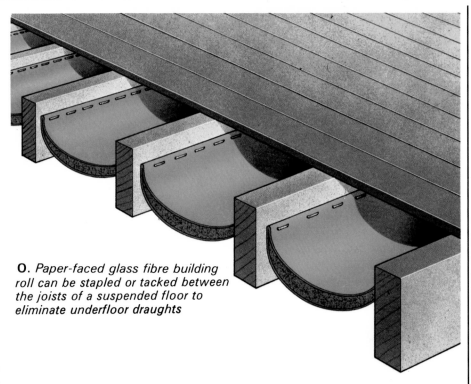

O. *Paper-faced glass fibre building roll can be stapled or tacked between the joists of a suspended floor to eliminate underfloor draughts*

which compress to form a very effective seal (fig. U). This can be used in conjunction with full carpeting in most instances, but is particularly suited to polished wood or tiled floors. When fitting, adjust the strip so that the fibres are very slightly bent when the door is closed.

Another solution is to use a 'rise and fall' excluder, particularly where a hard object—such as a door mat—has to be crossed. In this case, adjustable strip with an angled striking face is kept in place by a hollow moulding attached to the base of the door. In the closed-door position, the strip self-

levels (if it can be arranged, against the mat or carpet being used). As the door is opened the strip is forced upwards as its angled face strikes the floor covering (fig. V).

At the other extreme, a substantial gap of more than 20mm ought to be built up to reduce the eventual gap between the fitting and the base of the door. Threshold strips provide a partial answer, but you may find that these have to be fitted over thin battens to fill the extra space (fig. W). Battening used on its own and covered by carpeting can also act as an excellent seal and this inexpensive idea is well

P. *Gaps between weatherboarding and window frames can be sealed with mastic applied from a gun*

Q. *Draughtproofing the rear of a letterbox using a brushpile screen which is screwed into place*

R. *Draught-excluding strip is easily attached to the door base although plastics types are unlikely to last very long*

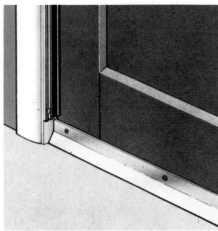

S. *A rubber seal set into a metal frame acts as a heavy-duty draught-excluder that is ideal for using on outer doors*

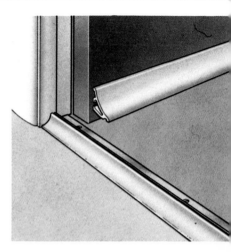

T. *A combination of threshold seal and door-mounted weather shield is the best option for heavy-duty applications*

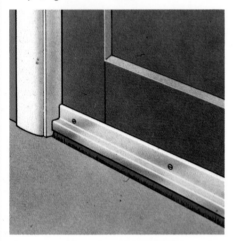

U. *Brushpile strip is easily fitted to the base of a door and is ideal where floors are uneven*

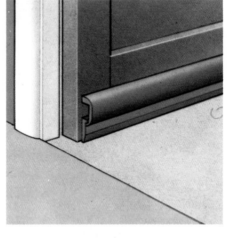

V. *A rise and fall excluder is an ideal draughtproofing aid where floor covering depths alter*

W. *A well-fitted door often needs no more than a threshold bar with its neoprene insert*

worth considering. Use padding in the form of offcuts of carpet to build up either side of the batten before laying the main carpet over (fig. X).

Dealing with other draughts

Make sure the loft trap or attic door is treated in the same way as others using the same methods of draught-proofing—strips of self-adhesive sponge are the cheapest, but any other door or window frame excluder can be used instead. It's important that this seal is efficient, since the amount of ventilation needed to prevent harmful condensation in the roof space can otherwise lead to howling draughts on the landing beneath, and heat loss into the attic itself.

Where downlighters and similar fittings are recessed into bedroom ceilings, fit chipboard boxes over them in the loft to prevent draughts through the opening.

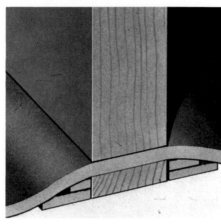

X. *If full carpeting is being laid, gaps under doors can be built up using a suitable thickness of timber batten laid across the threshold and beneath the carpet*

Then there's the letterbox. Here, you can fasten a piece of rubber or old carpet to the inside of the flap. But for a better-looking job, fit a stronger spring and line the slit with foam strip, or exchange the old flap for the new type with brush inserts. Another type fits behind the flap (fig. Q) and is easily screwed into place.

There is one last problem area: air ventilators. These may be fitted high up on outside walls, on the face of bricked-up chimney breasts, even in the floor surface, and can be a notable source of draughts. They should not be covered over permanently, and where they're fitted in rooms containing fuel-burning appliances they should not be covered at all. However, a sliding plastic hit-and-miss cover can be fitted over non-essential ventilators, and can be closed on windy days when draughts are a severe problem.

REPOINTING BRICKWORK

The mortar joints in brickwork protect a wall from the damaging effects of rainwater. So if the mortar shows signs of decay, replace it with fresh mortar to make a new seal

As long as brickwork is correctly designed and well built, it does not require much in the way of maintenance or repair work. But, as a building ages, the mortar joints between the bricks may begin to decay and crumble. Flaking joints in brickwork allow water to penetrate the wall and should never be neglected. The remedy for crumbling joints is repointing—clearing out the old mortar a short way and replacing it with fresh mortar to make a new waterproof seal.

Types of joint
The mortar between bricks can be finished in one of several ways; wherever possible, you should try to match new joints to the existing ones. However, if the old mortar is particularly badly decayed, you may not be able to see what type of joint has been used. In this case it is worthwhile making new weather-struck joints (fig. C).

The horizontal joints of this type have sloped surfaces which are slightly recessed below the upper brick and slightly overhanging the lower one. This slope allows water to run off quickly and prevents it from lodging on the lower edge of the joints, thus giving the wall further protection from rain and moisture. The vertical joints slope from one side to the other and match the angle of the horizontals above and below. Other types of joint commonly used in brickwork include:

Flush joint: When the mortar has almost dried, it is rubbed over with a piece of wood or old sacking to produce a surface flush with the surrounding brickwork (fig. E). This type of pointing looks particularly effective when used in conjunction with smooth-surfaced bricks.

Keyed or round joint: This is produced by running along the surface of the mortar with a semi-circular piece of metal to form a shallow, curved depression (fig. B).

Recessed joint: This is formed by scraping out the freshly-laid mortar to a depth of about 6mm below the brick surface, then smoothing the surface of the remaining mortar with a piece of wood the width of the joint (fig. D). Recessed joints look best on rough-textured bricks but should be used only where they match the existing pointing. If used on external walls in cold climates, the bricks must be hard and durable, otherwise water may collect and freeze on the ledges causing pieces of brick to flake off.

Equipment
For repointing brickwork, even if you are working over quite a small area of wall, you need a spot board on which to mix the mortar and a hawk for carrying the mortar to the work area from the board. For applying the mortar to the joints you need a pointing trowel, which resembles a small bricklayer's trowel, and for clearing out the old mortar use a shave hook with its pointed end cut off square.

If you are constructing weather-struck joints, you also need a *frenchman* for trimming away the excess mortar at the bottom of the horizontal joints. A suitable frenchman can be made from an old kitchen knife. Use a hacksaw to cut off the end of the knife, smooth off any burrs around the cut with a file, then heat the tip and bend it into a right-angle about 12mm from the end.

To guide the frenchman neatly along the joints when trimming, you need a straight-edged piece of timber which is held immediately below the top edge of the lower brick. Attach two pieces of hardboard to each end of the piece of wood so that when it is held against the wall, there is a slight gap allowing the trimmed mortar to fall through (fig. A).

Wherever possible, the mortar that you use for repointing should be mixed to match the composition of the existing mortar. If you do not know the mixing proportions of the original mortar, try using a 1:½:4½ (cement:lime:sand) mix or 1 part of masonry cement to 3 parts of sand. An exception to the rule is the softer type of facing brick, where you should use a weaker 1:1:6 mix.

Use as fine a grade of soft sand as possible, also called builders' or bricklayers' sand.

REPOINTING BRICKWORK

Working considerations

Repointing is generally best undertaken during warm weather as newly laid mortar is easily damaged by frost. However, avoid working in very hot weather, which dries out the mortar.

If you are working on a high wall, set up a platform or suitable scaffolding, so that you are working at chest height. Never be tempted to carry out pointing work standing on a ladder: you will not be able to reach the joints properly and you may fall.

If the area to be pointed is large, tackle the work in stages, finishing off the joints over an area of about 2m² before moving on to the next. Start work at the top left hand corner of the wall and move across and downwards.

Mortar for pointing should be mixed in small batches—enough for say one hour's work—and then used immediately. If you do mix too much, and some begins to dry out and harden before you come to use it, discard it and mix a fresh batch. Do not try to reconstitute hardening mortar by adding more water to it.

Preparing the surface

If there is paving below the wall to be repointed, lay down a large sheet of polythene before you start work to protect the concrete path from stray mortar droppings.

With the protective sheeting in place, gently scrape any lichen and moss from the surface of the brickwork, taking care not to damage the faces of any bricks.

When the brickwork is clean, start raking the joints, using the shave hook or a plugging chisel, to a depth of between 12mm and 20mm—if you clear out the mortar further than this, the wall may be damaged. Rake out the vertical joints—called *perpends*—first and then the horizontal, or *bed*, joints again taking care not to damage the bricks.

Make sure that the recess formed in the joints is absolutely square and that no traces of old mortar remain on the edges of the bricks (fig. 1). If you fail to remove all the old mortar, the fresh mortar will not adhere properly and will soon flake and crumble.

When all the joints in the area to be repointed have been raked out, brush them thoroughly with a stiff scrubbing brush to remove any remaining particles and dust (fig. 2).

In order to prevent too much moisture being absorbed by the surrounding brickwork from the fresh mortar, dampen the wall by flicking

1 To prepare the surface of brickwork for repointing, rake out the joints a short way with an old shave hook

2 Make sure that no traces of old mortar are left at the edges and brush down the joints to remove any remaining dust

3 Dampen the surface of the brickwork with a distemper brush and clean water to make sure that the new mortar will bond

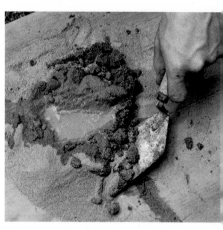

4 Mix up your first batch of mortar taking care not to prepare too much. Try to match the colour of the mix with that of the old mortar

thoroughly clean water over the surface with a distemper brush (fig. 3). However, take care not to use too much water or you will soak the brickwork and the fresh mortar will not adhere properly.

Handling the trowel

Opinions vary on the best way of using a pointing trowel, so it is best to experiment until you find a style that suits you before you start.

You may find that the easiest method is to roll the mortar down the hawk and divide it into 'strands'—as long as the trowel and about 12mm thick. Pick up each strand on the back of the trowel, along one edge, and flick it firmly into the waiting joint.

Weather-struck joints

Although slightly more difficult to construct than other types of brick

joint, weather-struck joints are well worth the extra trouble as they give the wall added protection against water penetration.

To fashion weather-struck joints, start by transferring a manageable amount of mortar from the spot board to the hawk and carry it to the work area. Using the pointing trowel, force some mortar well into the first few perpends. Use the trowel to form a sloping angle by drawing it down the edge of the brick on the right hand side of the joint, then cut off the excess mortar neatly with the edge of the trowel (fig. 7).

Move on to the bed joints above and below the filled perpends. Holding the trowel point upwards, press in more mortar, so that it is recessed to a depth of about 3mm at the top of the gap and slightly overhangs the edge of the brick at the bottom.

5 *Transfer a manageable amount of mortar to the hawk and divide it into strands as long as the trowel and about 12mm thick*

6 *Carry the hawk to the work area and pick up strands of mortar with the back of the pointing trowel. Force the mortar into the joints*

7 *If you are making weather-struck joints, form the sloping angle in the perpends by drawing the trowel down the edge of the brick*

8 *Tuck the mortar into the beds of weather-struck joints so that it is recessed under the top brick and slightly overhangs the lower one*

9 *Trim off the excess mortar at the bottom of the weather-struck joints with a frenchman, then brush the joints to remove waste*

10 *If you are making recessed joints use a shave hook, with its point cut off, to scrape out the freshly laid mortar*

When you have used up the first batch of mortar, make the rough slope already formed in the perpends neater by trimming off any remaining excess with the pointing trowel so the mortar is recessed 3mm on the right hand side.

Next, take the frenchman and straightedge to the wall. Holding the straightedge immediately below the lower edge of the bed joints, run the frenchman along the wall, with its tip pointing downwards, to cut off the excess mortar (fig. A).

When the mortar has begun to harden, rub the joints with a dusting brush to remove any remaining waste then move on to the next section.

Flush and keyed joints

Pointing brickwork with flush joints provides a neat finish and can be particularly useful on old brickwork

where the outer corners of the bricks have crumbled and the wall surface is to be redecorated.

Start as for weather-struck joints by filling perpends then bed joints. Press the mortar firmly into place with the pointing trowel, until it protrudes slightly out from the surface of the brickwork.

When the mortar starts to harden, rub along the joints with a piece of wood or old sacking working in the same direction, until the mortar is flush with the surrounding brickwork (fig. E). When completely dry, scrape over the mortar with a stiff piece of plastic to remove any excess particles of mortar dust.

To form a keyed joint, press the mortar well into the joints with the trowel, then smooth it to shape with a semi-circular piece of metal—an old metal bucket handle or a small piece

of metal piping are ideal for this task. Marginally less efficient is a piece of stout rubber hose. After rubbing the joints, trim the surplus mortar at the edges with the trowel.

Cleaning the brickwork

Although all the joints should be cleaned off as thoroughly as possible during the pointing process, it is difficult to achieve a completely clean finish by this means alone and some mortar will probably be left adhering to the edges of the bricks.

Never try to remove mortar which has been spattered on bricks while it is still wet, or attempt to wash it off with water. Instead, leave the excess mortar to dry out completely then use a stiff scrubbing brush to brush the soiled bricks. Remove large lumps of mortar on clay bricks by scraping with the side of a trowel. With calcium silicate bricks, lightly abrade the surface with a brick of the same colour to remove large pieces.

If marks still remain on the brickwork because the mortar has penetrated the surface, they can be removed with a very dilute solution of hydrochloric acid—1:10 by volume for clay bricks and 1:2 by volume for calcium silicate. Saturate the brickwork with clean water, then apply the solution sparingly with an old paint brush, taking great care not to get any on your skin or in your eyes. When the area has been thoroughly treated, hose down the brickwork to remove every trace. The surface of some types of brick can be affected by acid so, if in doubt, consult the brick manufacturer before embarking on treatment of this kind.

Colouring joints
To produce a matching or decorative effect in finished brickwork vegetable dyes, proprietary colourants and spe-

A. *To trim the excess mortar from the bottom of the weather-struck joints, use a frenchman and draw it along the top edge of a straight length of timber held just below the top edge of the lower brick. Attach a thin block of wood to each end of the timber to let the trimmed mortar fall through the gap. Make a frenchman from an old kitchen knife*

cial coloured cements are all available from builders' merchants and can be added to the mortar mix if desired. But because the colour will be altered by the texture of ordinary sand, you should use white sand in the mix, if possible. Remember also that cement with colour additives requires less water than is normally used.

If you use a vegetable dye, the final colour will be a lighter shade as the colour pales as the mortar dries; experiment first with small measured quantities of mortar and dye and allow them to dry out. When you have obtained the required shade in one of the experimental batches, mix up your first full batch and add the dye in an equal proportion.

If you are repointing part of a wall and want the colour of the fresh mortar to match that in the existing joints, rub the joints around the area with candlewax to prevent them from absorbing the colouring in the new mortar mixture.

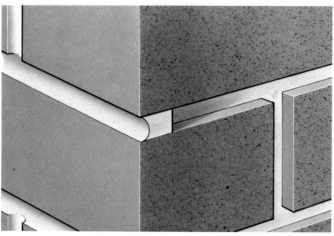

B. *Keyed joints are formed by smoothing the surface of the mortar with a rounded piece of metal*

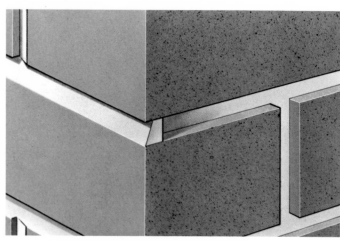

C. *The slope of weather-struck joints allows water to run off quickly, protecting the wall from rain*

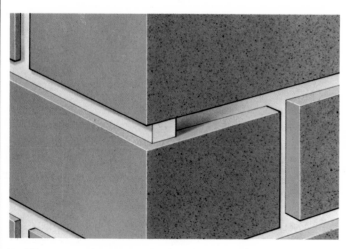

D. *The mortar in recessed joints is scraped out to a depth of about 6mm below the brick surface*

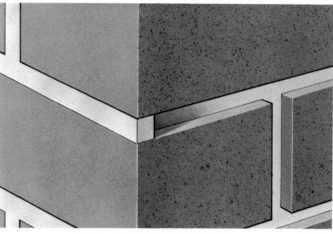

E. *Flush joints are produced by rubbing the mortar with a piece of wood to form a smooth surface*

REPLACING GLASS

Reglazing is an occasional household maintenance job that you can easily do yourself if the need ever arises. And with the number of decorative forms of sheet glass available, it is a novel way of changing appearances

Apart from the danger of exposed broken glass, a smashed window in the home is an open invitation to an intruder. You can reduce both risks by reglazing the window yourself. The job requires care but is straightforward and quick.

If you are reglazing a downstairs window it should not be necessary to remove the window from its frame. But if the window is upstairs, you need an extension ladder to reach the outside of the window. In this case, the job will take longer and you may find it more convenient to take the window out of its frame and reglaze it on a workbench at ground level.

A hinged sash can be removed from its window frame by unscrewing the hinges. Use an old knife to scrape out paint from the screw heads. To remove a sash from a double-hung window means removing woodwork, so in the case of an upstairs window, it may be better to work from a ladder.

If you decide to work from the ladder, secure it at the top by looping a safety rope through the rungs and around a suitable anchor point. Additionally, make sure the feet of the ladder are well anchored.

A useful tip is to wear an apron or workman's overall which has large tool pockets so that you can carry everything likely to be needed for the job. This will save countless trips up and down the ladder during the course of the installation.

Removing old glass
Take particular care when you are removing old glass from its frame. Always use heavy-duty (leather) gloves to pull out loose pieces (fig. 1).

Uncracked sections and stubborn slivers must be smashed out with a hammer. But before you do this, cover both sides of the glass with thick cloth or blanket to prevent chips flying through the air. For additional safety, wear safety goggles or old sunglasses at all times.

If you have removed the window from the main frame, cover it and lay it on several sheets of newspaper

Left: *It is sensible to replace the glass of a broken ground-floor window as soon as possible to deter would-be intruders. Choose replacement glass from the many decorative and strengthened types now available.*

REPLACING GLASS

Below: *Cross-section showing the normal method of glazing with putty. Triangular-shaped nails called sprigs are used to hold the pane in place against the back putty. These are then covered by more putty*

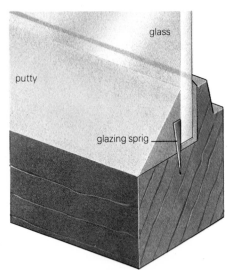

glass

putty

glazing sprig

Below: *Wooden beading can be used in place of the set of sprigs. This results in a neater looking finished job which many prefer to the more common putty glazing method where greater skill is required*

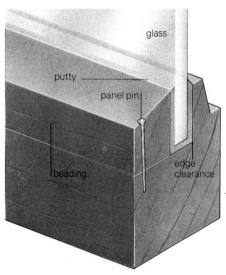

glass

putty

panel pin

beading

edge clearance

1 *Carefully work loose the large fragments of glass, then tap out the smaller pieces. Wear heavy-duty gloves when handling the glass*

2 *Use an old chisel or a hacking knife to remove hardened putty. Be especially careful of slivers of glass that may be embedded in this*

before you knock out the glass. This will make it easier to gather up the splinters afterwards.

After you have hammered out the glass, carefully remove the covering cloth and work loose fragments left in the frame. You should be able to prise out the glass quite easily, but if the putty is very old and hard and the glass refuses to be pulled out, cover the window with a cloth again and smash the fragments down to the level of the putty. Then, wearing eye protection, use a hammer and chisel to knock out the remaining putty with the glass embedded in it.

The old putty can be removed with a *hacking knife*—a tool specifically designed for this job—but a chisel will do the job nearly as well. Make sure that the chisel is an old one, well past its useful life, as it will become quite blunt when used in this way. Remove all the putty, including the *back* or *bedding layer* and take care not to damage the wood with whatever tools you use (fig. 2).

Measuring up the pane

When measuring up for the new pane of glass, always take the measurements twice: a mistake of only a few millimetres can make the pane unusable. Also, measure each opening within the main frame separately as small size differences between any two can go unnoticed until it comes to reglazing.

When you have determined the final height and width measurements, subtract about 3mm from each to allow

sufficient clearance in the frame—increase this to 6mm in the case of slightly warped frames.

When giving measurements to the glass merchant, it is customary to give the height before the width. This way, if you are buying frosted or patterned glass, the pattern will be the correct way up (vertical) when you install it.

The glass

Glass is now graded by thickness in millimetres—it was formerly graded by weight per square foot—and for most applications 4mm is adequate, although 3mm is sufficient for smaller windows. *Float glass* is now the most commonly used for general purpose work but cheaper *horticultural glass* may be used where viewing distortion is no problem—such as in a greenhouse.

For help and advice on the choice and safe use of glass, do not be afraid to consult your local glass supplier. Several types of glass can be used around the house and it is important to use a strengthened form where there is risk of breakage. For example, in the UK the Building Regulations state that only toughened or laminated glass should be used for balustrades which protect a difference in floor levels or which are used for shower screens.

Wired and laminated glass must also be used for floor-level windows, and those near to stairs (such as in a hall) can also benefit from these types.

A wide variety of decorative glass is available in addition to standard

frosted patterns; using these in place of clear glass for extra privacy is well worth considering.

Before you install the glass, place and check it for fit in the frame and, if necessary, get the supplier to make small adjustments. You can sometimes accommodate very small irregularities by turning the sheet upside down or around in relation to the frame and then trying it again.

Using putty

Putty needs to be of the right consistency if it is to hold the glass in place and form a watertight seal. And when first taken from the tin it is inclined to be too wet, rather sticky

3 Take particular care to clean out the upper rebate in a vertical sash window, but beware of glass slivers stuck in old putty here

4 Apply small nodules to the frame rebate so that sufficient back putty depth results. Use your thumb to force putty home

5 Push the replacement pane into position but apply pressure at the edges only. The back putty seal should be even and unbroken

6 Use a hammer or old chisel to tap the glazing sprigs home and slide the head along the glass to avoid cracking the pane

7 Trim off the back putty by a straight cut with the putty knife. Then apply the facing putty and smooth this down to finish

8 When the putty has matured, four weeks or so afterwards, it must be painted over to protect it from the weather

and consequently difficult to handle. Knead it gently between the palms of your hands or place it between folds of clean paper to remove excess moisture and oil.

There are two types of putty: linseed oil putty for wooden-framed windows, and metal casement putty for use with metal frames. The latter should also be used as a bedding seal if metal-framed glass—such as insulating glass —is fixed into a wooden frame. In this case, linseed oil putty is used to finish off the outside seal.

Nowadays, a glazing compound is widely used instead of putty—you apply it to the window frame in much the same way.

Installing the glass

Once you have checked the glass for fit, lay a strip of back (bedding) putty around the window frame (fig. 4). Where hacking off the old putty has exposed areas of bare wood, prime these and let them dry before you apply putty over them. Use your thumb to smear the nodules of putty around the insides of the rebates.

Place the glass in the frame and push it gently but firmly against the bedding putty. Push around the outside of the frame—not the middle—with a pad of cloth to protect you against any slivers of old glass left in the frame. As you do this, the putty will ooze out on the other side.

The bedding putty is necessary not only for providing a good watertight seal, but because it also takes up small irregularities in the trueness of the backing frame. A final depth of up to about 5mm is recommended, and you can ensure an even depth around the frame by locating small wooden spacers such as match wood.

The sheet of glass must be centred within the frame—you should already have had it cut to measurements slightly smaller than the frame's inner dimensions. The best way of doing this is to stick matchsticks between the glass edge and frame at odd points around the window; or use folds of thin wood or card to build up greater depths. Spacers should not be necessary if you can work on the window flat.

When the sheet of glass is properly bedded, by which time it should remain in position by itself, secure the glass on each side of the frame by tapping home a couple of *glazing sprigs* (fig. 6) These are small, headless nails, buried by the face putty when the glazing is completed. On larger windows, use more sprigs at 150mm spacings around the frame. Start with the bottom edge and then deal with the top and side edges.

To avoid breaking the glass, if you choose a hammer, hold the sprig next to the glass and then slide the hammer head along the glass to tap the sprig

down and below the level of the facing putty later added. Never lift the hammer from the glass surface, nor try to force a sprig home.

When this is done, you can apply the final (facing) putty. Start where you like and feed in little nodules of putty as you proceed around the edge, using the heel of your hand to press it fully home. The finished height of the facing putty must be no higher than the inside level of the frame, and therefore not visible from inside.

Finish the job by trimming off waste putty with a putty knife. Hold the flat edge against the pane of glass and run the knife along the edge of putty, pressing firmly downwards as you go

(fig. 7). If the knife sticks, wet the blade with water. Should the putty become unstuck as you drag the knife over it, push it back in firmly and continue trimming with the knife.

Finally, trim off the putty that has oozed out at the back of the glass level with the frame. When trimming be careful of small splinters which may still be left in the putty.

Wooden beading
Some windows use wooden beading in place of facing putty (fig. 11) and you can usually use this again when you set the new pane. Remove the side beading first—because it is longer and therefore more flexible—by bowing the ends towards you.

Then remove the small fixing nails afterwards by pulling them right through the beading—do not try to knock them back through the beading as this may split the wood. When you have removed all the nails, clean the beading with a medium grade of glass-paper. Any old putty on the back must be removed, as must the jagged edge left by the broken paint line where the bead joins the frame.

If the old beading is damaged and needs replacing, ask your supplier for *staff beading* in the length required. It is normally available in two sizes, so take along a piece of the old beading.

The mitred joints at the ends of glazing beads are most easily cut on a mitre block. If you do not have one, lay the new length beside the old one and use the latter as a cutting guide. It helps if both are taped or clamped together before cutting.

Beading is positioned as the sheet of glass is pushed home on the bedding putty. Fix the shorter (top and bottom) lengths first, using nails at 100mm intervals (fig. 12). For a really professional finish, punch in the glazing pins first so that the heads will not be visible when the beading itself is later decorated.

Use the point of a putty knife to remove bedding putty that has oozed out of the back and sides.

Decorating
Leave the freshly-bedded putty to mature for about four weeks before you paint it. But do not delay this final job for too long or the putty will shrink and crack, causing all sorts of problems later. When painting, carry the paint layer just beyond the edges of the putty and on to the glass in order to provide a better waterproof seal. Allow for this overlap when gauging the depth of putty required.

9 *For a beaded window, start by carefully levering off the wooden beading, especially if this is to be re-used for re-glazing*

10 *Much the same procedure is used as far as glass and putty removal is concerned. After making good, apply the bedding putty*

11 *Push the glass home against the bedding putty. Apply a small amount to the front glass and the nearby framework*

12 *Seat the wooden beading on this bedding seal and use small nails to fix the beading tight in place. Trim excess putty*

SOUNDPROOFING

● The two different types of noise ● How to identify impact and airborne noise from above and below ● Improving window and door insulation ● Reducing noise transmission in suspended and solid floors and walls

A. *If you live close to a main road, a railway line or airport, or if you suffer from noisy neighbours, the level of intrusive noise in your home may become intolerably high. Fortunately there is usually a way to bring the noise level down*

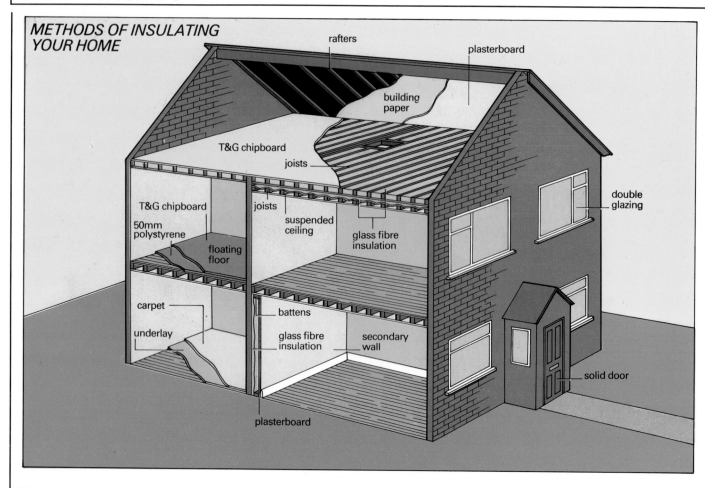

METHODS OF INSULATING YOUR HOME

rafters

plasterboard

building paper

T&G chipboard

joists

double glazing

T&G chipboard

joists

50mm polystyrene

suspended ceiling

glass fibre insulation

floating floor

carpet

battens

underlay

glass fibre insulation

secondary wall

solid door

plasterboard

Noisy neighbourhoods, and noisy houses, are an increasingly common cause for complaint in urban areas; even if you have the most considerate neighbours, intrusive noise is often intolerably high. Fortunately, there are a number of steps you can take to insulate your home effectively and efficiently against noises from within and without.

Much will depend upon whether your house has been built to take account of persistent local noise levels, and whether it has been designed to isolate noisy rooms from quiet ones. Indeed, a great deal hinges on the type of house you live in and on the type of noise concerned. But whatever the problem, there are ways of insulating your house which should bring the amount of noise down to acceptable levels—even though you may not be able to soundproof it completely.

The nature and types of noise

Sound is produced by the creation of variable waves in the substances through which it passes. These waves can pass through gases, liquids or solid materials and the sound you hear is determined by their nature; that is, by their frequency and intensity. When the frequency is fast, we hear high-pitched noises; when it is slow we hear low-pitched noises. Most

B. Above: *These are just some of the ways in which you can improve the level of sound insulation in your home, against both impact noise from indoors and outside airborne noise*

people can detect a wide range of frequencies—between 62 and 16,000 cycles per second—though this faculty will vary from person to person.

Noise level (or volume) is measured in *decibels* (dB). Decibels are points on a logarithmic scale which record the volume of noise produced in different situations. The higher the decibel reading, the louder the noise. But because the scale is logarithmic, doubling the volume of noise does not double the decibel reading—it only increases the decibels by about three.

Consequently, the difference between 60 decibels and 90 decibels is quite enormous; an appropriate comparison would be between the noise from a television in a living room (60dB), and heavy urban traffic at a distance of 5m (90dB). Conversely, halving the volume of noise reduces the decibel level by three points. The efficiency of insulation against sound is measured by the amount that it *reduces* the decibel level of any given sound.

C. Below: *Double glazing is a popular solution for cutting down airborne noise through windows. It must remain shut to be effective, so extra ventilation might be needed*

The degree to which a noise is annoying is dependent on a variety of factors. In certain circumstances, the ticking of the watch on your wrist (approximately 30dB) will be annoying, while in others the background noise of a television may not be. Much depends on your activity, the position and structure of your house, and the susceptibility of different people to certain types of noise.

Most importantly, you have to consider the source of the noise and this means understanding how the noise is reaching you. In this respect, it is important to bear in mind that sound travels into your home in two ways: through the air, when it is called 'airborne noise'; and through solid objects, when it becomes known as 'impact noise'. Bangs, thumps, footsteps and vibrations cause impact noise, but this in turn can create reverberations which produce airborne noise. Impact noises travel far faster and further in solid, dense objects while ironically, such objects are particularly effective in cutting out the passage of airborne noise.

Noise can come from outside the house–or from one part of the house to another–by both forms; that is, as both impact and airborne noise. Controlling and restricting the level of noise therefore means identifying its various sources and to do this it is essential that you understand how the sound travels into, or around, your home.

Airborne noise

Airborne noises are the most common invasion of your privacy and your moments of relaxation, but luckily they are also the easiest to deal with. They can range from aircraft and traffic noise, to the hi-fi system of the people in the house opposite, to the noise of children playing in the street outside.

Though levels of airborne noise are determined by a number of factors–your distance from its source, the sound absorbancy of the surrounding terrain, the position of natural 'screens' (trees, buildings, walls), these will probably be outside your control. In the end your last line of defence against airborne noise is to insulate your house against it.

Airborne noises from the outside will enter buildings through the weakest links; windows, doors and ventilators providing the easiest access. Consequently, the sound level close to the window will be mainly determined by the insulation value of the glazing. However, the average noise level in the room–which is what is important to the occupants–will be determined by the wall and window in combination. In this respect, the net insulation value of the room is always closer to that of the window than of the wall and so in

D. *When planning soundproofing you have to identify different noise sources; airborne–from cars and planes, and impact–from footsteps*

E. *If exterior doors do not fit well, you will suffer from high noise levels. The solution is to fit seals or build a separate porch*

general, the larger the window, the lower the insulation value (fig. C).

Because of its high density, even thin glass gives insulation ranging from 23dB for 3mm glass, up to 34dB for 25mm glass. But ill-fitting frames reduce these insulation values enormously. Firstly, then, check the seals on casement windows. On sliding sash windows, make sure that the tolerance between the sash and the frame is not wider than it need be. If necessary, glue and pin extra timber

strips to the frame side of the sashes to form a better seal.

On casement windows, overpainting of the edges will damage the effect of the seal because the paint builds up and prevents the frame from closing properly. If this is the case, scrape or burn off the excess paint before priming and painting both closing edges. When the paint has dried, fit one of the many types of seals that are currently available.

Seals which have been developed to

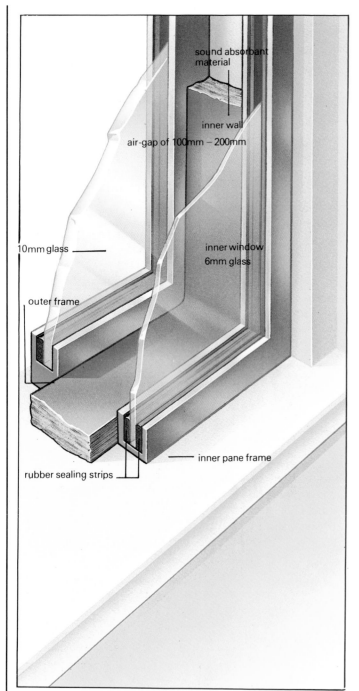

sound absorbant material

inner wall

air-gap of 100mm – 200mm

10mm glass

inner window 6mm glass

outer frame

inner pane frame

rubber sealing strips

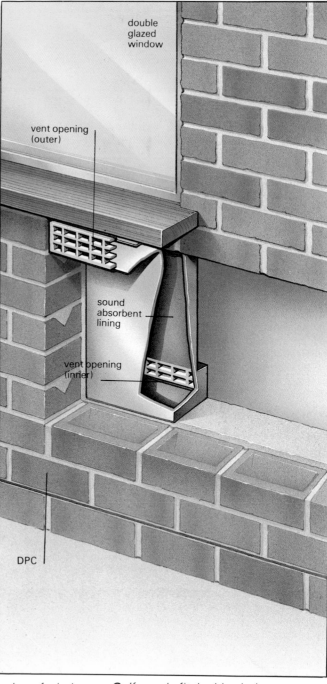

double glazed window

vent opening (outer)

sound absorbent lining

vent opening (inner)

DPC

save heat from escaping are useful in this respect because you can make them serve a dual purpose. Wherever possible, use compression seals, rather than brush seals, because they are more effective. Before doing so, however, make sure that the casement is capable of exerting the necessary compressing force: often only metal frames are sturdy enough to seal a compression joint.

Despite the density of glass, and the use of seals, the insulation value of a window is likely to be low unless it is double-glazed. However, while two thin sheets of glass, separated by a gap of less than 50mm, may be an efficient heat

F. *The best way to soundproof windows is to fit double glazing – in which case the air gap should be at least 100mm, with the outer pane thicker than the inner one*

insulator, such an arrangement may let in more noise than a heavy single pane of glass. This is because if both panes are of an equal thickness, they tend to produce a 'coincidence loss' for noises of a particular frequency. This will be heard as a 'hiss' on the inside. Therefore, where the width of the air-gap is limited to less than 100mm for practical reasons, use different weights of glass. With a gap of 50-80mm, and panes of different thicknesses, double

G. *If you do fit double glazing, you must consider ventilation. One way is to fit a staggered vent, lined with soundproofed material*

glazing gives an improvement of some 3-4dB over the same weight of a single pane of glass.

For sound insulation of greater efficiency, use a much wider gap between panes than you would for insulation against heat-loss – if possible as much as 200mm – and stick strips of absorbent lining in the reveals between the panes. Carpet strips, mineral-fibre board, or strips of foam plastic are sufficient to

H. *Loadbearing glass blocks make good sound insulators because of their thickness; but merely fitting thicker standard glass would have some benefit*

reduce noise escaping into the reveals or around the frames (fig. F). A single-glazed and well-sealed 4mm glass window is likely to have a sound insulation of about 22dB, whereas the value of a double-glazed unit – using 10mm glass in the external pane, a 200mm well-lined air-space, and 6mm glass in the internal pane – is likely to be in the region of 44dB.

You can improve the sound insulation of existing windows by installing secondary glazing behind them. Give the existing windows good seals first, particularly at the edges of opening casements and top ventilators. This may improve the insulation by as much as 10dB immediately. Use sliding panes as the secondary glazing, placing the frame at least 150mm behind the existing pane of glass.

Using heavy, lined curtains could improve the sound insulation still further, though give some thought to the loss of ventilation which this might

entail. Short periods of 'noisy' ventilation may be feasible, but if they are not, a ventilation gap beneath the window with staggered openings will baffle direct sound transmission; line the ventilation gap with absorbent material (fig. G).

Improving door insulation

Like windows, doors break the insulation qualities of solid brick walls, which are normally quite efficient. And because few doors are well-sealed, the insulation value of a wall can be as much as halved by the sound entering via the gaps around them. Your first concern is to make sure that the doors fit as well as possible. Where a door is warped or the frame is out of alignment, make this good.

Fitting seals around the edges of the doors can improve their insulation value by as much as 5dB immediately. The best seals, but also the most expensive, are the magnetic type used on refrigerators. Fit them into the rebate on the door frame to protect them and to form an unobtrusive and effective seal.

The threshold is the most difficult part of the door to seal and here you should use the type of threshold seal which has a raised bar containing a rounded, resilient

strip. Make quite sure that the bar is accurately aligned with the bottom of the door and that it is in contact with the complete length of the bottom rail. This will make the door more difficult to open and close, but will greatly improve the sound and heat insulation.

In particularly bad cases of traffic noise, or other persistent noises from outside, a good solution is to install an extra door by building a porch.

If necessary, or desirable, use sound-absorbent covering on the ceiling or walls of the lobby to form a sound lock. Alternatively, increase the sheer weight of the front door by lining it on the inside or changing the door for a heavier one.

Wall insulation

Many party walls are only of a single-brick thickness, and often a partition wall within a house is constructed only of timber and plasterboard. Because the weight of such walls is relatively light, airborne sound can easily pass through.

There are two things you can do to improve the insulation of such walls. The first is the most obvious method, but often the least practical: simply increase the weight of the wall itself by adding an extra leaf of brickwork. The increased solidity prevents the passage of significant amounts of airborne noise but the feasibility of such a step depends on the layout of your house and on whether it is possible to support the extra weight; certainly you should never build such a wall without adequate foundations. And although this method reduces the transmission of airborne noise, it will not reduce impact noise at all. You will still clearly hear banging of any sort from the other side (see below).

An alternative method for reducing airborne noise transmission, and which also reduces impact noise, involves constructing a false wall which conceals an insulating glass wool blanket. Along the ceiling, about 100mm from the noisy party wall, nail a 100mm timber lath parallel to the line of the wall. Hang a 75mm glass wool blanket from the lath by sandwiching the blanket between the timber and a strip of hardboard screwed or pinned along the length of the timber (fig. K). Make sure that the blanket hangs from the ceiling to the floor, without resting on the floor itself or touching the wall; this slight air gap all round is most important. On the inside of the room, erect a stud partition frame and clad the frame with two layers of plasterboard. When this has been done, finish the wall as you would any normal partition wall.

Use a similar method for insulating internal stud partition walls, and improve the insulation qualities of the wall surface still further by adding polystyrene sheets behind the sheet panels. Stagger the joints of the layers to avoid undue settlement and cracking (fig. K). In both these cases, the system works because of the interaction of air-space and sound absorbers.

As when double-glazing, use surfaces of different weights on either side of the wall wherever possible to reduce the risk of 'coincidence loss' by vibration. For the same reason, fit soft felt between the vertical wall and the top and bottom horizontal runners.

Noises from above and below

Noises from the room or flat above may be of both the impact and airborne type, but you will be unable to reduce their level simply by fitting acoustic tiles to the ceiling. Acoustic tiles are sound-absorbent; that is, they will only absorb the sounds created within the room itself. Likewise, soft furnishings, heavy curtains, and thick carpets will absorb – rather than reflect – noise.

Thick carpets, with heavy felt under-lays, prevent some impact noise from travelling through floors and ceilings into the room below, but are unlikely to improve the average insulation quality to any great extent. Other methods need to be employed, and much will depend upon the nature of the dividing floor. If you own a flat, you will need the co-operation of your neighbours to reduce the noise level from above effectively.

Suspended floors

Noise travels easily through normal suspended floors into the room below. Most annoying is the intrusion of impact noise from footsteps, furniture, and machines in the rooms above. Where the noises are not excessive, but are nevertheless annoying or distracting, one measure is to lay a 50mm layer of dry sand underneath the floorboards of the room above.

To do this, you must first make sure that the ceiling lining is capable of bearing the weight of the sand (or *pugging*, as it is known) and, if necessary, strengthen it by nailing the lining more firmly to the floor joists from below. To lay the pugging, you do of course have to remove all of the upstairs floorboards to gain full access. Afterwards, spread the sand evenly between the joists, including the narrow gaps at the edges. Pugging alone can improve the insulation properties of the floor by as much as 10dB – a significant amount.

With the floorboards removed and the pugging laid, you can now take the opportunity to restrict the passage of further airborne noise. Level the floor joists and remove any remaining nails.

I. *To insulate a suspended floor, raise the floorboards and lay dry 'pugging' sand between the joists. Then refit the boards over a glass fibre blanket*

21mm tongued and grooved boards or 19mm chipboard

glass fibre blanket

battens to create air gap

plaster

skirting board

air gap

50mm of dry 'pugging' sand

floor joists

Then lay a resilient quilt of glass fibre wool or mineral wool loosely over the top of the joists and overlapping up the edges of the adjacent walls. Select the first floorboards or sections of chipboard flooring and, on the undersides, mark the mid-points between the floorjoists. At these midpoints, nail or screw timber battens which will hold the quilt away from the flooring to provide an air gap. This is shown in fig. 1 and on page 190.

At the same time, the battens will allow you to cramp the floorboards together, because the object is to create a floating floor separate from the main structure. Therefore, do not nail the floorboards to the joists; any connection between the floor and the room below will enable impact noise to travel downwards.

Instead, cramp the floorboards together and fix them to the battens. Fix three or four boards together at a time. In this way the floor will be separate from the floor joists and 'float' on the resilient quilt. At the wall ends of the boards, draw the quilt up against the walls' surface where it will be covered by the replaced skirting boards. Fix these directly to the walls once the floor is laid, but leave a gap between the floor and the skirting boards to avoid creating a sound bridge into the room (fig. I). Such a method can improve the insulation of a normal suspended floor from about 35dB to as much as 50dB, so considerably reducing impact noise.

Solid floors

Most complaints about noise concern the transmission of sound from the room or flat above. This is especially the case in large blocks of flats, though if these were constructed properly, complaints need not arise. The problem is caused almost entirely by impact noise, which is transmitted easily through the solid floors, and is flanked by noise travelling through the concrete and into the adjacent walls. Virtually no airborne noise is involved.

A thick carpet, with two or three layers of thick foam underlay will improve the sound insulation greatly; but the best solution is to construct a floating floor, free from the structure through which the sound travels. The principle is much the same as the one used for suspended floors.

Again, it is essential that no solid connections exist between the floor surface and the building structure. Construct the floating floor by spreading a layer of expanded polystyrene, glass wool or mineral wool over the floor and constructing a timber raft above it. Remove the skirting boards first, then lay the blanket over the entire floor area. Lay 75mm × 50mm timber battens on top of the quilt at 50mm centres, but do not secure them to the floor.

Nail or screw 21mm tongued-and-grooved floorboards or 19mm chipboard to the battens. Take particular care at the wall edges; here, you should leave a gap between the floor and the walls so that any noises are not passed into the wall. Make sure that the skirting boards are separate from the floor so that they do not act as a sound bridge. Fix them directly to the wall with a slight gap between the floor and the skirtings.

An alternative method is to apply sound-damping flooring supports to the

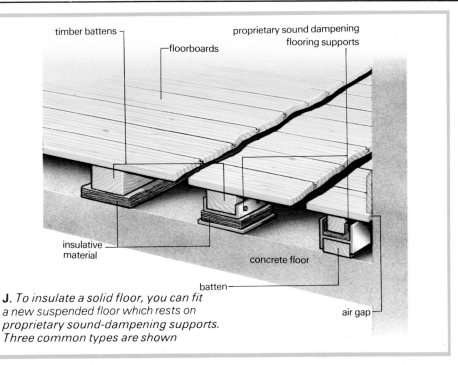

J. *To insulate a solid floor, you can fit a new suspended floor which rests on proprietary sound-dampening supports. Three common types are shown*

floor itself, so that the battens can be fixed to them. Such supports are available in a variety of designs, some of which rest on the floor and some which need to be embedded into the floor itself (fig. J). For the latter type, mark out the positions for the supports, then drill holes in the floor to accommodate the lugs. Fill the holes with mortar and push the lugs home. The battens then rest inside the support brackets (fig. J).

Noises are often caused by vibration of ventilation ducts, water pipes, machines and boilers. The most obvious answer is to avoid such a possibility at the planning stage by isolating potentially noisy machinery—but this is not always possible. An alternative solution is to pack pipes or ducts in an elastic or flexible material, such as fire-retardant glass fibre wool, or give flexible support to any solid connections through which the vibrations are transmitted. Rubber mountings inside brackets help reduce such noise transmission, and contribute to the general noise insulation.

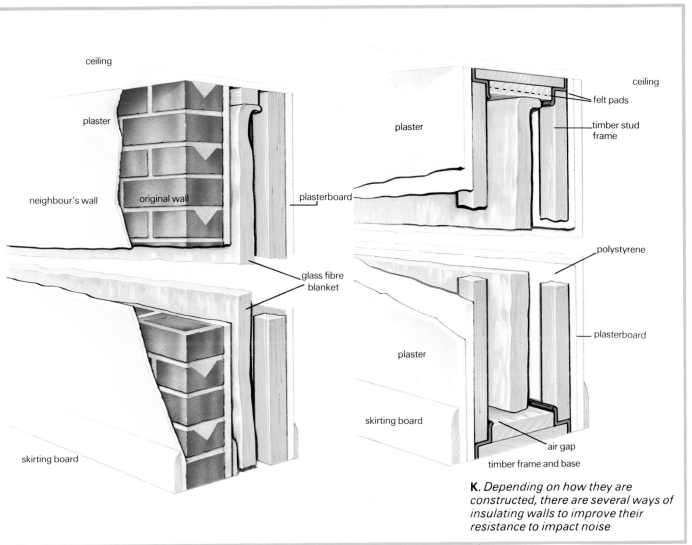

K. *Depending on how they are constructed, there are several ways of insulating walls to improve their resistance to impact noise*

1 Lay glass fibre or mineral wool blanket insulation in the loft to help absorb airborne noise entering through the roof

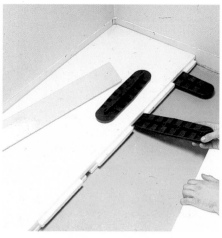

2 Absorb impact noise on floors by laying special clip-together polystyrene slabs. Remove the skirting boards first of all

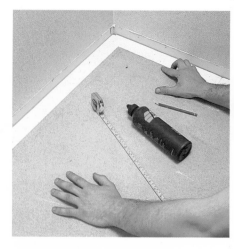

3 Cover the polystyrene with a layer of flooring-grade chipboard, laid so it just clears the walls all round. The skirting boards will cover the gap

4 Another solution, ideal for timber upstairs floors, is to lay sand pugging and add a floating floor. Start by prising up the floorboards

5 Get a professional to check that the ceiling can take the weight. Then pour in the sand and level it 50mm thick with a notched spreader

6 Next, lay glass fibre insulation blanket across the joists, and sandwich it against the wall with a board until you re-lay the floor

7 Use timber battens to secure the boards together in panels three or four boards wide. Make sure there are no gaps between the boards

8 Lay each group of boards over the fibre blanket, butting the panels tightly up against one another and leaving a gap all round the edge

9 Complete the job by replacing all the skirting boards to hide the perimeter gap, and trim away any excess insulation with a sharp knife

BRICKWORK REPAIRS

Left: *All the tools necessary to complete the repairs to any building with cracked brickwork*

Cracked brickwork is unsightly, even dangerous and if neglected, will deteriorate further. Routine inspection and maintenance can stop the rot before it becomes expensive

Despite its importance, the brickwork of a house needs relatively little maintenance to keep it in good order. But as a result, it is often neglected to the point where it ceases to do its job properly. Under these circumstances, penetrating damp and a shabby-looking exterior are often the result.

Loose and crumbling bricks, minor cracks, bad pointing, and plant growth are all defects which can easily be tackled with a small investment of time and effort. And although you will not be able to repair more serious cracking until the cause has been put right, monitoring the damage will give you an idea of where the source lies.

Settlement
The most serious cause of damage to brickwork, settlement, occurs when the material surrounding the foundation of a building moves. For example, where earth under the building breaks up and shifts, support for the weight above disappears and causes the unsupported parts to drop. The result is cracks in the brickwork and internal structure which vary in size according to the problem.

Among the many causes of settlement, mine workings below the building can result in underground subsidence which is eventually transferred to the surface. Settlement often occurs when houses are built on rubbish tips which have not been allowed to settle and decay properly. Tree roots close to the building can severely disturb the foundations. And clay soil can shift considerably, depending on whether it is wet or dry.

Testing for subsidence
Before dealing with cracks, either around window or door frames or on outside walls, find out whether the movement which has caused them has ceased. On very small cracks this is not really necessary.

Glue a small square or slide of glass across the widest part of the open crack to check if the ground is still moving. Using a rigidly setting adhesive such as an epoxy resin, secure the square on both sides and at each corner. Glass has very little tensile strength, and any movement, however slight, in the wall will cause the slide to crack. Alternatively, you can fill the crack with plaster of Paris; this also cracks very easily. You must continue to monitor the test for at least three months. If there is no cracking in this time you can assume earth movement has ceased.

If the settlement proves to be persistent you must have the foundation underpinned; this is a difficult and expensive job and is best left to the professional who will be able to guarantee his work.

Cracks around doors and windows are not usually attributable to a fundamental subsidence. More often the damage results from distortion in the actual door or window frame. This is very common in new houses where new wood may shrink as it dries changing the shape of the frame as it does so. The simple remedy is to fill

Below: *Soil movement on settlement will cause cracks to occur in the brickwork above*

the cracks with an outdoor flexible mastic, which does not set hard like mortar or filler and so is able to cope better with subsequent expansion or contraction of the frames.

The porous nature of bricks

Some of the clay bricks used in building are soft and porous, and may crack or flake as a result of freeze/thaw cycles. In a wet autumn, bricks, especially unfinished ones, tend to become saturated; and when the temperature falls, the water freezes and expands, cracking the bricks.

The symptoms of frost damage are, typically, pock marks and flaking of the surface of the brick face. Where damage is not too extensive you can paint the bricks with several coats of clear silicone fluid, which repels the water, binds the substance of the brick, and so minimizes the damage. Where the bricks are badly cracked, however, you must replace them.

Replacing damaged bricks

To replace damaged bricks all you need in the way of tools are a plugging (pointed end) chisel, a club hammer and a pair of safety goggles to protect your eyes from flying masonry chips.

To start with, chip away all the surrounding mortar from one of the damaged bricks. Then use the chisel to break up the brick and remove it piece by piece. To dislodge subsequent damaged bricks hammer the chisel along the mortar joints, and, in the case of double-thickness walls, chisel off the outside half of bricks laid across the wall (fig. 2).

On cavity walls you must take great care to ensure that no debris falls down into the cavity, because this can

1 *A fairly typical example of some cracked brickwork. In this case the weight of the window sill has helped develop the fault*

2 *To extract the first brick, start by chipping out all the old mortar from around the brick with a plugging or cold chisel*

3 *Run the chisel along each side of the brick doing your best to work the brick free and clear out the mortar*

4 *Use a bolster (bricklayer's) chisel to break up the brick for easy removal. Make sure no debris falls into a cavity wall*

5 *Once the bricks, or brick pieces, have been completely loosened, they can easily be extracted from place with the bolster*

6 *When the first brick has been removed the remaining bricks in the jigsaw can be extracted with relatively little chipping away*

cause a moisture bridge between the two walls above the DPC.

Once all the loose brickwork has been removed sweep the hole with a wire brush to clean the new surface to which you will apply mortar.

It is important that replacement bricks match the rest of the brickwork and the pointing style is consistent with the rest of the walls. Where the building is old and the brickwork is weathered you should use old replacement bricks. Old bricks can be obtained fairly easily from demolition yards or builders.

One way to match the colours exactly, if the right bricks are unavailable, is to rub one of the original bricks very hard over the face of the replacement. For the pointing mortar it is an easy matter to achieve a colour match by adding special mortar pigments to the mortar.

Choose the mortar mix to suit the types of bricks in use and the exposure conditions. Under normal conditions a 1 : 1 : 6 (cement : lime : sand) mix is generally acceptable. But for the softer type of facing brick, a 1 : 2 : 9 (cement : lime : sand) mix is usually

satisfactory. For very hard, dense bricks used in situations of extreme exposure, a $1 : \frac{1}{4} : 3$ (cement : lime : sand) is best. Your local supplier should be able to advise you on the right mix.

With the richer cement mixes you should watch for possible shrinkage of the joint, which could lead to hair-line cracking at the brick/mortar interface.

Make up the mortar mix, and spread it evenly about 10mm thick on the bottom of the hole in the wall, and on the top and sides of the brick (fig. 11).

Then fit the brick carefully into the hole, remove the excess mortar with a

7 Gradually enlarge the hole by removing all affected bricks. Then clean up all surrounding mortar joints ready for fresh pointing

8 Once you have cleared the area, all surfaces must be cleaned up. Use a hard wire brush to remove any reluctant mortar

9 Finally, use a soft brush to get rid of all dust and dirt. Failure to do this will prevent the fresh mortar from tying in properly

10 Choose a mortar mix to suit the types of bricks in use. Under normal conditions a 1:1:6 mix is generally acceptable

11 Once the mix has been made up, use a trowel to spread some on the bottom of the hole in the wall. It should be about 10mm thick

12 Before laying the first brick, spread some more mix on the top and sides of the brick; again, it must be about 10mm thick

trowel, and repoint to match the existing pointing. Continue in this way until the whole section of brickwork has been replaced.

As you replace the bricks it is important to keep the face of the brickwork clean. Remove any vestiges of mortar when the pointing is dry with a stiff wire brush. If this fails to shift all the debris you can use an acidic chemical cleaner. However, such a solution is corrosive to skin, so take great care. Proprietary cleaners often clean bricks of not only cement or mortar stains but algal growth and atmospheric staining. Follow the manufacturer's instructions carefully, using the solution either neat or diluted as required.

The solution is brushed or sprayed on, and when the effervescent action stops you must wash it off with clean water. Heavy contaminations may require a second treatment.

Plant life

Plants, despite their attractive appearance are not very kind to brickwork—their roots tend to penetrate any loose spots in the pointing, especially on older houses, thus weakening the brickwork. You would be wise to train climbing plants up properly fixed trelliswork. One plant that you should actively discourage is the lichen which although giving the brickwork a weathered appearance also helps water to penetrate it and this can also damage the brickwork.

The damp-proof course

Where bricks are damaged beneath the DPC you must render down about 500mm from the DPC using sharp sand and cement with a waterproof liquid additive. Remember do not bridge the DPC because moisture will inevitably permeate.

13 Then fit the brick carefully into the wall and continue building the wall up. Remove any excess mortar as you go

14 Make sure that there is plenty of mix in the last hole and then insert the final brick. Use the trowel handle to tap it straight

15 Use the remaining mortar to fill in any surrounding cracks that you have cleaned out, then mix up your pointing mortar

16 Use the pointing mortar to make good all the mortar joints. A good colour match can be achieved with a mortar colouring

17 Wait till the mortar has almost dried and then clean off any traces of mortar on the bricks with a hard wire brush

18 Finally clean up the entire area with a soft brush. If chemical cleaners are used on the brickwork, follow the instructions carefully

WINDOW SILL REPAIRS

Left: *Rot is the biggest enemy of wooden window sills. Often replacing the damaged areas with new wood is the only practical solution*

Putting a projecting ledge—a sill—of some material between the window and the wall below stops this happening and prevents penetrating damp. But this means that the sill itself has to cope with the water flow and so it is constantly exposed to wear.

Damage to sills is often the result of faults in the basic design or construction of the window and sill and reaction to former repairs.

Some typical sills are shown below. They project well beyond the frame of the window itself so that rainwater is directed well clear of the supporting wall. Note that any projection beyond the width of the window opening is for the sake of appearance only—and does nothing to improve the function of the window sill itself.

In older houses, particularly, the window frame is often deeply recessed —perhaps flush with the inside surface of the wall. In this case, and where the window frame itself has no sill, a separate sill has to be provided and these are prone to trouble.

It is important that the top surface is sloped (or 'weathered') away from the window so that rainwater does not settle. A rounded sill edge also encourages water run-off. For wooden and smooth stone or concrete sills, the

Window sills are constantly at the mercy of the elements and so need occasional maintenance and repair, not only to look good but also to perform their job properly. Repairing most types of sill is not as difficult as it seems

The purpose of a window sill is to protect the wall underneath the window from rain. Although this may not seem necessary—after all, the rest of the wall is not protected in this way—rainwater striking the glass panes forms a concentrated, downward-running cascade which could penetrate a masonry wall or start rot in wooden siding.

Types of window sill

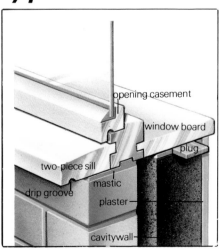

Tongued-and-grooved sill

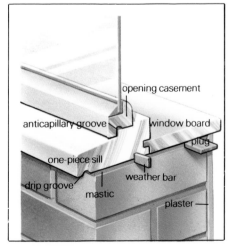

Projecting sill

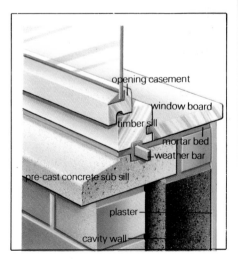

Composite sill

195

slope need not be very great; for the rougher clay tile or brick sills, a steeper slope is necessary.

Unless rainwater runs off quickly, wooden sills may rot and stone or cement sills crack through frost action. Paint finds it difficult to adhere to damp surfaces and combined with the action of sun it can easily blister and peel, leaving the sill even more vulnerable to attack from the rain.

A drip groove on the underside of the sill is a small but important feature. Whatever the angle of slope on the top surface, some rain inevitably creeps around the front face of the sill; accummulated drips then work along the bottom edge and onwards to the wall—where they can attack the joint with the sill. The drip groove prevents this by halting the water's progress, causing it to form into larger droplets that then fall harmlessly to the ground.

Some sills are formed in one piece with the rest of the window frame. Others—either by design or following a repair—are installed separately and if any joint between the two is left unprotected or badly sealed, you can expect trouble. One type of sill which is particularly prone to damage at the joint with the frame is shown in fig. A where a repair has been made.

In other designs, a galvanized steel *water bar* may be used to prevent water from tracking along constructional joints to the inside. This will be bedded on edge in a lead-packed groove in the main section of a stone or concrete sill. The bar fits a corresponding groove in the underside of a fixed wooden frame or top sill to give complete protection from draughts and wind-driven water.

Irregularities in the design of the window frame may also spell trouble for the sill beneath it. The basic rule is that each part of the frame ought to overhang the part beneath it, and that all 'horizontal' surfaces should slope slightly towards the outside.

Other sill types

Fig. 24 shows a stone subsill—widely used with sash windows in masonry walls—where the frame itself is recessed in the window opening, and where the frame's own sill is too short to reach the outer surface of the wall let alone project from it. This type of sill, which has a weathered top surface and a drip groove—also called a throat—is wider than the frame and is built into the brickwork on each side.

Another type of sill makes use of plain clay roofing tiles or quarry tiles.

Hand-made tiles are rough-surfaced and fairly porous, and so should be laid at a comparatively steep slope of about 30° to the horizontal; machine-made and quarry tiles need less. Two staggered layers of tiles are laid to prevent rainwater seeping through to the brickwork beneath—the bottom course is laid with the tile nibs along the outer edge, hanging down to form a crude drip groove.

Dealing with design faults

If you want to avoid recurring problems, it is important to correct any design faults during the course of routine maintenance or repair work.

Start by checking the drip groove. Appearance can be deceptive: there may be a drip groove, but well hidden under layers of paint. Probe around to see if you can find one and, if you

1 Use a pointed tool and knife to explore the extent of rot in the wood. Expect trouble at exposed joins in old sills

2 Carefully mark an angled cut line on each side and well clear of the rot, and use a tenon saw (*backsaw*) to remove the rotten section

3 Chisel into sound wood to the rear, levelling the wood as you proceed, so that the replacement pieces fit snugly

4 From direct measurement, cut the replacement sill sections. Carve or rout a drip groove to join the existing one

5 Where sill rot has spread to nearby framework, a replacement section must be fitted. Build this up from suitable pieces of timber

6 *It is sometimes easier to shape wood in situ. Use countersunk fixing screws, and a plane to reduce the wood to matching section*

7 *Before permanent fixing, apply liberal quantities of wood preservative to the contact areas, working it well into the cracks*

There is little you can do to correct poorly made tiled sills except remove and replace them. But only do this once you are sure that it is the slope which is causing the trouble.

Similarly, there is little you can do about design faults in a window frame without replacing the frame completely. Where the upper frame sections do not overhang lower ones properly, it may be possible to fix additional thicknesses of wood to the frame. But unless this is done carefully and the joints between the timber very well sealed, it may prove more of a problem than the original fault.

However, if the joints between a wooden sill and the frame are exposed and letting in water, simply rake out the old jointing material and pack the cleaned gap with suitable mastic or filler before repainting.

8 *Apply suitable adhesive to the contact areas between the old and new parts of the sill. Use a water resistant adhesive*

9 *Carefully position the new section and immediately drill holes for a secondary fixing using countersunk plated screws*

10 *Check the accompanying pieces for accuracy of fit, and then glue and screw these into position. Use filler to make good gaps*

do, scrape the recess completely clear then prime and paint it, taking care not to repeat the fault.

Where there is no groove, you might be able to rout or chisel one. But a stop of some form is a much easier solution which should work just as well. You can make the stop from a length of quadrant (or even square) beading and fix it to the underside of the sill with impact adhesive, about 35mm back from the front edge. Make sure that the sill is sound and properly painted around the site of the stop and repaint the entire underside once the stop is in place.

Next check that the sill slope is steep enough. Puddles of water on the upper surface indicate real trouble and will quickly cause rapid decay. Prod a wood sill with a pointed blade or bradawl to check for wet rot, and

look for fine cracks and flaking on stone or concrete sills—typical signs of an inadequate slope.

A wooden sill is easily corrected by planing it to a suitable slope, though you can do this only if the timber is sound and deep enough.

A stone sill can be repaired and sloped by forming a mortar fillet on top. But this usually means that the back edge of the sill would come close to wooden parts of the window frame; you should first carefully chip away part of the sill in order to lower it.

Remove all dust and loose particles, then paint the surface with PVA adhesive so that the new mortar mix of one part cement to three of sand adheres properly. Run over this with an offcut of timber to give the slope you want, then remove the former and shape a rounded front edge.

11 *Plane the new sill pieces to the same section as the existing sill, then sand down wood and filler ready for painting*

WINDOW SILL REPAIRS

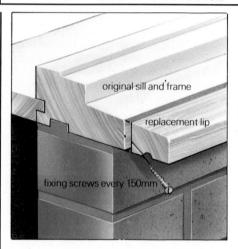

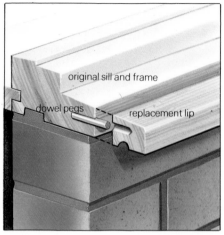

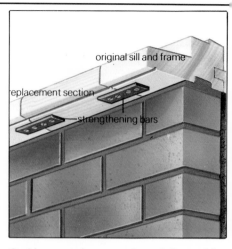

A. *To renew a lip, form a matching piece and fix this using glue and countersunk fixing screws angled in behind the drip groove*

B. *An alternative method is to use dowel pins to fix the new lip section in position, in which case in situ sill shaping is advisable*

C. *New sections can be reinforced by fixing strengthening bars to the underside. Ideally, these should be countersunk, filled and concealed*

Rotten window sills

If you have caught the rot in good time you may need to do nothing more than burn off all the paint on the sill, scrape the surface back to sound timber, and flood the area with wood preservative before repainting.

But if the damage is at all extensive, it is sensible to cut out the affected part and replace it. Some joinery stockists sell ready-shaped sills and if you can find one which has the same profile as your sill (or nearly so), it can be used for patching gaps. Otherwise you have to trim a piece of suitable timber to the correct shape.

As an alternative, replacing the whole sill with new material often makes better sense; patching involves making joints that may themselves let water in, thus creating further rot problems to repair.

Most modern wooden sills are made of softwood—usually redwood—which is perfectly suitable providing it has been properly treated with pressure-impregnated preservative.

Hardwood is a better material for sills because of its resistance to decay, but there are problems. Susceptibility to surface 'checking' may make traditional materials difficult to paint while some hardwoods such as Ramin have poor resistance to decay.

You may be able to find a suitable all-plastics sill. Obviously, this cannot rot but the wood at the joint between it and the existing frame will still be susceptible to damage. Do not cover wooden sills with a plastics covering such as sheet laminate. Almost certainly you will not be able to make the edges and joints completely watertight and any water entering these could cause rot very quickly.

12 *A damaged concrete sill is better removed in its entirety using a club hammer and bolster. Remove sections at a time*

13 *Failure of a concrete sill may mean that accompanying woodwork has to be removed also. Chisel this away until you reach sound timber*

14 *Paint the existing timber with two coats of preservative and one coat of primer, allowing time for each coat to dry*

15 *Measure and cut a piece of replacement timber and nail or screw this into place. Apply two coats of preserver, one of primer*

Replacing a sill

If the sill is formed in one piece with the window frame, you must cut it free at a suitable point in order to replace the whole sill. If possible, arrange the cut so that the joint with the new sill will be covered by the next window frame member up. Otherwise simply cut off a generous width of sill, well beyond the depth of the rot. Power sawing tools are useful for this operation—you could use a circular saw or a jigsaw.

Clean up the cut face of the remaining part of the sill by chiselling and planing until it is smooth and flat. Treat the face generously with preservative (fig. 7).

The new sill is bonded firmly to this surface. Although galvanized screws driven in at angles from below through the two pieces might do in some cases,

a better solution is to make dowel joints between the two as shown in figs A and B.

Whatever main method of fixing you choose the two surfaces must also be glued together, using a urea or resorcinol formaldehyde adhesive. When the wood is well bonded, rake out all the gaps between the new sill and the wall or the old sill and flood them with preservative. Finally, pack the gaps with a suitable waterproof mastic.

To repair just a small section of sill, cut out the affected part with a saw and chisel then use this as a template to cut the patching timber to size. Thoroughly treat the new wood—especially the cut ends—with preservative, then glue it in place with a urea or resorcinol formaldehyde adhesive—not ordinary PVA woodworking adhesive. Finally, screw the patch

to the existing sill using galvanized screws countersunk well below the surface. Cover the heads with mastic or filler and if even greater strength is needed, fix a metal strap to the underside of the sill (fig. C).

Stone or concrete sills

Non-timber sills rarely need much more than patching. Stone and concrete sills are easily patched with a 1:3 mortar mix, using a timber formwork arrangement similar to that used for increasing the surface slope. Tiled sills are best patched by replacing the damaged tiles themselves, on an individual basis.

However, badly cracked or decayed sills may need replacing altogether and the best way of doing it is to cast a new concrete sill in situ, using shuttering.

16 *Remove any loose bricks from the support area so that they may be remortared. Remove all traces of the old mortar and dampen the area*

17 *Prepare some mortar and then replace the line of bricks that you have removed. Allow the mortar to dry for 24 hours*

18 *The next stage is to make the shuttering for casting the new concrete sill. Use a bevel gauge to transfer angles in the brickwork*

19 *Construct the shuttering from suitable pieces of timber. Use a length of half-dowel to form the drip groove in the sill underside*

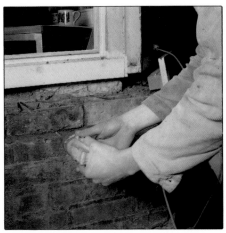

20 *Drill 25mm holes in the mortar of the support bricks so you can use 100mm nails for fixing the shuttering in place*

21 *Offer up each section of the shuttering to check for fit and then nail these into place to form a snug box round the window*

22 *Secure the box by tacking bracing struts between the window frame and the shuttering, but take care not to damage the woodwork*

23 *Dampen the brickwork and trowel in the mortar. Chop and tamp this into place to fill even the smallest cavity*

24 *Slope off the top, then leave the mortar to dry for 48 hours before removing the box. Cover to protect from rain if necessary*

Although the job can be very tricky with the existing window frame in place, the chances are that it too will need replacing if the sill is beyond reasonable repair.

Painting

Prevention is much better than cure, so making sure that your window sills are properly painted is a good investment and an important household maintenance job.

Perhaps the most important point is to ensure that the woodwork is not damp when it is painted, as this quickly leads to blistering and peeling.

The old paint will probably have to be removed completely if it is in poor condition and in this case burning off is better than using stripper because it keeps the wood dry. Sand the surface smooth afterwards and treat any knots with knotting compound to seal them. Rub a fine wood filler into the surface to seal the grain—do not forget the ends of the sill. Finally paint with primer, undercoat and two top coats, or use one of the new microporous paints instead.

Hardwood sills often develop small cracks, causing subsequent fracture and flaking of paint. The answer is good preparation; one treatment is to scrub thinned wood primer into the grain and then seal it with filler before applying another coat of primer.

Painting stone or concrete can also cause problems. Ordinary oil paint will mix with the alkali salts in the stone and soften or flake, unless you use an alkali-resistant primer first. It is far better to use emulsion or masonry paints, both of which resist alkalis fairly well.

25 *To repair a stone sill, rake out all loose material and use a wire brush to scrape all surfaces as clean as possible*

26 *Mix up some exterior stone filler and fill cracks and surface indentations, carefully forming edge sections in stages*

27 *When the filler has dried, use sandpaper to smooth this down, feathering the edges where it meets the original stonework*

28 *Dust the sill carefully and apply one coat of stabilizer over the entire sill. Allow this to dry before decorating*

USING FILLERS

Left: *Fillers may be ready mixed when you are dealing with small areas, but for larger areas it is more economical to mix a powder filler with water. The advantage of mixing the filler yourself is that you can vary the consistency according to the needs of the surface. When you wish to achieve a mirror-like surface as in French polishing you can use a grain filler which fills the timber pores*

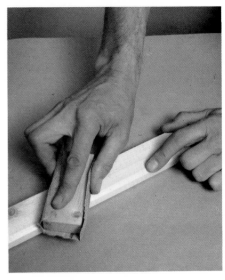

1 *When working on new wood you must start by rubbing down the timber with a medium grade glass paper (sandpaper)*

Paint applied over rusty metal or knot-ridden wood will neither look attractive nor last for very long. Yet careful preparation with primers and fillers provides a good base for paint and protection against moisture

Getting a smooth, flawless finish on most materials is not just a question of applying the final surface coating of paint or other covering. Often, a great deal of hard work is required to prepare the material beforehand. Without adequate and careful preparation the finish is likely to be poor, resulting in uneven, pitted surfaces, eventual flaking of paint and possible damage to the material itself because it has been inadequately sealed.

There are two stages in preparing any material for painting. The first is to prime its surface thoroughly with special paint—this has the effect of sealing it from intruding damp and

preventing corrosion or rot. It also provides a key for subsequent coats of paint.

The second stage is to use an appropriate filler to hide defects in the material and to fill holes and cracks caused by wear and tear. Only when the filler has been smoothed down with abrasive paper can undercoats and a topcoat be applied successfully.

Choosing wood primer
A wide variety of wood primers are available but it is essential to choose the one best suited to the type of wood you are painting and the use to which this will be put.

2 *Next clean the timber by rubbing gently with a soft cloth soaked in white spirit (turpentine) to remove grease which would repel the primer*

Knotting: Although not strictly a primer, knotting compound (knot sealer) seals the wood and provides a key for the top coats of paint.

Most new wood available at a reasonable price contains knots which mark the places where branches meet the trunk of the tree. After the tree is cut down, sap and resin tend to rise to the surface by way of the knots as the timber dries out, since most of them run at right-angles to the main grain of the wood.

Later, as the wood looses its moisture and becomes seasoned, the knots shrink and gaps appear between them and the surrounding timber. Often the knots shrink so much that they fall out altogether and leave unsightly holes which must be filled before painting. Patent knotting compound prevents this happening by sealing the knot and the area around it, stopping any further shrinkage and filling the small gaps and cracks which have consequently appeared.

General purpose primer. This oil-based paint will perform well on bare wood, and is the type you should generally use, unless you require a special treatment.

Lead primer: This is the traditional primer for bare wood or metal, but it is now rarely used since modern substitutes perform as well and are safer. Lead primer is usually available in red, pink and white—the darker colours containing a greater concentration of lead. However, check the contents carefully since some manufacturers add dye to their primers to make them appear heavily lead-based.

Because lead-based primers are highly toxic, great care must be taken when using them. Even if the primer is covered in many layers of paint it is still potentially dangerous and should never be applied to any surface which children might bring into contact with their mouths. For the same reason, keep lead primer well away from your mouth and wash your hands and face directly after you have made the application.

Acrylic primer: This is a non-toxic primer suitable for internal use where the need is more to protect the wood from knocks than weathering. It can be applied to almost any type of material besides wood and fulfils the function of providing both a primer and an undercoat.

Aluminium primer: As its name suggests, this type of primer consists of minute particles of aluminium suspended in a clear varnish solution. Once dry, it forms a tough grey-coloured base and is particularly good for sealing heavily resinous woods such as pine. Because of these sealing qualities, knotting the wood prior to using this primer is not strictly necessary. But aluminium primer should never be applied to wood which has not been thoroughly seasoned or the effect will be to trap damp and speed up the rotting process.

Priming wood

Whether you are priming old wood which has been cleaned off, or new timber fresh from the woodyard, this is a job that requires plenty of care and patience.

Preparing old timber: When faced with old timber where the paint is badly pitted or is loose and flaking, your first task is to remove all the loose material and get down to a smooth, firm base.

Any thick layers of paint which have accumulated can be removed using a good, reliable paint stripper but this is a time consuming process and it is often far easier to use a blowlamp or hot air gun. When working, keep the flame on the move to avoid burning the wood. Apply only as much heat as is needed to loosen the paint then scrape this off with a shavehook or knife.

You may not need to remove all the old paint unless it is particularly loose or lumpy—the idea is to get down to a firm base and then prime.

Once all loose and flaking paint has been burned off, smooth down with a piece of abrasive paper (sandpaper) mounted on a block (fig. 6). The whole surface should then be completely degreased and washed down with a solution of sugar soap. Make sure that any sticky residue is thoroughly washed away with clean water and leave the surface to dry before proceeding with the priming.

Preparing new timber: Most new wood is brought already planed and merely needs to be sanded to a smooth finish before you seal any knots.

Apply knotting compound with a soft cloth, covering each knot and the area about 10mm around it (fig. 3). Leave it to dry for at least twenty-four hours and then apply a second coat, trying to fill any small gaps not covered by the first. Two coats of knotting should generally be enough, but if gaps still remain in and around the knots a further application may be necessary. Finally, smooth the knotting level with the surrounding timber using fine abrasive paper mounted on a block. Note that the final surface can only be as good as its base.

Clean the surface by rubbing gently (fig. 2) with a soft cloth soaked in white spirit (turpentine). The timber should now be ready for priming.

The primer itself can be applied with a soft paint brush but make sure you cover all the areas of bare wood thoroughly, especially end grains (fig. 4). Most types of wood require only one coat but certain timbers—especially those with a deep or pronounced grain—need either two coats or else a covering of fine surface filler to get them perfectly smooth. If more than one coat is necessary lightly rub down the surface between coats with fine abrasive glasspaper.

3 You must apply knotting compound to every knot and the area of timber about 10mm around it in order to prevent it shrinking

4 Once the knotting compound has dried you can apply the primer to all areas of bare wood—especially the end grain

5 *To remove thick layers of old flaking paint use a blowlamp to burn it off. Keep the flame moving to avoid burning the wood*

6 *Apply only as much heat as is necessary to loosen the paint and then scrape it off—for corners use a shavehook*

7 *Once all the loose and flaking paint has been removed you must smooth down any rough edges with a piece of abrasive paper on a block*

Wood fillers

Once the wood has been thoroughly primed, all holes and cracks should be covered with an appropriate filler. Be wary of instructions accompanying fillers which claim that they can be applied without the need for primer beforehand. If this is done the timber will be inadequately protected and is likely to shrink—eventually causing the paint to flake off.

Cellulose/plaster filler: This is the most common type of wood filler and is suitable both for interior and exterior woodwork. It is available ready-mixed or in powder form for mixing with water to the required consistency.

Plastic filler: Although expensive, the two part plastic fillers—usually used for repairs to car bodies—are useful when some degree of structural strength is needed. They are often used to fill joints in wood which have worked their way apart or for large holes which cannot be bridged by ordinary fillers.

Fine surface filler: This is available in ready-mixed or powder form and because it is of a finer consistency than other fillers, it is useful for filling small dents or imperfections in the grain prior to painting.

Natural wood filler: A number of fillers are available which are designed to blend with the natural colours of the wood so that it can be varnished or stained afterwards. But take care to match natural fillers with the wood you are using by trying them out first on a piece of waste. They're also known as wood stoppers.

Filling wood

Minor deficiencies in primed surfaces are not always obvious so begin by examining the surface of the wood carefully. Run your hand over the timber a few times to search out small dents and cracks.

Hair-line splits should be covered with fine surface filler but larger cracks can only be bridged by building up successive layers of filler.

Filler will not adhere to dusty surfaces so remove any loose material from the cracks with a soft paint brush. Finally, any nail and screw heads liable to rust should be covered with an oil-based paint before you fill them.

If the filler is in powder form, it must be mixed with water before use. About two and a half volumes of filler to one volume of water is suitable for small cracks, but very absorbent surfaces and deep splits require less water. Gradually add the water to the powder until you get the right consistency and stir the mixture thoroughly so that all the lumps are removed to leave a smooth workable paste for you to apply.

Press the mixture into each hole with a filling knife or the plastic spreader supplied with the filler (fig. 8). Try to finish just above surface level and clean off any excess filler before it hardens with the blade of the knife or with a damp cloth.

Once the mixture sets hard—usually in about two hours—it should be sanded to a smooth finish, level with the surrounding wood, using fine

8 *Press the filler mixture into each hole with a filling knife, finish just proud of the surface and clean off any excess before it sets*

sandpaper on a block. If you can, 'feather' away the edges of the filler so that the patch will be invisible once it is covered with paint.

Preparing building boards

The techniques used to prime and fill man-made boards are similar to those used for ordinary wood, but there are a number of extra points to consider before tackling the job.

Hardboard: This is surprisingly porous despite its strong, hardwearing surface and tends to absorb paint patchily. A number of special hard-

9 *First rub the whole surface of the metal vigorously with a wire brush in order to get as near to metal as possible*

10 *Next paint a rust remover on to the metal, leave it for two or three hours, scrubbing occasionally, then wash it off. Repeat if necessary*

11 *Apply one or two coats of metal primer on to all exposed surfaces of the metal, taking great care to cover holes and cracks*

board primers are available to cope with this but if you intend to paint over it, the surface can also be sealed effectively with a thin coat of emulsion paint (latex paint) applied evenly.

Chipboard: This has a porous, rough surface which looks shoddy if it is prepared badly, so give it at least two coats of primer. A layer of surface filler may also be necessary. Take care to smooth the surface well.

Blockboard and laminboard: These are surfaced with a thin wood veneer and can therefore be treated in the same way as wood.

Primers for metal surfaces

Most metal is prone to oxidation or rusting and unless the surface is sealed, corrosion quickly sets in. If left unchecked, holes develop and rust bubbles distort the surface. Exterior metalwork exposed to the air is prone to atmospheric corrosion, so items such as guttering and down pipes need a primer which seals the surface effectively and completely.

Lead primers: Lead-based primers are particularily good for protecting metal and keeping rust and corrosion at bay. However, as they are highly toxic you should, if at all possible, use a different kind of primer which would be safer.

Bitumen: A cheap method of priming metal objects such as guttering and drainpipes is to coat them with bitumen paint. Although this gives more than adequate protection from corrosion it cannot be painted over until it has weathered for a number of

years in the wind and rain.

Zinc primers: Zinc chromate or zinc phosphate primers are expensive but effective primers of metal. They are usually used to touch up small areas of corrosion on pieces of metal that are open to weathering, such as dents in car bodywork.

Priming metal

The first step on both new and old metal is to remove all traces of rust and get down to bare metal before priming. Old paint can be removed from metal with a blowlamp and a stripping knife. The rust can then be cleared off by rubbing vigorously with a wire brush (fig. 9). Any odd spots should be removed.

Where rust and corrosion are particularly difficult to shift, treat the surface with rust remover—a gel-like substance which helps dissolve rust as well as inhibiting its further development. Paint it on to the affected areas taking care not to let it touch your bare skin (fig. 10). Leave it for two or three hours, scrubbing it occasionally with a wire brush to loosen the rust. Afterwards, thoroughly wash down the surface with warm, clean water before priming the bare metal.

Apply primer to all areas which are likely to be exposed to corrosion, especially around holes and cracks which have appeared in the surface. Two coats will usually be necessary to do a proper job.

Metal fillers

Because of the effects of weathering

and corrosion, holes and cracks are common in metal surfaces. But, after the metal has been cleaned and thoroughly primed, these can often be repaired by using one of the many fillers suitable for the purpose.

Plastic filler: Particularly suited to metal repairs, these give good structural strength and can easily be built up in a number of layers to cover even large splits. Plastic fillers usually come as two packs which need to be mixed together before use.

Sealing bandage: A very useful method of sealing cracks in metal pipes as well as strengthening them is to wrap sealing bandage around the affected area. These are self-adhesive gauze or plastic strips which can later be covered with bitumen paint to give a tough, watertight finish.

Repairs in plaster

Very large holes in plaster can be repaired only by coating the wall or ceiling with two coats of mixed plaster but hairline cracks and splits are dealt with more easily.

Start by raking out any loose material from the cracks and if necessary, use a bolster and hammer to cut the plaster back to a firm edge. Any dust still remaining can then be removed with a paint brush.

Any flaking or chalky plaster can be stabilized and made ready for the filler by applying a penetrating primer or masonry sealer. Cellulose or plaster fillers are best for the job since they are flexible and allow for movement in the material over a period of time.

WINDOW SECURITY

- **Choosing the right lock** ● **Lock finishes** ● **Fitting to wooden windows** ● **Fitting to metal windows** ● **Surface or flush mounting** ● **Key operation** ● **Providing night-time ventilation**

2 Replace an existing casement handle (cockspur) with a lockable version. Make new screw holes for the cockspur

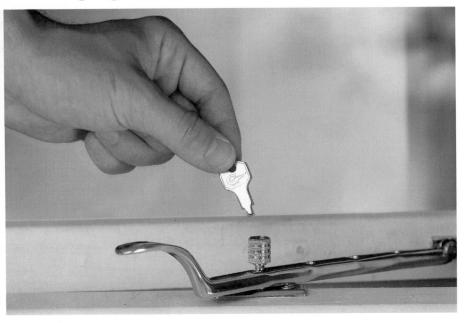

Everyone fits a lock of some sort to the front door to keep burglars at bay, and usually remembers to bolt the back door when going out or at bedtime. Yet the average house has a number of far weaker points—the windows—that present an easy way in for the determined intruder, even if he finds them closed. With break-ins increasing rapidly, it makes sense to

1 Fit a locking casement stay in place of the existing stay. Secure the stay by attaching the locknut and turning the key

tackle window security as a matter of high priority.

There is a wide range of window locks on the market at present, and it's a

relatively simple matter to decide which type to use for windows of different styles and types. Some are designed solely for casement windows, for example, some for sashes, while others can be fitted to any window type. The majority are surface-mounted, so installation involves little more than driving a few screws; even flush-fitting types just require a hole of the right depth and diameter to be drilled in the window, ready to receive the lock body.

The most secure locks are key-operated types using unique keys, like a door lock. Many of the window locks on the market

3 Offer a surface-mounted frame lock up to the frame and mark the position of the keeper. Drill the bolt hole and chisel out its recess

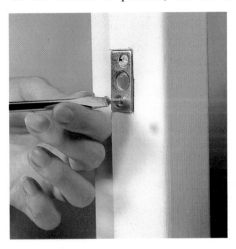

4 Screw the keeper plate into position in the recess, making sure it is square to the window when this is closed

5 Shoot the lock bolt so you can use it as a guide to positioning the lock body on the window itself. Drive the screws and add the covers 205

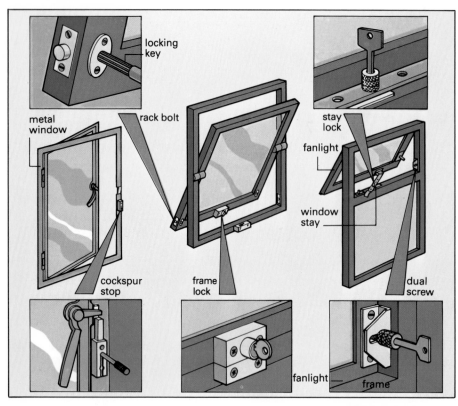

A Above: *Locks for casement windows and fanlights come in a wide range of styles, and each one is designed to be used at a particular position on the window. Often two should be fitted*

B Below: *Locks for sash windows generally work on the principle of preventing the two sashes from sliding past each other. Most lock the sashes closed, but acorn stops (top right) allow some ventilation*

are operated by a universal key, and there's nothing to stop a burglar carrying a selection of these round with him. Look at this point when you're shopping if you want a high level of window security.

Apart from choosing a particular type of lock, there are several other points to check before you go ahead and fit it. For a start, it's important that the opening part of the window is a good fit within its frame; if it's not, the lock may not work properly. Adjust hinge positions, plane high spots that are binding, fit new sash cords, tackle rust spots on metal windows—in fact, do whatever is necessary to get the window into perfect working order. Look out also for signs of rot in woodwork, which may weaken the window and make it difficult to achieve a secure fixing.

Take note of any windows with particularly narrow frames; you may be restricted in the type of lock you can fit, and recessed types will probably be quite out of the question because drilling a hole would seriously weaken timber of too small a cross-section. You must also be careful when fitting locks to windows containing sealed double glazing units; carelessly-drilled holes could damage the edges of the units where they are housed in their surrounds. Modern plastic-framed windows can pose problems too—it's very difficult to fit conventional window locks to them, and it's best to seek advice about providing extra security from the window manufacturer.

Most locks are designed to lock the window shut. However, there may be situations where you want to lock the window in a slightly open position—for night-time ventilation, for example. Some locks allow this facility, but there is always a risk that a partly-open window can be opened by force; the very fact that it is not tightly closed affords an intruder some leverage.

Whatever type of locks you decide to fit on your windows, there are two important points to remember. The first is that to be effective, the locks you fit must be used—whenever you leave the house, and at night. With some types, the lock operates as soon as the window is closed, and this is clearly the best type to fit if you are at all forgetful. The second point concerns keys. It's best to keep the key for each window lock close to the window, so it can be reached easily in an emergency—you might need to use the window as an escape route in the event of a fire, for example.

Locks for casement windows
One of the simplest ways of securing a casement window is to use a casement stay lock (fig. 1). You replace the existing

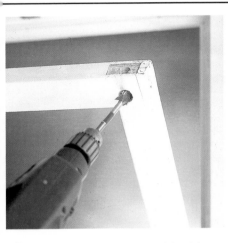

6 Mortise rack bolts are ideal for securing pivot windows which close flush with their frames. Drill holes for the bolt and key

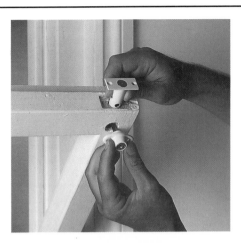

7 Chisel a recess in the frame edge for the bolt faceplate, then slide the bolt in to check its fit before offering up the lock

8 Shoot the bolt to mark the frame, then drill a hole at that point and fit the small keeper plate. Test that the bolt engages smoothly

9 On narrow casements, fit a slim two-part lock instead. Drill pilot holes for the screws in the casement and screw the pin in place

10 Use the pin position to align the slotted bracket on the window frame itself and screw it on. Check that the two parts mate

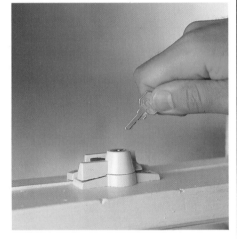

11 On sash windows, unscrew the existing fitch pattern catch from the top of the inner sash and replace it with a lockable type

12 To fit dual screws, drill a hole in the top rail of the inner sash and part-way into the bottom of the outer one. Fit the barrel

13 Next, drive in the threaded locking pin to check that it engages correctly in the hole drilled in the outer sash rail

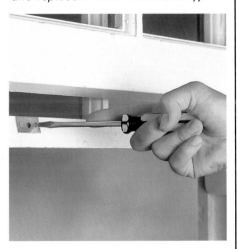

14 Complete the installation by fitting the small metal keeper in place over the hole. Then close the window and insert the pin

stay pin with a special locking type which prevents the casement stay from being lifted. You usually have to replace the casement stay at the same time, since the size of its holes may not match the size of the new lockable pin.

Another simple way of improving window security is to fit a locking casement handle (cockspur) in place of the existing one (fig. 2). However, neither of these types is suitable for existing steel windows, where the casement stay pin and cockspur may be an integral part of the window frame.

Frame locks (fig. 3) can be installed on all sorts of wooden casements and fanlights, without the need to remove or replace the existing window furniture. They come in a range of types, but all work on the same principle of shooting a bolt into a recess in the window frame.

Pivoting windows can also be secured by frame locks of this type, but because of the way they close within their frames it is often better to fit mortise rack bolts instead (fig. 6). These fit within holes drilled in the window surround (fig. 7), so are invisible from outside and relatively unobtrusive indoors. Two types are available: one is operated by a simple turnkey that shoots and withdraws the bolt, the other actually locks in the closed position (fig. 8).

Where the frame is too narrow to accept a rack bolt, a slim two-part lock can be fitted instead. This has a surface-mounted block or bracket screwed to the frame and a plate or recessed nut on the casement itself (fig. 10). When the window is closed a locking nut is screwed in place through the frame block to hold the window closed.

Locks for sash windows

Because of the sliding action of vertical sash windows, most of the available locks work by preventing one sash from sliding past the other. One of the easiest to fit is a locking fitch fastener (fig. 11).

Dual screws are an alternative way of locking the sashes together. Here, a hole is drilled right through the top rail of the inner sash and part-way into the bottom rail of the outer one. Then a threaded barrel is screwed into the hole (fig. 12), and a screw bolt is driven through the barrel into the outer sash with a special key (fig. 13). The hole in the outer sash rail is reinforced with a metal keeper plate (fig. 14).

Acorn stops are small lockable pegs that are fitted to the inner face of the outer sash to prevent it from sliding down past the inner one. Depending on where they are positioned, they can lock the window closed or allow it to be opened slightly for ventilation. To fit them you simply drill a hole in the sash stile (fig. 15), fit the acorn stop (fig. 16) and add the striking plate on top of the inner sash. It's best to fit stops at both sides of the window.

You can also use surface-mounted locks—again, one at each side of the window. To install them close the window, attach the lock body to the inner stile (fig. 17) and shoot the bolt to mark the position for the hole in the outer sash. Drill this, fit the keeper and test the lock's action (fig. 18).

Security grilles

All the window locks in the world may not stop a determined burglar, and if you have a window that is particularly at risk—in a basement, for example—consider fitting security grilles.

15 *Acorn stops can be fitted part-way up the sash stiles. Mark the position of the keeper, then cut out the recess*

16 *Test the plate for fit, then screw it into position. To use the lock, simply insert the brass pin in the hole*

17 *You can also secure sash windows with surface-mounted locks. Screw the lock body in place after drilling the bolt hole*

18 *Check that the lock engages smoothly in the recess, then lower the outer sash and fit the small keeper plate*

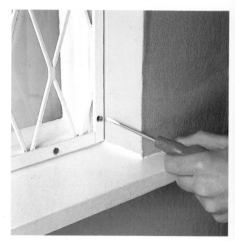

19 *Provide additional protection for at-risk windows by fitting security grilles. Fixed types are cheapest*

ALL ABOUT WOOD

- ● TYPES OF SOFTWOOD AND HARDWOOD
- ● TIMBER CONVERSION ● SEASONING
- ● SHRINKAGE ● TIMBER SIZES
- ● SAWN OR PLANED? ● BUYING TIMBER

After centuries of use, timber still remains the most commonly used material in the building and furniture industries despite the upsurge in the use of plastics and pre-moulded metal. Timber has good structural strength and is relatively easy to work, but much of its popularity lies in its beauty, warmth and individuality which is unmatched by any other constructional material.

Timber is cut as efficiently as possible from a very wide variety of trees. The mature wood from the centre of a tree is termed 'true wood' or 'heartwood' although the correct name is *duramen*. This is the most sought-after timber—even though it is more expensive—as it is more stable, less likely to shrink, and less liable to insect attack than the rest of the tree as the cells contain little of the sugar and starch needed for the growth of the outer layers of wood.

These remaining outer layers of wood are known as 'sapwood' or *alburnum*. Sapwood is light in colour, and soft and spongy when compared to heartwood. The foodstuff contained in this timber makes it very liable to pest attack until treated.

Although frequently used for box and crate carcassing, it is only recently that sapwood has been used for more ambitious jobs. This is largely due to the escalating costs of timber in general, and recent improvements in preserving and artificially seasoning the inferior timber. Now, sapwood is used for all but the finest cabinet work.

Hardwoods and softwoods
There is great confusion about the terms 'hardwood' and 'softwood'— indeed, many people refer to deal, pine and fir when they talk about softwood. But while pine and fir are species of tree, 'deal' is a technical term—now obsolete—describing a size of softwood or its origin.

Most softwood trees have spiky leaves and are coniferous (larch, a deciduous tree, is an exception). Branches frequently form in whorls

of two or more at the same level.

The softwood most commonly used in the UK is from the tree *Pinus sylvestus*, and is known as Redwood. Other names for this include Red Deal, Yellow Deal, Archangel Fir, Swedish Pine and Scots Pine.

Other softwoods in common use are Cedar, Western Red, Douglas Fir, Hemlock, Parana Pine, Pitch Pine, Quebec Yellow Pine, Western White Pine, Sitka and Spruce.

In other countries, native or imported softwoods generally include varieties of pine, larch, spruce and cedar. In South Africa, the most widely available softwood species are the South African pine, honey wood and jelutong, while eucalyptus is generally used for fence poles and the like. Some species such as white cedar are naturally resistant to rot and insect attack: others, such as Southern yellow pine, need preservative treatment for outdoor use.

Hardwood trees have broad, flat leaves and are deciduous—yew and holly being the well-known exceptions. Branches usually grow at different levels and never more than two at the same level.

Unlike softwoods, which now are specifically grown and forested, most hardwoods—especially tropical ones— occur at random and are naturally growing. This makes felling and collection difficult, consequently prices are high. This and diminishing stocks

1. *African Mahogany—the cheapest and most readily available mahogany, a hardwood used for general construction and joinery, as well as for veneers*
2. *African Walnut—an easily worked hardwood, which is suitable for pannelling, joinery and flooring*
3. *Afrormosia—stronger and harder than Teak which it resembles, used for furniture and flooring*
4. *Agba—hardwood which is suitable for joinery and constructional work as well as panelling*
5. *Australian Oak—not a true oak but similar in hardness, it is typically used for flooring*

1. *African Mahogany*

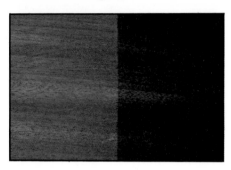

2. *African Walnut*

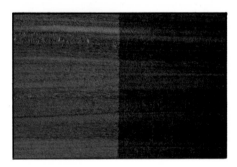

3. *Afrormosia*

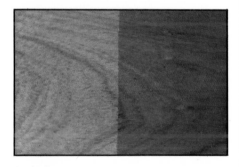

4. *Agba*

5. *Australian Oak*

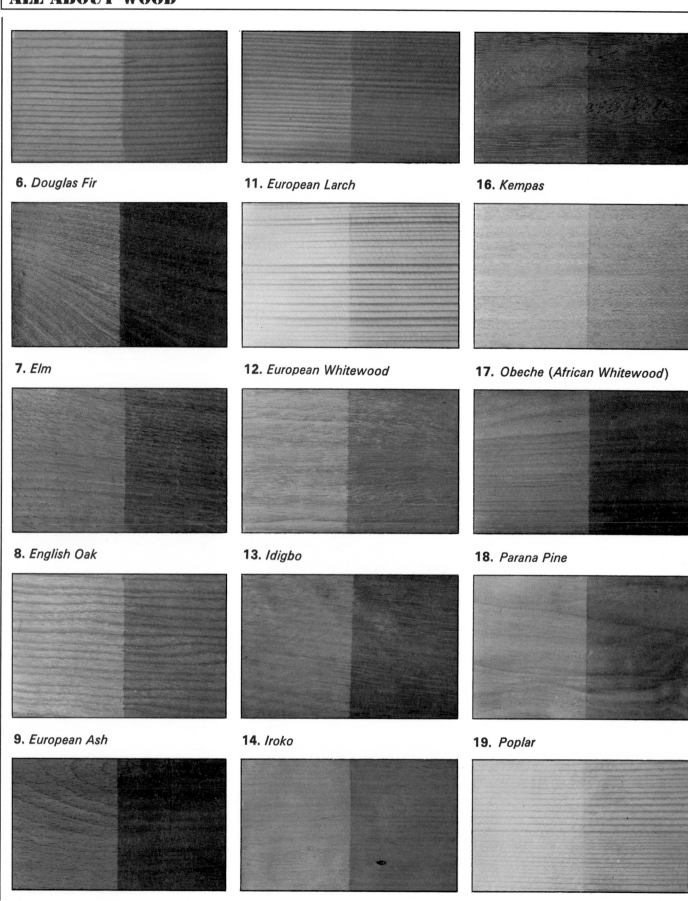

6. *Douglas Fir*

11. *European Larch*

16. *Kempas*

7. *Elm*

12. *European Whitewood*

17. *Obeche (African Whitewood)*

8. *English Oak*

13. *Idigbo*

18. *Parana Pine*

9. *European Ash*

14. *Iroko*

19. *Poplar*

10. *European Beech*

15. *Jelutong*

20. *European Redwood*

have increased interest in lesser-known hardwood species which up to now have been disregarded as being value-less. Utile is a good example of the 'new' hardwoods.

Other hardwoods commonly available in the UK include home-grown or European English Oak, Beech, Ash, Elm, Sycamore, Birch and Walnut. More exotic hardwoods include Mahogany, Gabon, Agba, Utile, Sapele, Teak, Balsa (which may be a surprise), Ramin, Iroko, African Walnut, Meranti, and Japanese Oak.

Because many of the woods have superb decorative value, they are often

Left: *More hardwoods and softwoods*
6. Douglas Fir—a most important softwood for general building work, joinery, and heavy constructions
7. Elm—relatively cheap hardwood with good strength and appearance, a favourite for furniture
8. English Oak—fine-looking hardwood used for its extreme durability in a very wide variety of applications both indoors and out
9. European Ash—widely distributed hardwood which works and finishes well, but too flexible for heavy-duty structural work
10. European Beech—hardwood which is stronger than oak, works well, but prone to decay unless treated
11. European Larch—one of the hardest softwoods and very resistant to decay, so often used for posts
12. European Whitewood—not a strong hardwood but suitable for normal joinery
13. Idigbo—a hardwood which can be used for a variety of jobs ranging from panelling to general construction
14. Iroko—hardwood used for high class joinery, flooring and veneers
15. Jelutong—lightweight hardwood good for carving and special carcassing where lightness is required
16. Kempas—hardwood good for door sills but has problem resin which needs treatment before painting
17. Obeche (African Whitewood)—a hardwood used for cabinet making and general joinery
18. Parana Pine—softwood suitable for interior joinery, but variable strength makes use in structural applications suspect
19. Poplar—widely distributed hardwood which is soft, woolly and light
20. European Redwood—softwood which is strong but variable, used for all building work but knots may present a problem

cut into thin veneers and used to face lesser timbers or man-made boarding.

Conversion

Turning a tree trunk, or *bole*, into a plank is called conversion and there are two stages in the process: sawing and seasoning. Branches are rarely used as growth tends to be uneven.

There are various methods of sawing a trunk, and the art is to cut this—without wastage—in a way that allows the resulting planks to season properly. Conversion has to take place before the outside of the trunk has had a chance to dry out, in the process shrinking and cracking (fig. E).

Plain sawing is the commonest, simplest and least wasteful of the two basic methods of cutting up timber, but the resulting grain pattern, or *figure*, is rather plain and the boards made are more likely to distort.

Plain sawing is done in two ways. First, there is the *flat cut* (fig. A), where the log is cut into slices complete with the wavy edge of the outside surface. By comparison, the outside of a *billet sawn* log is first trimmed, then cut into thick planks or *billets*. These are then sawn into thinner planks (fig. B).

Quarter sawing is the second method of cutting up a log (fig. C). The process is more time consuming and wastage is greater, but the resulting additional expense is offset by two important characteristics: the board may have an exceptionally fine grain when cut in this way—which is good for decorative work—and is much less likely to warp because shrinkage is usually at an even rate.

Rare and therefore expensive, highly decorative timbers such as Rosewood and Honduras Mahogany are usually cut into veneer thicknesses. For plywood and blockboard construction, some cheaper woods—such as Birch, Gabon and Pine, are also cut into veneers.

Knots in wood are particularly decorative in veneer work, though they are avoided as much as possible

21. Sapele—mahogany as hard as oak used for veneers and furniture work
22. Sitka Spruce—a strong softwood with good working properties
23. Sycamore—hardwood which is strong and works well, useful for turnery and veneers
24. Utile— similar to Sapele but less figured and slightly coarser
25. Western Red Cedar—a rather coarse, straight-grained softwood which works well but requires care over finishing

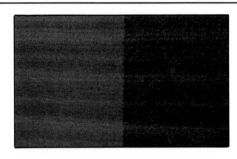
21. *Sapele*

22. *Sitka Spruce*

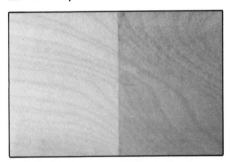
23. *Sycamore*

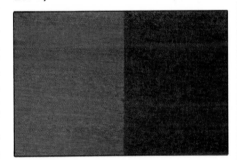
24. *Utile*

25. *Western Red Cedar*

Conversion of timber

A. *Least wasteful of the sawing methods, flat cut or slab sawing yields two different types of plank according to the position within the log*

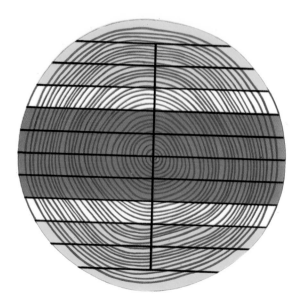

B. *For a billet cut, the log is first trimmed then cut into thick planks to yield wood which has a grain pattern similar to slab sawing*

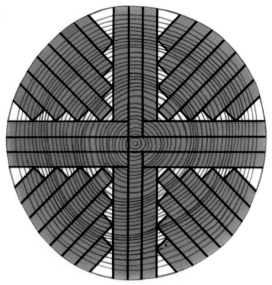

C. *The true method of quarter sawing producing all quarter sawn planks is labour intensive and wasteful, but the grain pattern is desirable*

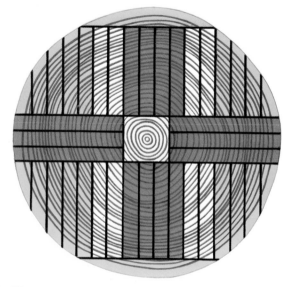

D. *The modern method of quarter sawing does not produce so many quarter sawn boards as the old method but is more economical in its use of wood*

in constructional timber. Burrs, those lumps which for no apparent reason grow on the base and sides of a tree, sprout bunches of young branches and these explain the profusion of knots here. A veneer cut from this area of a tree is therefore highly prized for its decorative effect.

Another area commonly used by veneer manufacturers is the part of the tree where a trunk divides into two main branches, known as 'crotch wood', the fork of a tree.

Seasoning
Seasoning is the process of allowing—or forcing—wood to dry out so that its moisture content equals that of the atmosphere.

Natural seasoning brings the moisture content down to between 15 and 17 per cent, which makes the wood suitable for outdoor use and general construction carpentry. But used indoors, timber seasoned in this way is likely to shrink and warp as further drying out takes place.

Forced seasoning by kiln drying to a great extent overcomes these problems, as it brings down the moisture content to much lower percentages. But no matter how timber for indoor use is seasoned, it is advisable to lay it up in the room in which it is to be used for as long as possible before starting work. Two weeks is not too long in homes with central heating.

Lay the timber flat or on edge, with spacers between successive layers and between the timber and the floor. The spacers should be of equal thickness, and placed in line above each other at roughly 500mm centres. This allows good air circulation and ensures even acclimatization with the atmosphere in the room.

Shrinkage

Shrinkage occurs as moisture is removed from the wood. As there is more moisture in the sapwood—the outer layers of a tree—this is where the greatest shrinkage occurs.

Directionally, shrinkage is most marked along the wood rings—known as *circumferential shrinkage*—but about half this rate also takes place radially. The least amount of shrinkage occurs in the length of the log.

The main, and most commonly noticed effect of shrinkage seen on plain sawn boards is 'cupping' (fig. K).

This results from the variable shrinkage rate of growth rings of different circumference, the longer ones on the outside shrinking more than the short circumference rings on the inside. Variable shrinkage of this sort may affect other sections of timber depending from what part of the trunk they are cut (fig. G).

Timber sizes

Metric timber is sold in three ways: by *metre super* (or square metre), by *metre run* (linear metres), and *per cube* (or cubic metre). Of these, the commonest in small woodyards and shops is pricing by metre run. The price charged is so much per metre length for a specific section of timber.

Under the metric system, softwood timber is cut and sold in units, or modules, of 300mm (about a foot in imperial measurement) beginning at 1.8m and rising in these increments to a maximum of 6.3m. The various standard metric cross-sectional sizes in which softwood is available are summarised in the table on page 214, along with details for hardwood.

You may find that you need to buy slightly more material than you require if you are working to imperial measurements (unless wood is still available to you in this form). But some establishments are prepared to cut to your exact needs.

Hardwood sizes follow a different system. Lengths normally begin at 1.8m and increase in 100mm steps, although some rarer hardwoods are imported in lengths shorter than 1.8m. Thicknesses range from 19mm to 125mm. Widths normally start at 150mm and increase in 10mm steps.

E. *Heartshake is a fault caused by decay working outwards from the pith of a tree. Circumferential shrinkage is also shown*

F. *Tangential shakes occur as the sapwood separates from the summer growth, either during growth or in seasoning*

G. *Warping of timber is influenced by the region of the log from which it is cut, being most pronounced on boards from the edge of the tree*

H. *Twisted grain seriously weakens the timber and normally should not be considered for use*

I. *End shrinkage splits usually follow the medullary rays and are caused by shakes, poor felling or seasoning*

J. *Thunder shakes, caused by stresses in the growing tree, greatly weaken timber, and should be cut to waste*

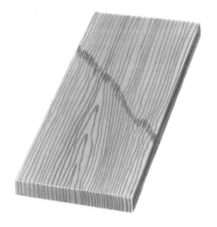

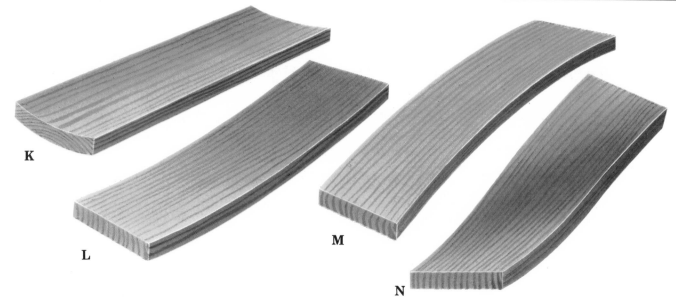

Above: *Whereas it may be possible to rectify cupping (K) by planing edges level, there is not much you can do for other faults such as bowing (L), springing (M) and twisting (N). Most of these faults result from bad stacking*

Prepared or planed timber

All timber is now sold by its nominal size, that is how it measures in its rough sawn state. When ordering prepared or planed timber—usually termed PAR, in the UK which stands for 'planed all round'—you get timber slightly smaller than the size quoted. The normal allowance for planing is between 3mm and 3.5mm overall, so a piece of timber of nominal size 25mm × 50mm sawn should measure about 22mm × 47mm when planed.

It is important to allow for this variation when planning the work and cutting routines.

Choosing timber

Bad planing can reduce the nominal measurement by as much as 5mm overall and this is one of the points to watch for when selecting matching timber sizes. But timber quality is also important.

Softwoods are graded in the countries in which they are grown, and the rating system varies. Swedish boards are graded 1 to 6; those 1 to 4 are considered best quality, 5ths are called standard, whilst 6ths are unsorted low quality.

Russian timbers are graded so that 1 to 3 are graded best quality, 4ths and 5ths are used for carcassing, whilst 6ths are mainly used for packing case material and similar coarse jobs.

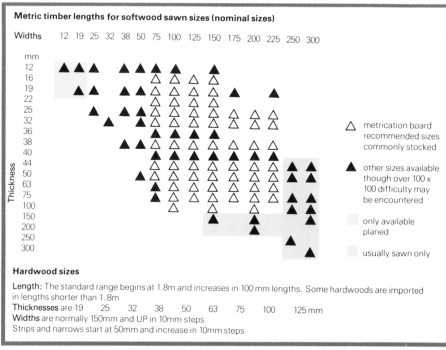

Metric timber lengths for softwood sawn sizes (nominal sizes)

Widths: 12 19 25 32 38 50 75 100 125 150 175 200 225 250 300

Thickness (mm): 12 16 19 22 25 32 36 38 40 44 50 63 75 100 150 200 250 300

△ metrication board recommended sizes commonly stocked

▲ other sizes available though over 100 × 100 difficulty may be encountered

only available planed

usually sawn only

Hardwood sizes

Length: The standard range begins at 1.8m and increases in 100 mm lengths. Some hardwoods are imported in lengths shorter than 1.8m

Thicknesses are 19   25   32   38   50   63   75   100   125 mm

Widths are normally 150mm and UP in 10mm steps.

Strips and narrows start at 50mm and increase in 10mm steps

However, the average timber yard or DIY shop sells a medium range of unsorted timber which is mostly suitable for building work and general joinery. It is often possible to find timbers of better than average quality by sorting through such a pile of unsorted timber. Select your own wood, taking the best of what is there.

Look for straight-grained, knot-free timber which has no splits or shakes (fig. I) and look along the end edge to check for cupping or ring shakes. Whenever you can, pick timber as near to quarter sawn as possible—where the ring growth is close and even—so that later shrinkage is much less likely. In softwood, the closer together the rings, the better is the quality of the timber. The reverse is true of hardwoods.

Reject any timber that is badly twisted or warped without further question. Its use in constructions may cause long-term problems as well as posing initial difficulties in working. Some defects in softwoods may not be considered so in hardwood. For example, large knots in English Walnut and Elm, and small 'pin knots' in Oak are acceptable and sometimes desirable. But mahoganies, Sapele and Teak should be free of all but the slightest defects. Other timber defects are shown in figs K to N.

MARKING AND CUTTING TIMBER

- **TYPES OF SAW**
- **MARKING UP**
- **STARTING A CUT**
- **SAWING TECHNIQUES**
- **ANGLED CUTS**
- **HAND SANDING**

It is surprising just how much you can undertake in the way of carpentry projects simply by mastering the most basic skill of cutting timber squarely and accurately to length.

Many different types of saw are available, all designed for specific cutting jobs. In general woodwork, the most commonly used are the handsaw and the backsaw (fig. 9). These are further classified according to the number and shape of their teeth.

Handsaws can be broken down into rip saws, crosscut saws and panel saws, each of which make different cuts and with varying degrees of roughness. For the beginner, a panel saw will prove the most useful.

Backsaws can be divided into tenon saws and dovetail saws (fig. 9). Again for the beginner, only the tenon saw is really necessary—use it for joint-cutting and for cutting battens below 100mm × 25mm in size.

A solid working surface is essential for quick and accurate saw cutting. If you do not already have a work bench of some sort, an old table covered in 6mm hardboard and used in conjunction with a home-made bench hook (figs 11 and 12) should see you through most of the cutting jobs you will encounter.

For detailed work at a later stage, you may need to add a vice to the bench. Alternatively, you could invest in a collapsible work bench which serves as a work surface, large vice and drilling rig all in one. Making a purpose-built work bench is covered further on in the course.

Measuring and marking up
Any slight errors made in measuring and marking will multiply when you come to start sawing and may ruin your project. The best way to avoid a mistake is to check every measurement twice.

Having selected the piece of timber to be worked on—the workpiece—inspect it carefully. With a try square, determine which are the straightest adjacent side and edge and mark them in pencil (figs. 1 and 2). Always work from these when using any measuring

Left: *The correct position for sawing across a piece of timber with a panel or crosscut handsaw. Movement of the sawing arm is unobstructed, the saw is held at about 45° and the head is looking straight down over the blade*

215

or marking tool—this will ensure that the marks are consistent. A try square is an essential marking tool and costs very little.

For measuring, use a steel rule or boxwood rule where possible: you may need a steel tape on longer pieces of timber or boards, but this is not so accurate.

Mark out distances in pencil, using a 'vee' mark as shown in fig. 2—this tells you exactly where you have measured to and is another tip for avoiding errors. Where possible, cut out marks altogether by using the try square and rule as shown in fig. A.

Where accuracy is essential, mark cutting lines with a sharp knife—preferably a marking knife—not with a pencil. The scored line made by a knife is thinner, and therefore more accurate, than a pencil line. Also, it serves to break the outer fibres of the timber, thereby stopping the saw cut from fraying.

As you scribe a cutting line, use the try square to guide you (fig. 3). Your free hand should control the try square without obstructing the marking knife. Keep the stock of the try square flush against the face or edge of the workpiece, with the blade flat on the surface you are marking. The edge of the blade should line up exactly with the points of the vee pencil marks.

Using a marking gauge

Scribing with a marking gauge (fig. 6) often saves a great deal of laborious measuring and marking. Marking gauges are cheap and make life easier when marking out joints. The technique takes a bit of practice to master, so you should experiment on wood offcuts before starting any serious scribing work.

To scribe a mark, arrange the workpiece with the gauge nearest you. Make sure that the sliding block is flush against your face side or edge, then roll the gauge towards you until the needle touches the wood (fig. 6). Keeping the gauge at this angle, run it away from you down the workpiece to scribe the line. Avoid applying excessive pressure as you do this: if the needle digs in too far, a wavering line will result.

To scribe a line down the middle of a workpiece, set your marking gauge to roughly half its width and make a mark from the face edge. Make a mark from the opposite edge in the same way, adjust the gauge, then continue making marks from either edge until the two marks coincide.

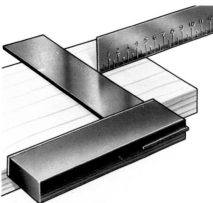

A. *Where possible, measure your timber with just a rule and try square. This saves time and is more accurate than lining up the square with pencil marks*

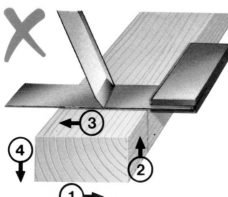

B. *Marking timber—the wrong way. If you mark continuously right round the workpiece, your lines may not meet when you get back to the starting point. With thick or rough timber, this leads to crooked cuts*

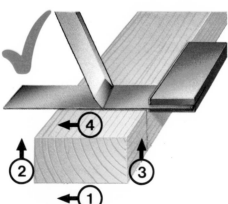

C. *Marking timber—the right way. Mark the face first, then the two edges, then the back. Note that both sets of parallel marks are made in the same direction, not in opposite directions*

Solving marking problems

Occasionally, you may come across a piece of timber which is difficult to mark up because of its shape and size.

To find the length of a workpiece longer than your rule or tape, measure a certain distance along it from one end then measure the same distance from the other end. Mark both points and measure between them. Add this to your two original measurements to get the overall length.

If you need to find the centre of this piece, simply divide your third measurement by two and mark off.

Dividing a piece of hardboard into equal strips can become extremely confusing unless the overall width divides exactly. Provided that no great accuracy is called for, you can get round the problem by running your tape or rule across one end of the workpiece and angling it until you get a measurement which is easily divisible by the strips required (fig. 7).

Mark off each division then repeat the process at the other end of the workpiece. Scribe the cutting line for each strip against a rule or straight edge, lined up with these marks (fig. 8). If the board is narrow enough do this with the marking gauge.

Before you start cutting the strips, bear in mind that some wood will be lost during the cutting process—using a panel saw, about 1.5mm per cut. This wastage is known as the kerf. For really accurate work, make allowances for it on each strip.

Sawing timber

The first important rule about sawing timber is that you should always saw on the waste side of the cutting line. Where accuracy is vital—as in furniture or shelf making—this means that you should always allow 5mm-10mm waste wood between one piece of timber and the next. For this type of work never be tempted to economize by simply dividing the timber into the required lengths—inaccuracies creep in, compounding as you work down.

Your sawing position is also crucial: get this right and you are well on the way to getting a perfect cut every time. The main picture shows the correct stance. Note that you should stand slightly 'sideways on' to the workpiece, not straight in front.

Starting the cut

Make sure that your workpiece is firmly held and will not 'jar' as you saw. If you are using a bench hook, arrange the workpiece so that as much of it as possible is supported on the bench. Use your free hand to press the timber against the raised lip of the bench hook as you saw.

To start the cut, line up your saw blade against the cutting line and rest it against your thumb (fig. 11). Keeping your thumb still and the saw at the optimum angle of 30 to 45 degrees, make a few short strokes towards you until you have grazed the wood. As you do this, look along the saw blade and keep your face side and face edge cutting lines in view.

As you get into your stroke—that is, start sawing in both directions—try to saw in a 'bowing' motion to keep the cut firmly fixed on both cutting lines. Keep the saw at right-angles to the workpiece, to ensure an accurate cut across the timber.

Well into the cut, lengthen your stroke to make as much use of the saw blade as possible. At the same time, bring down the heel of the saw to ensure that you follow the lines on the two visible surfaces. Use short, sharp strokes to stop the undersurface of the wood from fraying as you finish off the cut.

Sawing with the grain

The need to saw a piece of timber lengthways with the grain can usually be avoided, simply by buying the correct-sized timber to start with.

But if long-grain sawing is unavoidable, place the timber or board across two trestles at about knee height. Support the timber with your free hand and knee. Position your body so as to give free movement to your sawing arm with your body weight balanced over the cut.

Use a cross-cut or panel saw for boards up to 15mm thick, and for plywood and hardboard; use a rip saw on heavier timber.

If the timber begins to pinch the saw blade—causing inaccuracies—open up the kerf with thin wedges.

Although the optimum cutting angle for long grain cuts is normally 45 degrees, cut thin sheet material and plastic-faced boards at 10-15 degrees to the workpiece.

If the saw wanders to one side of the line, gently bend the blade back in the opposite direction until the correct cutting line is achieved, occasionally turning the board upside down to check that your line is straight.

1 Slide your try square up and down the workpiece as shown to find out which two sides form the most perfect right-angle

2 Having decided this, mark the two sides as 'face edge'—with a vee mark—and 'face side'—with an 'f'. Always work from these

3 To scribe a cutting line, hold the try square as shown. If you are working to pencil marks, ensure that you line up the square properly

4 Set a marking gauge against your rule as shown. When the slide is as near as you can get it, tighten the lock slightly to hold it

5 Make final adjustments by holding the gauge as shown and tapping it sharply on the bench. Check with the ruler after each tap

6 To scribe with the gauge, tilt it towards you until the needle just touches the wood then run the gauge away from you down the timber

Making 45 degree cuts

To make 45 degree cuts quickly and accurately, carpenters use a mitre block (fig. 12) or mitre box. These are available quite cheaply from do-it-yourself shops and builders' merchants.

Hold your workpiece firmly against the block as you cut. Rest the block itself against a bench hook or, alter-natively, clamp it in a vice.

Always use a backsaw to do the cutting, keeping the blade flatter than usual—although the cut may take longer, you will avoid accidental damage to the box itself.

Hand-sanding timber

Nearly all hand-sanding work should be done with a cork sanding block—available cheaply from most do-it-yourself shops. You have a wide choice of woodworking abrasive paper—including garnet paper, glasspaper and silicon carbide to name but a few. But each carries a grading number on the back referring to its grit size, which is a guide to its abrasive properties. Often, there will also be a more general classification—coarse, medium or fine.

Coarse grade paper is too abrasive for most sanding work, so you should rely only on the medium and fine grades. Try out the fine grade paper first and, if it works, stick to it for the whole job.

The key to sanding along the length of a piece of timber is to use long, uniform strokes—keeping with the grain at all times. Short strokes tend to create hollows and ridges.

To sand the end grain, use the technique shown in fig. 13. Always start by smoothing down the four edges, keeping your paper flat on the bench. This will stop them from fraying as you block-sand the rest of the grain.

7 Measurements which do not divide exactly can be made divisible by angling your rule. Mark off, then repeat on the other side

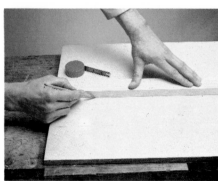

8 Having marked the divisions, use a rule, straight edge or—where possible—a marking gauge to turn the marks into cutting lines

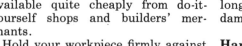

9 A handsaw and two backsaws. From top to bottom: general-purpose panel saw, tenon saw, and dovetail saw—used for intricate work

10 When you are dealing with damp or unseasoned timber, waxing the saw blade first with a candle will make sawing easier

11 Start saw cuts with the blade up against your thumb. Use short, sharp strokes to begin with then lengthen them as the cut grows

12 Using a mitre block. Steady the block as you saw, by holding it against a bench hook or clamping it in a vice

13 Chamfer the edges of a piece of timber as shown before you sand the end-grain. This will prevent the wood from fraying

---

TIP FROM THE TRADE

Q When sawing wet timber, my crosscut saw keeps jamming. Any ideas?

A The saw will run more freely if you lubricate the whole blade by rubbing it over, either with the end of an old candle or with a small lump of raw lamb fat. If you have a large quantity of wet or green timber to cut, have your saw re-sharpened with the teeth set to a coarser angle—ie, with their points splayed farther apart.

FIXING WOOD TO WOOD

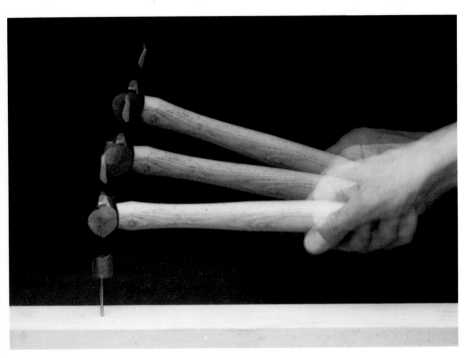

- ● **USING A HAMMER**
- ● **NAILING TIPS**
- ● **REMOVING NAILS**
- ● **DRILLING HOLES**
- ● **DRIVING SCREWS**
- ● **BUYING GUIDES**

Nails and screws are the two most important fastening devices used in carpentry, but how well they do their job depends almost entirely on how correctly they are used.

Tools
The two hammers used most frequently in carpentry are the claw hammer and the cross-pein, or 'Warrington'. The first is useful for levering out old nails and lifting floorboards while the second is more suited to finer nailing work.

If you are starting a tool kit, opt for a 450g claw hammer and a 280g Warrington. Later, you can add a 100g 'pin' Warrington for light, accurate nailing and pinning.

For burying nails below the surface of the wood, you need a set of nail punches (nail sets). These come in various sizes—to suit different sizes of nail—and help to avoid bruising the wood with the hammer head.

Some kind of drill is essential for screwing work. A power drill is the obvious choice because of its versatility but where there are no power points or access is limited, a wheel brace (hand drill) will serve well.

To drill larger holes by hand, you need a swing brace (fig 1) and a set of special bits—not a priority for the beginner's basic tool kit.

Good quality screwdrivers are essential to any tool kit and cabinet screwdrivers, with blades of about 300mm, are the most useful. Two of them—one with an 8mm tip and one with a 6.5mm tip—should cover you for most jobs. To deal with crosshead, Philips or Pozidriv screws, you need screwdrivers with the appropriate tips.

Using a hammer
Using a hammer properly requires a little bit of practice. Take a firm grip right at the end of the handle and form your arm into a right-angle, looking straight down on the work as you do so. Start the nail by tapping it lightly, keeping your wrist controlled but flexible and letting the hammer head do the work. Increase the power of your stroke slightly as the nail goes in but at no time let your arm waver—if you do, you will either miss, or bend, the nail.

On well-finished work, remember not to drive nails right in—leave a

1 *If you are drilling large clearance holes, use a swing brace. When the point emerges, turn the wood over and drill from the other side*

2 *Start short nails with a cross-pein hammer. Tap gently with the wedge end until they stand firm, then drive in with the hammer face*

3 *Very small nails and pins should be held with a pair of pliers. Use the cross-pein hammer to hit the nail with fairly gentle taps*

bit protruding for the hammer and nail punch to finish off.

Start light nails or tacks with the cross-pein by tapping gently with the wedge end of the hammer head. Drive them home with the hammer face using a number of fairly gentle taps rather than trying to knock them in with one blow, which will probably bend the nail. Very short nails can be held with a pair of thin-nosed pliers until driven in far enough to stand on their own.

Nailing techniques

For accurate, well-finished work, nails alone do not normally make a strong joint. However, if the nails are angled in opposition to each other, a reasonable joint can be made. When used in conjunction with one of the modern, woodworking adhesives, a very strong joint can be achieved. The panel on page 221 shows some common nailing techniques. Seldom are nails driven straight—a stronger joint can be made if they go in at an angle or *skew*.

When nailing two pieces of wood together, nail the smaller to the larger. Avoid nailing into hardwoods altogether: if you must, drill a pilot hole first, slightly smaller than the shank of the nail.

Removing nails

The claw hammer is used to remove partially driven nails. To avoid damaging the surface of the wood, place a small offcut under the hammer head before you start levering (fig 5). Extract nails with a number of pulls rather than trying to do the job in one.

Use pincers to remove small nails and pins which are difficult to grip with the claw hammer. Rock the curved face of the tool on the wood surface to draw the nail smoothly out.

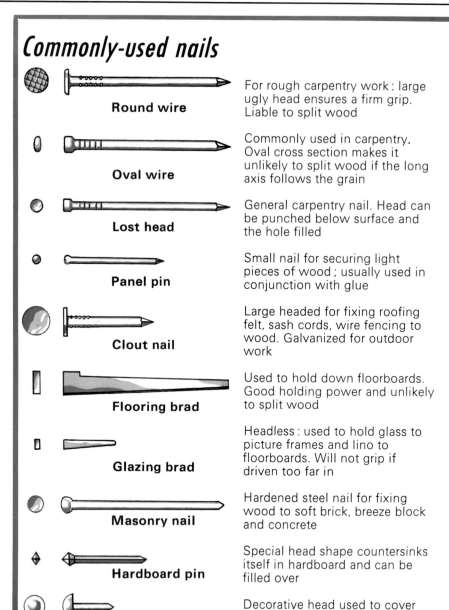

Commonly-used nails

Round wire — For rough carpentry work: large ugly head ensures a firm grip. Liable to split wood

Oval wire — Commonly used in carpentry. Oval cross section makes it unlikely to split wood if the long axis follows the grain

Lost head — General carpentry nail. Head can be punched below surface and the hole filled

Panel pin — Small nail for securing light pieces of wood; usually used in conjunction with glue

Clout nail — Large headed for fixing roofing felt, sash cords, wire fencing to wood. Galvanized for outdoor work

Flooring brad — Used to hold down floorboards. Good holding power and unlikely to split wood

Glazing brad — Headless: used to hold glass to picture frames and lino to floorboards. Will not grip if driven too far in

Masonry nail — Hardened steel nail for fixing wood to soft brick, breeze block and concrete

Hardboard pin — Special head shape countersinks itself in hardboard and can be filled over

Upholstery nail — Decorative head used to cover tacks in upholstery work

4 *Use the claw hammer to remove any partially driven nails. Slide the claw under the nail head then give it several short, sharp pulls*

5 *To remove large nails and to avoid damaging the wood, slip a block of wood under the head of the nail. This increases the leverage*

6 *Use pincers to remove nails which are difficult to grip with a claw hammer. A series of sharp pulls avoids leaving a large hole*

Nailing tips

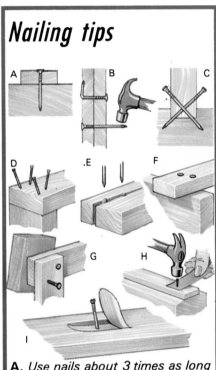

A. Use nails about 3 times as long as the workpiece. Always nail smaller to larger. **B.** On rough work, clench-nailed joints are much stronger. **C.** Skew-nailing is one of the best ways of securing a housing joint. **D.** When nailing into end-grain, drive in nails at opposing angles. **E.** Driving more than one nail along the same grain line risks splitting the wood. **F.** Nail small battens overlength to avoid splitting the end. Afterwards, saw or plane off the excess. **G.** Avoid 'bouncing' by placing a block under the workpiece. **H.** Small nails can be positioned with the aid of a cardboard holder. **J.** Secret nailing. Prise up a sliver of timber with a chisel.

Special-purpose nails

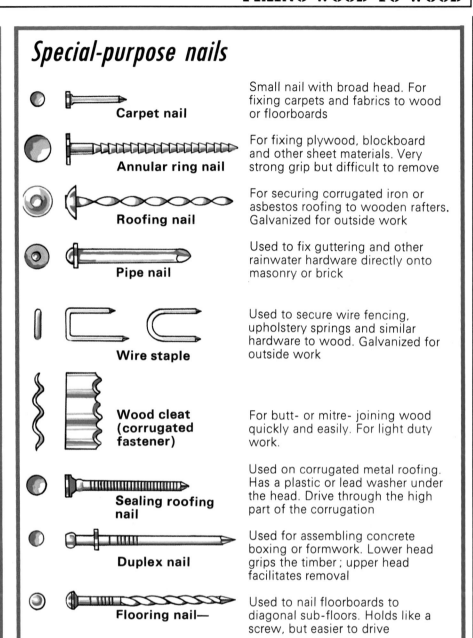

Carpet nail — Small nail with broad head. For fixing carpets and fabrics to wood or floorboards

Annular ring nail — For fixing plywood, blockboard and other sheet materials. Very strong grip but difficult to remove

Roofing nail — For securing corrugated iron or asbestos roofing to wooden rafters. Galvanized for outside work

Pipe nail — Used to fix guttering and other rainwater hardware directly onto masonry or brick

Wire staple — Used to secure wire fencing, upholstery springs and similar hardware to wood. Galvanized for outside work

Wood cleat (corrugated fastener) — For butt- or mitre- joining wood quickly and easily. For light duty work.

Sealing roofing nail — Used on corrugated metal roofing. Has a plastic or lead washer under the head. Drive through the high part of the corrugation

Duplex nail — Used for assembling concrete boxing or formwork. Lower head grips the timber; upper head facilitates removal

Flooring nail— Used to nail floorboards to diagonal sub-floors. Holds like a screw, but easier to drive

Drilling screw holes

All screws must have pilot holes made before they can be driven home. For screws into softwood smaller than No. 6 gauge, make these with a bradawl. Drive it into the wood with its chisel point across the grain, to avoid splitting.

Screws into hardwood and screws into softwood larger than No. 6 gauge need two pilot holes. One is for the thread—the pilot hole—and one for the shank—the shank hole.

For all except the largest pilot holes, use twist drill bits. Those for pilot holes should be the same size as the screw core to which the threads are attached. Those for the shanks should match them exactly.

When drilling pilot holes, mark the required depth on the drill bit with a piece of masking tape. This will tell you when to stop and helps prevent the drill chuck damaging the workpiece should you overdrill.

As with nailing, where two pieces of wood are to be fixed together, screw the smaller to the larger. Drill the shank hole right through the smaller piece so it is pulled down tight as the screw is driven home. If the shank hole goes only part of the way through you will find it very hard to pull the top piece of wood down tight and may risk breaking or damaging the screw. Brute force should never be used—it indicates that either the thread hole or the shank hole is too small.

Countersinking

Countersinking is normally the easiest way of recessing screw heads flush with, or below, the surface of the wood. The recess is made with a countersink bit (fig 7) after the pilot has been drilled, to the same depth as the countersunk screw head. Take particular care if you are countersinking with a power drill or the recess may accidentally become too large.

Counterboring

If the wood being fixed is thicker than the length of the screw shank, drill a hole the same size as the screw head part-way through the wood, and fill the hole afterwards with a plug of wood or a length of dowel.

TIP FROM THE TRADE

Q How can I avoid getting hammer bruises on the surface of the wood I am nailing? And how can they be removed?

A The hammer face must hit the nail head exactly at right angles, so check that you are holding the hammer correctly. Also, clean the face of the hammer after every few nails by rubbing it on an offcut of wood; this will get rid of dirt from the nails and help prevent the hammer 'skidding'. Small bruises can usually be removed by ironing with a hot iron and wet cloth—the steam causes the compressed wood fibres to swell and fill the depression.

7 For flat-head countersunk screws, use a countersink bit. Drill a hole of the same diameter as that of the screw head

Screws: types and uses

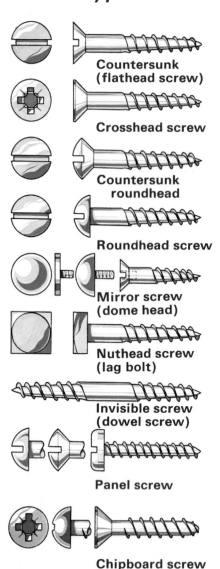

Countersunk (flathead screw)
Used for general woodwork. The head sinks in flush with or slightly below the wood surface

Crosshead screw
Used for general woodwork, but needs a special screwdriver which does not slip from the head

Countersunk roundhead
Used for fixing door-handle plates and other decorative fittings with countersunk holes. The head is designed to be seen

Roundhead screw
Used for fixing hardware fittings without countersunk holes. The head protrudes from the work

Mirror screw (dome head)
Used for fixing mirrors and bathroom fittings. The chromed cap threads into the screw head to hide the screw. Do not overtighten

Nuthead screw (lag bolt)
Used for fixing heavy constructions together and heavy equipment to timbers. Tighten with a spanner

Invisible screw (dowel screw)
Used for invisible joining of two pieces of timber.

Panel screw
Used for fixing thin sheets of metal and plastic. Cuts its own thread as it is screwed in. Various types of head are available

Chipboard screw
Used for securing chipboard and its derivatives. Various types of head are available

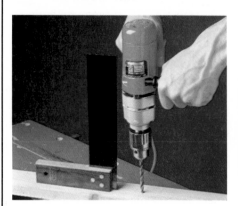

8 Always hold a drill at right-angles to the surface so that you drill a straight hole. Rest a try square next to the bit and use it as a guide

9 When you are drilling horizontally with a hand-operated wheel brace, grip the handle with your thumb towards the wheel

10 A pump action screwdriver should be held with both hands. Make sure the screwdriver is squarely on the screw head

Drilling techniques

Using the correct drilling technique makes all the difference to the quality of the finished work. Whether your drill is power or hand operated, you should always hold it at right angles to the work surface so that the pilot hole is straight. If you find this difficult, rest a try square upright near the bit and use it as a guide.

With twist drills, operate the drill in bursts and lift it frequently to allow debris to escape. To give yourself as much control as possible, always hold the drill with both hands and never press too hard—you are bound to overdrill.

Keep the chuck key taped to the cable, so it is handy whenever you want to change drills.

Using a hand-operated wheel brace requires slightly more effort, but gives more control than a power drill. When drilling vertically, grip the handle with your thumb on top. Turn the wheel steadily to avoid knocking the drill out of line.

To drill horizontally, grip the handle with your thumb towards the wheel (fig 9). Alternatively, where a side handle is fitted, grasp this in one hand while you turn the wheel steadily with the other.

Driving screws

Always make sure that the tip of your screwdriver is in good condition and that it fits exactly into the slot in the screw head. A blade which is too narrow or rounded damages the slot, while too wide a blade damages the wood as the screw goes in.

When using a pump-action screwdriver, hold it firmly in both hands—one on the handle, the other on the knurled collar just above the bit—and make sure that you are not off-balance (fig 10). Any loss of control could cause the blade to slip out of its screw slot and damage your wood.

To make screwdriving easier, the screws can be lubricated with wax or candle grease before driving. Brass screws are quite soft and to prevent damage when screwing into hardwood, the resistance can be lowered by driving in a steel screw first.

Build a bunk

Start by cutting all the timber to length, following the cutting list below, and label every component to avoid confusion later. Assemble the two end frames first, spacing the groups of rails 25mm apart. Each group of three rails consists of a pair 100mm wide flanking one 50mm wide. The rail at floor level is 75mm wide.

Next, get a helper to prop up the end frames so they can be linked by the four long side rails. Each is aligned with the lower 100mm end rail at top and bottom, and is secured with domed or covered screws.

Secure the base support rails to the inner face of the long side rails and the lowest end rails, with fixing screws at 100mm centres.

Saw and rasp the ends of the ladder stiles to a smooth curve, and drill 25mm diameter holes in the inner stiles at the spacings shown overleaf to take the ladder rungs. Screw the inner stiles to the outer ones, slot in the rungs and screw the completed ladder in position.

Finish off by adding the short front side rails. Then cut the bed bases to size and screw them to their support rails all round.

Cutting list

The list quotes finished lengths of timber. When buying the timber, add on at least 15mm to each length to allow for cutting wastage.

Legs: 4 No. 50mm x 50mm x 1480mm

Side rails: 4 No. 100mm x 25mm x 2065mm; 2 No. 100mm x 25mm x 708mm; 2 No. 50mm x 25mm x 708mm

End rails: 8 No. 100mm x 25mm x 760mm; 4 No. 50mm x 25mm x 760mm; 2 No. 75mm x 25mm x 760mm

Base support rails: 4 No. 50mm x 25mm x 672mm; 4 No. 50mm x 25mm x 1929mm

Outer ladder stiles: 2 No. 50mm x 25mm x 1250mm

Inner ladder stiles: 2 No. 50mm x 22mm x 1038mm

Plywood leaves: 2 No. 760mm x 1929mm x 9mm

Ladder rungs: 3 No. 25mm chromed steel tube x 649mm

Use 32mm No.8 countersunk wood screws and white PVA adhesive on the frame: on the bed rails use the covered type (page 222). Use 25mm No. 6 screws on the bed bases.

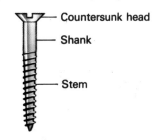

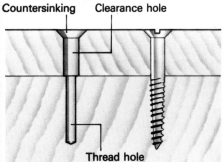

A. *Drill two pilot holes for each screw—the top one to accept the shank in a 'push fit', the bottom one usually two sizes smaller*

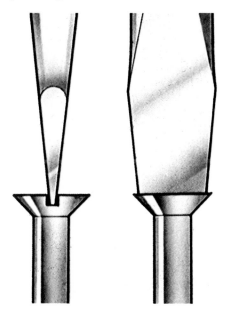

B. *See that the screwdriver blade fits the screw head exactly and that the tip is kept ground square. If not, you risk 'chewing up' the screw*

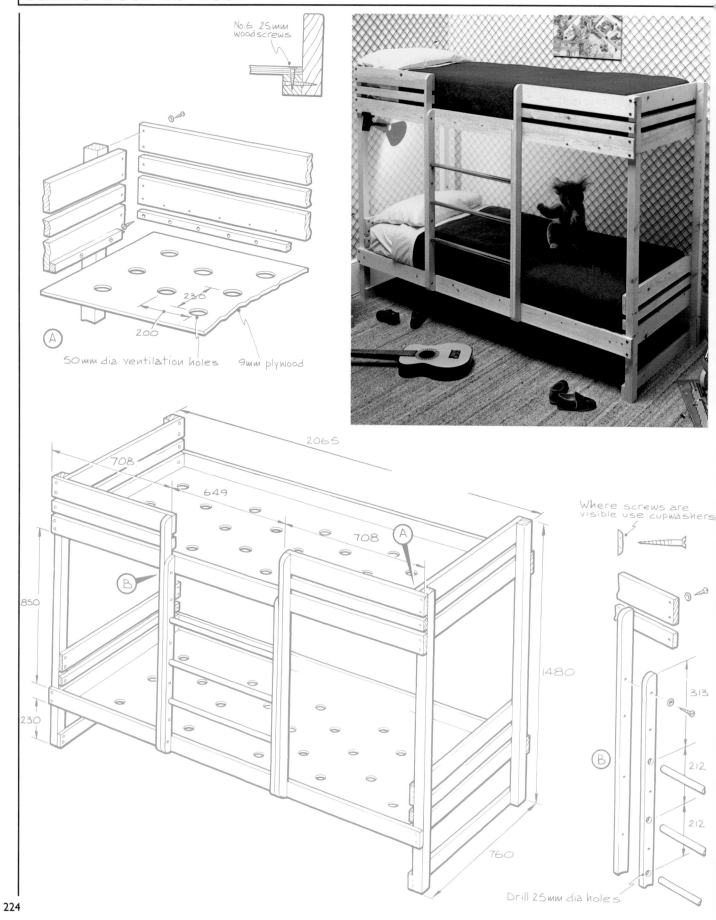

No.6 25mm woodscrews

A 230 200

50mm dia. ventilation holes   9mm plywood

2065

708

649

708   A

Where screws are visible use cupwashers

B

850

230

1480

760

313

B

212

212

Drill 25mm dia holes

FIXING TO WALLS

The fixing of any object—light or heavy—to a wall must always be done with a proper fixing device to make the attachment a secure one. Fixing devices provide the grip a nail or screw needs to give holding power.

Only masonry nails can be banged into a brick or block wall—and still provide holding power—without first boring a hole for a fixing device.

The type of fixing you need is determined by the weight of the object to be fixed and the type of wall it is to be attached to. For solid walls, there are three basic methods of fixing—masonry nails, plugs and screws, and plastic compound with screws. Bolts are sometimes used to fix very heavy objects. For timber-framed walls, special cavity fixing devices are available for use where there is no stud handy.

Before making a hole in any type of wall, however, first check that there are no pipes or electricity cables running across it, by using a small metal detector.

Fixing tools

Tungsten carbide-tipped masonry drills are specially designed for drilling in brick, cement, concrete and tiles. There are two types of drill bit available—those for use with hammer or impact drills, and those for non-impact use with a wheel brace or simple electric drill. If the latter is used, it should be set at its lowest speed and preferably with the speed controller set to about 600-800rpm. Failure to use the correct type of bit will result in the tip either shattering or burning.

The size of drill bit you use is determined by the size of your chosen screw and fitting. For example, with most domestic wall plugs and using a No. 8 gauge (4.2mm) screw, you would use a No. 8 gauge drill and a No. 8 gauge wall plug.

A hand boring tool and club hammer can also be used to make the required

Right: *A wide range of wall fixings specially designed for stud partition walls is now available. The types shown here are (from top): Fischer captive nylon toggle (retaining strap is cut off when fixing is complete); expanding plug (wings are forced out as screw is driven); plasterboard plug; collapsing steel anchor (two types); Rawlnut*

- ● FIXING TOOLS
- ● PLASTIC FILLERS
- ● FIXINGS FOR HOLLOW WALLS
- ● WALL PLUGS
- ● BOLTS AND NAILS

hole, although obviously this is a slower method. Whatever method you use to make the hole, you must wear goggles as protection against flying masonry.

Fixings for solid walls

A solid wall could be made of either concrete, brick, or lightweight cellular or aggregate building blocks. Any of the basic fixing methods can be used on brick or concrete walls. But breeze block or clinker walls need special fixing devices, the holes for which must be drilled. This is because the blocks break up easily as the fixing device is inserted unless there is a clean hole—and it is more difficult to control a hammer than a drill.

Wall plug and screw fixings

Wall plugs can be used to fix most of the usual household objects such as shelves, cabinets and wall ornaments. There are various types of plug fixing and they all require a pre-drilled hole.

When using an electric drill, remem-

1 First mark the exact position of the fixings and then carefully drill the holes—a cardboard box is useful for catching the debris

2 When the holes have been drilled to correspond to the size of plug and screw being used, simply push the plugs carefully into place

ber to press firmly so that the masonry drill bit bites into the wall. Keep the drill steady and draw it back regularly to clear away the debris and to allow the bit to cool.

To ensure that the drill tip does not slip on a hard surface such as tile, place a piece of adhesive tape over the spot to be drilled.

To make a hole with a hand boring tool, first tap the tool with the club hammer to penetrate the plaster and then hit it more firmly when you make contact with the brickwork.

Continue to do so until the required depth is reached, turning the tool slightly in a clockwise direction after each hammer blow to prevent it getting stuck. Always blow out any dust before inserting the fixing device.

The most common types of wall plugs are those made of plastic or fibre. Aluminium plugs are also available but the plastic kind are the most popular because they are waterproof and do not rot, expand or contract.

Plastic plugs (fig. A) sometimes have protruding teeth to grip the surrounding material, while the composition of fibre plugs is such that it expands (fig. B) to give a secure fixing.

All plugs are coded to correspond with the standard screw sizes and should always be slightly longer than the lengths of the threads on the screws being used. **Drill a hole slightly deeper than the length of the screw** (minus the thickness of the item you are fitting). With some plugs, the shank of the screw should not enter the plug: others are devised so that the plug surrounds the whole screw, so follow manufacturers' instructions. You can regulate the depth of the hole you drill by sticking marking tape at the appropriate length on the drill. Only insert the drill as far as the tape and you have

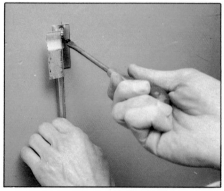

3 Hold the fixture in position and screw it to the wall. Fibre wall-plugs expand to grip the masonry as the screw is turned

A. *Expanding plastic plugs can be used with three different screw sizes*

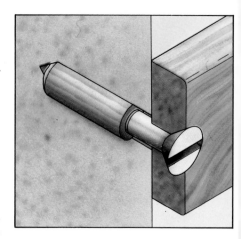

B. *The traditional fibre plug allows the screw to form its own thread*

the correct depth.

Also, try to get the plug sunk right into the masonry so that the surface plaster is not damaged as the screw is turned into position.

Occasionally, the thickness of the object to be fixed is less than that of the screw shank. If this is the case, the plug must be sunk further into the masonry. You can do this by inserting the plug into the hole and screwing in the screw. Continue tightening until the shank is about to enter the plug then take out the screw and attach the object to the wall.

The wall plugs designed specifically for aggregate or cellular block walls have teeth or ridges to grip the surrounding material and fins which prevent them from rotating as you turn the screw.

The Rawlnut is another fixing device for use on aggregate blocks. This has a sleeve which compresses against the surrounding material as the bolt is tightened (fig. C). Both types can also be used in brick or concrete walls.

C. *The Rawlnut is suitable for fixings in solid and hollow walls*

The old-fashioned wooden plug is not often used these days, mainly because each one has to be hand cut to size. However, if you do decide to use them make sure that they fit tightly—a slight taper at the end of the plug helps to fit it right to the back of the hole. Solid wooden plugs must be drilled out with a pilot drill before the screw can be inserted.

Plastic compounds
These were usually made from asbestos fibre and cement base, but were withdrawn from sale a few years ago on safety grounds. Modern plugging compounds which do not contain asbestos are now available, and if anything offer even better fixings in irregular holes.

To provide a really strong fixing with a plastic compound, the back of the hole needs to be wider than the mouth—scrape it out with the screw if this is not already the case. Then moisten a little of the compound to a smooth consistency and mould it into

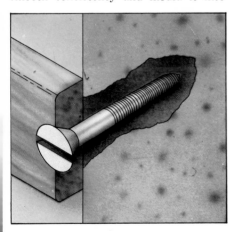

D. *Plastic compounds are ideal for use when the hole has become too large for the particular fixing*

a suitable shape (fig. D). Force it into the hole, using the packing tool normally provided with such compounds. The other end of the packing tool should be pointed—with this pierce the compound ready for the relevant screw.

Light objects can be fixed immediately, but heavier objects should not be fixed until the compound is hard.

Another type of compound which can be used in all types of masonry is Kemfix, made up of a chemical adhesive—consisting of a capsule containing polyester resin and quartz granules plus a phial of hardener. The capsule and phial are inserted in a pre-drilled hole and crushed.

Special stainless steel studs and

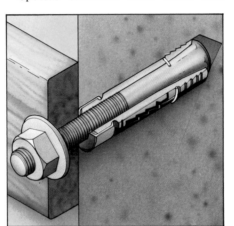

sockets are available for use with this adhesive. Attachments made with this fixing do not exert expansion stresses in the masonry. Fixings can, therefore, be made exceptionally close to the outside edges of walls without breaking up the masonry.

Masonry bolts
Masonry or anchor bolts are used where heavy, wooden loadbearing frameworks are to be fixed to a wall and can be used on all types of solid masonry. Bolts of up to 10mm diameter are suitable for 230mm thick brickwork but for 115mm brickwork, 6mm is the largest recommended size.

In this case a hole needs to be drilled to the diameter of the bolt (fig. E), avoiding mortar joints and the corners of the bricks. The metal plug inserted into the hole expands as the bolt is tightened up and grips the surrounding material.

Masonry bolts are available in a variety of head styles, such as one which accepts a hook and eyelet.

E. *Masonry bolts offer heavy-duty fixings in concrete and brickwork. Various bolt types are available*

Below: *This chart shows how pull-out loads depend on plug size and screw diameter. In general terms, fixings are stronger in concrete*

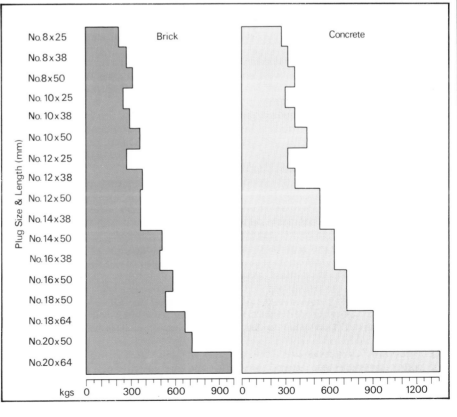

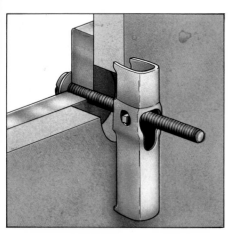

F. *A gravity toggle provides a good fixing for plasterboard partitions and other types of hollow wall*

Masonry nails

Masonry nails are available in two types, one of which has a straight shank and the other a twisted shank to improve its penetration into exceptionally hard materials.

The 28-70mm straight shank nail is the standard size and is suitable for fixing shelving battens, skirting boards, wall panelling and so on to solid walls. Medium straight-shanked nails of 22-86mm can be used for fixing similar objects into slightly harder walls. The twisted shank nails vary in size from 38-89mm and should be used only for heavy-duty fixing.

Masonry nails create a strong holding power by compacting the finely-ground material around them as they penetrate the wall.

When using such nails, always drive them in at right angles to the wall and ensure that they penetrate at least 13mm—but not more than 19mm—into the masonry. Remember to allow for the depth of your plaster both when estimating the length of nail required and when driving it in.

Nails with straight shanks should be driven into the walls with gentle hammer blows which hit the head of the nail straight on. Twisted shank nails must be started off with light hammer blows but can take heavier blows once they have got a grip on the masonry. When banging in masonry nails, wear goggles to protect your eyes from flying chips and dust.

Always use an engineer's ball-pein hammer when banging in masonry nails. The heads of most other types of hammer are made of a softer metal than the nails themselves and could well chip as you use them—never underestimate the dangers of this 'flying shrapnel'.

Hollow walls

Internal partition walls often consist of some form of lining—such as plasterboard—fixed to timber supports. The stud partition wall is a common example of this. Special fixing devices are needed for such walls as those for solid walls would simply fall out—there being nothing for the nails or plugs to grip. The Rawlnut and certain types of nylon plug are the only exceptions to this.

The best means of fixing objects to hollow walls is to drill through the lining to the timber supports (studs). These are usually positioned at 300, 400 or 600mm intervals (406mm in older houses) and can be located by tapping along the wall—a dull sound

G. *The spring toggle is specially designed so that the load is spread over a wide area of the cavity wall*

indicating a stud. If you are in any doubt, probe the area with your finest drill bit to confirm you are in the right place for the stud.

If the proposed fixing site of the object does not correspond with a stud, one of the large number of fixings available for hollow walls can be used.

Fixings for hollow walls

All fixings for hollow walls have one thing in common—they provide support behind the lining when the screw has been tightened.

The metal toggle (fig. F) is the most popular type of fixing. This either relies on gravity to open it up as it is pushed through the wall or it is spring-loaded (fig. G).

Fixing an object with a toggle is a simple matter—undo the toggle and insert the bolt through the object to be fixed. Then, after attaching the toggle to the end of the bolt, fold it flat and push it through the hole. As soon as it is pushed through the wall, the toggle

opens up and is pulled against the wall as the bolt is tightened up.

However, make sure that you get this fixing method correct the first time—unscrewing the bolt means that the toggle will fall into the cavity and be lost forever. The same applies to the nylon or plastic anchors which are used on hollow walls with screws instead of bolts.

A nylon toggle is available which remains in place when the screw is removed—this is made up of a toggle bar, a slotted collar which remains on the outside of the wall, and a ridged nylon strip which joins the other two parts together.

To use this type of fixing, first push the toggle through the wall and slide

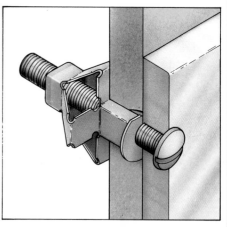

H. *The ribbed legs of the Interset give extra rigidity to this permanent fixing for plywood or chipboard*

the collar along the ridged nylon strip into the hole—the strip may need to be cut off flush with the collar. Having done this, you can insert the screw.

A particularly strong fixing can be made on even the flimsiest of linings—such as hardboard—by using a plated steel cavity fixing, called Interset (fig. H). This has rigid legs which fold at predetermined points giving maximum support to the object.

Obviously, hollow walls cannot bear the large loads that solid walls can. One way of increasing their capacity is to fix a batten across two studs and then screw the object to the batten. Attaching a batten with several hollow wall fixings is also a sensible way of spreading the load which would otherwise fall on a single fixing device. To make a secure job, use No. 12 (4.6mm) screws to fix the batten.

If the correct screws are not used with each type of fixing, they are unlikely to perform properly and may eventually pull out of the wall.

GLUING AND CRAMPING

- ● ADHESIVES
- ● TYPES OF CRAMP
- ● PREPARATION
- ● USING ADHESIVES
- ● FITTING CRAMPS
- ● IMPROVISED CRAMPS

Above: *You can improvise a cramp for simple gluing jobs simply by using terylene (polyester) cord and a short piece of dowel—which is used as a turn-key to tighten the web*

Modern adhesives have made it possible for amateur carpenters to construct wooden furniture which in the past only skilled craftsmen could have tackled. Work which would have once needed precise joints can now be joined simply with strong wood adhesive—using cramps to hold the wood in place while this is drying. You can choose from a variety of cramps according to the size of the wood.

The term glue properly refers to pure animal or vegetable glue. Other types, which are resin based, are known as adhesives. The success of your gluing depends on choosing the right kind of glue for the job.

Choosing the right adhesive
The glue or adhesive you use will depend on the type of wood you want to join together, the surface conditions, the kind of stress the join will be subjected to and whether a temporary or permanent join is wanted.

Pay particular attention to the temperature in the workshop. Most adhesives need a warm atmosphere in which to set. Make allowances too, for hard or resinous woods: these require a sap-resistant adhesive.

Polyvinyl acetate (PVA)
PVA adhesive ('white glue') is among the most useful for general-purpose woodwork. Available ready mixed in easy-to-use plastic bottles, it is applied directly to the wood which is then cramped. At normal room temperatures, the setting time varies from 30 minutes to three hours depending on the brand used.

PVA is a strong adhesive. It does not stain timber but, if smears are left on the surface, it will show through varnish as a light patch. So any smears must be wiped away quickly with a damp cloth. It is not completely waterproof, although outdoor grades are available, and will not adhere very readily to resinous or very hard woods such as teak.

Urea formaldehyde adhesive

This is a good adhesive for hard, resinous woods. Its gap-filling properties also make it ideal for gluing loose-fitting joints—such as those found in furniture making and repairs. It resists moisture better than PVA.

Resorcinol formaldehyde

This woodwork adhesive provides the greatest strength and is the most water resistant, so it is ideal for outdoor work and boatbuilding. It is also a good gap-filling adhesive.

When adhesives have to be applied to timber treated with preservative, use urea formaldehyde or resorcinol.

Animal glue (Scotch glue)

This old fashioned glue is made from animal pelts and bones. It comes both in cake or granular form and in liquid form. The cake or granular varieties need to be melted down in a glue pot with water at a temperature of 65°C and used while still hot. These do not stain timber and dry to a medium brown colour which matches most polished or stained woods. They are not waterproof.

Unlike the granular variety, liquid animal glues can be used cold. Again they are not waterproof and do stain some woods—especially oak—so excess glue should be wiped off with a damp cloth before it can do any damage to the wood.

Animal glue has largely been made obsolete by more modern adhesives but is still the best to use when constructing frameworks for upholstered furniture. The stresses which the frame undergoes while being upholstered may cause adhesive-made joints to fracture.

For mending or renovating antique furniture, use an alburnum (sapwood) based Scotch glue. This has the same expansion and contraction rate as old-fashioned Scotch glue, which is different from that of modern adhesives. Never mix old and new glue on one piece of furniture.

Synthetic resin cements

This type of adhesive is almost completely waterproof and comes in a variety of forms—powder, semi-liquid or two-part (adhesive and hardener). It can be used for outdoor work and small boat-building. The setting time depends on the temperature of the surroundings—the warmer the air around the workpiece the faster it sets.

Impact (or contact) adhesives

Wood stuck to wood with this type of adhesive tends to move after a time. It is therefore not strong enough for furniture making and is better suited to fixing laminates and tiles.

The surfaces to be stuck together are both coated with the impact adhesive and are then left to dry separately according to the manufacturer's instructions. Afterwards, the two surfaces are brought together to make an instant, strong bond.

Impact and contact adhesives are the only types which do not require cramping while they set. But as a bond is formed instantly, you should ensure that the mating surfaces are aligned.

Epoxies

Almost any material can be stuck with epoxy adhesives but for woodworking, PVA and formaldehyde adhesives often prove to be both cheaper and easier to use. Epoxies are made up of two parts —a resin and a hardener—which must be mixed together. Setting time can vary between one hour and 24 hours.

Cyanocrylate adhesives

Extra care must be taken when using these 'super glues'. Manufacturers claim that one small spot of the adhesive and a little pressure will stick almost anything to anything in moments, although they don't stick wood well. They will certainly stick skin to skin, so be careful and make sure that children do not get anywhere near them.

Safety precautions

Many adhesives are highly inflammable and some also give off toxic fumes. Make sure that you work in a well ventilated space and that there are no naked flames about.

Anyone who is prone to dermatitis should wear gloves or a barrier cream as glues contain skin irritants. If the glue should get on to unprotected skin and cause burns or an allergy rash, seek medical advice. If it gets in your eyes, wash it out with plenty of warm water and, again, seek medical advice.

Types of cramp

The type of cramp you should use depends on the size of the wood you are gluing.

G cramp: Sometimes also known as a C-cramp, this most versatile type of cramp gets its name from its shape. G cramps have a mouth capacity of

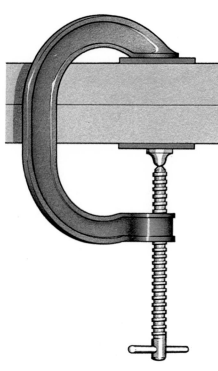

A. *This G cramp is the ideal choice when you want to hold smaller pieces of wood or awkward shapes as the glue sets*

between 25mm and 250mm or 300mm and are mainly used for cramping pieces of wood to a bench and for holding down veneer or laminate while the adhesive dries.

Variations on the basic G cramp include deep-mouthed cramps—which reach further across the workpiece— and small, sliding bar G cramps. The latter are smaller and easier to use than conventional G cramps and are useful for holding small pieces of timber in place.

Sash cramp: Sash cramps are used to cramp larger pieces of timber, such as doors and window frames. Consisting of two adjustable stops on a long bar, they come in different lengths up to 3m long with extensions (fig. B). One stop is adjusted by sliding it along the bar and securing it with a pin: the other tightens like a vice jaw. Because of their size, sash cramps are expensive to buy. They are, however, obtainable from hire shops.

Web cramp: This consists of a long loop of nylon webbing, running through a ratchet, which can be tightened and released using a spanner or screwdriver (fig. 7). The web cramp cannot apply as much pressure as a sash cramp, but it is cheaper and is quite adequate for light and medium weight gluing jobs.

You can make an improvised form of

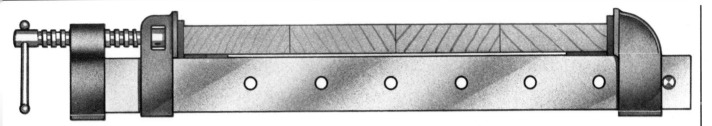

B. *Large scale gluing of things like long pieces of wood requires one or more sash cramps to hold the work really securely along its whole length while the glue is setting*

web cramp by using strong cord and two short pieces of dowel (fig. 8). Tie a double thickness of the string around the object to be put under pressure then use the dowel to twist the strands together until the tension cramps the wood firmly. Use the second piece of dowel to hold the first in place.

Preparation

If you are using liquid animal glue, make sure that it is fresh—most have a limited life and will cease to work properly if they are old.

Most, but not all, adhesives are effective only on surfaces which are free from moisture, dust and grease. Unless the instructions with your adhesive specify special gap-filling properties, the surfaces should also be reasonably smooth.

Always 'dry assemble' your work to begin with. Blow out dust from any inaccessible corners of the work, then fit the pieces together. Having made the necessary adjustments and re-cleaned the joints, mark each part to

eliminate the possibility of getting things in the wrong order on final assembly. Make sure that you sand and finish off any areas which would prove too inaccessible after gluing.

Mixing and applying adhesives

Before you start mixing and applying your glue or adhesive, make sure that all the necessary cramping equipment is well to hand—it will be too late to search for it once the glue is mixed.

If there are any small holes or cracks in the wood, fill them at this stage. A good filler can be made by mixing a thin glue or adhesive with some sawdust: if you use sawdust from the same wood, the finished joint will be barely noticeable.

When making up a mixed glue or adhesive, use a small piece of wood and an old china teacup or saucer. Follow the manufacturer's instructions to the letter, taking particular care when water has to be added.

Use another, preferably flat, piece of wood to apply your glue or adhesive or apply it straight from the container. Again, you should follow the instructions carefully and make sure that each surface to be coated receives an even covering. Glue invariably shrinks as it dries—causing stresses and strains which will weaken the joint unless the coat is even.

Cramping techniques

Unless you are using impact adhesive, you should cramp the wood as soon as

the joint has been made. Whichever type of cramp you use, you must be careful that the surface of the wood does not get scratched and damaged by the action of the cramp while the glue is setting. You can either use some newspaper or alternatively, to prevent the metal cramp jaws from bruising the surface of the wood, ensure that there is a small block of wood between the two (fig. 3). Make your blocks, or *cushions*, from offcuts.

When using a G cramp, make sure that the jaws and cushions are positioned as far over the joint as possible (fig. 3) then tighten the cramp to finger-tight. Where two pieces of angled, or wedge-shaped, wood are being cramped, position a second cramp at right-angles to the first (fig. 5) to stop the parts slipping.

Use a sash cramp in the same way as a G cramp. Make sure the sash is exactly square to the workpiece or distortions may result. During cramping, the bar of the sash will tend to bow in towards the workpiece, so place small wedges underneath to keep it straight.

When using a web cramp, or its improvised alternative, ensure that the webbing runs around firmly fixed parts of the workpiece. Otherwise, you may break one joint as you are trying to cramp another.

If you are making an improvised web cramp, make sure that it is of a really strong material like terylene (polyester) cord.

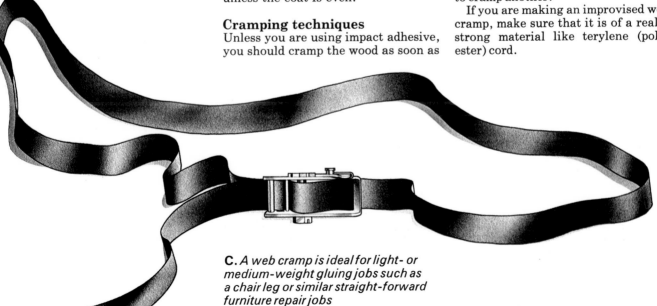

C. *A web cramp is ideal for light- or medium-weight gluing jobs such as a chair leg or similar straight-forward furniture repair jobs*

1 Mix glue to the right consistency, if necessary, then apply it with a stick or straight from the glue bottle onto the surface of the wood

2 With the wood on the bench, wipe off any excess glue to prevent it staining and place the wood in whichever cramp you are using

3 Place a block of wood between the wood you are gluing and the cramp to cushion the work and protect it while it is in the cramp

4 Tighten the cramp and if any excess glue is squeezed out of the joint wipe it away. Leave the wood in the cramp for the required time

5 If cramping wedge-shaped pieces of wood together, use a second cramp at right-angles to the first to stop the wood slipping

6 If gluing long pieces of wood, use several sash cramps on alternate sides of the wood. Protect it with cushion blocks and paper

7 For light- or medium-weight gluing jobs use a web cramp. Run the webbing through the ratchet and tighten steadily

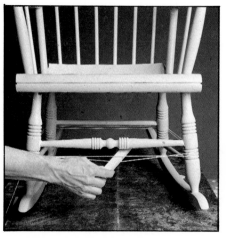

8 Make an improvised web cramp using polyester cord and a short piece of dowel. Use double-thickness cord around the object being glued

9 Use the dowel to twist the strands together until the tension cramps the wood firmly. Use a second piece of dowel to hold the first

USING A CHISEL

- ● **TYPES OF CHISEL**
- ● **PARING**
- ● **CUTTING MORTISES**
- ● **BUYING CHISELS**
- ● **CUTTING HOUSINGS**
- ● **CHISEL SAFETY**

Above: *To use a chisel successfully and safely, when paring vertically or horizontally, it must be kept under complete control. A chisel should be sharpened regularly to maintain its cutting edge*

Knowing how to use a chisel correctly is one of the most important aspects of carpentry. And once you have mastered the skills and techniques involved, a whole new range of do-it-yourself projects becomes possible.

Types of chisel
The chisel is the basic wood-shaping tool and is used for paring, cutting joints and chopping out areas of wood for hinges and other fittings. There are various types of chisel for different uses, the basic types being:
Bevel edged chisels have tapered edges which allow the chisel to get easily into tight corners. They are ideal for cutting dovetails and shallow housings, such as hinge recesses, and for vertical paring. But because much of the steel in the blade is ground away to form the bevel, the blade lacks strength. A bevel edged chisel should not be used for heavy work or for work that involves any lever action.
Firmer chisels have strong blades of rectangular cross-section which make them stronger than bevel edged chisels and thus more suitable for heavy work such as fencing, frame construction and notching out for pipes running over joists.
Mortise chisels are the strongest chisels of all and are designed to withstand both continual striking with a mallet and the levering action required when cutting the mortises for mortise-and-tenon joints. The heavy square cross-section of the blade prevents the chisel from twisting in the mortise, thereby ensuring neat and accurate finished work.

Mortise chisels of good quality have a leather washer between the shoulder of the blade and the handle to reduce the jarring caused by striking with the mallet.

233

USING A CHISEL

Paring chisels have long blades of either firmer or bevel edged type. The long blade is so designed for reaching into awkward corners and for paring out long housings such as those used in bookcase and staircase construction. Because they have long blades, paring chisels should never be struck with a mallet or used with a lever action. This can cause the brittle metal to snap and may be dangerous.

Buying chisels

Bevel edged and firmer chisels are available in a wide range of widths from 3mm to 38mm. Initially, a set of 6mm, 12mm and 25mm chisels should be adequate for most requirements. Mortise chisels do not come in such a range of sizes and it is unlikely that anything other than 6mm, 8mm and 12mm mortises will ever be required. Buy paring chisels only when the need for a particular one arises.

Always select chisels that have smooth handles and make sure that the handles feel comfortable in your hand. Modern chisels usually have handles made of shockproof, splinter-proof plastic. Traditionally, chisel handles were made of boxwood or beech and although these are still obtainable, they are an expensive alternative to plastic. If you prefer wood, pick chisels with handles made of beech which is much cheaper than boxwood but not as tough.

Always check that the blade is secure in the handle and that the blade and handle are in line. If the blade is wrongly aligned, the chisel will be incapable of producing good work. Check also that the blade is flat across its face—if it is not, it will be impossible to sharpen correctly.

Chisel safety

Chisels are often supplied with plastic guards which fit over the end of the blade. If the chisels you choose do not come supplied with guards, it is well worth buying a set. Always replace the guard when you have finished using a chisel in order to protect the cutting edge, and to prevent accidents.

When working with a chisel, always keep both hands safely behind the cutting edge. Except for vertical paring, when the work is secured by your hand, hold the work firmly in a vice or cramp it to the work bench.

Trying to force a chisel leads to lack of control and a possible accident, so always use two or three thin cuts rather than one thick one.

Horizontal paring

Horizontal paring is a technique used when constructing joints—such as housing joints for supporting the ends of shelves and halving joints used in framework. These consist of slots across the grain of the wood and are normally made with a bevel edged chisel which is able to get into the corners of the joints.

When making such a joint, define the area of the slot by marking out width lines on top of the wood, and width and depth lines on both sides. Make a saw cut, slightly to the waste side of each width line and cut down to the depth line. If the joint is particularly wide, extra saw cuts can be made in the waste to make chiselling-out easier.

1 For horizontal paring, hold the wood securely in the vice so that it does not move as you chisel. Rest your elbow on the bench

2 Hold the chisel with both hands, keeping them behind the cutting edge and pare angled cuts adjacent to the sawn guide lines

3 When the angled cuts are half way across the wood, turn it around in the vice and finish the cuts from the other side

4 Turn the chisel over so that its bevel edged side is facing down, and slap the handle with the palm of your hand to remove the waste

5 Turn the wood in the vice again, and remove the remainder of the waste from the other side. The bevel edge should be facing up once more

6 When most of the waste has been cleared, work the chisel across the joint with its blade flat against the wood to remove fine shavings

7 To sever any remaining fibres in the corners, work the blade into each corner with the chisel held in one hand

8 For vertical paring, place the wood on a bench hook and support the end with a timber offcut. Keep your head over the work

9 Remove slivers of wood, gripping the blade between your fingers. Hold your thumb over the handle to provide downward force

Hold the wood securely in the vice so that it will not move as you work and make sure that it is horizontal (fig. 1). Hold the chisel in both hands, safely behind the cutting edge, with the elbow resting comfortably on the bench. This gives extra control over the chisel's movement.

Start by chiselling out the waste adjacent to the sawn lines, making angled cuts to half way across the wood (fig. 2). Push the chisel firmly, holding it at a slight angle, keeping your arm horizontal and level with the work. When the cuts are half way across the joint, reverse the wood in the vice and complete the angled cuts from the other side (fig. 3).

Now turn the chisel over so that the bevel is facing downwards and remove the bulk of the remaining waste by slapping the handle of the chisel with the palm of your hand (fig. 4). Because the bevel side is facing down, the chisel blade works its way up to the surface and no levering action is needed to clear the waste. Again chisel only half way across the joint, then turn the wood around and work from the other side with the bevel side of the chisel facing upwards once more (fig. 5). If you chisel right across the joint, the wood will break and splinter out on the other side.

When most of the waste has been removed, work the chisel across the joint, keeping it absolutely flat across the bottom, to shave off the last fibres of wood (fig. 6). Finally, hold the chisel vertically in one hand and work the blade into the corners to clean them out and sever any remaining fibres (fig. 7).

Vertical paring
Vertical paring is necessary when you wish to round off a corner or to make a curve in a piece of wood.

Hold the wood on a bench hook, to protect the surface of the work bench, and support the other end, if necessary, with a timber offcut of the same height as the hook (fig. 8). Hold the chisel upright in both hands with the thumb of the upper hand over the top of the handle to give control and downward force. The lower hand steadies the work and also grips the blade of the chisel between the index finger and the knuckles of the other fingers. Keep your head over the work as you pare away the wood.

Mark the required curve on the wood and cut off the corner, to an angle of about 45 degrees, with a tenon saw. Holding the chisel as described, pare off the corners left by the saw cut. Keep paring off the corners, taking off thin slivers of wood not more than 1mm thick (fig. 9). If you take off thicker cuts than this, the extra effort involved may cause you to lose control of the chisel.

Work as closely in to the curve line as possible, then finish off by smoothing with a file.

10 To sharpen the blade of a chisel, hold it at an angle of about 30° onto an oilstone. Rub the blade in a figure of eight motion

Cutting a mortise
A mortise is a rectangular slot cut into a piece of wood into which a tongue—called a tenon—from another piece of wood is fixed. The mortise and tenon make a strong joint which is used to form T-shapes in frames. The mortise should always be made with a mortise chisel—the width of the chisel's blade determines the width of the mortise.

To mark out a mortise accurately you need a mortise gauge. Using a chisel of the exact width of the planned mortise, set the gauge to the chisel blade and mark out the width lines on the wood. With a try square as a guide, draw the two setting-out lines which determine the length of the mortise.

When cutting a mortise, the wood should be held securely on a solid part of the bench rather than cramped in the vice: as the chisel is struck with a mallet, it would dislodge the wood from a vice. Use a G cramp to hold the wood firmly in position and protect the top surface with a timber offcut.

11 When a fine burr begins to form, turn the blade over. Rub it over the oilstone keeping the blade flat upon the surface

Make sure that the tail of the cramp is beneath the work or injury may result. Drive the chisel into the wood with a mallet—never use a hammer to hit a chisel as this may damage the handle, making it uncomfortable to use.

Start by driving the chisel into the mortise to dislodge a deep wedge of waste. Use three separate strokes of the chisel to remove the wedge, making it equal on both sides. Keep your body behind, and in line with, the workpiece. Work, with a series of small chops, from the centre towards one of the setting out lines keeping the chisel in the same vertical plane at all times. Stop at the line, turn the chisel round and approach the other setting out line with a further series of chops.

Clear out the waste and dislodge another wedge in the centre to the depth of the finished mortise. A band of tape wrapped around the chisel blade to the required depth makes a good depth indicator. Chop up to both setting out lines, again to the required depth.

If you are cutting a mortise to go right through the wood, chop to half way from one side then turn the wood over and work from the other side. Never chisel all the way through to the other side or the wood will split.

Sharpening chisels

No matter how correct your technique or how expensive your chisels, you cannot produce good work with a blunt chisel. You should always check that cutting edges are sharp before use and hone them if necessary.

Chisels are sharpened on oilstones which are made in three grades of grit—coarse, medium and fine. Coarse grade stones remove large particles of steel and are therefore needed only when a cutting edge is chipped or badly damaged. Medium stones are used for normal sharpening of the blade and for dealing with small nicks in the cutting edge. Fine stones hone the blade to a sharp edge. For sharpening on oilstones, you also need a light oil.

Chisels have two angles to their cutting edge: the ground angle of 25° and the honed angle of 30°. The ground angle is formed on a powered grindstone and only occasionally needs regrinding.

To hone a chisel, apply a liberal amount of oil to the stone and hold the blade at an angle of about 30° against the stone (fig. 10). Keep the blade square to the stone and rub it in a figure of eight motion to distribute wear evenly over the stone. When a burr—known as a wire edge—begins to form on the flat side of the blade, turn the chisel over, Rub the flat side across the stone to remove the wire edge, keeping the blade perfectly flat upon the stone (fig. 11). If you raise the chisel handle, however slightly, the flat side of the blade becomes bevelled.

When the wire edge has been removed, return to the bevelled side of the blade. Rub each side of the blade in turn, using less and less pressure, until a razor sharp edge is produced.

Cutting a mortise

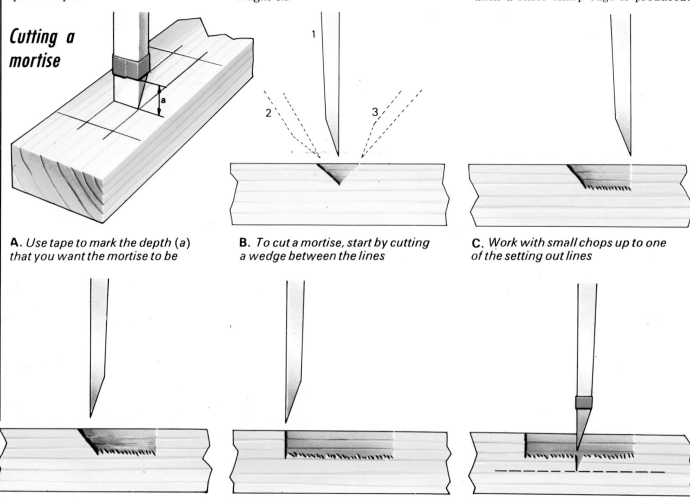

A. Use tape to mark the depth (a) that you want the mortise to be

B. To cut a mortise, start by cutting a wedge between the lines

C. Work with small chops up to one of the setting out lines

D. Reverse the chisel and start again from the centre

E. Work towards the other setting out line with a further series of chops

F. Place tape on the blade and repeat down to the required depth

HALVING JOINTS

- JOINT TYPES
- TEE HALVINGS
- CUTTING PARTS
- CROSS HALVINGS
- MARKING UP
- ASSEMBLY

The halving joint is a model of strength and simplicity, with the two parts interlocking fully to provide resistance to twisting. The joint can be reinforced with adhesive, using screws, or by driving dowel pegs through holes bored in both components

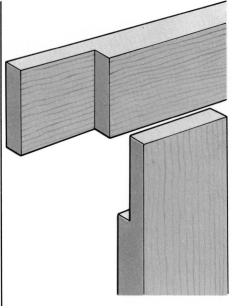

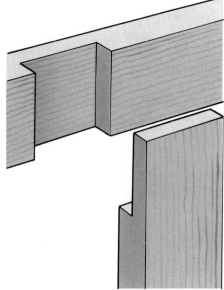

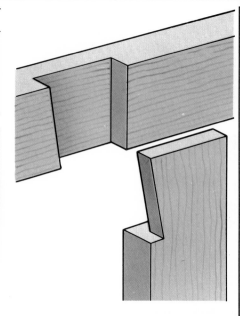

B. *The corner halving is used where two members meet at their ends*

C. *The tee halving joint consists of a pin and a socket*

D. *A stronger tee halving is made by sloping one edge to form a shoulder*

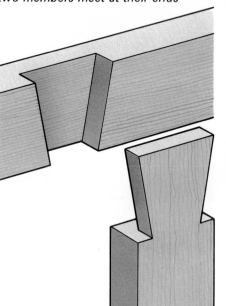

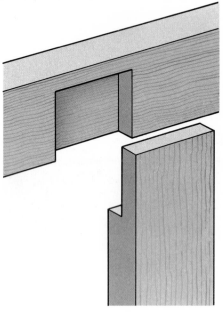

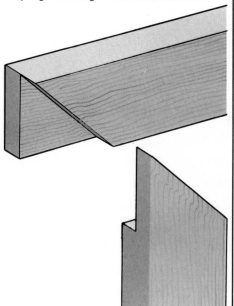

E. *In the dovetail halving, both of the edges are sloped*

F. *A stopped tee halving produces a neat finish to the work*

G. *The mitred corner halving can be used if the surface is to be moulded*

The halving, or half-lap joint—one of the most versatile woodworking joints —is used in all kinds of framework from delicate side tables to a full-framed timber building. So, for building hardwood and softwood frames or repairing damaged timber around the house, a practical knowledge of halving joints is a real asset.

Halving joints are so-called because both members of the joint are halved in thickness so that the faces of the finished assembly are flush with one another. There are three basic types

of halving joint: the tee halving, the cross halving and the corner halving.

The tee joint is often used in cabinet framework where the end of a rail meets another piece some distance from the end (fig. C). To produce a neat finish, the joint can be stopped— cut short of the cross-piece of the 'T'— so that the outside edge does not show the end grain. But a stronger joint is made if one of the edges is sloped to provide a shoulder, so that the two members can be separated in one direction only (fig. D).

Alternatively, both edges can be sloped to produce a dovetail halving joint (fig. E). This type of joint is often used as an intermediate rail on a long table to prevent the sides from bowing.

The cross halving is used where two members have to cross each other without increasing the thickness of the frame, such as in the diagonal stays of tables and chairs (fig. A).

The corner halving is used where the members meet at their ends, for example the corners of a rectangular frame (fig. B). A mitred corner halving

1 Where halving joints are to be assembled in pairs, mark up each pair at the same time so that they come out to the same length

2 To construct a tee halving joint mark out the socket section then mark the shoulder line for the pin on the back of the cross-rail

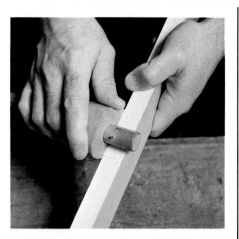

3 Set a marking gauge to half the thickness of the wood and then carefully scribe the depth lines for the socket part of the joint

4 Use the marking gauge to scribe thickness lines on the pin, then mark the area of waste onto the pin and socket with a pencil

5 To saw the pin, position the wood vertically in the vice and make a notch in the wood by drawing back the blade of the tenon saw

6 When you have cut a notch about 5mm deep in the end of the wood, saw down to the shoulder line on one side of the piece

7 Turn the piece of wood around in the vice, then saw down to the shoulder line on the other side of the pin section

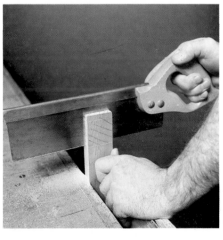

8 Next, hold the saw horizontally and cut down to the shoulder once more to remove the remaining V-shaped piece of wood

9 Hold the wood on a bench hook and cut away the waste wood, taking care not to saw into, and weaken, the neck of the pin

239

is often employed when the surface has to be moulded (fig. F).

The interlocking parts of a halving joint are known as 'pins' and 'sockets'. The tee halving joint consists of a pin cut in the cross rail and a socket in the side rail into which the pin is fitted. Corner halvings consist of a pin in each member, and cross halvings of two sockets.

Marking up the pieces

Where halving joints are to be fitted in pairs, be sure to mark up each pair of pieces at the same time to make certain that they come out to the same length (fig. 1).

On rough-sawn wood you can mark out the cutting lines in pencil, but for hardwood or softwood furniture you should scribe the lines with a marking knife held carefully against the side of a try square. Bear in mind that the knife leaves quite deep marks in the wood, so mark heavily only the areas you intend to cut or you will spoil the finished appearance of the halving joint.

The procedure for marking up a tee halving joint is as follows:
● Mark the width of the cross-rail across the face of the side rail and half-way down both edges.
● Mark the shoulder line across the back of the cross-rail at a distance from the end about 6mm longer than the width of the side rail (fig. 2). Continue this line across the edges of the wood.
● Set a marking gauge to half the thickness of the pieces of timber. Scribe a short test line on one of the edges, then turn the gauge around and mark the same surface from the other side. If the two marks merge into one, the gauge is set. If not, adjust it until they do.
● With the gauge set correctly, scribe depth lines for the socket part of the joint on both edges of the side rail (fig. 3).
● Gauge the thickness of the pin along the edges, and across the end of the cross rail, then mark the waste area on both pieces (fig. 4).

Sawing the pin

When sawing the section out of the cross rail to form the pin of a tee halving joint, the 'rip' cut that runs in the same direction as the grain must be made before the cross-cut across the grain.

Place the wood vertically in the vice, in a low position to prevent vibrations which might cause the saw to jump off the wood. Using a tenon

saw (backsaw), notch the corner of the wood on the waste side at the far side of the gauge line by drawing the blade of the saw back (fig. 5). Use your thumb to guide the blade and continue sawing gently, letting the saw handle drop slowly until the blade is in the horizontal plane.

When you have cut a groove about 5mm deep in the end of the wood, saw down to the shoulder line on one side of the piece (fig. 6). Afterwards, reverse the wood and, remembering that the waste will have changed sides, saw down to the shoulder line on the other side (fig. 7). Finally, hold the wood vertically in the vice once more and saw out the V-shaped piece of wood left inside the cut (fig. 8).

To make the cross-cut, hold the wood on a bench hook and, cutting

to the waste side, remove the waste wood with a tenon saw, taking care not to cut into, and weaken, the neck of the pin (fig. 9).

Finish off by clamping the wood horizontally in the vice and cleaning out the angle of the L-shaped cut with a chisel, paring across the grain (fig. 10).

Cutting the socket

When you have completed the pin section of the joint, hold it temporarily in place on the marked-up side rail to make certain that the measurements for the socket are accurate. Make minor adjustments if necessary.

Secure the wood horizontally in the vice and make a saw cut, slightly to the waste side of each width line, down to the depth line. Pare out the

10 Clamp the wood horizontally in the vice and clean out the angle of the L-shaped cut with a chisel, paring across the grain

11 When the socket section of the joint is complete, temporarily assemble the pieces and saw off the excess wood at the end of the pin

12 If the fit of the assembled joint is too tight, plane a shaving off the edge of the pin. Take care not to remove too much wood

13 If a particularly rigid finished joint is required, drill through the joint and secure it with a glued dowel peg

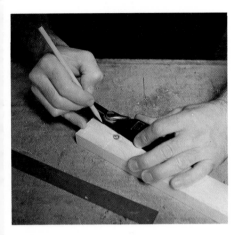

14 To mark out the pin of a dovetail halving, use a sliding bevel to obtain an equal angle on each shoulder

15 To cut the pin, position the wood in the vice so that one of the sloped lines is vertical and cut down to the shoulder line

16 Cut down the other sloping line and then position the wood in the vice sideways. Cut down the halving line

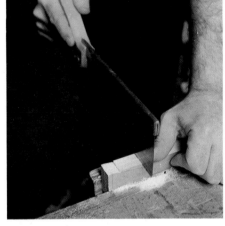

17 To complete the pin of the dovetail halving, cut away the wide shoulder and the two wedge-shaped side shoulders

18 To mark up the socket section of the joint, place the pin over the other piece and trace the shape with a marking knife

waste with a bevel edged chisel as described on pages 233 to 236.

Mark up and cut the pins for corner halvings and the sockets for cross halvings as described above.

Assembling the joint
When you come to assemble the members of a tee halving, you may find that the fit is too tight. In this case, plane a shaving off the edge of the pin rather than trimming the side of the socket.

In addition, you may find that the pin does not bed down sufficiently to produce a flush surface. If this is the case, check that the bottom of the socket and the cut face of the pin are flat. If they are not, use a wide chisel or a flat file to level them. Bear in mind that the joint should, as far as possible, be assembled only once

before gluing in place: too many trial assemblies loosen the parts. Before gluing the joint, cut off the excess wood at the end of the pin (fig. 11).

Apply a liberal amount of PVA adhesive to both surfaces to be joined and cramp the joint as described on pages 229 to 232. To avoid marking the wood, pad the jaws of the cramps with timber offcuts. Before the glue sets, check again that the joint is tight fitting and wipe off any excess adhesive with a damp cloth.

Tee halving joints should be given extra strength by nails or screws (see pages 219 to 224), or if a particularly rigid joint is required you can drill through the joint and secure it with a glued dowel peg (fig. 13).

Dovetail halving joints
Although more complicated to construct than the tee halving, the dovetail halving is a useful joint because it can withstand sideways tension without being screwed or pegged. Although the construction technique is similar to that for a tee halving, the marking up procedure and the order of cutting are quite different:
● Mark out the shoulder line of the pin around the piece of wood with a try square and marking knife.
● Mark up the sloping lines of the dovetail, using a sliding bevel to obtain an equal angle on both sides of the wood (fig. 14).
● Use the marking gauge to mark the halving lines as above, and pencil mark all the waste areas. Position the wood in the vice at such an angle that one of the sloping lines is in the vertical plane.
● Using the tenon saw, saw down the first sloping line to the shoulder mark (fig. 15).
● Reposition the wood in the vice so that the second line is now vertical and saw down this line.
● Saw down the halving line as described above.
● With the wood held horizontally in the vice cut away the wide shoulder and the two short side shoulders with a tenon saw (fig. 17).
● Clean up the edges and corners of the halved dovetail with a bevel-edged chisel.
● To mark up the shape of the socket section of the joint, place the pin over the other piece of wood and trace the shape of the pin onto the wood with a marking knife (fig. 18).
● Use the marking gauge to score the halving lines onto the edges of the wood and pare out the waste as described above.

Hat and coat stand

Mark the topmost housing 80 mm below the top of the post

Pegs measure 220, 205, 190, 175, 160, and 145 mm long: fit the longest at the top, the shortest at the bottom.

Subsequent housing on the other three faces are separated by the thickness of one peg.

Cut the hooks—notches 20mm wide and 15 mm deep and 25mm from one end of each peg

Cut the housing half as deep as the peg thickness.

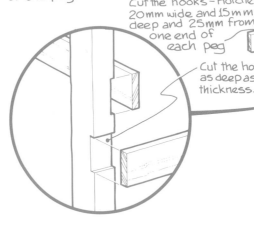

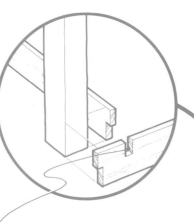

1700mm

Use actual wood thicknesses to mark the sizes of the cut-outs in the four legs. Assemble them, then insert the central post.

This attractive and functional hat and coat stand is both inexpensive and easy to construct. There are no complicated joints, difficult markings or cutting to do, and the whole project can easily be completed in a day.

The biggest faults with hat and coat stands are a general lack of stability, and the way clothing can easily fall off in an untidy heap. This stand will solve these irritating problems. The rebated lips cut in the pegs, projecting in a spiral procession from the central post, will grip a hat or coat thrown carelessly over them. The projecting base, constructed with sturdy halving joints, gives the whole stand a steadiness that will resist most efforts to topple it.

The stand can be constructed from hardwood or softwood. Your choice will be determined by appearance and how much you wish to spend. Whatever your choice, buy wood that's planed all round 242 (PAR). Note that wood is sold by its

nominal size, but the actual sizes are reduced by the planing process. Here it is essential to use the actual wood to mark out the various housing joints.

Cutting list

Part	Material	No.	Size
centre post	50 × 50mm wood	1	1700mm
peg 1	50 × 25mm wood	1	220mm
peg 2	50 × 25mm wood	1	205mm
peg 3	50 × 25mm wood	1	190mm
peg 4	50 × 25mm wood	1	175mm
peg 5	50 × 25mm wood	1	160mm
peg 6	50 × 25mm wood	1	145mm
base	75 × 25mm wood	4	314mm

Miscellaneous: 32mm oval wire nails or brass screws and screw cups, glasspaper, PVA adhesive and filler, paint or varnish.

314mm

MORTISE & TENON JOINTS

- ● JOINT TYPES
- ● MARKING MORTISES
- ● CUTTING PARTS
- ● DIMENSIONS
- ● MARKING TENONS
- ● ASSEMBLY

Above: *A typical mortise and tenon joint incorporating a secret haunch to stop the components twisting*

A. *A conventional haunched through joint of the type found on many older window and door frames*

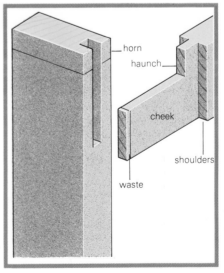

The strength of a joint connecting two pieces of timber depends on three factors: the size of the gluing area, the way in which one piece of timber encases the other, and the accuracy of the finished work. A strong joint is one in which one component encases the other in such a way as to ensure a large gluing area without either component being unduly weakened. The mortise and tenon joint satisfies these requirements best of all.

Types of mortise and tenon

Mortise and tenon joints are used in a wide variety of work, ranging from coarse carpentry through joinery to the finest cabinet work. Their most common applications are in roofing, window frames and door frames, stud partitions, and tables and chairs.

The component parts of the joint are known as the *stile*—the vertical member which usually holds the mortise—and the *rail*—the horizontal member usually with a tenon at each end. In the simplest mortise and tenon joint, used only in the roughest carpentry work, the rail fits straight in to a mortise in the stile (fig. B). More usually, though, the rail is trimmed to leave 2-6mm shoulders on either face (fig. A). These effectively hide any gaps—such as those caused by a slack-fitting tenon or by careless cutting-out of the waste in the mortise.

This type of mortise and tenon joint is called a plain joint. It can also be classified according to the way in which the mortise and tenon meet.

243

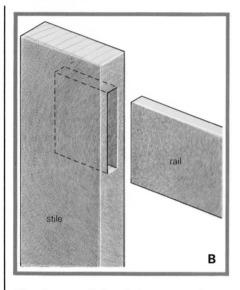

B

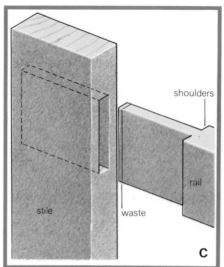

shoulders

rail

stile

waste

C

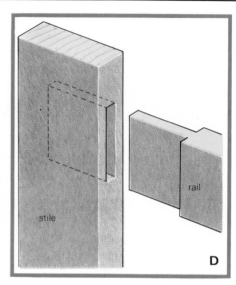

rail

stile

D

The four traditional forms are shown (figs C to F)—*through, stub or 'blind', through wedged,* and *foxed wedged.*

An additional complication—*haunching*—is sometimes introduced to stop the rail from twisting, and to take strain off the tenon (fig. A). And on large rails, the gluing area can be increased by employing a double tenon with haunching (fig. G)—the strongest mortise and tenon joint.

Some of the above permutations are occasionally combined, making the whole business of mortise and tenon joints look far more complicated than it really is. For example, on high-quality door frames you may find that some of the joints are of the foxed wedged double tenon type.

In fact, the only joints which are really difficult to make are those where the stile and rail are moulded —requiring you to scribe and cut complicated shapes. These are described further on in the course.

Rules for dimensions
The thickness of the tenon should be around one-third of the thickness of the stile, but should be set finally to match the width of the nearest available size of chisel.

The width of the tenon should not exceed five times its own thickness, which in turn will determine whether a single or double tenon is used. But if the joint is positioned at the top of the stile, it is usual to divide the tenon width into three parts—two for the tenon and one for the haunch (fig. K). Where the frame of which the joint is a part is to take a panel of some sort and is grooved, the haunch forms part of this. Otherwise, it is customary to make a groove to match a *secret* haunch (fig. 13).

Where the rail is wide—over about 75mm—it is usual to employ a double tenon. In this case, you can either divide the rail width by four and take each tenon width as one-quarter (fig.

B. *A simple stub joint in which the tenon has no shoulders. This is used only for the simplest frameworks*

C. *In the plain through joint, the tenon passes right through the stile and is trimmed off after assembly*

D. *For a stub joint, the mortise in the stile must be cut to exceed the length of the tenon by 3-5mm*

E. *For a through wedged joint, wedge room must be cut on either side of the mortise. The wedges are driven in after the joint has been assembled*

F. *The foxed wedged joint, which incorporates secret wedges, is little used today thanks to the strength of modern woodworking adhesives*

G. *A double haunched joint has exceptional strength. The waste between the tenons is cut with a coping saw taking care not to weaken the tenons*

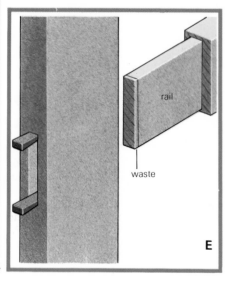

rail

waste

E

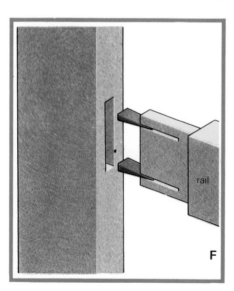

rail

F

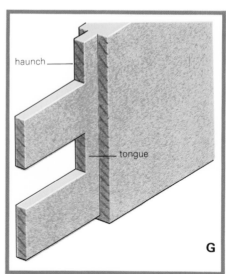

haunch

tongue

G

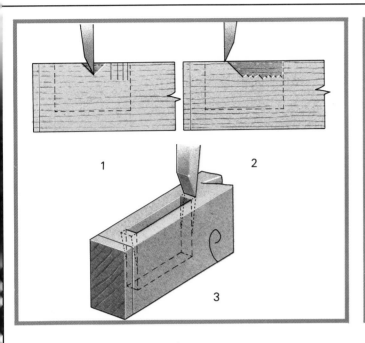

H. *Start a mortise from the centre (1) working outwards. Move back to the centre (2) then out to the other end (3) Trim to the edges then cut wedge room if needed*

I. *Initial marking out on both the stiles and rails is best done with the relevant pieces of timber cramped together. Mark the waste first, then the rail width*

1 *To mark out a tenon, the mortise gauge must be set to the nearest convenient chisel size. Adjust the pin spacing as necessary*

2 *To find the middle of a piece of timber with a mortise gauge, try it from both sides until you get the pin marks to match up*

3 *After you have marked the tenon on the rail and mortise on the stile, reset the gauge and mark out the tenon width*

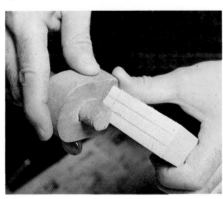

4 *Use a conventional gauge to mark out where the haunch will be cut. Make sure that you have set it to the correct width*

G) or divide it by three and make the distance between tenon centres one-third of the rail width.

If you are making a stub tenon joint, the depth of the mortise should exceed the length of the tenon by 2mm. The gap allows for excess glue which might otherwise force the joint apart as soon as it has been assembled. When you are cutting the mortise for a stub tenon, make sure that there is at least 4.5mm of wood between it and the outer edge of the stile.

When marking and cutting a mortise at the end of a stile, it is customary to leave excess waste material known as a *horn*—between 25mm and 35mm is usual on a standard-sized door frame. The horn helps stop the stile from splitting as the mortise is cut and also protects the frame in transit to its final position, where the waste is trimmed off.

Marking up a simple frame

If you are making a framework which incorporates joints at the ends of stiles, do not forget to allow for the extra length taken up by the horns when you compile your cutting list.

Rail lengths for a framework are normally taken as the overall width of the frame, allowing you plenty of waste material. But if you are using through mortise and tenon joints, add on 12mm to the overall frame width: this gives you 6mm waste on each end, removed when the joint is finally 'cleaned up'.

245

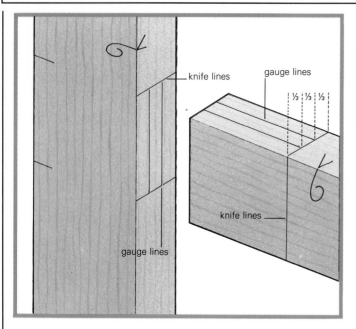

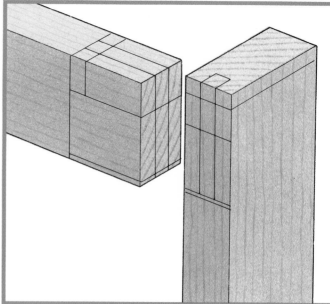

J. *A marked-out plain through mortise and tenon joint ready to be cut. The lines marking the mortise and corresponding tenon width are made with a mortise gauge*

K. *This more complicated haunched stub joint is at the top of the stile. If you get confused when marking out, shade in the waste areas in pencil*

With your timber to hand, test each piece for true and mark on face sides and face edges (see pages 215 to 218). Lay the pieces out as they will appear in the finished frame, face edges innermost and face sides uppermost.

Designate and mark the stiles 'left' and 'right', and the rails 'top' and 'bottom'. You can also mark the joints A-A, B-B and so on, though the marks should be on waste wood which will be removed later.

Next, place the stiles side by side on the bench, face sides uppermost and face edges outwards, and cramp them together with a small G cramp. Remember to place offcuts between the jaws of the cramp and the workpiece to protect the latter from becoming bruised (fig. I).

With a try square, marking knife and rule, mark off one waste end or horn—whichever is appropriate—on both pieces. Follow by marking the finished lengths of the stiles. The material left represents either waste or another horn.

Your next job is to mark the positions of the mortises and, if you are making a wedged joint, the 'wedge room' on either side of them. Again, use the try square, marking knife and rule, but score deeply only those areas which are to be cut. Mark very fine lines on the rest of the timber.

If you are making a through tenon joint, separate the stiles and mark around them individually. Start at the face edge and work around the timber so as to end up at the edge below it.

Make fine lines at each edge of the workpiece to enable you to continue around it without having to score across the whole surface.

When you have finished marking the stiles, cramp the rails in the same way and mark off the overall lengths. Do not forget to add an extra 12mm waste if you are making through mortise and tenon joints. This will be planed off when the joint is assembled.

Mark the lengths of the tenons as described above—together with the haunches where necessary (figs I and K). Finally, separate the rails and continue the lines right around each workpiece.

Marking mortises

At this stage, you are ready to mark the widths of the mortises on each stile. By far the easiest way of doing this is with a mortise gauge (fig. 1), a tool similar to a marking gauge but with an adjustable scribing pin in addition to the standard fixed one. You are well advised to go to the trouble of buying or borrowing a mortise gauge, rather than trying to 'make do' with existing tools.

Start by releasing the set screw on the stock and adjusting the distance between the pins to match the width of the chisel you are using to cut the mortise out. Next, you must adjust the stock so that the distance between

5 *The saw cuts for the haunch groove are best made with a dovetail saw, but if you do not have one, use an ordinary tenon saw*

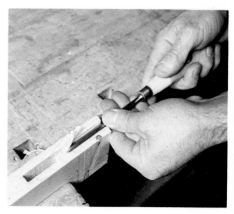

6 *After you have made the saw cuts, chisel out the waste wood in the groove with an appropriately-sized bevel-edged chisel*

it and the moveable pin allows you to centre the pins on the timber.

To check this, place the stem of the gauge flat on the workpiece with the stock face to the face side, then roll the gauge until the pins make indentations in the surface. Repeat the operation from the side opposite the face side. If the two sets of marks coincide, the pins are centred and you can tighten the stock. If they do not, adjust the stock until they do.

With the pins centred and the stock back against the face side, roll the gauge away from you to mark the **mortise widths on the stiles (fig. 2).** Keeping the gauge on the same setting, mark around the rail ends to give you the necessary width of the tenons.

If shoulders or haunches are included in the joints, reset the gauge to the appropriate dimensions and mark them out with the stock against the face edge (fig. 3). Use an ordinary marking gauge to mark the depth of the haunch to be cut across the end of the stile (fig. 4).

If you must use an ordinary marking gauge instead of a mortise gauge, always work from the same face side and edge—resetting the gauge for each mark you make.

Cutting the mortises
The techniques for chiselling out a simple mortise are described in detail in pages 233 to 236. Briefly, the best procedure for an effective result (page 236) is as follows:
● Cramp the workpiece securely to a solid part of the bench.
● Drive the chisel into the marked-out mortise to dislodge a deep wedge of waste. Use three separate strokes of the chisel.
● Work in a series of small chops from the centre of the mortise to one end, removing waste as you go.
● Turn the chisel around and work back to the other end in the same way.
● For a stub (blind) mortise, wrap a piece of tape around the chisel blade to give you the required depth. Continue removing waste in the same way then trim all sides.
● For a through mortise, continue chiselling until you get half way through the wood then turn the workpiece over and restart the mortise from the other side.

Where necessary, the 'wedge room' outside the mortise must also be chiselled. Line up your chisel on the appropriate line with the bevel pointing towards the centre of the mortise. Chop downwards at an angle of about

7 *The easiest way to start off large mortises is to drill a series of holes within the confines of the marking out lines on the stile*

85° to finish the wedge room 3-5mm from the end of the mortise.

For a haunch groove, you need to make two saw cuts: one to the waste sides and one to the depth of the groove (fig. 5). You can use a tenon saw (backsaw) for these, though if you have one, a dovetail saw is easier to manage. Once you have made the cuts, remove the waste with a suitably-sized bevel-edged chisel (fig. 6).

When cutting large—over 12mm wide—through mortises, you can save yourself a great deal of hard work by drilling a series of overlapping holes before you start chiselling. The bit should be slightly smaller than the width of the mortise and of the woodworking, high-speed, flat type if used with an electric drill. For a brace and bit, use a Jennings-type woodworking bit (fig. 7).

9 *On large section timbers, use a panel saw or crosscut saw to make cuts with the grain. Make sure that the timber is well supported*

8 *Afterwards, remove the rest of the waste wood with a mortise chisel, held as shown and used in the correct sequence*

To avoid splintering the wood, drill through from one side until the tip of the bit just breaks the surface of the other. At this point turn the workpiece over and finish the holes from the reverse side. Use wide and narrow mortise chisels or heavy firmer chisels to remove the rest of the waste.

Cutting the tenons
The procedure for cutting a simple tenon is the same as that for cutting the pin in a halving joint (see pages 237 to 242). Make the longitudinal cuts first, then the cross cuts, cutting to the waste side of the line at all times (figs. 9 to 12). Afterwards, clean up the tenons with a bevel-edged chisel.

Where a rail is too long to place vertically in the vice, arrange it at an angle, parallel to the bench and firmly clamped. Many craftsmen prefer

10 *Crosscutting—such as cutting away the shoulders around the tenon—can be done with a dovetail or tenon saw and a bench hook*

this set up for all tenon cutting, so it is worth trying in any case.

Haunched tenon: Make the longitudinal cuts as normal, but remember that one will be shorter than the other to allow for the haunch itself. Afterwards, cut the haunch, the cheeks and finally the shoulders.

Double tenon: To remove the space between double tenons, first make the longitudinal cuts. Remove the waste with a coping saw (fig. 14), then saw off the cheeks and the shoulders. As with all tenons, clean up the finished cuts with a chisel.

Assembling non-wedged joints

When you have cut all the joints, assemble the frame (or construction) in a dry run—without glue—to check the fit. The joints should require no more than light tapping with a hammer—using an offcut to protect the work—to get them to interlock.

If greater force is needed, dismantle the frame and make small adjustments. While the frame is together, set out whatever cramps are necessary and cramp up the frame without adhesive. Check that it is square by measuring the diagonals, which should be equal in length.

Tidy up the inside surfaces of the frame with a finely set plane and glasspaper. You can, if you wish, apply a finish to the inside edges of the frame timbers at this stage. But mask off the mating surfaces of the joints first to keep them clean for when you apply the glue.

Finally, glue and sash-cramp the joints (see pages 229 to 232), using offcuts of timber to protect the workpieces. Wipe off any excess adhesive while it is still wet.

Wedged joints

Cut wedges for the joints from offcuts of waste wood. Do this as carefully as possible, since you cannot test them in a dry run with the tenon in place. Make adjustments to the widths of the wedges where necessary, then glue and cramp up the assembly.

In the case of a through wedged joint, drive the wedges in once the tenon is in place in its mortise (fig. 16).

Finishing

When the joints are thoroughly dry, remove the cramps. Cut off all the waste—horns, pieces of wedge, through tenon ends—with a fine saw, cutting no closer than 1mm to the work. Afterwards, use a finely set plane and glasspaper on a sanding block to complete the finish.

11 *Make the angled cuts with the workpiece once more secured in the vice. Here, the secret haunching above the tenon is being cut away*

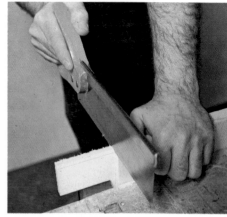

12 *Take extra care when you cut out the final pieces of waste. Even at this stage, a slip can still ruin the finished joint*

13 *The finished rail, showing the sloped secret haunch which will become invisible when inserted into its matching slot on the stile*

14 *When making a double joint, use a coping saw to cut away the waste between tenons. Take care not to stray outside the marked lines*

15 *Assembly of all mortise and tenon joints is made easier if you first bevel away the edges of the waste on the tenons with a sharp chisel*

16 *On a through wedged joint, the wedges are tapped in as far as they will go then the waste on the tenon is trimmed off*

Using a sawing jig

A sawing jig can be used to cut precision tenons, but you will still have to mark out and cut the mortise.

The jig used here consists of a flat baseplate with two saw guide pillars, sprung to hold the saw blade upright. It's held against the edge of the bench with nylon dowels slotted into the underside, like a bench hook. The design of the jig means that the saw is used in the same direction for all cuts; the workpiece itself is moved to the required angle and is held against reinforced nylon dowels inserted in the baseplate. An adjustable angle bracket and selector head are used to gauge the width of cut; and a depth stop allows you to cut accurately to a pre-set depth.

Right: *The jig enables you to make a wide range of wood joints*

1 *Place the workpiece against the saw guides as shown and set the angle bracket against its edge to give the joint width*

2 *Reposition the workpiece with its end against the angle bracket, insert the saw in the guides and saw to the depth required*

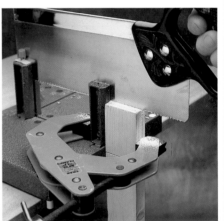

3 *Repeat this for the other side of the tenon. Then clamp the workpiece in line with the jig's front saw guide and cut out the waste*

4 *One joint the jig cannot help with is the matching mortise. Use the accurately-cut tenon as a guide to marking up the slot*

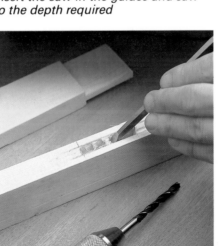

5 *Drill out the waste to depth required using a depth stop on the drill bit, then clean up the mortise with a sharp chisel*

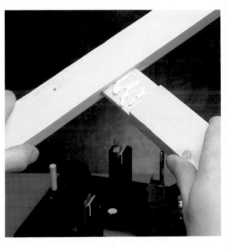

6 *Test the fit of the tenon in the mortise. When you are satisfied, apply glue to the tenon and then assemble the joint*

Make a teapot stand

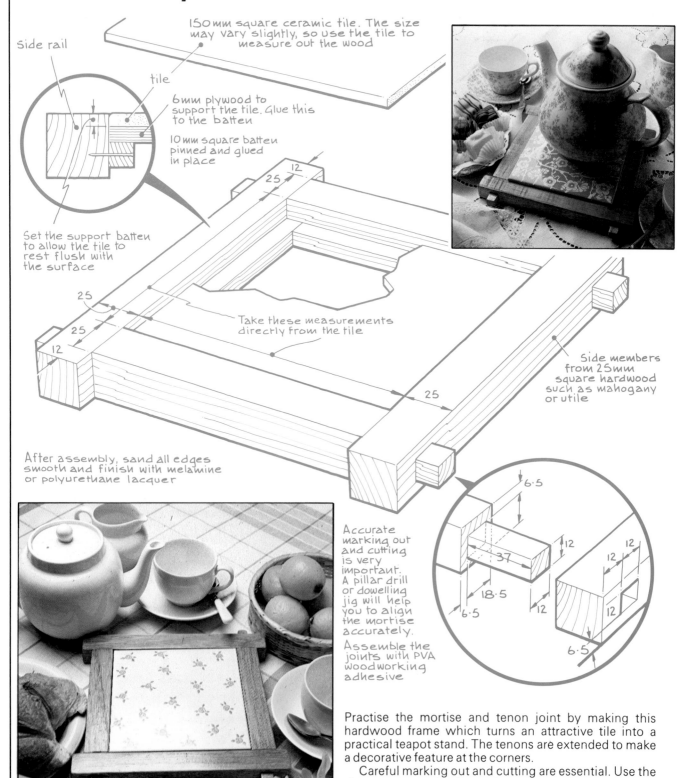

Side rail

150mm square ceramic tile. The size may vary slightly, so use the tile to measure out the wood

tile

6mm plywood to support the tile. Glue this to the batten

10mm square batten pinned and glued in place

Set the support batten to allow the tile to rest flush with the surface

12
25

25
25
12

Take these measurements directly from the tile

25

Side members from 25mm square hardwood such as mahogany or utile

After assembly, sand all edges smooth and finish with melamine or polyurethane lacquer

Accurate marking out and cutting is very important. A pillar drill or dowelling jig will help you to align the mortise accurately.

Assemble the joints with PVA woodworking adhesive

6.5
37
18.5
6.5
12
12
12
12
12
6.5

Practise the mortise and tenon joint by making this hardwood frame which turns an attractive tile into a practical teapot stand. The tenons are extended to make a decorative feature at the corners.

Careful marking out and cutting are essential. Use the tile to measure the dimensions shown. Ensure accurate mortises by using a drill stand or dowel jig to drill a pilot hole at right angles. Square this with a chisel. Cut the tenons with a fine-toothed tenon saw and assemble the frame with care.

MITRE JOINTS

- ● **MARKING MITRES**
- ● **TRIMMING WASTE**
- ● **VENEER KEYS**
- ● **CUTTING MITRES**
- ● **REINFORCEMENT**
- ● **DOWELLED JOINTS**

A mitre joint is a neat way of joining two pieces of timber at an angle. The ends of the pieces are cut so that the line at the butt joint is a diagonal across the corners of the meeting members. For example, if two sections of timber meet at 90° the mitre cut would be 45° (fig. A).

The simplest and most common mitre joint uses timbers of equal section butt joined together with adhesive and pins. It is typically found in decorative objects—such as picture frames.

Marking out

To mark out a mitre you will need a pencil, marking knife, rule, try square and a means for marking angles—either a combination square or a sliding bevel.

The *combination*, or *sliding, square* (fig. 1) is capable of marking angles of

90° and 45° and has a sliding rule which may be adjusted to give projections from 1mm to approximately 260mm. It is extremely useful when the blade of an ordinary try square is too long, because it can double up as an adjustable try square.

The sliding bevel—with the aid of a protractor (fig. 2)—can be set to any angle, the blade being locked in position until released.

Start marking by deciding the overall dimensions of the frame to be made and then add 5–6mm to both ends of each separate component to allow for waste. Measure and rough-cut the individual pieces of wood, marking each face side and edge with the proper identification marks. Then, using a rule, marking knife and try square, carefully mark out the overall dimensions on the face edge of each work-

piece, allowing enough for waste.

If the frame is longer one way than the other, mark opposite pairs together to avoid confusion.

If the mitre is to be cut across the wide surface, or 'side' of the piece, use one of the angle marking aids and a marking knife to set out the cut on the face side. Slide the combination square or sliding bevel up to the knife and score across the timber. Mark across the next edge at 90° to the side then finally mark the angle across the surface opposite the face side.

If the mitre is to be cut across the narrow surface, or 'edge', of the piece start by marking the overall dimension line with a try-square allowing for waste across the face edge; and then mark the face edge to the mitre angle with the sliding bevel or combination square. Next mark the sides at right angles with a try square, and use the bevel to mark the surface opposite the face edge as a mitre.

Cutting the mitre

It is quite possible to cut a mitre by holding the workpieces at an angle in a vice and sawing them direct. But for greater accuracy and ease of handling use a mitre block or, better still, a mitre box (fig. C). Both of these devices are available from tool shops but generally cut only 45° angles.

Cramp the block or box in a vice, or fix it to a worktop with large G-cramps. A fine toothed saw should be used to cut into any moulding on the work-piece and not out of it. This ensures

Above, left: *Mitre joints are mainly used for making frames. They can be strengthened by the various methods shown, including dowels, veneer inserts and plywood tongue*

A. *The simplest mitre joint is where two pieces of wood meet at right-angles. In this case the mitre angle is 45° across the join*

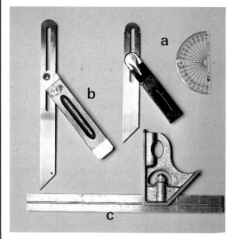

1 *Essential tools when marking out mitre joints are a protractor (a) and either a sliding bevel (b) or combination square (c)*

2 *Set the required mitre angle on the sliding bevel with the protractor and use it to mark out the cut lines on the workpiece*

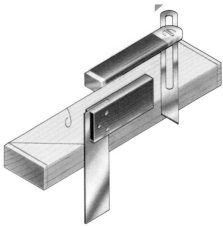

B. *Using a try square and a sliding bevel to mark up a mitre. It is important always to allow a short length for waste when marking up*

C. *A mitre block (above) and a mitre box (right). Mitres need to be cut very accurately if the resulting frame is to be square. Sawing guides*

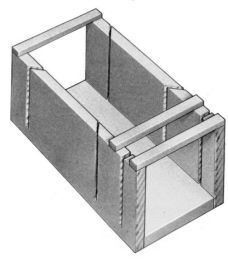

such as these help a great deal to keep the saw steady

3 *Use a mitre box to guide the saw when cutting 45° mitres. Hold the workpiece tight. Packing underneath it will protect the base of the box*

4 *Adjustable mitre jigs are not expensive and they can be used to guide the saw on cuts at a number of different angles*

5 *Use a mitre shooting board to trim off the waste from a mitre which has been cut across the face side of the workpiece*

6 *Use a donkey's ear and a plane to trim off the waste from a mitre which has been cut across the face edge of the workpiece*

7 *Use a picture framer's cramp to hold the components of a mitre in position while you pin them together and let the adhesive set*

8 *Alternatively use a proprietary clamp system which sets strong springs into the wood and leaves small indents which are later filled*

that the rag of the saw cut is at the back of the joint and not on the face.

Always remember to saw slightly to the waste side of the cut and trim off the excess afterwards with a plane.

Trimming off the waste
Large sections can be angled in a vice and trimmed freehand, taking great care and using a fine-set No. 4 smooth plane or a block plane.

Small sections may be more accurately trimmed with the aid of a *mitre shooting board* (fig. 5) for mitres in the width or side, and a *donkey's ear* (fig. 6) for mitres in the thickness, or edge, of the work piece.

Neither of these work aids are readily available, but you may also find them in a specialist shop. When using the mitre shooting board, plane away from your body to trim right-

hand mitres and towards you for left-hand mitres.

The donkey's ear will give the best results if you first of all plane away from you, to just beyond the centre of the work, then place the work on the other side of the stop, reverse the plane and trim towards you. Finally, reverse the procedure for a last, straight-through trim to finish the mitre neatly and cleanly.

Joining mitred frames
The big problem when joining simple mitres is that the adhesive acts as a lubricant—causing the pieces of the frame to slide about and making the use of sash cramps impossible.

Light frames can be joined together using adhesive and pins. Use a picture framer's cramp to hold the mitres in position while the pins are driven home, then tap them below the surface with a fine pin punch and fill.

Another method of clamping mitres

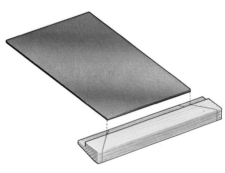

D. *Make sure that the cut lines for the mitres in a picture frame cross the rebate so that the glass fits exactly in the frame*

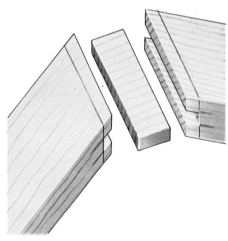

E. *Strengthening a mitre joint with a tongue insert. The extra gluing area provided makes the mitre less susceptible to warping or splitting*

in light to medium section timbers uses special spring clamps (fig. 8). This clamping system, which is relatively cheap and easy to use, employs three sets of spring clamps in different sizes to suit different sections. The springs—which are set into the frame using a special tool—hold the mitre together by closing spiked ends onto the frame, one at each corner, rather like a hawk's talons. The indentation they produce is relatively small and can be either ignored or filled.

Larger frames can be joined together with a web cramp or a simple straining twine (see pages 231 and 232). Both of these tools should be used with L-shaped wooden blocks, the outer corners of which must be well rounded to allow the web or cord to move around them.

Place clean paper between the block and the workpiece to stop the block sticking to the work. Once the web or cord is tensioned, check the frame for square by measuring the diagonals, which should be equal.

Stronger types of mitre joint
The *cross-tongued* or *feathered-mitre* joint gives a greater gluing area in the mitre and is used where sideways movement is likely to occur (fig. E). Grooves are cut in the faces of the mitres into which a tongue, or feather, is then inserted. The tongue should be cut either from matching timber—in which case the grain must run at right angles to the mitre faces—or from multi-layer plywood.

The thickness of the tongue can vary between one quarter and one third of the thickness of the timber and will considerably strengthen the joint.

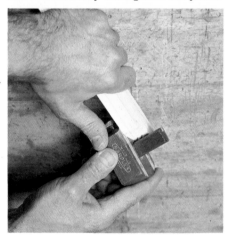

9 *To make a cross-tongued mitre, mark out the width of the tongue with a mortise gauge and use a dove-tail saw and chisel to remove the wood* 253

10 *When the tongue groove is cut, glue the frame together with the strengthening tongue inserted as shown above*

11 *Using a coping saw to trim out the waste tongue when the glue has set lessens the likelihood of disturbing the mitre joint*

12 *For a really neat finish, pare away the last few slivers of the tongue insert with a sharp, bevel-edged chisel*

The width of the tongue depends upon the size of the frame section, but a measurement based on one fifth of the face width is about right.

To mark out the grooves, set a mortise gauge to the width of the chisel you will use which should also match, exactly, the thickness of the tongue. Then set the gauge so that the two points are evenly spaced across the thickness of the mitre and mark parallel lines along the mitre face (fig. 9). To mark the groove depth, use a marking knife and combination square or sliding bevel and make a faint line on the face across which the mitre has been cut parallel to the edge of the mitre. The line should be half the tongue's width plus half a milli- metre from the mitre edge. Use a try square to carry these lines across both edges of the piece.

Set the piece in a vice so that the mitre face is horizontal and use a dove- tail saw or fine tenon saw (backsaw) to make two saw cuts to the waste side of the groove. Chisel out waste.

When all of the grooves are cut, piece the frame together to ensure everything fits. Make any adjustment necessary for a good fit and, when all is well, glue the frame together. The best cramping method to use for this type of joint is the spring system used in conjunction with G-cramps across the thickness of the section. Trim off the waste after the adhesive has set completely (fig. 12).

Veneer keyed mitre joints

Keyed mitres are used to strengthen edge mitred joints, especially those which are to be veneered. Cut the mitres and check that each side is of the correct length, then assemble

F. *Edge mitres are best strengthened by using veneer inserts like these. Always make sure that the grain of the veneer crosses that of the mitre*

the frame without glue to ensure it goes together well. Mark each pair of mitres on the face side, A-A, B-B and so on until all are marked.

Next, take a pair of mitres and place them in a vice, ensuring that the correct angle is maintained—use a try square or sliding bevel to check this. Using a fine saw with a veneer thickness kerf of approximately 2mm, make opposing angled cuts across the corner of the frame (fig. 13). Check that the cut will take the veneer you propose to use; if the veneer is too tight a fit, open the cut slightly using either a thin file or a piece of glass paper fixed to a steel rule with double-sided tape.

When all of the joints are cut and ready, apply adhesive to the mitres and assemble the frame using either spring or sash cramps. If sash cramps are

13 *For a veneer keyed mitre joint, cramp the mitre in a vice and use a panel saw to cut angled slots for the veneer*

14 *Cut slivers of veneer so that the grain runs across that of the work piece, glue them in place and trim off the waste*

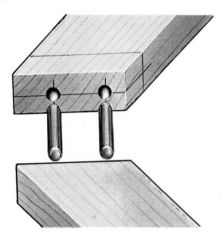

G. *Dowel inserts provide the best way of strengthening a mitre joint and are completely invisible when the work is finished*

15 *To strengthen a mitre with dowels first mark the position of the dowel centre line across the mitre as shown*

16 *Extend your original line across the face of the mitre to mark out the sites of the dowels which you are inserting*

17 *Use a marking gauge to find the exact centre of the mitre face and mark where the scribed line crosses the track of the gauge*

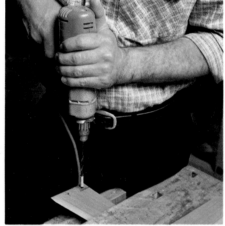

18 *Drill out the holes for the dowels at these points. Use masking tape on the drill bit to control the depth of the hole*

19 *Insert the dowels, check for fit then score them, to let the adhesive flow. Finally, glue the frame together and cramp it*

used (see pages 230 and 231), they must be prepared with protective waste blocks before you apply the adhesive. Two cramps should be placed underneath the frame close to the mitres; the other two go on top of the frame at right-angles to the first pair and also close to the mitres.

When the frame is in place tighten the cramps so that they are just squeezing the protecting waste blocks against the frame.

Check that the mitres are correctly placed and insert the pre-cut veneer slips—which should be coated with adhesive—with the grain running at right angles to the mitre. Carefully tighten the cramps and ensure that the mitres slip evenly, if at all, so that the frame remains entirely square and does not twist.

When the adhesive has set, remove

the frame from the cramps and cut off any excess veneer with a dovetail saw.

Dowelled mitre joints
This is the neatest of the strong joints discussed in this section, and also one of the strongest.

To make a dowelled mitre without a specialized dowel jig start by marking, cutting and trimming the mitres. The number and size of the inserted dowels will obviously depend upon the section of the frame and how strong you wish the joint to be. The diameter of the dowel should not be greater than one third of the thickness of the timber. And as the length may also vary, it is preferable to have a long dowel on the inside of the frame and a short dowel towards the outer corner.

Place one pair of mitres together and with a rule and sharp 2H pencil, mark

the position of the dowel or dowels (fig. 15). Use a try square to continue these lines across the face of the mitre.

Take a marking gauge and set this to half the thickness of the section. Next, mark a line down the length of the mitre face (fig. 17) and place the work in a vice with the mitre face horizontal and with a centre punch, 'dot' the dowel hole centres; that is, where the gauge line crosses the pencil lines exactly.

Select the appropriate dowel or drill bit and drill the holes. Wrap some masking tape around the drill to act as a depth guide and preferably get an assistant to watch that the drill is kept vertical to the mitre face. Then cut the dowels to length and groove the sides with a tenon saw to allow air and excess adhesive to escape from the holes. Assemble the frame as before. 255

Making picture frames

Apart from the sorts of joints already described, one job where neatly cut mitre joints are absolutely essential is when making picture frames. There is a huge range of picture frame mouldings available nowadays, and it's far cheaper to make up your own frames than to buy professionally-made types.

The starting point is the height and width of the picture you want to frame (complete with mount, if one is being used). Measure these, then subtract twice the width of the picture frame rebate from each measurement; this gives you the inside dimensions of the frame. Mark these on the inside faces of the mouldings, remembering to allow for the triangular waste section that results when cutting successive lengths from one strip of moulding. Cut the mitres with a very fine-toothed saw.

20 *Mark the length of each moulding on the inner edge, and indicate on the back which way the mitred cut will be angled*

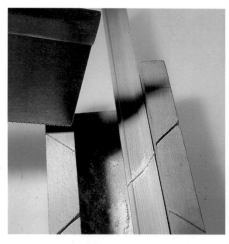

21 *Line up the mark on the moulding with the appropriate guide slot in the mitre box, and hold the moulding securely as you cut it*

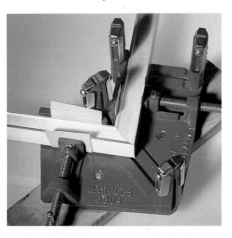

22 *After cutting all the mitres, sand the ends lightly, apply woodworking adhesive and clamp each joint in turn. Let them set overnight*

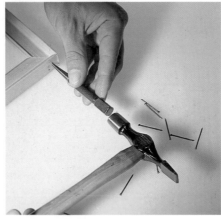

23 *Remove all the clamps and strengthen the joints at each corner by tapping in panel pins. Use a punch to drive in the pin heads*

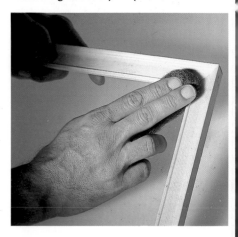

24 *Fill the holes left by the panel pin heads, and any slight gaps at the mitre joints. Then rub the whole frame down with fine wire wool*

25 *Whether you are painting or varnishing the frame, apply several coats for a good finish. Sand down lightly between coats*

26 *Lay the glass in the frame rebate, then the mounted picture and its backing board. Secure the back with 15mm panel pins*

27 *Stick a trimmed piece of brown paper to the back of the frame. Twist in the screw eyes one third the way down each side, and add the wire*

Make your own mitre tools

The three mitring tools shown here are invaluable for cutting quick, accurate mitres. Making them is itself useful practice in mitring, and once made, they should last you for many years.

All three can be made from odd pieces of wood, as most of the dimensions are not critical. The best wood to use is a hardwood, such as beech, but if this is not available, use any timber which is well seasoned—and warp- and knot-free. Make sure that it is planed squarely.

The easiest tool to make is the mitre box. Assemble the basic U shape—you can extend the front to provide a clamping strip if preferred—taking care that everything is square. Then mark and cut the three angled cuts, making sure that both your marking and cutting are very accurate. Use a tenon saw (backsaw) for the cuts, cutting the slots on each side simultaneously.

With a mitre box, the mitre shooting board is quite easy to make. Make up the base and the running stop, checking that the edge of the running stop is planed quite straight. Use the mitre box to cut the V-block accurately then fit this in position. You can cut the V-block without a mitre box by careful marking and cutting with a tenon saw.

Make the donkey's ear by careful marking out and cutting in the same way as for the other two tools. The stop is quite simple to cut with a saw, or using the shooting board. Plane the long edges of the base and running stop to accurately marked, 45° lines.

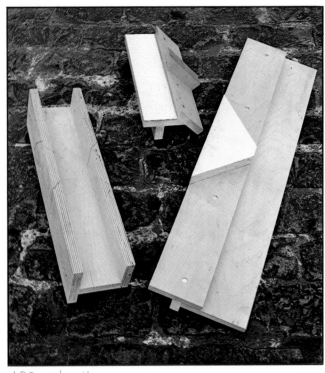

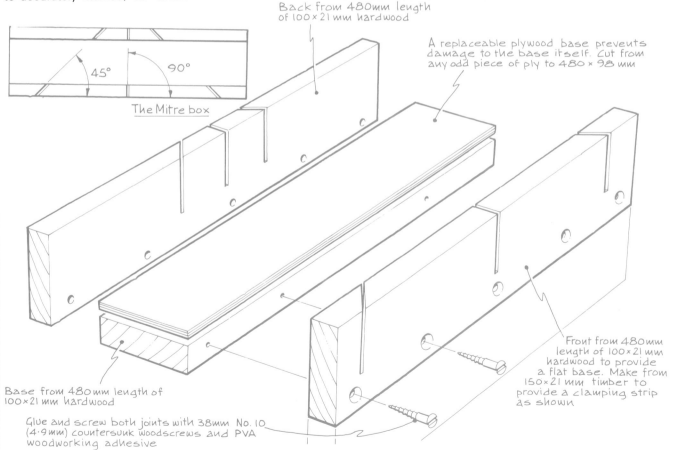

The Mitre box

45°   90°

Back from 480mm length of 100×21mm hardwood

A replaceable plywood base prevents damage to the base itself. Cut from any odd piece of ply to 480×98mm

Base from 480mm length of 100×21mm hardwood

Glue and screw both joints with 38mm No.10 (4·9mm) countersunk woodscrews and PVA woodworking adhesive

Front from 480mm length of 100×21mm hardwood to provide a flat base. Make from 150×21mm timber to provide a clamping strip as shown

Cutting list
All timber parts should preferably be made from a hardwood such as beech, but any well seasoned. warp- and knot-free timber is suitable.

The Mitre box
Base: 480mm × 100mm × 21mm
Front: 480mm × 100mm (150mm to provide a clamping strip) × 21mm
Back: 480mm × 100mm × 21mm
Additional materials: Scrap plywood, 10. 38mm No. 10 countersunk woodscrews, PVA adhesive

The Mitre shooting board
Base: 650mm × 175mm × 16mm
Running stop: 650mm × 100mm × 16mm
V block: 215mm × 100mm × 44mm
Additional materials: Scrap laminate, 3 75mm No. 10 countersunk woodscrews, PVA adhesive

The Donkey's ear
Base: 300mm × 100mm × 25mm
Running stop: 300mm × 100mm × 25mm
Clamp block: 300mm × 50mm × 25mm
Stop: 138mm × 38mm × 38mm
Additional materials: Scrap laminate 10 38mm No. 10 countersunk woodscrews, PVA adhesive

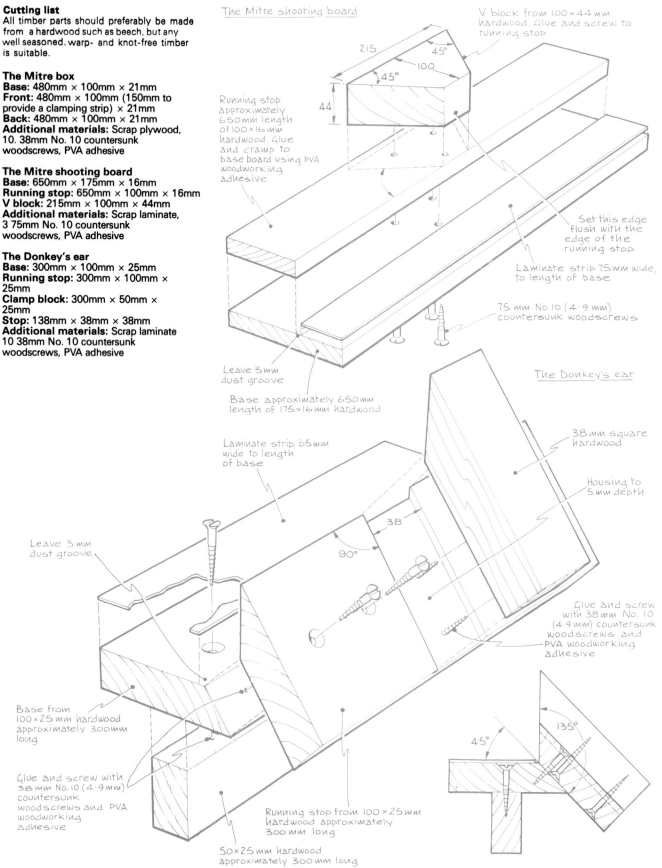

The Mitre shooting board

V block from 100×44mm hardwood. Glue and screw to running stop

215

45°

100

45°

44

Running stop approximately 650mm length of 100×16mm hardwood. Glue and cramp to base board using PVA woodworking adhesive

Set this edge flush with the edge of the running stop

Laminate strip 75mm wide, to length of base

75 mm No.10 (4·9mm) countersunk woodscrews

Leave 3mm dust groove

Base approximately 650mm length of 175×16mm hardwood

The Donkey's ear

Laminate strip 65mm wide to length of base

38 mm square hardwood

Housing to 5mm depth

Leave 3 mm dust groove

38

90°

Glue and screw with 38 mm No. 10 (4·9mm) countersunk woodscrews and PVA woodworking adhesive

Base from 100×25 mm hardwood approximately 300mm long

Glue and screw with 38 mm No. 10 (4·9mm) countersunk woodscrews and PVA woodworking adhesive

Running stop from 100×25 mm hardwood approximately 300mm long

135°

45°

50×25 mm hardwood approximately 300 mm long

DOVETAIL JOINTS

Left: *To make a perfect dovetail you need very few special tools, but a great deal of patience and skill*

1 *To set out the dovetails, first mark out the thickness of one board across the other allowing just under 1mm for wastage*

- ● **TYPES OF DOVETAIL**
- ● **MARKING OUT**
- ● **GLUING UP**
- ● **THROUGH JOINTS**
- ● **CUTTING OUT**
- ● **LAPPED JOINTS**

The ease of use and strength of modern adhesives means that nowadays there is less need for complicated joints like the dovetail. But although the dovetail is one of the most difficult joints to manufacture, it is definitely the best joint to use in the construction of traditional furniture which is expected to stand up to hundreds of years of wear. In such cases the use of adhesives can lead to the joint breaking as a result of vibration. Furthermore, the dovetail is one of the most attractive joints for something like a linen chest.

Dovetails can be made both by hand and machine. Simple proprietary jigs for the do-it-yourselfer are available but best of all are the special hand-held power routers which will produce a perfect dovetail within a few seconds.

Types of dovetail

There are four distinct types of dovetail used in cabinet and joinery work: the *through dovetail* which shows both sides of the corner joint (fig. A); the *lapped dovetail* which shows on one side but is concealed on the other (fig. B) as in drawer fronts; the *double lapped dovetail* (fig. B) in which only a thin line of end grain is visible; and finally, the

secret mitre dovetail where the joint is entirely hidden.

The component parts of the joint are known as the *dovetail*—the female part, and the *pin*—the male part. Usually the pin, at its widest, is about half the width of the dovetail. However, the tails can be up to five times the width of the pin. For very strong work the pin and dovetail may be of equal width; this is called a *cistern dovetail*, and is nearly always the rule in machined joints. The *slope*, *rake* or *bevel* of the dovetail is the angle which gives the joint its strength. The *slope* is measured as a proportion of the width over rise—1 in 5, 1 in 6, 1 in 7, or even 1 in 8: 1 in 5 is usual for work where strength is more important than appearance, and 1 in 7 or 8 where the reverse applies. It is essential for the integrity of the joint not to exceed these extremes.

One important difference between cutting dovetails and other joints is that of wastage. In the manufacture of all other joints it is normal to mark out the timber and joints, leaving an additional 6mm of waste, which is removed after assembly. In the case of dovetail joints, however, it is rare to leave on any waste; and even when it is, as in through dovetails

2 *Now decide a suitable width for the pins and mark lines for the two end pins about two-thirds of this width in from each edge*

3 *To divide the distance between the lines into the number of dovetails needed, lay a ruler at an angle to make it easily divisible*

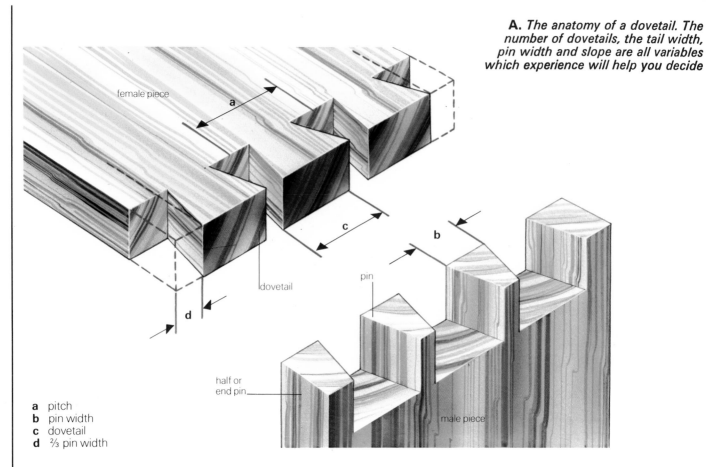

A. *The anatomy of a dovetail. The number of dovetails, the tail width, pin width and slope are all variables which experience will help you decide*

female piece

a

c

pin

b

dovetail

d

half or
end pin

male piece

a pitch
b pin width
c dovetail
d ⅔ pin width

and the male side of lapped dovetails, the maximum amount left should be 1mm—any more than that will lead to inaccuracies.

When you prepare materials for dovetails you must mark and cut them to the exact length, including any waste, and the ends must be shot square with a plane. Two adjoining sides need not be of the same thickness as you can adjust the length of the tails. The exception to this is the secret mitre dovetail in which the

adjacent sides must be of equal and even thickness to allow the mitres to meet.

The through dovetail
It is normal when constructing a dovetail joint to set out and cut the dovetails first, then set out and cut the pins, and then glue up the joint.

To set out the dovetails, first mark the thickness of one board across the surface of the other (fig. 1). You can allow just under 1mm for wastage. Repeat on the other boards.

There are no absolute rules for the pitch or spacing of the pins, so first choose an arbitrary pin width; half the board thickness is a good guide. Then draw a line, two-thirds the size of the pins, down both sides of the face of this, the female piece of board. Now, with the help of a ruler laid along the base line of the joint, decide how many dovetails the width of the board demands (say four). Lay the ruler with the 0 mark on one pin line, and angle it until the 4 mark

4 *Extend the ruler marks to the base line of the joint using a try square placed square against the end of the board*

5 *Set a pair of dividers to half the pin width. Place one point on the marked line and mark out the pin width on the base line*

6 *Now you must decide the slope of the dovetail, having regard to the strength and appearance of the joint. Mark it with a sliding bevel*

(or a multiple of 4, such as 8) touches the other (fig. 3). The intermediate points 1,2,3 (or their multiples) then indicate equal divisions. Mark these points and extend them to the end of the board to indicate the centre of each pin (fig. 4). Set a pair of dividers to half the pin width, place one leg on the pin centre at the base line and mark to each side to indicate the pin width (fig. 5).

Now draw in the slope from these points. There is no hard and fast rule for this other than the practical limits set out above.

Mark the slope with a sharp pencil, using either a sliding bevel or a hardwood or zinc template (fig. D) as a guide. Then project the lines across the end of the board with the help of a try square, and down the other face of the board with the sliding bevel or template. Mark waste areas with a cross. Now you can cut the dovetails.

Place the board in a vice so that the tail lines are vertical, and, using a fine dovetail or tenon saw (backsaw), cut exactly along the lines. For greater accuracy saw along all the right inclined lines first, and then all of the left ones. Insert a coping or scroll saw blade into the cut and remove all but 1mm of the waste, then finish off with a sharp bevel edge chisel.

It is essential for the neatness of the joint to remove only the exact amount of waste. To do this, place the board on a bench with a piece of waste timber under the joint area. Set

7 *Clamp the work upright in a vice and use a try square and a sharp pencil to extend the lines of the dovetails over the end of the board*

8 *Shade all the waste areas to avoid confusion when you cut, then clamp the board so that one side of the dovetail is vertical*

9 *Using a tenon saw, cut exactly along all the lines on one side. Then clamp the board so that the other lines are vertical, and cut these*

B. Below: *The lapped dovetail, where a lap is left on the outside face of the pins to hide the end grain, is generally used when making drawers*

Below: *The double lapped dovetail, where the laps cover both the end grain of the pins and the dovetails, is used only in fine cabinet making*

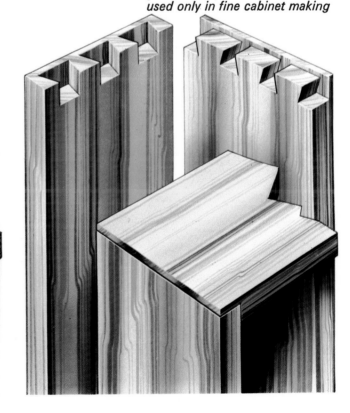

the chisel on the base line, bevel out, and hit it very hard with a mallet. Do this on both sides—you will probably find that one hard blow will suffice in most cases to cut neatly through the waste.

Having completed the dovetails you must now turn your attention to cutting the pins.

Place the male piece of timber vertically in a vice, and rub a piece of blackboard chalk across the end grain. If the wood is light, use dark chalk, and vice versa. Lay the female piece of timber over the male, line up the dovetails accurately with the end of the latter, then, using a sharp engineers's steel scriber, trace the position of the pins (fig. 12) carefully onto the end grain.

Use a small try square and a hard, sharp pencil to project the lines to the depth lines on both sides of the board, and mark the waste wood clearly with a cross.

First cut the vertical lines, as with the dovetails, using a dovetail saw.

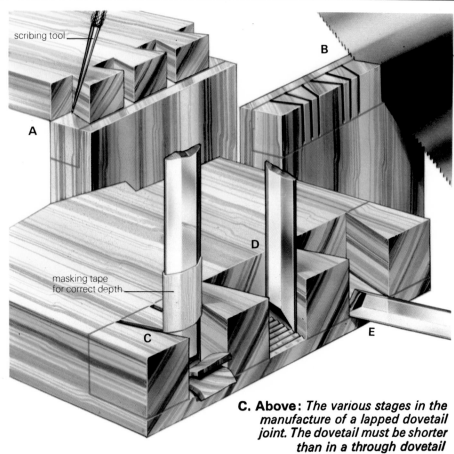

scribing tool

masking tape for correct depth

C. Above: *The various stages in the manufacture of a lapped dovetail joint. The dovetail must be shorter than in a through dovetail*

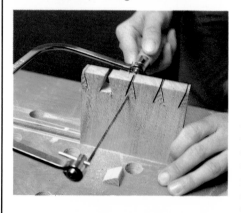

10 *Insert a coping or scroll saw into the saw cuts then turn the blade through 90° and cut out all but 1mm of the waste wood*

11 *To cut out the exact amount of waste, lay the work on a piece of waste board then place a bevel edged chisel on the line and hit it*

Then remove most of the waste with a coping or scroll saw, and finish with a chisel in exactly the same way as you did with the tails, except that you must angle the chisel to cope with the sloping sides of the joint. To make assembly easier you can lightly chisel away the inner surfaces of the dovetails (fig. E).

You can now put the joint together, but you must not knock it together fully because a dovetail is always more successful if only fitted once. The joint should be a really tight fit, with no play once it is assembled, and knocking it apart again after a trial fitting may damage the pins on one or both the components.

Gluing up
Before gluing up, clean the inside surfaces of the joint with a fine set plane, then finish off with glasspaper. Take care not to remove more than a minimum amount of material from the actual joint area. If you wish to apply varnish or wood lacquer to the boards before joining, you must mask the joint areas because both substances inhibit adhesion.

Prepare some pieces of scrap wood with notches that fit over the pins as in fig. E and then glue and cramp up

the joint. Remove excess adhesive with a sharp knife before it sets. When the adhesive has set remove the cramps and battens and clean up the exterior with glasspaper on a block.

It is more than likely that if you have never attempted a dovetail before there will be one or two gaps

D. Below: *To mark out the slopes of the dovetail it is simple and quick to make a template either from strong cardboard, or better still zinc or aluminium plate*

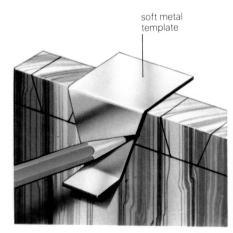

soft metal template

12 To mark out the pins, rub some chalk over the end grain, and carefully trace the dovetail with an engineers' steel scribe

13 Extend all the lines down both sides of the board to the base line of the joint. Shade the waste, then cut the vertical lines as before

14 Remove most of the waste with a coping or scroll saw, then finish off with a chisel. Remember to angle the chisel to cope with the slope

between the tails and pins. The skilled craftsman would cut thin wedges of similar end grain and drive them into the gap. Far easier, and probably more successful for the average DIY man, however, is the process known as bishoping. Apply some spittle or hot water to the end grain around the gaps to expand the timber, then tap it with the ball of a light ball-pein hammer to close the gap. Alternatively, pack the gaps with a mixture of glue and fine sawdust (fig. 16).

Lapped dovetails

Lapped dovetails are the most commonly used joints for drawer sides, or where the joint must not show on one face of the assembled construction.

Essentially, the setting out and cutting of the lapped dovetail is the same as for the through dovetail. However, there are a few differences.

Firstly, you must leave no waste on the tail (female) side. Then, trace the full thickness of the tail on the inner face only of the pin (male) side. Use a marking gauge to mark the depth of the pins and the length of the tails. It is usual to leave about one-quarter of the thickness of the pin side to form the lap.

The tails can be cut in the same way as for a through dovetail. You can then mark out the pins. This is done in a similar way to the through dovetails, but in this case the front edge of the tails is lined up with the

15 Finally clean up the faces of the joint with abrasive paper. Apply glue only after you have partially fitted it together in a dry run

Dovetails and chisels

Most bevel chisels do in fact have a slight thickness of square edge (see below). This can make it difficult to clean out the roots of the dovetails, and it may be necessary to remove some of the thickness with a fine grindstone. Be careful, however, not to overheat the chisel and thereby cause it to lose its hardness or 'temper'.

E. Far left: Chamfer the edges of the tails to aid assembly of the joint
Left: To efficiently cramp the joint, use a waste wood batten with cut outs

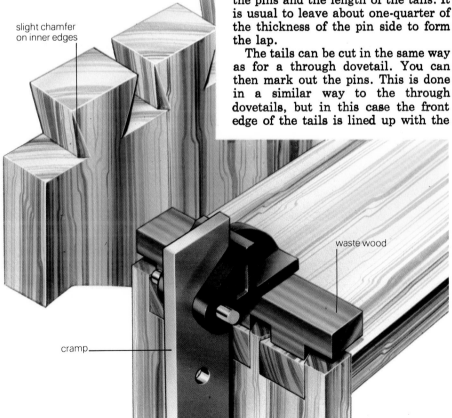

slight chamfer on inner edges

waste wood

cramp

16 To fill in any gaps due to cutting errors you can make a small quantity of very fine sawdust, and mix it with glue

17 When the mixture has been formed into a thin, workable paste, rub it into the gaps, pressing it down with the blade of a chisel

lap as shown in fig. C. It is in the cutting out of the pins where the main differences between the through dovetail and the lapped dovetail lie. The pins need more chisel work because you cannot saw straight through.

To start with, set the tail piece vertically in the vice and, with the fine dovetail saw, make diagonal cuts as shown in fig. C. Follow by paring out the corners with a chisel. Next, clamp the piece of board firmly to the bench, and use masking tape to set a cutting depth on the chisel. This depth must be 0.5mm less than the length of the tails. Hold the chisel almost vertically and, working backwards from the outer edge to the tail piece thickness line, aim to cut out each bit of waste wood to the required depth in one blow. Having worked all the way back, turn the chisel almost through 90° and carefully clean out the base of the cavity.

Finally glue and cramp the joint in exactly the same way as for the through dovetail.

Using a dovetail jig

For keen woodworkers, there are various drill attachments and power routers available which can form dovetails in seconds. All of these require some practice and setting up for use, and, as they are all different in design it is best if you follow the manufacturer's instructions for the one that you are using. Because one side of the joint will show rounded parts while the other shows the familiar square ones, machine-made dovetails are not as attractive for through dovetails as they are for either lapped or secret mitred dovetails. The machine made joints feature tails and pins of equal size, and the male and female parts of the joints are reversed.

19 Both pieces of wood are clamped into the machine. With the bit spinning, push the guide into the slots until it bottoms

21 The peculiarity of the machine-made dovetail is the rounded shape at the bottom of the cut—you can square it with a chisel

18 All you need for machine-made dovetails. Several proprietary jigs are available and most make both through and lapped joints

20 A piece of clear tape on the edge of the top piece prevents the bit pulling up splinters and encourages a neat cut

22 The machine comes into its own on the lapped dovetail— a practical way of making drawers— where the rounded side is hidden

A collector's box

This charming miniature box is just the thing to store your collection of mementoes or precious objects. And with its rich mahogany finish, it will itself be an object to treasure.

The basic frame is made from solid mahogany, held together with through dovetail joints. These provide a strong construction and an attractive decorative feature. Making the frame will give you plenty of practice at making these joints.

Mark out and cut the four sides. Make the joints before separating the top and bottom along the cutting line: this ensures that the panels match exactly.

Glue the top into a rebate. You can fit the bottom as shown, or rebate it too, for a neater finish. Fit hinges and a box lock, and your box is complete. Sand the surface, and finish to a high gloss.

Cutting the dovetails

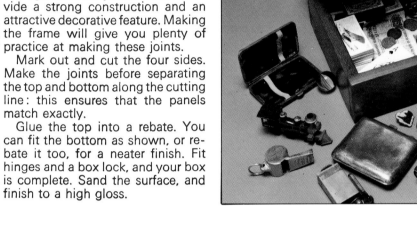

Stop the rebates in the front and back 6mm short of the end

Rebate (see opposite) Cut before assembly

18   20
      3
7
- 23 -   27
7   3
20   24
7   3
18 12   20
          12
     12

Cutting line

36

Mark the pins from the dovetails after these have been cut

Mark out and cut dovetails on each corner as shown. Mark the cutting line, but do not separate until all the joints are made

Cross section of box

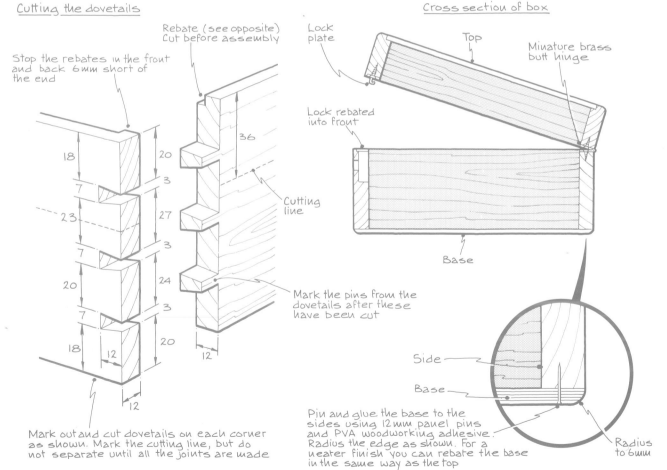

Lock plate

Top

Miniature brass butt hinge

Lock rebated into front

Base

Side

Base

Radius to 6mm

Pin and glue the base to the sides using 12mm panel pins and PVA woodworking adhesive. Radius the edge as shown. For a neater finish you can rebate the base in the same way as the top

DOVETAIL JOINTS

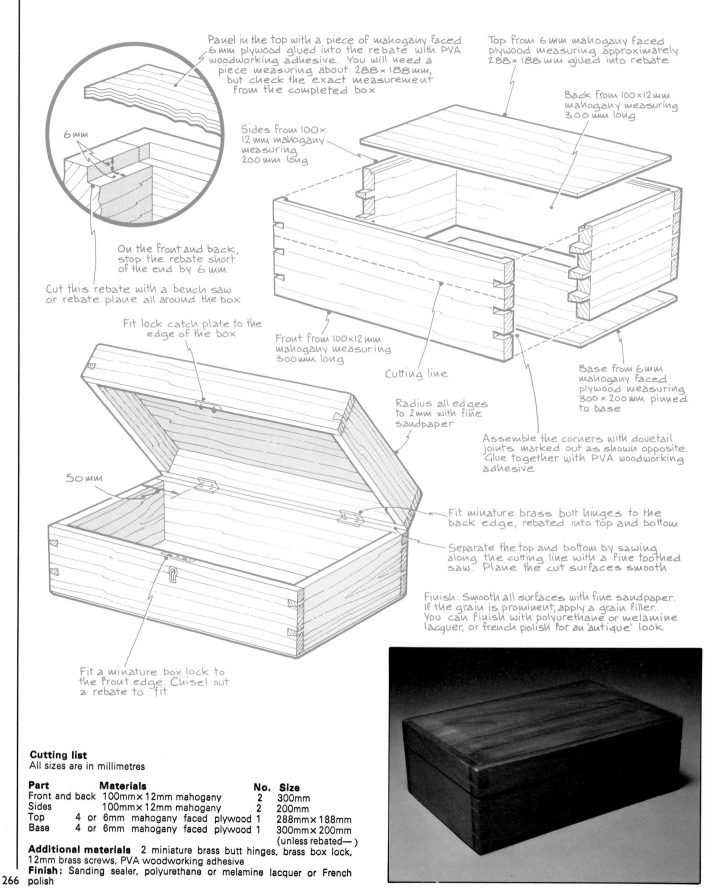

Panel in the top with a piece of mahogany faced 6mm plywood glued into the rebate with PVA woodworking adhesive. You will need a piece measuring about 288×188mm, but check the exact measurement from the completed box

Top from 6mm mahogany faced plywood measuring approximately 288×188mm glued into rebate

Back from 100×12mm mahogany measuring 300mm long

Sides from 100× 12mm mahogany measuring 200mm long

6mm

On the front and back, stop the rebate short of the end by 6mm

Cut this rebate with a bench saw or rebate plane all around the box

Fit lock catch plate to the edge of the box

Front from 100×12mm mahogany measuring 300mm long

Cutting line

Radius all edges to 2mm with fine sandpaper

Base from 6mm mahogany faced plywood measuring 300×200mm pinned to base

Assemble the corners with dovetail joints marked out as shown opposite. Glue together with PVA woodworking adhesive

50mm

Fit miniature brass butt hinges to the back edge, rebated into top and bottom

Separate the top and bottom by sawing along the cutting line with a fine toothed saw. Plane the cut surfaces smooth

Finish: Smooth all surfaces with fine sandpaper. If the grain is prominent, apply a grain filler. You can finish with polyurethane or melamine lacquer, or french polish for an 'antique' look

Fit a miniature box lock to the front edge. Chisel out a rebate to fit

Cutting list
All sizes are in millimetres

Part	Materials	No.	Size
Front and back	100mm×12mm mahogany	2	300mm
Sides	100mm×12mm mahogany	2	200mm
Top	4 or 6mm mahogany faced plywood	1	288mm×188mm
Base	4 or 6mm mahogany faced plywood	1	300mm×200mm (unless rebated—)

Additional materials 2 miniature brass butt hinges, brass box lock, 12mm brass screws, PVA woodworking adhesive
Finish: Sanding sealer, polyurethane or melamine lacquer or French polish

266

STAINS & VARNISHES

- ● **TYPES OF STAINS**
- ● **FUMING WOOD**
- ● **WAXES AND OILS**

- ● **USING STAINS**
- ● **BLEACHING**
- ● **VARNISHES**

Below: *Wood stains and varnishes not only allow you to finish projects to the colour of your choice, they also help to show off the beautiful variations in grain pattern to their very best advantage*

Probably more practical projects are ruined by poor finishing than anything else. And it is not just enhancing natural grain and timber colour which makes good finishing so vitally important. Care at this final stage will help to protect timber from dust, dirt, fungal attack and the damaging effects of weather. Apart from this a good finish will also make timber easy to keep clean.

It is choosing the right finishing material for the type of timber or man-made board being used that causes most problems. And the choice is almost endless.

Stains

With the current trend of retaining natural timber colour, particularly for domestic furniture, the once common practice of staining timber has declined. But stains can still have their uses where, for example, mixed timbers are used and a uniform colour is needed or where grain patterns need to be accentuated—as with some softwoods. Stains can also be used to good effect making cheap materials look more expensive.

There are three readily available types of stain—water, spirit and oil based. Cheapest of these are water stains but they can often be difficult to apply. Because water stains penetrate deeply into timber surfaces and produce the cleanest finish they are often the first choice of professional wood finishers.

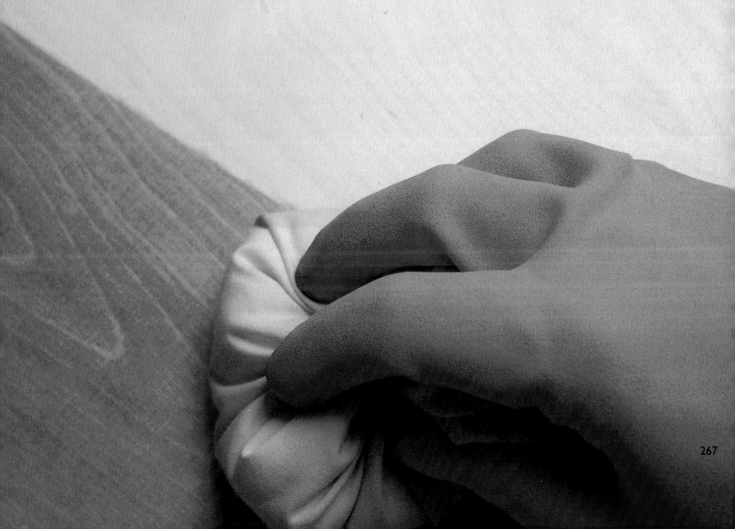

1 Oil-based stains can be bought ready-prepared but tend to hide, rather than enhance, the grain. Apply with a soft brush, using long strokes

2 After coating with oil stain, leave for two or three minutes, then wipe off along the grain with a soft cloth. Now leave for 24 hours to dry

3 Proprietary teak oil has largely replaced traditional oil finishes. Apply it with a stiff brush or cloth pad, rubbing well into grain

You can make up a stock solution of stain by mixing 50g of dye crystals in 0.5 litres of hot water. To this you also add one tablespoon of 0.880 ammonia and a teaspoon of household detergent. Both the ammonia and detergent act as degreasing agents and reduce the surface tension of water allowing for deeper penetration.

Vandyke brown (walnut crystals): As the name implies this dye can give various shades of brown depending on the degree of dilution. It is often used on oak and walnut and will give mahogany a rich brown colour.

Potassium bichromate: This is most effective on timber containing tannin. The colour can vary from light orange to dark brown on mahogany. With oak it produces greenish-brown tones.

Sulphate of iron (green copperas): Can turn oak and sycamore grey. When dissolved in water this dye makes a clear liquid, but if it is applied too strongly you can end up with oak stained bright blue! You can use this dye on mahogany to make it resemble walnut.

Ebony crystals: This stain produces an almost black finish.

All these dyes are available from specialist suppliers, and can be made into solutions using water, oil or methylated spirit. Make sure you state which base you will use when ordering a dye; if in doubt, ask for the supplier's advice.

When you make up a strong solution you will need to remove traces of sediment by straining the mix through a fine nylon mesh. You will also need to bind the solution. With water-based stains add a teaspoon of glue size; add French polish for spirit-based stains, and turpentine and gold size for oil based stains. You can use an old pair of tights to make a strainer.

Aniline dyes are certainly the material for the more adventurous when it comes to colouring wood. They are available in a whole host of shades including purple, maroon, crimson, magenta, orange, yellow, brown, blue, green and black.

Using stains

Water stains tend to raise the grain, but you can easily overcome this by first dampening the surface with clean water after the timber has been thoroughly prepared. Simply let the surface dry then rub down using 00 flour paper.

You should apply the stain with a wide, soft brush or a cloth pad. Use long, even strokes and be prepared to wipe away excess stain with a dry, lint-free cloth. When the surface is dry, rub along the grain with 220 grit wet or dry abrasive paper, then lightly rub down again with 00 flour paper. You can use any type of finish **over water stains to seal and protect the surface.**

Oil-based stains can usually be bought ready-prepared. Although they do not raise the grain on timber surfaces, they are not as transparent as water stains and often tend to hide the grain rather than enhance it.

Again, apply the stain with a wide, soft brush and leave for two to three minutes. Then wipe off, along the

4 Results with three different wood stains, showing varying effects on the same piece of timber. Note how grain pattern is enhanced at the same time that the wood is coloured

grain, using a soft cloth. Leave the work for 24 hours before lightly abrading the surface to a smooth finish with 00 flour paper.

With oil stains you do run the risk of lifting the stain, leaving unsightly patches when a wax finish is applied. But you can avoid this by applying two coats of shellac-based finish, such as French polish, before waxing. There are also some modern synthetic finishes which may not take on top of an oil stain. The only ways of determining this are to conduct some

5 Water stains tend to raise the grain. After you have prepared the timber, dampen the surface with water and allow the workpiece to dry

6 Follow by rubbing down the surface with 00 grade flour paper—you will not need to exert much pressure for a smooth finish

7 Apply the stain with a wide, soft brush or a cloth pad. Use long, even strokes to achieve good overall colour and avoid overcharging

8 You can wipe off excess stain from the work with a piece of dry, lint-free cloth, but be careful not to snag this against the wood grain

9 When the stain is dry, rub along the grain with 220 grit wet and dry then lightly rub down with 00 grade flour paper before finishing

preliminary tests on scrap wood or contact the manufacturers concerned.

Spirit stains are difficult to apply and often fade easily. Also, because the spirit base dries rapidly, you can find yourself with ugly brush marks on your work—one reason why professionals rarely use this stain unless the timber surface is greasy.

While spirit stains can be bought ready-mixed, you can make up your own solutions using 25g of spirit soluble dye in 1 litre of spirit. The best way to apply spirit stain is with a spray gun but you can improve the way it brushes by adding 20 parts of stain to two parts shellac and one part pure turpentine. Again, some

synthetic finishes are not suitable for use with spirit stains and you should check first.

Use a wide, soft brush to apply the stain, starting from the middle of the work and brushing outwards. Keep a spirit-soaked rag to hand in case you need to rub out any hard lines. After about 30 minutes, lightly abrade the surface with 00 flour paper and seal with two coats of shellac-based polish.

Fuming
Fuming is a traditional colouring process in which ammonia vapour reacts with tannin in timber to darken it. This process turns oak a blue/grey colour, turning to rich brown when

the timber is treated with boiled linseed oil. However, various types of oak should not be mixed in one job if fuming is to be employed, as they will react differently and colour balance will be lost.

Both mahogany and walnut are well suited to fuming and some outstanding effects can be achieved if chestnut is subjected to the process.

Before attempting to fume finished work, carry out a trial to ensure you can achieve the required colour. Take an offcut of timber and place it in a 'chamber' like the one shown in fig. A. This can be made up from polythene sheet and should be as airtight as you can make it. Place saucers containing 0.880 ammonia into the chamber and, after a while, remove the offcut and treat a small portion with linseed oil **to check colour density. This should be done at intervals until you are satisfied with the results.**

Having noted the time taken to fume the offcut to the required colour, proceed in exactly the same way for the workpiece.

Bleaching
Bleaching is another chemical treatment which can be applied to wood. Here the process is used to lighten colour, remove dark patches, even out the natural colour or prepare for staining with unusual colour.

The simplest bleach to use is oxalic acid. Dissolve crystals of this in hot water until it reaches saturation—when no more crystals can be made to dissolve—then, if the work is of a delicate nature, dilute it slightly with

10 *Wax is the traditional furniture finish. To prepare carnauba wax —which is a hard wax—shred or grate enough to fill two dessert spoons*

11 *Next add an equal volume of beeswax. This can be sliced quite easily with a carpenters' chisel or grated—small chips are best*

12 *Place the grated portions of beeswax and carnauba in a suitable container—such as a cocoa tin or boil-proof jar—before proceeding*

13 *The final component in the mix is ordinary turpentine. Again add enough to fill two dessert spoons, and stir it together with the dry ingredients*

14 *Lower the container into a pan of boiling water and keep the water simmering until the contents have melted. Remove the jar from the water*

15 *Add more beeswax, together with enough turpentine to fill two-thirds of the jar. Return to hot water, stir until melted, then allow to cool*

more water.

Apply the solution sparingly with a brush until you get the required effect. Then wash down the work to 'kill' the bleach, first with a borax solution (14g of borax per litre of water) and then with fresh water.

Remember that oxalic acid is a poison and should be kept out of the reach of children—ideally in a locked cabinet. It is also illegal to make up solutions in food or drink containers such as milk and lemonade bottles. Always wear rubber gloves when handling oxalic acid.

Proprietary two-part bleaches are more reliable than oxalic acid, but their formulae vary and it is vital that you follow the manufacturer's instructions to the letter.

Finishing with wax

Wax is the traditional furniture finish and the best to use is beeswax, **which varies in colour from brown through orange to pale yellow. It is also** available in a bleached white form. Other major waxes are *carnauba* and *cerestine*—both hard—and paraffin wax which is soft. In order to get a workable material, these are often mixed with beeswax and turpentine.

To apply carnauba wax, first shred or grate enough of it to fill two dessert **spoons, then place this in a tin or jar with equal parts of grated beeswax and** turpentine. Lower the tin into a pan of boiling water and keep the water simmering until the contents have completely melted.

Remove the tin and add more grated beeswax, together with enough turpentine to fill two-thirds of the tin.

Return the tin to the hot water and leave it until the new mix has melted, carefully stirring the contents at intervals, then put it to set in a cool place. Providing the mixture is kept covered, it will last virtually for ever.

Apply this polish with a shoe brush, scrubbing across the grain to make sure it is well filled. When the work is fully covered, leave-it for 24 hours and then burnish along the grain using 000

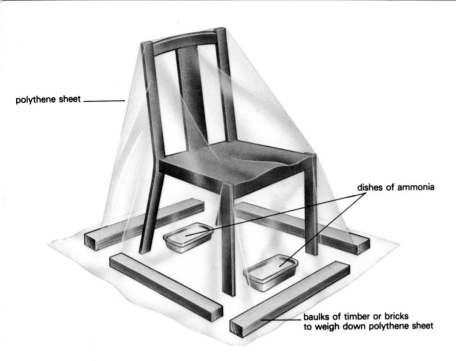

polythene sheet

dishes of ammonia

baulks of timber or bricks
to weigh down polythene sheet

A. *Make your own fuming chamber for traditional ammonia staining using an old chair as shown. Take great care however, to weigh down the edges of the sheeting or fumes may escape*

wire wool. Finally buff with a soft cloth. You will have to repeat this process two or three times each week for a period of one month before you get the lustre typical of traditionally finished antique furniture.

The whole process can be speeded up by adding lighter fuel to the original mix as it is cooling. Equally, you can stop the wax from soaking too far into the wood by applying two coats of brushing cellulose sanding sealer or spirit sanding sealer to the work before finishing. Both should be thinned to a milky consistency and applied with a brush working across the grain. When the sealant is dry—cellulose 10–15 minutes, spirit 30–45 minutes—rub down the surface using fine grade glass or garnet paper.

Oil-based finishes
These are probably the simplest of all finishes to apply, but you need a great deal of time and patience to get satisfactory results. The oil—usually linseed—is applied to the work and burnished every day for a period of four to six weeks, though the process can be speeded up by first applying a sealer such as sanding sealer or a wash coat of shellac varnish.

Careful preparation of both oil and surface is necessary. You can use boiled or raw linseed, but a mixture of

both in equal parts is probably the best. Simmer oil for 15 minutes and then add an eighth measure of turpentine. You can also add a small measure of terebine to speed drying—but be warned that this reduces the ability of the finish to withstand even just warm heat.

The surface of the work should be first prepared with a sealer, then lightly sanded down with flour paper. Rub in the oil itself with fine silicon carbide paper—360–400 grit is best—papering along the grain until a sludge is produced. Remove this afterwards with a clean cloth, wiping across the grain, then lay the work in a dust-free atmosphere for 24 hours.

The whole process must be repeated each day until you get a satisfactory finish. Finally, apply a coat of medium wax polish with a soft cloth.

You might find during application of the oil that it becomes too tacky to work properly. In this case a few drops of turpentine sprinkled on a buffing pad will soften the surface and make application easier. Equally you might find, after polishing the work, that oil sweats out. All you need do here is to wipe over the surface with a small measure of methylated spirits.

Teak oil: This proprietary finish has largely replaced the traditional oil type. Prepare and seal the work in the usual way then apply the teak oil with a stiff brush or cloth pad. Rub it well into the wood grain using 360–400 grit silicon carbide abrasive paper or 000 grade steel wool. Repeat the process two or three times and then

finish by buffing with a soft cloth. Bear in mind that oily, resinous or greasy timbers—such as teak—should be wiped over with methylated spirit before the teak oil is applied.

Lacquers and varnishes
Traditional varnishes, made from natural resin, have now been largely superseded by synthetic materials—properly called *lacquers*—which are both easier to apply and control. Applying varnish and French polish is an art in itself and is covered further on in the course.

Plastic lacquers are the modern answer to both varnish and polish. Not only are they easier to apply but they are naturally rapid drying and give an almost instant finish. Generally they offer excellent heat properties and react less easily to chemicals than traditional materials.

Polyurethane forms the base of the best known plastic lacquers and offers a tough, hard wearing surface. But a better product, because it allows timber to flex, is urea/melamine lacquer. Both types harden by chemical reaction and, in theory, can be applied initially in thick coats. In this way it is easier to ensure coats of lacquer are free from runs, tears and curtains.

For general purposes the one-pot lacquers, with the catalyst already mixed-in, are ideal. But in specialist situations like floor finishing, two-pot lacquers, where the catalyst must be added just before application, are more suitable. Here it is vital to follow the manufacturer's instructions regarding mixing and quantities.

Remember that the pot life of some two-pot mixes is as little as 20 minutes, so mix only as much as you need. Also, check with manufacturer's instructions on the suitability of stains, fillers, thinners and any special paints used in conjunction with these lacquers.

In practice, most lacquers are thinned for the first and second coats, while third and final coats are applied straight from the pot. Lay on the lacquer with a good quality varnish brush as wide as the work will allow. When each coat is thoroughly dry, rub down with fine glasspaper, brush off the dust and remove any fine residue with a soft cloth dampened in white spirit or the manufacturer's recommended thinner.

The final coat can be left as it is but if you want a more traditional finish, apply a thin coat of beeswax as described above.

Renovating a chest of drawers

The chest of drawers in the pictures is typical of the kind of furniture which you can often find cheaply, but in a poor condition, in junk shops or at auctions. With care and the right materials, you can restore the finish to achieve a result as good as that shown in the picture above.

Remove all the old varnish or paint using a stripping paste as shown on the right. At the same time, you can inspect the piece for any weak joints or damage to the wood. Repair these by regluing, or, if necessary, by making new parts. Small holes can be repaired with a wood filler.

Wipe down the wood with water to remove all traces of the stripper and sand to a fine surface. It is now ready for refinishing. You can use stain to add colour and bring out the grain before lacquering. Finish with at least two coats of polyurethane lacquer, sanding lightly between coats.

SUCCESSFUL DRILLING

- ● **HAND-HELD DRILLS**
- ● **DRILL STANDS**
- ● **CUTTING MORTISES**
- ● **DOWEL JOINTING**
- ● **ANGLE DRILLING**
- ● **BUILD A STOOL**

Drilling holes to a high degree of accuracy is extremely difficult—even using a good quality drill fitted with the correct bit. The required angle and depth can be maintained only by careful preparation of the material to be drilled and by keeping a constant check on the drill itself.

A hand-held drill is perfectly adequate for rough work—where pin-point accuracy is not needed. And if the material is correctly marked out and the drill properly positioned, a high degree of accuracy can still be achieved.

For really fine work a vertical drill stand is essential. This holds both the workpiece and the drill so that a hole of exactly the correct angle and depth can be made in the material.

Hand-held drilling

The key to successful hand drilling lies in preparing and marking out the material to be drilled, and in positioning the drill correctly.

Before you start, measure and mark each of the holes to be drilled, in pencil, across the surface of the material. Then use a centre punch (or a bradawl on softwood) to make a small indentation at each of the marks. This ensures that the drill bit can be positioned correctly and that it does not wander once drilling starts. Without switching the drill on, carefully position the point of the bit using the indent as a guide. Drill a pilot hole first and then select a suitable sized bit to finish the hole to the correct diameter for the screw you are driving.

A. Right: *Accurate drilling is made easy by the use of a bench drill stand. This allows you to hold the workpiece steady while drilling to an exact, pre-set depth*

Wherever possible the workpiece should be held securely during drilling, although this may not always be feasible or necessary with large items or those which are fixed permanently. Securing the workpiece ensures that the drill can be positioned more accurately and that the unit does not move during drilling (fig. 1).

A vice on a workbench is often useful depending on the shape of the workpiece and the angle of drilling. As an alternative, the workpiece can be secured to the bench, or some other suitable surface, using G-cramps (C-clamps) or a bench holdfast. This is especially useful if you want to exert downward pressure on the drill or if you need to hold pieces of material which cannot be secured in a vice.

Make sure that the workpiece is sandwiched between two offcuts of wood at each end to protect it from damage, and raise it away from the bench (fig. 2). Thin, pliable materials—such as sheet metal—should be clamped to a wooden backing to prevent them flexing during drilling.

Once the workpiece is firmly held the drill can be moved into position. Before you start drilling check that the body of the drill is at right-angles to the workpiece. Alternatively, line it up with a try square before you start and use this as a guide during drilling (fig. 4). Many drill manufacturers make a simple drill guide to help you to position the drill and to hold it in the correct position while you make the hole.

Even if you manage to make a hole at the correct angle it is often difficult with a hand-held drill to guarantee a pre-set depth. This is essential when drilling for fixings—such as screws and dowels—which require an exact depth for maximum strength.

A rough depth gauge can be made by marking the bit with chalk or crayon or by wrapping a piece of tape around it. Once the marked part of the bit comes level with the top of the hole you have reached the required depth and can stop drilling (fig. 5).

A more accurate gauge—or depth stop—can be made by fitting a small piece of wood around the upper part of the bit. This is especially useful if you have a large number of holes of the same depth to drill (fig. 6).

First fit the bit you intend to use into the chuck and mark the depth of the proposed hole in chalk on its side. Make a careful note of the distance from the chalk mark to the bottom of the chuck and then cut a piece the same length from a 25mm square batten (fig. 7).

Secure the cut piece in a vice and drill a hole through it lengthways. Try to keep the bit in the centre of the gauge and if possible avoid splitting the wood. With care you should be able to drill through the gauge and continue until it is resting just below the chunk. Holes can then be drilled using the depth stop as an accurate marking gauge. As an alternative, many manufacturers make a metal depth stop which slides on to the bit and is held by a grub screw (fig. C). This is particularly useful if you need to drill to different depths.

1 For accurate drilling by hand, the workpiece should first be firmly held—preferably in a vice mounted on a workbench

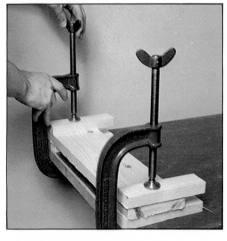

2 As an alternative, secure the workpiece using G-cramps. Sandwich it between two offcuts to prevent it becoming bruised

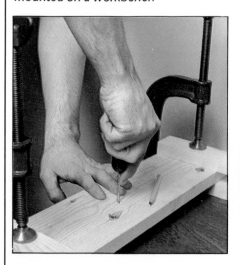

3 Mark out the position of the holes in pencil and then use a centre punch or bradawl to indent the surface of the workpiece

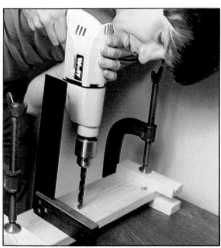

4 Make sure that the body of the drill is correctly aligned. A try square placed next to the workpiece can be used as a guide

5 A rough depth gauge can be made by marking the bit with chalk or by carefully wrapping a piece of tape around it at the correct depth

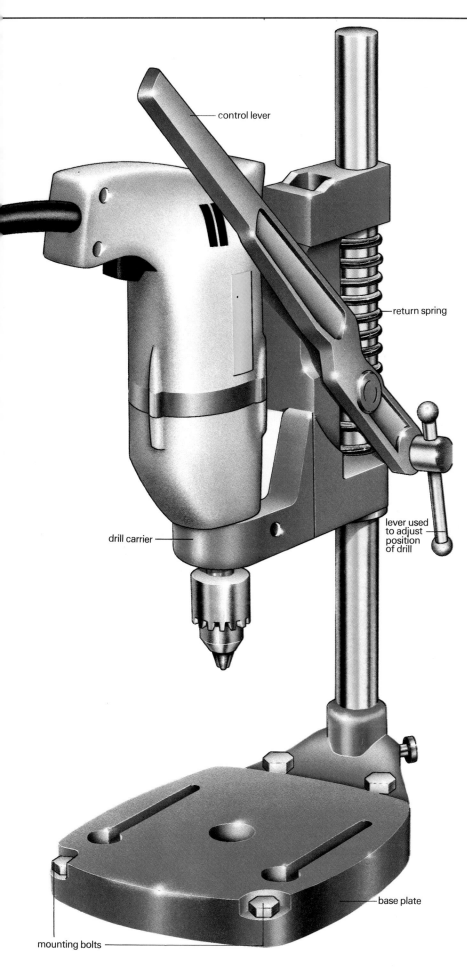

control lever

return spring

lever used
to adjust
position
of drill

drill carrier

base plate

mounting bolts

Vertical drill stands

Accurate drilling is made easy by the use of a drill stand. This can be fitted to a workbench or any flat area where you are drilling. The stand holds both the workpiece and the drill steady so that holes can be drilled at an exact angle and depth.

Fig. B shows the component parts of a basic drill stand. This consists of a base plate on which the workpiece rests and a vertical metal column above it which carries the drill and allows it to slide up and down. The position of the drill is controlled by a lever mounted halfway up the column.

When buying a stand the first point to consider is whether or not your drill, or one you are considering buying, will fit the stand. A wide range of drills can be fitted into some drill stands while other models are designed to take only one specific drill—usually the manufacturer's own brand.

You should also consider whether the stand is suited to the type of work you intend to tackle. The stand itself should be made of good quality materials robust enough to withstand rough treatment. It should also be comfortable to use, and have all the component parts within easy reach.

Check carefully the maximum size of material the stand can hold. The depth of the workpiece is determined both by how far above the base plate the carrier can be set, and by the clearance under the drill once a bit has been fitted. The maximum width of the workpiece is governed by the amount of room between the drill bit and the column—often known as the *throat*. You should also check the maximum depth that can be drilled in one operation by pulling the carrier down on its operating lever.

The base plates of many stands can be swivelled through 360°. This allows greater flexibility—especially in the size of workpiece that can be handled. If the stand is arranged so that the carrier overhangs the edge of the workbench, larger pieces of work can be accommodated—the maximum size being limited only by the height of the bench above ground level (fig. 11).

Before you buy the stand check that it is fitted with a depth stop. This is an adjustable fixture which prevents you drilling too far into the workpiece (fig. 12). If the stand you want to buy has no stop, check whether this can be supplied as an attachment.

B. Left: *A drill stand consists of a base plate and a vertical metal column which carries the drill*

275

6 *An accurate depth gauge can be made by fitting a small piece of 25mm square batten around the upper part of the drill bit*

7 *To make the gauge, carefully measure the depth of hole to be drilled and cut a wooden stop to ensure the bit goes no further*

8 *Before using the drill stand, check that the base plate is firmly bolted to the bench, or screwed to a large, flat board*

9 *The workpiece is held to the base plate by a special clamp which slides up and down the vertical metal column*

10 *Alternatively, a machine vice can be fitted to the base plate. This allows the workpiece to be positioned even more accurately*

11 *The base plates of many drill stands can be swivelled through 360°. This allows larger pieces of work to be accommodated*

If the drill stand is to be effective, the workpiece must be held securely in place. A drill stand or machine vice bolted to the base plate of the stand will hold most small items.

For larger workpieces or more complex tasks a special stand table might be more appropriate. This does not clamp the material, but holds it against a vertical fence so that it can be adjusted more easily. Many tables also tilt, enabling you to drill holes at angles other than 90°.

Using a drill stand

Before using the drill stand, first check that it is securely fixed to the bench. It can be bolted permanently to the bench, or screwed or bolted to a large wooden board so that the whole assembly can be mounted in a vice.

Next check that the workpiece is firmly held in the stand or machine vice. You may find it useful to build up the area in front of the base plate with a plank of wood so that the workpiece can lie flat.

Most stands have a hole in the middle of the base plate directly under the bit so that you can drill right through the workpiece without damage. However, if you are drilling wood it is a good idea to place a scrap piece of timber underneath to prevent splintering. If you are drilling to a pre-set depth, adjust the depth stop accordingly and make a few test drills in a piece of scrap material first (fig. 13).

All the same safety precautions which apply to standard hand-held drills should be followed when using a drill

stand. In particular, fitting a drill chuck guard can prevent serious accidents and stop flying material.

Cutting mortises and dowelling

Cutting mortises and making dowelling joints are essential woodworking jobs—although they are usually very time consuming. By using a drill stand you can carry out both of these tasks quickly and accurately.

To cut a mortise joint from a board, first mark its proposed position on the face of the board. Adjust the depth stop so that the bit will not continue right through the workpiece and then drill a series of closely-spaced holes between the marked-out lines. To complete the joint clean up the slot with a chisel. (Figs. 14 and 15 show how a housing can be similarly cut out).

For a really professional finish a *mortiser* or *mortise drill* can be fitted instead of an ordinary twist or wood bit. These not only cut a neat slot but clean it out at the same time. The mortiser is a drill bit inside a square, four-sided chisel (fig. 16). The bit rotates to cut a circular slot down the middle of the joint while the chisel cleans up the sides and squares off. The mortise drill is a bit with longitudinal rather than spiral cutting edges. By moving the wood slowly from side to side the bit cleans out the slot and drills to the required depth.

A common drilling job, where extreme accuracy is called for, is in the making of dowel joints. Not only do the holes for the dowels have to be precisely at right-angles to the boards, but they also have to be accurately aligned with each other. If this is not done properly the two boards will not mate and a weak joint will be produced.

A vertical drill stand will help you make dowel joints with great ease and accuracy but a hand-held drill can be equally effective if used with a dowelling jig. These jigs vary in design from one manufacturer to another, but they all have the basic purpose of aligning one hole with another so that a dowel can be inserted accurately.

If you have two pieces of wood to join by dowelling, start by laying them both flat on a bench as if they were already joined. Carefully mark the position of the dowels by drawing lines across the edge of both boards using a set square.

Separate the boards and clamp the jig in position across the end of each board in turn. By carefully aligning the jig with the marks you have already made on the edge of the board, the jig can be centred and the dowel holes drilled. Most jigs have a dowel bit guide into which the bit is fitted during drilling. This keeps the bit aligned at right-angles to the board so that a hand-held drill can be used. Various sizes of drilling guide are supplied to suit the standard sizes of dowelling bit.

Even if you do not have a dowelling jig, dowel joints can be made with the help of a drill stand and dowel centring pins. The dowel centring pins are inserted into the top of each set of holes once they are drilled so that the positions for the second pair of dowel holes can be marked (fig. 19).

To use the dowel centring pins, first mark the position of the holes on the first board and then drill them to the required depth using the drill stand. This guarantees that the holes are made at the correct angle and to matching depths.

Then fit the dowel centring pins into the holes, pointed ends facing outwards. Bring both boards together in the position they are to be fixed and the pointed ends of the centring pins will mark the second board exactly where it should be drilled. The drill stand can then be used to make the second set of holes and the dowels cut and inserted (see pages 251 to 258 for more details of how to strengthen other joints with dowels).

12 *The vertical column should be fitted with an adjustable depth stop. This allows you to gauge the drilling depth to the finest degree*

13 *Once you have set the depth stop, make a number of test drillings in a scrap piece of wood before starting on the workpiece*

C. Below: *A home-made depth stop can be made from a small length of wood (right). Alternatively, you could invest in an adjustable metal stop*

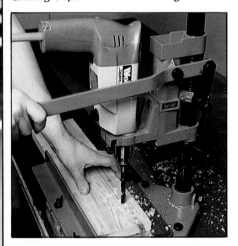

14 *A housing joint can be cut in a board with the help of a drill stand. First drill a row of holes across the face of the board*

15 *The joint can then be cleaned up and the sides squared off with a chisel. However, take care not to split the wood while you do this*

Confined spaces

A number of drilling aids are available to help you work in areas where space and access are limited. These enable you get into places where an ordinary hand-held drill might be too large and awkward.

Angle drilling attachment: A right-angle drilling attachment allows you to hold the drill body vertically while drilling horizontally—or vice versa. The attachment takes the place of the chuck and is screwed directly on to the spindle. It is especially useful when working above head height or below floor level—when drilling through joists for channelling cable for example.

To fit the angle attachment, you must first remove the existing chuck. To do this, place the chuck key in position and give it a sharp tap with a mallet in an anti-clockwise direction. The chuck can then be unscrewed by hand. Afterwards screw the angle attachment into the spindle and tighten it to the body with the spanner or Allen key (hex key wrench) usually supplied with the attachment.

Flexible drive shaft: This is a long, flexible shaft—about 1m long—which can be attached to a hand-held drill so that the drive can easily be taken into confined or awkward spaces.

If you are intending to use this device, make sure that the drill body is well supported. A vertical drill stand can be used, but a horizontal stand—usually used for holding a grinding wheel—is more usual. For added safety the stand should be anchored to a large, flat board so that it can be transferred easily and safely.

Flexible drives may have either a plain, rounded shaft which fits into the chuck, rather like a drill bit, or a threaded end which allows it to be threaded directly on to the spindle shaft. The working end may have a fixed chuck or a spindle so that a range of chucks can be fitted.

Drilling at angles

A drill guide is an extremely useful attachment that can be used to ensure accurate drilling at right angles (or any other pre-set angle) to a surface that cannot be positioned under a drill stand. The adjustable side arms hold the drill at the required angle, and the sole plate can be used with a fence for accurate edge drilling too (fig. 20).

One final feature of many modern electric drills is the ability to drive screws when fitted with an appropriate screwdriver bit (fig. 21)—a very useful feature on repetitive work.

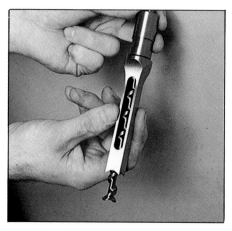

16 For a really accurate finish, you should use a mortiser—a special type of drill bit mounted inside a square, four-sided chisel

17 When using the mortiser, fit an adjustable fence to the base plate: this allows you to move the workpiece during drilling

18 Fit the mortiser and use it to cut out the joint. Slide the workpiece along the fence as the work progresses

19 Drill stands also help you to make accurate dowel joints. Centring pins allow you to line up one hole with another

20 A drill guide can be fitted to the body of the drill to ensure accurate drilling angles when the drill has to be used freehand

21 Many modern drills—especially cordless ones—can be used to drive screws effortlessly into pre-drilled pilot holes and clearance holes

Build a stool

Accurate drilling is always important, but this project depends on it. Although the construction is basically very simple, you will need to drill holes to an accurate depth and at an accurate angle.

Start by making up the top, which is made from three pieces of timber joined with dowels. Drill the dowel holes by hand, using dowel centre pins, or use a drill stand or dowel jig. Cut the finished block to shape with a bow saw or power jig saw and profile the edge.

Drill four angled holes in the top. You can do this by hand, using a bevel guide to set the angle, or clamp the workpiece on an angled block under a drill stand. Drill the holes to the depth indicated. This is best done using a Forstner bit, since it leaves no centre hole. With other types of bit, be careful not to allow the centre to break through on the upper side of the seat.

Drill the legs in the same way. The drawings show two ways to clamp the dowel to prevent it moving.

Assemble all the parts, then sand down carefully and apply three coats of lacquer.

SUCCESSFUL DRILLING

Cutting list

All sizes are in millimetres. Timber is planed all round PAR (dressed four sides, D4S)

Part	Material	No.	Size
top	100 × 32mm softwood (PAR)	3	280mm
legs	32mm diameter dowel	4	440mm
upper rails	21mm diameter dowel	2	210mm
lower rails	21mm diameter dowel	2	230mm

Additional materials: PVA woodworking adhesive, 10mm dowels
Finish: Polyurethane or melamine lacquer

Make the top from three sections of 100×32mm or 100× 38mm planed all round softwood 280mm long. Reverse the grains and join them with 10mm hardwood dowels and PVA woodworking adhesive. Mark out and cut a 280mm diameter circle from the assembled board using a power jigsaw, band saw or bowsaw

Make the legs from 32mm softwood dowel. Join them to the top with PVA woodworking adhesive

Make the rails from 21mm softwood dowel. Join them to the legs with PVA woodworking adhesive

Finish: Sand smooth and seal with polyurethane or melamine lacquer

You can drill the fixing holes in the top by clamping the whole top at an angle, supported on blocks of scrap wood. To prevent the dowels from moving when drilled, you can make up a simple jig like those shown, using pieces of scrap wood. Clamp the leg in place, set the whole jig to the required angle and position for drilling

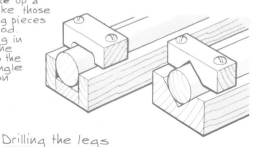

Drilling the legs

Drilling the top

Leg fixing holes. Position them 90° apart on a 170 mm diameter circle

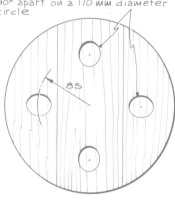

85

Fixing hole   Dowels   Radius the edges to 50mm

Drill the fixing holes at this angle to the diagonal through opposite holes

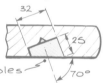

32

25

70°

Fixing hole drilling details

Clamp the legs as shown opposite, then set to this angle for drilling the holes

77°   25

Leg 440mm long from 32mm diameter dowel   21

Dimensions of the legs and rails

Rail holes, positioned at 90° from each other around the dowel

Upper and lower rails. Cut two of each from 21mm diameter dowel

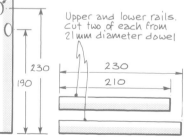

230

190

230

210

YOUR WATER SYSTEM

- **HIGH- & LOW- PRESSURE SYSTEMS**
- **STORAGE TANKS**
- **INDIRECT SUPPLIES**
- **DIRECT SUPPLIES**
- **HEATING SYSTEMS**

Domestic water systems come in two main types:

High-pressure systems, in which water at 'mains pressure' is supplied directly to all the taps and other water-using appliances.

Low-pressure systems, in which the water supply to most taps and appliances is via a cold-water storage cistern in the attic, only the kitchen tap(s) being supplied directly from the mains.

Cold water comes to your house from the water authority mains via a smaller, service pipe. This pipe may have been installed specifically to serve your house or you may share it with a neighbour. Either way, it will be controlled by a water authority stopcock somewhere on the edge of your, or

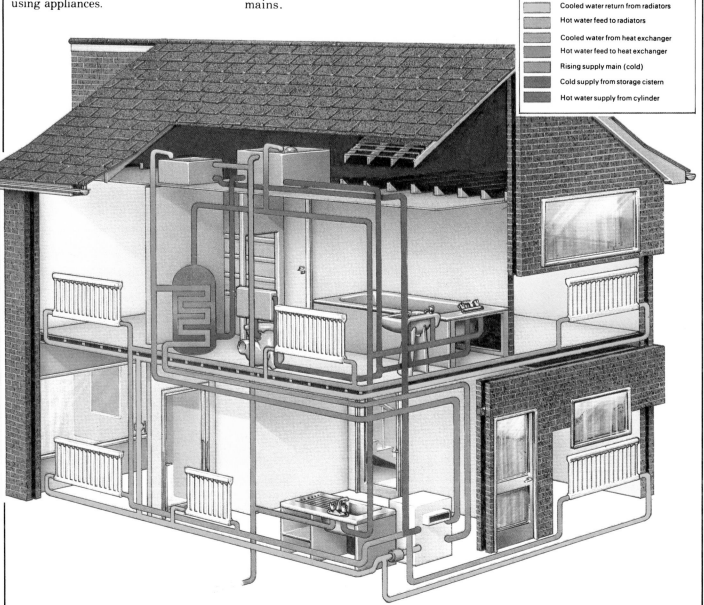

	Cooled water return from radiators
	Hot water feed to radiators
	Cooled water from heat exchanger
	Hot water feed to heat exchanger
	Rising supply main (cold)
	Cold supply from storage cistern
	Hot water supply from cylinder

Above: *A typical British low-pressure water system incorporating two hot water circuits – one for the hot taps and one for the radiators. Water for each system is stored in the two loft tanks which are fed by the rising main.*

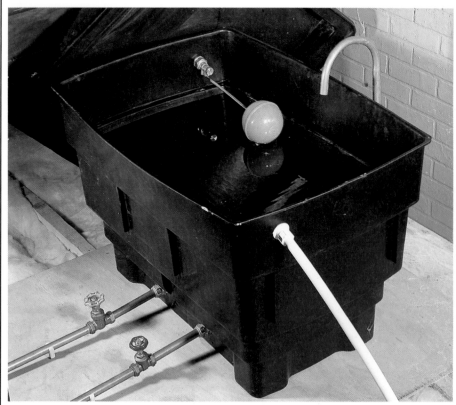

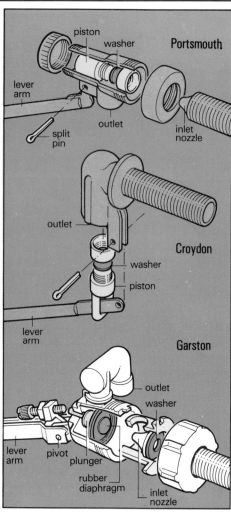

your neighbour's, property. The stop-cock is sunk below ground (usually about a metre) and is encased in brick-work, concrete, or a stoneware pipe to provide access. To mark the site, a small cast-iron casing is usually fitted at ground level.

From here, the service pipe runs to your house and becomes known as the rising main. At the point where it enters, a further stopcock—known as the consumer's, or house, stopcock—is fitted. This one is your own property and, because it controls all water entering the house, it is as well to know where to find it.

The most common place is under the kitchen sink, where a branch of the rising main directly supplies the kit-chen cold tap with drinking water. The other most likely locations are under the stairs, or below floorboards im-mediately inside the front door.

The cold storage tank
After the branch to the kitchen cold tap, the rising main runs to a cold storage tank or cistern, normally in the roof space. Older storage tanks are made of galvanized iron, which is both heavy and prone to rust. These have now been replaced by the lighter, more hygienic, plastic tanks.

The storage tank helps to iron out
irregularities in the mains supply and

Above: *Storage tanks are kept topped up by means of ballvalves, of which there are three common patterns. Gate valves allow parts of the system to be isolated*

also provides an emergency reservoir if the supply is cut off.

The rising main's supply of water to the top of the tank is controlled by a ball-valve similar to the one in a WC cistern. At the base of the storage tank you will find the main water outlet. The stored water flows through here under the pressure of gravity and then branches off to supply the rest of your house's water requirements.

The hot water supply
In household plumbing, cold water is converted to hot either directly or in-directly. Direct heating means that the cold water comes into direct contact with a heater—normally a boiler or an electric immersion heater—then flows straight to the taps.

With indirect heating—usually com-bined with central heating—the water heated by the boiler is itself used to heat up fresh cold water. In this system, the two hot water circuits are separate and heat is transferred from one to the other by means of a heat exchanger.

The hot water cylinder, a copper

tank heavily insulated to guard against heat loss, is common to most hot water installations.

In direct systems, it houses the electric immersion heaters—if fitted—and acts as storage tank to keep your hot water supply as constant as possible. In an indirect system, the cylinder has the additional function of housing the heat exchanger.

The direct flow
The flow of water in both direct and indirect systems relies on the prin-ciple that hot water always rises above the cold water around it. So, in a direct system, the flow starts with cold water running to the base of the hot water cylinder.

If a boiler is fitted then the flow continues from the cylinder down to the base of the boiler. As the water is heated it rises out through the top of the boiler, up to the top (crown) of the hot water cylinder and then on to the hot taps.

If immersion heaters are fitted in-stead of a boiler, the flow is greatly simplified. The water runs from the

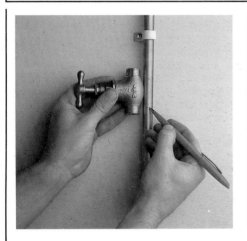

1 To fit a stopcock or gatevalve in a pipe run, first turn off the supply and drain the pipe. Then mark the amount to be cut out

2 Use a hacksaw to cut out the section of pipe squarely. Then spring the cut ends into the fitting and tighten the nuts

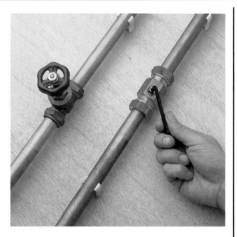

3 Fit gatevalves rather than stopcocks on low-pressure pipe runs . Open Ballofix valves with an Allen key

storage tank to the base of the hot water cylinder and is heated: it then rises straight out of the cylinder and on to the hot taps.

The great disadvantage of direct systems is that water, when it is heated above 60°C (140°F)—or 80°C (180°F) in soft water areas—deposits scale similar to kettle fur. This can block up pipework and boilers alike unless adequate precautions are taken.

The indirect flow
The easiest way of understanding an indirect hot water flow is to visualize two independent 'loops' of water. The first loop consists of the water used to feed the hot taps.

This flows from the cold storage tank to the base of the hot water cylinder, where it comes into thermal contact with hot water on the other loop (via the heat exchanger). As the water is heated, it rises out of the cylinder and on to supply the taps.

The other loop supplies the boiler, heat exchanger and—if fitted—the radiators. Here, fresh water flows to the base of the boiler from either the storage tank or from another separate tank, known as the 'expansion tank'.

Once in the boiler, the water is heated and then rises out to feed the heat exchanger and radiators. After the water has given up its heat, it flows back to the boiler for re-heating.

Because the water in this loop is hardly ever changed, the problems of scaling are greatly reduced.

The expansion tank
The indirect arrangement works best when an expansion tank is fitted to supply the boiler loop. This makes the loop almost completely independent of

the one supplying the hot taps.

The tank is supplied with water from the rising main via another ball-valve. So, if the loop needs topping up with water because of evaporation, the process is automatic. In practice, changes in the water level inside the expansion tank are barely noticeable.

To guard against the build-up of high pressures in the hot water system, overflows or vents are fitted.

In a direct system, only one pipe is needed. This runs to the top of the cold storage tank, either from the crown of the hot water cylinder or from a branch off the hot water service pipe.

In an indirect system, an additional vent is installed at the top point of the primary circuit.

Turning off the hot water
Whatever your hot water system, the hot water which reaches the taps comes from the top of your hot water cylinder. It does so because of the pressure of the cold water entering the cylinder beneath.

So, if you cut off the cold water supply at the base of the cylinder, no further hot water will rise from the top. Most hot water cylinders have a gate valve for this purpose, fitted at the cold water inlet. Those that do not, invariably have a stopcock somewhere on the pipe between the inlet and the cold storage tank.

Wet central heating
Wet central heating, in which hot water is used to heat the house via a system of radiators, adds an additional complication to plumbing installations. But if you can imagine the radiators and their pipes as being part of the boiler 'loop' in a basic hot water

system, the whole thing becomes easier to understand.

Some older installations work on the direct principle in which hot water heated by the boiler flows to the radiators as well as to the hot taps. Because this system is uneconomical and causes scaling, it has been replaced by indirect installations.

Here, the water which flows to the radiators is on a pump-driven loop like the one used to supply the heat exchanger. So the water flowing through the radiators hardly changes, and there is very little chance of scaling and corrosion occurring.

Consequently, the system can use a mixture of metals—copper pipes and thin, lightweight steel radiators rather than the heavy and very expensive cast iron radiators and pipes used in direct systems.

Radiator systems
The pipework used to supply the radiators may take one of two forms. In the simpler, one-pipe system, hot water flows from the boiler to each radiator in turn and then back to the boiler again. Although this cuts down the amount of pipework needed, it allows hot and cooled water to mix during the run. Consequently, the last radiator in the run often remains cool however hard the boiler is working.

In the two-pipe system, the pipework is arranged so that cooled water leaving the radiators cannot mix with the hot water entering them. The radiators therefore heat up faster, as well as remaining at the same temperature.

Sizing of inward and outward piping in the radiator circuit is matched to the given radiator load—so pipe sizes can vary throughout the system. 283

Where to turn the water off

If you are unlucky enough to have a leak or a burst pipe, your first step must be to cut off the water supply. Do this as near to the offending area as possible so that inconvenience is kept to a minimum.

Hot water pipe or tap: Look for a gate valve on the pipe which runs into the base of the hot water cylinder or boiler. Before you turn it, make sure that all heating apparatus is off.

Cold water pipe or tap (low pressure systems): Trace back along the relevant pipe until you come to a gate valve. If there is none between the burst and the cold storage tank, you will have to block the tank outlet. To do this, nail a cork slightly larger than the outlet hole on to the end of a piece of timber (fig. B). By 'remote control', you can now insert the cork into the outlet and prevent further water from leaving the tank.

Should the outlet prove impossible to block, drain the tank instead. First tie back the ball valve to a piece of timber stretched across the tank: this will stop fresh water from entering. Now, turn on your bath and washhand basin cold taps, until the tank is fully drained.

Cold water pipe or tap (high pressure systems): Turn off the house or water authority stopcock. The house stopcock is usually located on the rising main in the kitchen, quite often under the sink.

Leaking galvanized storage tank: A leak here will probably be due to a rust spot which has eaten its way right through the metal. Once you have tied back the ball valve and drained the tank, you can cure the leak by drilling out the rust spot and fitting a nut, bolt and washer into the hole (fig. A).

Burst lead pipe: A crack in a lead pipe can be temporarily stopped by ramming in a matchstick and then rubbing the area with candle wax. Follow this by binding up the repair with strong tape and keeping any relevant gate valves at half pressure until a proper repair can be carried out.

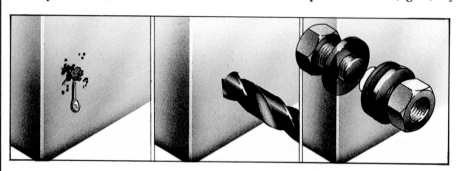

A. *A leak in the tank can often be fixed by plugging the hole with a bolt. Use a soft washer between the two metal rings for a watertight fit*

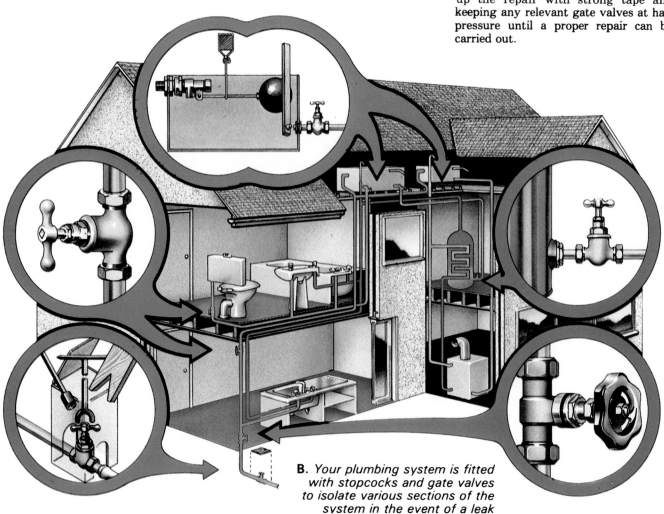

B. *Your plumbing system is fitted with stopcocks and gate valves to isolate various sections of the system in the event of a leak*

YOUR WASTE SYSTEM

- **TWO-PIPE SYSTEMS**
- **SINGLE STACKS**
- **CLEARING BLOCKED WASTE TRAPS**
- **ONE-PIPE SYSTEMS**
- **TRAP TYPES**

Above-ground drainage systems are governed by a variety of regulations and local bye-laws (ordinances). Plans of all proposed alterations to your existing system must be submitted to the building control department of your local council. The inspector there will be able to authorize the plans and also give guidance and advice.

Above-ground drainage—the parts of the waste system linking water-using appliances to the drains—is a vital part of any house. Understanding how it works enables you to clear blockages quickly and effectively and gives a useful insight into how future additions to your plumbing can be made.

Three main types of above-ground drainage systems are in common use, although variations and modifications are frequently used.

In the *two-pipe system*, found in British homes built before the 1930s (fig. A) soil and waste discharges are piped separately to the ground drain. 'Soil' describes effluent from the wc; 'waste' describes water not contaminated by 'soil', including washwater. The two pipes may or may not be provided with ventilation pipes (revents) to balance out pressures in the system, depending on its size.

A variation of the two-pipe system is still occasionally used for bungalows, but seldom on two-storey houses as the amount of pipework is considered extravagant.

The hopper head used in this system for collecting bath and basin waste at each floor can become foul-smelling in hot weather, and its waste pipe blocked by dead leaves and suchlike at other times. This causes the hopper to overspill, leaving stains on the face wall of the building.

In the *one-pipe system*, (fig. C) used in Britain and several other countries, the soil and waste water discharges into a single, common pipe which runs down an outside wall. Individual ventilating pipes (revents) from the discharge pipes, which carry the waste from the appliances, are all connected to a main ventilating pipe whose outlet is above roof level. In Britain, the one-pipe system can be seen on good-quality housing built between 1930 and 1950, but has since been superseded by the *single-stack* system (fig. B) for most forms of housing below five storeys.

Here, the soil and waste water discharges into a single pipe or *stack*, built into the structure of the house. The top of the stack, which rises through the roof, normally provides

the sole means of ventilation.

The efficient working of a single-stack system is dependent on all the branches being as short and as closely grouped on the stack as possible. Suitable methods of achieving this are shown in fig. J.

Where a discharge pipe over the recommended length has to be installed, an extra vent pipe is run from the pipe near the appliance to a point at least one metre above the nearest entry to the stack. This balances out the pressures in the system which might otherwise result in the siphonage problems described below.

Because it is contained within the structure of the house, access to a single-stack system can often prove more difficult than to older systems.

This is outweighed, however, by the saving on pipework and by the protection afforded against frost damage.

Sub-stacks and gullies
In single storey houses, appliances are sometimes connected to a *sub-stack*—a short stack which runs directly to the ground drain and is ventilated independently of the main stack.

In many houses, waste water discharge from the kitchen sink runs to a separate gully (fig. A) which has its own waste trap (see below) and con-

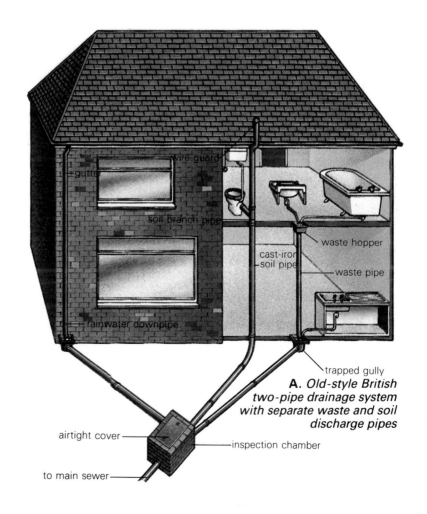

gutter

wire guard

soil branch pipe

rainwater downpipe

waste hopper

cast-iron soil pipe

waste pipe

trapped gully

A. *Old-style British two-pipe drainage system with separate waste and soil discharge pipes*

airtight cover

inspection chamber

to main sewer

D. *Hand-basin design when a 36mm branch pipe (D) is used: the maximum slope (θ) depends on pipe length L between trap and vent—about 1.5° for 1.5m, 2° for 1.25m, 3° for 1m, 4.5° for 0.75m. A trap of 75mm seal depth and 32mm diameter is needed*

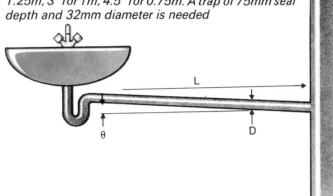

E. *Bidet design calls for use of a 42mm branch pipe, and the slope of this (θ) must be between 1° and 2.5° (a drop of between 18mm and 45mm per metre). L must normally be no more than 1.7m. A trap of 75mm seal depth and 38mm diameter is needed*

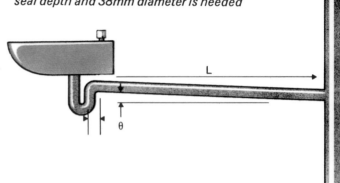

nection to the ground drain. In houses employing a two-pipe system, the gully will be below the hopper head. In single-stack systems, the discharge pipe from the sink is connected below the gully grid but above the level of the water in the trap. This arrangement is commonly known as a *back inlet gully*.

Some local authorities permit other waste water appliances—such as washing machines and showers—to be discharged into the gully. The rules here are the same as those governing the sink discharge pipe (fig. H).

Waste traps
To prevent foul air entering the home, simple devices known as *traps* are employed on each and every discharge pipe. A trap is little more than a depression or a bend which retains water but does not interfere with the flow of water through the pipe it serves. This *water seal* prevents air on the drain side of the bend from entering the room.

Traps come in a variety of shapes according to their function and fitting, and may in fact be incorporated

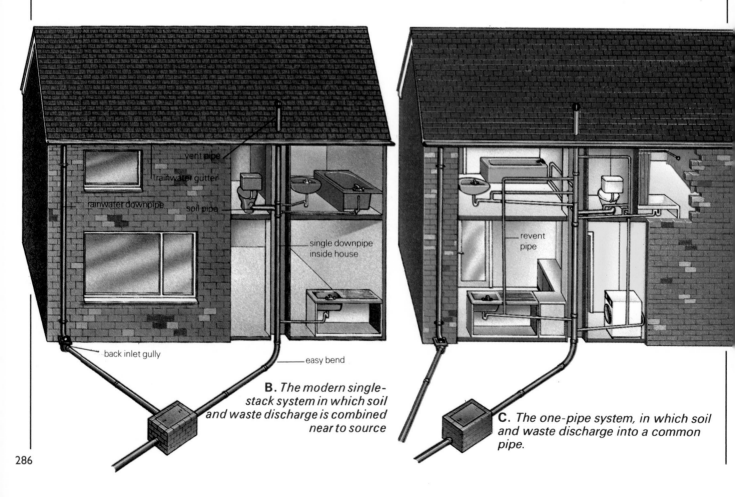

B. *The modern single-stack system in which soil and waste discharge is combined near to source*

C. *The one-pipe system, in which soil and waste discharge into a common pipe.*

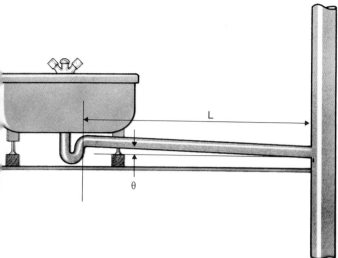

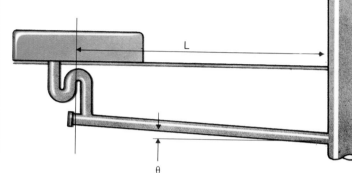

G. *Shower base using an 'S' trap, for which bath design conditions apply. Again, a 3-4m length is possible if a 42mm trap is fed to a 55mm discharge pipe—this prevents the waste pipe running full, reducing suction on the trap which might otherwise empty it*

F. *Bath design using a 'P' trap. Slope of the discharge pipe must be between 1 and 5 (18 to 90mm/m) and its length kept to less than 3m. A 3-4m length can be fitted using a 42mm trap (with short 50mm tail pipe) into a 55mm pipe*

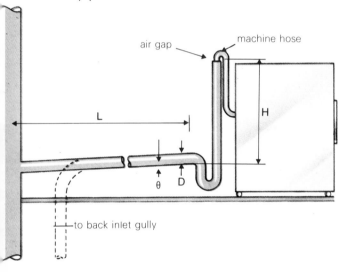

H. *Plumbing in a washing machine. Slope (θ) of 42mm discharge pipe is between 1 and 2.5 (18 to 45mm/m), L must be less than 3m, H between 600mm and 900mm (depends on machine). Low-level outlets must be piped to a back inlet gully*

I. *Two arrangements for providing ventilating pipes, needed when more than two bends occur in any branch pipe or when long pipe stretches require relief venting. The alternative system (beneath) is better because it avoids unsightly pipework*

within an appliance. 'P' and 'S' shaped traps are the most common, though they are now being superseded by the modern *bottle* trap. These are all used directly beneath the discharge outlet of baths, basins and sinks.

The water seal is the important part of the trap and the depth of water must be maintained. Loss of the trap through *self-siphonage*, *induced-siphonage* or *evaporation* can result in fumes or waste entering the house.

Self-siphonage occurs when a reduction of pressure occurs within the 'drain' part of a system, resulting in

an individual appliance losing its seal when flushed or drained. Induced-siphonage occurs under similar conditions, but in this instance one appliance—such as a wc when flushed—sucks out the trap of another appliance where this trap is weaker or of incorrect depth.

Problems of evaporation may occur in long hot spells if an appliance is left unused for any length of time. An outside appliance is particularly prone and the best thing that can be done to prevent the loss of water depth in the trap—making it useless—is to try to

arrange for someone to flush the appliance from time to time.

In rare instances *blow-back (compression)* may occur when there is a burst of unusually high pressure in a system. A discharge high in the stack released shortly after another is nearing the bottom—and being slowed down by the bend there—causes the air between the two to become slightly compressed. Sometimes this pressure is sufficient to 'blow' the traps of lower waste appliances (bath, basin, bidet, sinks, shower) but not those of the wc.

J. *Design points of a single-stack system take into consideration the length and slope of individual discharge pipes according to the appliance they serve. Under no circumstances should pipe runs be level or very steeply sloped as both cause problems within the system as a whole*

vent

If the distance of the stack from a window opening is less than 3m, the termination point must be a minimum of 900mm above the window

The diameter of branch discharge pipes for single wc pans is usually 100mm although 75mm can be used for some siphonic models. 'P' or 'S' trap connections can be used. Pipe length should be less than 6m, and its slope greater than or equal to 1° (18mm drop per metre). A downwards drop on the discharge pipe should not exceed 1.5m— longer connections must be extended upwards and a discharge stack and a 'P' type wc used

basin

bath

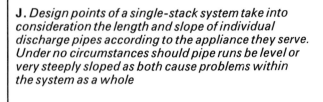
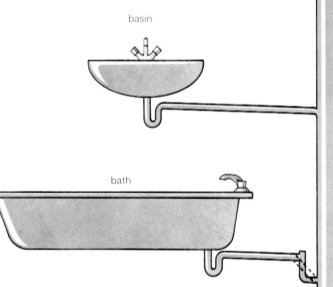
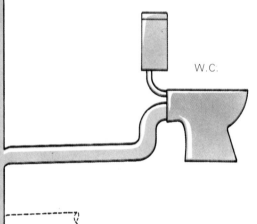

W.C.

Care is needed where waste and soil discharge pipes meet on the stack. To prevent wc discharge backing up a smaller diameter branch—such as that for the bath— the latter should be connected to the stack so that its centre line is at least 200mm below the wc outlet centre line (as shown, using a parallel branch). Alternatively, the bath pipe can be located so its centre line is at least 200mm above the wc pipe centre line (dotted line shows the arrangement). Similar rules to this 200mm clearance apply to opposed small diameter branch pipes

sink

Branch pipes should be kept as short as possible and under no circumstances should the diameter be reduced in the direction of flow. Bends should be kept to a minimum and be of as large a radius as you can manage

The minimum distance between the bend at the base of the stack and the first branch connection on the stack is 450mm, a condition suitable for houses up to three storeys high. The bend radius should be as large as possible, but 200mm is the minimum. An alternative bend arrangement consisting of two 45° bends is shown alongside

slow radius bend

drain

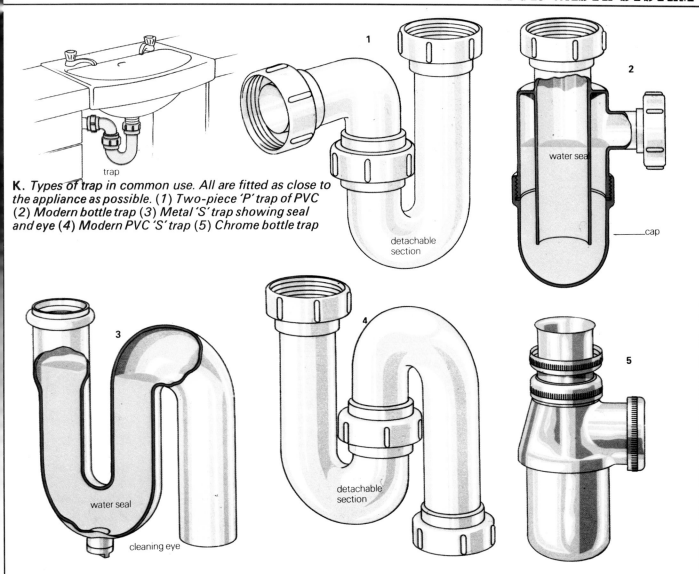

K. *Types of trap in common use. All are fitted as close to the appliance as possible. (1) Two-piece 'P' trap of PVC (2) Modern bottle trap (3) Metal 'S' trap showing seal and eye (4) Modern PVC 'S' trap (5) Chrome bottle trap*

Blow-back may also occur if discharge from one appliance (such as a wc) is allowed to force itself into a lesser discharge branch (such as that for a bath). This will occur if the centre lines of both discharge pipes meet at a common point—a mistake all too easily made when considering additions to a discharge stack. Fig. J shows how the two can be fitted.

Every type of trap has some form of access for clearing blockages. Older traps have a small screw-in metal *eye* fitted to the lowest part. The newer, two-piece traps made of PVC are simply unscrewed if a blockage occurs. The access plate near to a wc is normally large enough to permit rodding in the event of a blockage.

Drainage requirements
The requirements governing aboveground drainage systems may seem unnecessarily complicated but failure to observe them can result in frequent blockages and the kind of siphonage problems described above.

In older houses, poor or haphazard installation of the various discharge pipes is often the most common cause of blockages.

Figs. D to I show the design points to watch for when planning the drainage for a new appliance or checking on the efficiency of your existing system.

As a general rule, discharge pipes should be kept short and as free from bends as possible. Each must be connected independently to the relevant stack or pipe. In single-stack systems, the connections are best made as close together as possible.

Adding discharge pipes
When planning the run of a discharge pipe for a new appliance, bear in mind that it should follow the design recommendations in figs D to I as closely as possible—even if this restricts your choice of site.

Waste water discharges from two-pipe systems can usually run to the hopper head on the first floor, or to the gully on the ground.

Soil discharges present more of a problem as it is nearly impossible to break into old, cast-iron or earthenware soil pipes. Unless the branch fitting to the existing wc can be dismantled and replaced with a ready-made twin-branch fitting. it will generally prove easier to replace the entire soil pipe with one made of more workable PVC material.

Waste and soil discharge connections to a single stack are much more straightforward. Providing the site of the extra appliance is carefully chosen, and the run of the discharge pipe planned to join the stack close to an existing branch, then normally all you have to do is change this for a new fitting which has the extra discharge pipe socket you need. You could get this professionally fitted.

289

Clearing blocked traps

Use an adjustable spanner or wrench to undo the eye in a metal 'P' trap and gouge out the blockage using a screwdriver or stick. Apply sealing compound before you replace the eye

Try a plunger before attempting to dismantle a trap. Stuff a damp rag into the overflow—or use suitable tape —and bale out all but a small depth of water before you start using the plunger

A plunger, ideally with a metal plate above the rubber cup, must be jerked vigorously up and down to create sufficient water pressure inside the trap to remove a wc blockage

REPLACING GUTTERS

- ● **PLANNING A SYSTEM** ● **BUYING PARTS**
- ● **REMOVING OLD GUTTERS AND DOWNPIPES**
- ● **FITTING BRACKETS** ● **FINISHING OFF**

Above: *When you come to fix the downpipe of a PVC gutter system, secure a plumbline with a nail or drawing pin to the fascia board immediately behind the outlet. This gives you a guideline for positioning the pipe clips down the wall*

However well they are maintained, old metal gutters and rainwater downpipes may eventually begin to show signs of decay. If decay is far advanced, it is well worth replacing the whole system with PVC guttering.

PVC rainwater systems have several advantages over the various metal types. They do not corrode, nor do they require painting for protection — though they can be painted to suit colour schemes. Because PVC guttering is light, sections of it are easier to handle than their metal counterparts—an important consideration

when you are working on a ladder. Being cheaper than cast iron, PVC has virtually replaced it for home building and renovation work. It is available in a range of cross-sections, including the traditional half-round shape.

Planning the new assembly

Sections of PVC guttering can be joined together in different ways (see also pages 147 to 152). But with all types of half-round guttering, you fix the system to the exterior of the house in more or less the same way. The gutter sections are clipped into brack-

ets screwed to the fascia boards beneath the eaves of the roof. The downpipes have wrap-around pipe clips which are screwed directly to the walls. Some other systems require no brackets for the gutters because they are screwed directly to the fascia boards themselves.

You can cut sections to any length required using a fine-toothed hacksaw.

Before you take down the existing guttering, measure it carefully to give you the lengths for the new gutters and pipes (fig. 1). Count and measure the stop-ends, outlets, shoes, swan

REPLACING GUTTERS

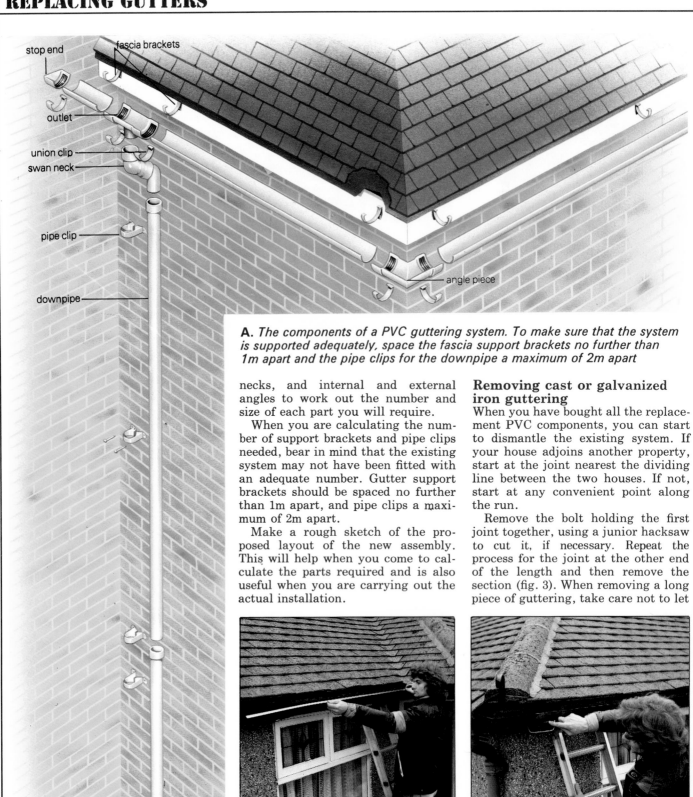

stop end

fascia brackets

outlet

union clip

swan neck

pipe clip

downpipe

angle piece

shoe

A. *The components of a PVC guttering system. To make sure that the system is supported adequately, space the fascia support brackets no further than 1m apart and the pipe clips for the downpipe a maximum of 2m apart*

necks, and internal and external angles to work out the number and size of each part you will require.

When you are calculating the number of support brackets and pipe clips needed, bear in mind that the existing system may not have been fitted with an adequate number. Gutter support brackets should be spaced no further than 1m apart, and pipe clips a maximum of 2m apart.

Make a rough sketch of the proposed layout of the new assembly. This will help when you come to calculate the parts required and is also useful when you are carrying out the actual installation.

Removing cast or galvanized iron guttering

When you have bought all the replacement PVC components, you can start to dismantle the existing system. If your house adjoins another property, start at the joint nearest the dividing line between the two houses. If not, start at any convenient point along the run.

Remove the bolt holding the first joint together, using a junior hacksaw to cut it, if necessary. Repeat the process for the joint at the other end of the length and then remove the section (fig. 3). When removing a long piece of guttering, take care not to let

1 *Before you take down the existing guttering, measure it carefully to give you the lengths for the new gutters and downpipes*

2 *The bolts holding the old gutter together may be corroded. In this case saw through them using a junior hacksaw*

3 *Lift the freed guttering out of its brackets and take it to the ground making sure that the weight does not catch you off balance*

4 *If the fixing screws of a fascia bracket are too corroded to unscrew, use a claw hammer to lever it away from the board*

5 *You should be able to remove the swan neck of a downpipe by hand but if not, knock it out gently with a hammer*

its weight catch you off balance while you are on the ladder.

When you have removed a section and taken it to the ground, unscrew the supporting brackets from the fascia board. If the fixing screws of a bracket are too corroded to unscrew, use a claw hammer to lever them away (fig. 4). Do not knock upwards with the hammer when you are trying to dislodge a stubborn support or you may crack the tiles immediately above.

If you are dealing with Ogee-section guttering, either unscrew the fixing screws holding the lengths to the fascia board, or, if they are corroded, cut through them with a junior hacksaw. If these methods fail, use a bolster to lever between the gutter and the fascia boards.

Some cast iron systems are supported by brackets which are screwed to the ends of the roof rafters. To gain access to the fixing screws on such brackets, you may have to remove the slate or tile immediately above it with a slate ripper. In this case, it may be easier to saw through the brackets and fit the new system directly to a fascia, if you can add one.

When you come to dismantle a downpipe, start by removing the outlet section at the top and if fitted, the swan neck. You should be able to dislodge these by hand by pulling upwards but if not, use a hammer to knock them from place (fig. 5). Remove the downpipe brackets by levering out the pipe nails with a claw hammer. Where necessary, hold an

offcut of timber against the wall so that you get more leverage on the hammer.

Assembling the new system

Before you erect the new guttering, check that the fascia boards are in a sound condition. It is well worth taking the opportunity to repaint the fascias before fixing the new guttering.

Scrape off any paint that has formed in ridges around the old guttering, then wash down the fascia and when dry, apply primer to any bare wood. When this has dried, key the surface by rubbing it over with a medium grade of glasspaper. Paint the boards with two undercoats and one top coat then leave them to dry out before erecting the new guttering.

Boards in particularly bad condition may have to be replaced altogether. This is not always a particularly easy job, and you may find it involves disturbing the lowest course of slates or tiles on the roof.

To assemble the system, begin by fixing the supporting brackets. Place one bracket at the top end of a run to correspond with the old one, and one at the bottom end in a similar position (fig. 7). Attach a length of string between the two brackets and make sure that it is taut. Check the string with a spirit level to make sure that it slopes towards the outlet position—the correct slope need be as little as 25mm in a 15m run—then use it as guide for positioning the intervening brackets. It may be that you can fix all the new brackets in the positions of the old ones. But check constantly that both the spacings and the fall are correct.

6 *Before you start to assemble the new guttering, use a spirit level to check that all the fascia boards are horizontal*

7 *To assemble the system, begin by screwing the supporting fascia brackets firmly into place along the fascia board*

When you come to an internal or external angle at the corners, hold the appropriate part in place and mark the **appropriate bracket positions: these** vary according to the brand of system that you are installing.

When you have marked all the bracket positions, drill holes for the mounting screws into the fascia boards and screw each bracket home. With all the brackets in place, you can start to position the guttering lengths within them.

Cutting and fitting
When you are cutting new gutter lengths, it is important to make sure

that the cut ends are square. You can do this by fitting a spare section over the piece to be cut and using it as a template to draw the cutting line (fig. 9). Once you have sawn through a section, smooth the cut edges with a medium file.

Start fitting the guttering at the top end of a run. Clip the lengths into position in the brackets and join sections together, following the manufacturer's instructions.

Because PVC tends to expand and contract, even with quite small temperature variations, some systems make allowance for movement at each joint. In this case, the union clips

holding sections together have marks on either side with which the ends of adjoining gutter sections are aligned. The resulting gap between sections allows for maximum expansion and contraction without weakening the new seal.

If you are faced with the problem of connecting the new guttering to a neighbour's iron system, special adaptor fittings are available for joining the two materials. Dry out and clean the end of the iron section, using a wire brush to remove any traces of rust. Apply sealing compound to the mating surfaces and then press the adaptor into place (fig. 12). You can now join the PVC section, following the manufacturer's instructions.

Fitting a downpipe
Unlike cast iron systems, the swan necks for PVC guttering are not manufactured in one piece. Instead they are made up of an offset socket, an offset spigot and an offcut of pipe (fig. A). The length of pipe determines the angle of the bend, thus giving you more flexibility in positioning the downpipe than you would have with cast iron or galvanized metal.

To erect the downpipe, fix a plumbline with a nail or drawing pin to the fascia board behind the outlet. You can then use the string as a guideline down which to mark the pipe clip screw positions.

Place one of the clips around the bottom of the offset spigot, hold it temporarily in place on the wall, and mark its screw holes. Next, measure and cut the length of pipe to fit between the socket and spigot. To

8 When cutting a new piece of gutter to length, make a pencil mark on the underside of the section at the correct distance from the end

9 Fit a spare gutter section over the piece to be cut. Align its edge with the pencil mark and draw the cutting line

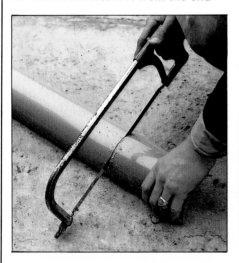

10 Hold the length of guttering in place and cut through the line with a hacksaw. Smooth the cut edges with a medium file

11 To join PVC guttering to a cast-iron system, clean the end of the iron piece, then apply some sealing compound to the area

12 Fix the special adaptor fitting into the end of the iron gutter and clean off the underside with the point of a screwdriver make sure that the cut end of the pipe is square, mark the length to be cut then wrap a paper template around the pipe at the mark (fig. 13). Bore the holes for the pipe clip screws into the wall (fig. 14), plug the holes with wall plugs, then fit the swan neck in position (fig. 15).

Fit the downpipe down the wall, joining the sections according to the manufacturer's instructions, and fix a pipe clip at each joint to support the pipe. Finally, fit the shoe piece that lets into the drain or soakaway at the bottom of the pipe and attach the last clip (fig. 17).

Once the whole assembly has been fitted and joined, test the system by emptying a bucket of water into the gutter at the highest point of each run to check that there are no leaks.

13 *When cutting a piece of downpipe to length, wrap a paper template around the pipe to make sure the cut edges are square*

14 *Attach a plumbline to the fascia board behind the outlet and use it as a guide to mark and drill the pipe clip screw holes*

15 *In masonry walls, plug the holes with wall plugs, place a clip around the pipe, then screw it into place on the wall*

16 *Working down the plumbline fix the downpipe sections to the wall. Fit a pipe clip over every joint of the pipe*

17 *Finally, fit the shoe piece that lets into the drain or soakaway at the bottom of the pipe and attach the last clip*

Install a water butt

Rainwater is ideal for watering indoor or outdoor plants. Instead of letting it run to waste, you can divert some of it into a storage barrel ready for use.

You can buy a purpose-built plastic barrel with a tap from garden stores, or use a metal oil drum and fit a tap.

The rainflow from a whole roof will fill a barrel very quickly, so use the flow from a garage, shed or outhouse. Build a brick plinth to support the barrel alongside the old soakaway. Shorten the original pipe and fit a swan neck bend to divert the flow into the barrel. Fit a clip at the point where you join in the new section.

You must fit an overflow pipe to the barrel. This should be routed to the original drain. If there is sufficient rainfall, this arrangement should maintain a constant supply in the barrel, ready for use.

The plinth makes it easy to fit a bucket or watering can under the tap. To prevent the area from becoming muddy, you can lay a small concrete slab in front of the plinth, on which to rest the bucket or can.

Stand the barrel on a plinth so you can fit a bucket under the tap. You can make a simple plinth like that shown by laying bricks on a concrete footing

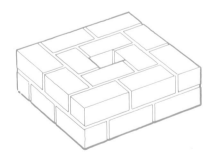

Alternatively, use concrete blocks or even heavy timber, but remember that when full, the barrel will be very heavy

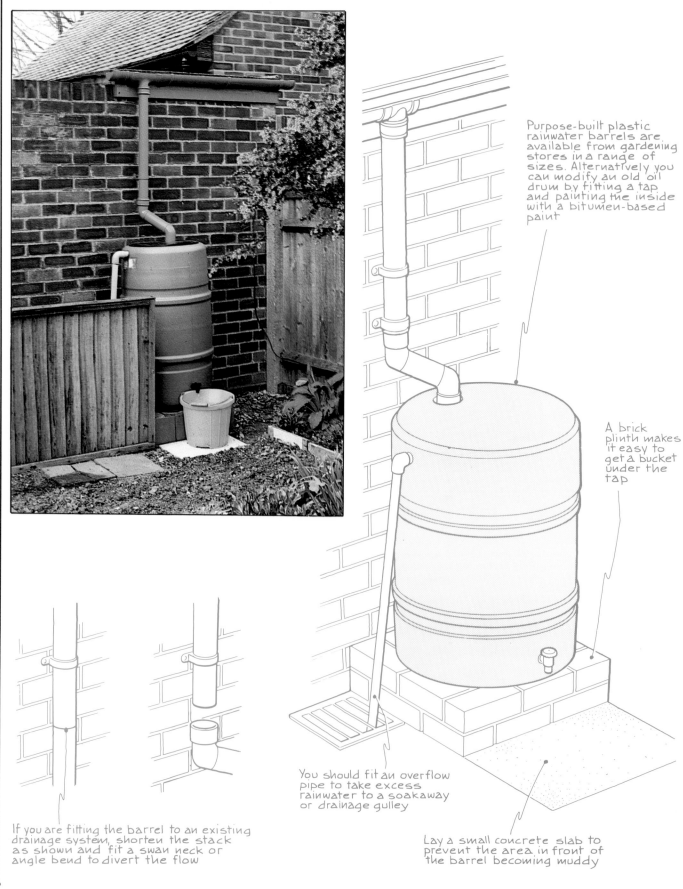

Purpose-built plastic rainwater barrels are available from gardening stores in a range of sizes. Alternatively you can modify an old oil drum by fitting a tap and painting the inside with a bitumen-based paint

A brick plinth makes it easy to get a bucket under the tap

If you are fitting the barrel to an existing drainage system, shorten the stack as shown and fit a swan neck or angle bend to divert the flow

You should fit an overflow pipe to take excess rainwater to a soakaway or drainage gulley

Lay a small concrete slab to prevent the area in front of the barrel becoming muddy

PLANNING A SHOWER

- **SHOWER TYPES**
- **WATER SUPPLIES**
- **ENCLOSURES**

- **THE RIGHT SITE**
- **DRAIN RUNS**
- **INSTANT SHOWERS**

Taking a shower is the ideal way to freshen up, much more convenient than having a bath and considerably cheaper. Among the other benefits of a shower are its constant running temperature, and the possibility of fitting it away from the bathroom to avoid early-morning congestion.

You have the choice of converting existing room space to form an enclosure (fig. A), or of buying one of the many prefabricated enclosures (fig. B) now on the market—many of which come complete with fixtures and fittings.

If you plan to make your own enclosure, base the design of this on the use of a prefabricated shower base. This considerably simplifies the all-important drainage arrangements, which are often the greatest problem where the bath is not used. From a

safety point of view, make sure you provide adequate lighting and room for movement.

On the plumbing side, hot and cold water supply pipes have to be laid on as well as drainage, and these points go a long way towards influencing your choice of site. At the shower, the hot and cold water can be mixed by

> **WARNING**
> In some countries, electrical, plumbing and drainage work is required by building regulations and supply authority rules to be carried out only by a licensed tradesperson. It should be stressed that unlicensed tradespersons must not undertake the work outlined here.

A. *Purpose-built shower enclosure, here incorporating a traditional tank-fed shower mixer*

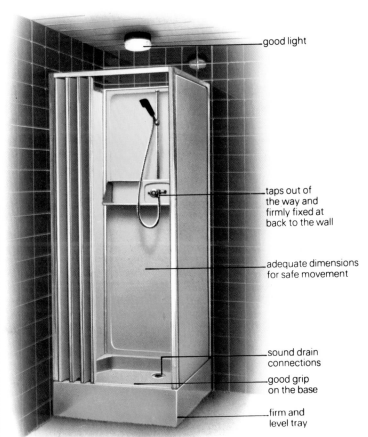

good light

taps out of the way and firmly fixed at back to the wall

adequate dimensions for safe movement

sound drain connections

good grip on the base

firm and level tray

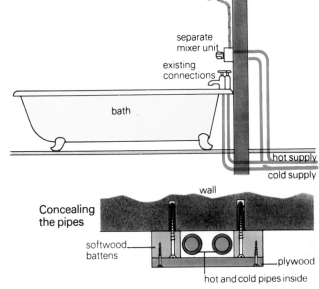

separate mixer unit

existing connections

bath

hot supply

cold supply

wall

Concealing the pipes

softwood battens

plywood

hot and cold pipes inside

B. Left: *A prefabricated shower base can be located wherever plumbing and drainage present no problem. Observe commonsense safety precautions*
C. *If you choose to use your bath as a shower base, an independent hot and cold water supply permits some freedom in locating this. Box off exposed piping as shown*

297

D. *Interrupting existing hot and cold water supplies in order to feed the shower control requires some care. Mixer controls should be fed by independent hot and cold water supplies wherever possible to avoid water starvation—hence temperature fluctuations—when taps in other parts of the system are turned on. To ensure equal hot and cold water tap pressures at the mixer, see that the cold water supply comes from the same system as supplies the hot water system, or from one alongside it. The two diagrams show two typical supply interruption points. Adequate water pressure is essential: the head of water must be at least a metre, but preferably more for optimum flow. Raising the supply cistern is one way of achieving this*

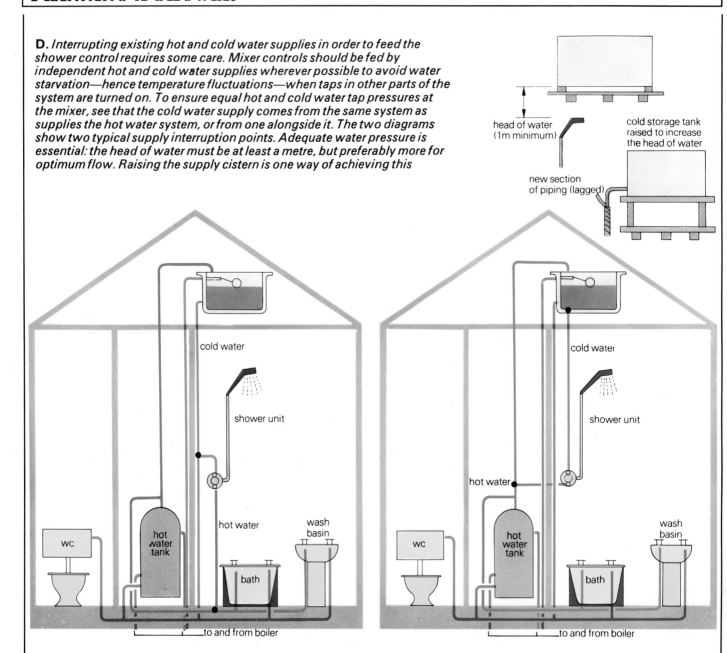

head of water (1m minimum)

cold storage tank raised to increase the head of water

new section of piping (lagged)

cold water

shower unit

hot water

wash basin

WC

hot water tank

bath

to and from boiler

cold water

shower unit

hot water

wash basin

WC

hot water tank

bath

to and from boiler

independent taps or by a single control. Supply pipework and the shower head connection can be concealed beneath tiling, perhaps behind a false panel fixed to the wall.

Another alternative is to provide a shower over a bath, either by fitting combination bath/shower mixer taps in the way described on page 310, or by laying on piping for an independent shower. With this arrangement, you have no shower base or drainage to worry about.

If it is difficult or impossible to lay on a suitable hot water supply, then an electric 'instantaneous' shower or gas heater may provide the answer, although both have disadvantages compared to a two-pipe shower. The

instantaneous electric shower has a slower flow rate, and the gas shower needs ducting to the outside (it is usually attached to an outer wall). However, instantaneous showers have improved dramatically over the past few years and are well worth considering.

The water supply

For proper operation of a shower, there must be sufficient water pressure at the shower rose. In many British houses, the water pressure at most taps (both hot and cold) is provided by a cold water storage cistern, mounted above the level of the water outlets. The higher the cistern above the outlet, the greater the pressure will be; the vertical distance measured from the

bottom of the cistern to the outlet is called the *head*. For a shower, the head is measured to the rose and ideally should not be less than 1.5m, though in simple plumbing systems a head of 1m may be sufficient.

If the head is between about 1m and 1.5m, then an adequate shower may be achieved if you can keep connecting pipework runs short, and with very few bends.

For heads of less than a metre, or where it is not possible to have short simple pipe runs, there are three main solutions. The first is to install a *flow booster*—a type of electrical pump which increases the pressure. Operation is automatic.

The second solution is to *increase the*

height of the cold water storage cistern by raising it up on a sturdy wooden platform. But there may not be room in your loft to do this. Another solution is to use an *instantaneous shower* connected directly to the cold water mains.

In some areas of the UK, houses do not have cold water storage cisterns; instead, all cold taps and so on are supplied direct from the mains. Hot taps are usually supplied from a conventional hot water cylinder fed from its own small cistern. Such *direct systems* are mentioned on pages 281-284. With this arrangement it is not possible to fit a conventional mixer type shower: it would contravene water regulations. You can either fit an instantaneous shower or perhaps modify your plumbing so that the shower is fed from a suitable, conventional cold water cistern.

Sometimes the whole house system, including the hot supply, is fed direct from the mains, and showers designed to work with this system are readily available. In Britain, a fully direct system like this will almost certainly use a 'multipoint' type gas heater: you should consult both your gas board and your water authority about the possible problems of connecting a shower to such a supply.

E. *A built-in shower enclosure is a desirable feature of any well-appointed bathroom, but can of course be incorporated wherever there is room to spare. Note the hinged screen of strengthened or laminated glass*

Temperature fluctuations
Water starvation in either hot or cold supply pipes can cause temperature fluctuations in the shower, which could be annoying or even dangerous. It is very sensible to buy a shower that is thermostatically controlled, or at least has a temperature limiting device so that the water never gets dangerously hot.

For showers in an indirect plumbing system, it is a good idea to use separate hot and cold supply pipes that do not feed any other fittings—then turning on any other taps in the home will have no effect on the flow.

Drainage considerations
Although deciding how to supply water to a shower can be tricky, it is usually possible to get over the problems one way or another. Leading the dirty water away, though, to a soil stack or waste water drain often presents far more constraints. PVC piping, being easy to work with, is the logical choice for this sort of job. But breaking through walling, both internal and external, is usually necessary if the discharge pipe is to remain completely

hidden from view. And unlike hot and cold supply piping, the discharge branch cannot be taken under the floorboards unless the run is between, and almost parallel to, the joists underneath.

Your choice of site for the shower must therefore take into consideration drainage arrangements almost to the exclusion of everything else.

In Britain, the Building Regulations limit the run of the branch discharge pipe to a length of 3 metres and to a slope of between 1° and 5° (equivalent to a drop of between 18mm and 90mm per metre length).

An 'S' trap can be employed if a pipe drop is required (fig. F), such as when underfloor drainage is possible, but otherwise a 'P' trap is preferable— shallow ones are available if space is tight. Use pipe of 42mm diameter.

If the shower base discharge pipe can be arranged to go directly through the wall and connection has to be made to an outside soil stack or waste hopper, much of the fall can be arranged externally.

Use professional help if you have

to break into a cast-iron stack, though it is usually easier to replace the whole stack with the PVC equivalent so that the shower and any future additions to the system involve the minimum amount of work.

Installing a shower base
The first stage of the job is to prepare structural work—such as a timber frame for the enclosure—if this is necessary. Thereafter the sequence is:

In the UK, alterations to existing plumbing installations are strictly controlled by local water authority by-laws. Because of this, you should inform your local water board of your plans at least seven days before work starts. As well as giving practical advice, they will warn you against any possible infringement of their regulations.

In addition to this, new waste pipe installations should have Building Regulations approval, which should be obtained from the local authority.

Run hot and cold water supply pipes to the point where a connection is made with the shower controller.

Follow carefully any recommendations made by the shower manufacturer as to where to break into the supply. Use 15mm copper piping and "T" connections to connect with your existing hot and cold water pipes, keeping bends to a minimum and pipe runs as short as possible. Use either compression or capillary fittings—the latter are cheaper, and neater looking. See pages 307 to 310 for information on working with copper pipe.

Remove the shower base (or tray) and its accessories from the protective wrapping, taking care not to scratch or damage these parts. Lay fixing accessories on the floor close at hand —but not in the immediate working area—in a logical order ready for use.

Lay the shower base on a protective groundsheet, and locate the tubular legs in the sockets welded on each side of the steel shower support frame. Fix the frame to the wooden shower support, which may be flooring grade chipboard (particleboard) or similar.

Secure each leg to its socket upstand using self-tapping screws.

Assemble the adjustable feet but hand tighten only as later adjustment is necessary. Place the base on its feet.

Fix the waste outlet to the shower base, incorporating the sealing washers provided and using a waterproof mastic to complete the seal. Use a holding spanner while tightening the larger nut with an adjustable spanner.

Attach a short length of pipe to the trap and temporarily secure the trap to the waste outlet, then mark on the wall the exit position of the pipe.

Cut a hole through the wall big enough for the discharge pipe at this point. You will find it easier to remove a small section of skirting first if you find that this is in the way.

Reposition the shower base, then using a bradawl, mark the floor fixing points of its supporting board.

Check the level of the shower base, ensuring that the trap has sufficient ground clearance, and tighten the fixing nut on each leg.

On solid floors it is difficult to drill and plug for eight screws and still have perfect alignment—especially as the holes have to be angled so that the shower base does not impede the actual screwing process. It is easier to fix the support board on its own to the floor, attaching the feet later.

Temporarily link together the trap with a short length of pipe, arranged to protrude through the wall near to where it is to discharge into a hopper or stack. If you have the choice, it's easier to direct the pipe to a hopper.

If discharge is made to a soil stack, mark a point on the stack which is level with the protruding pipe ('A' in fig. F) and another point a little below this so that a drop of between 18 and 90mm per metre is obtained ('B') for satisfactory discharge.

Assemble a replacement triple socket, boss branch and pipe socket and then gauge the length of the piping which has to be removed from the stack in order to fit these. Transfer the measurement to the stack in such a way as to embrace points 'A' and 'B' (fig. F), with the pipe socket coinciding with the latter.

Cut out the stack length with a fine-toothed saw, taking precautions or using assistance to keep the upper and lower lengths in position afterwards.

Dismantle the triple socket from the boss branch and pipe socket. Push the triple socket into the top part of the stack as far as it will go. Then fix the boss branch and pipe branch on to the lower part of the stack. Complete

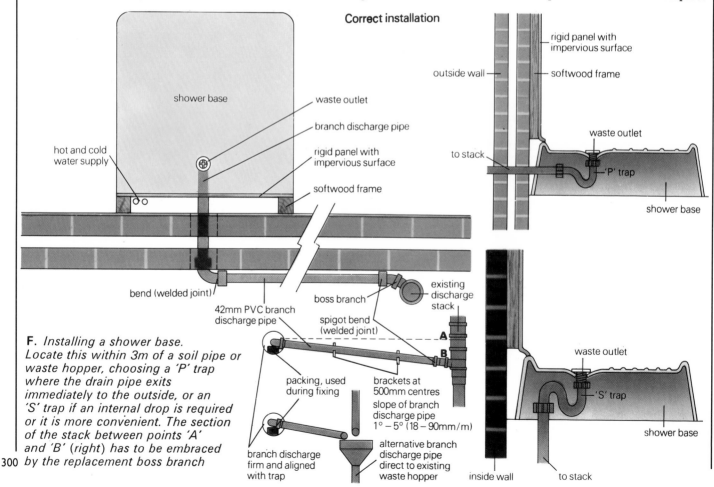

Correct installation

shower base

hot and cold water supply

waste outlet

branch discharge pipe

rigid panel with impervious surface

softwood frame

bend (welded joint)

42mm PVC branch discharge pipe

boss branch

spigot bend (welded joint)

existing discharge stack

packing, used during fixing

brackets at 500mm centres

slope of branch discharge pipe 1° – 5° (18 – 90mm/m)

branch discharge firm and aligned with trap

alternative branch discharge pipe direct to existing waste hopper

rigid panel with impervious surface

outside wall

softwood frame

to stack

waste outlet

'P' trap

shower base

waste outlet

'S' trap

shower base

inside wall

to stack

F. *Installing a shower base. Locate this within 3m of a soil pipe or waste hopper, choosing a 'P' trap where the drain pipe exits immediately to the outside, or an 'S' trap if an internal drop is required or it is more convenient. The section of the stack between points 'A' and 'B' (right) has to be embraced by the replacement boss branch*

G. *A shower enclosure can be incorporated in an under-stairs conversion where other simple washing facilities may also be provided for use by occasional guests. Lack of privacy may pose a problem, however*

Install an electric shower

An instant electric shower is an attractive proposition if use cannot be made of conventional hot and cold water supplies. In most instances, connection of the heater is direct to the mains water supply—so a shower of this type is especially useful if a hot water cylinder is not incorporated within the system. Pressure and flow variations within the system may have a marked effect on temperature stability, however. The heater needs direct and permanent connection to the electricity supply through a double-pole isolating switch. The appliance must be earthed, and protected by a 30amp fuse. For additional safety, site the heater well away from the direct spray at the shower, and locate the switch outside the bathroom or shower enclosure.

You can interrupt the rising main at any convenient point. Remember to keep the pipe run as short and as straight as possible. Most instant showers require a cold water supply which has a minimum static pressure of one bar (equivalent to a water head of about eight metres) which should be available from most mains supplies. In most houses, though, you cannot use a cistern-fed supply because the head will not be great enough.

In some countries you must by law have electric and plumbing work done by licenced tradesmen. Heater suppliers usually provide a complete installation service.

the fitting by pushing the triple socket down into its final position.

Insert the spigot bend into the boss branch, attach brackets to the outside connecting length of the discharge pipe and fit this into the spigot bend. Twist the boss branch until the supporting brackets on the discharge pipe make contact with the wall.

The discharge pipe from the inside of the house should by now meet the discharge pipe attached to the stack, and the two can be marked for cutting so that you can fit a 90° bend where the inner pipe leaves the wall. Remove both pipes and cut these to final length.

Replace all pipes, the longer (outside) one with its fixing brackets in place. The shorter (inner) length is fixed first to the trap and then to the bend. Screw the trap to the waste outlet of the shower base. It is essential that all pipes and fittings are perfectly aligned and that no force is used to keep them in place. Make minor adjustments if necessary.

Mark and fix supporting brackets, normally required only for the outside length. Make alignment marks at each of the fittings.

Dismantle pipework and fittings that require solvent welded joints, prepare the joints and reassemble as before.

If the discharge pipe is to be led to an outside hopper, cut the protruding pipe close to the wall and fit a 90° bend. Attach whatever length of pipe is necessary to complete the run to a convenient point above the hopper, and provide support brackets.

Make good the hole through the wall using a proprietary filler paste. There are now aerosol foam sprays on the market which are waterproof, allow for expansion or contraction, and are easier to work with than the more traditional compounds.

Test the pipework, first for stability (proper support and correct joining) and then for watertightness, using a pail of water until connection is made with the supply system.

Connection of the hot and cold water supply pipes to the shower controller (or regulator) is made in the course of assembling the shower enclosure, and the procedures should follow exactly those stipulated by the manufacturer. The valve and spray piping are attached to a mounting panel attached to the wall or set into the wall along with piping. With self-contained shower enclosures, the mounting panel is attached to the rear of the cubicle with a waterproof gasket arrangement.

Completing the enclosure

Once the shower base installation is complete, you can attend to the completion of the shower enclosure. This is a relatively simple job if you are using a prefabricated kit, which often requires little more than a few minutes with a screwdriver. Built-in enclosures requiring woodwork, tiling and other jobs (not forgetting suitable sealing at the joints) take much longer to make but can be matched completely to the design of the room.

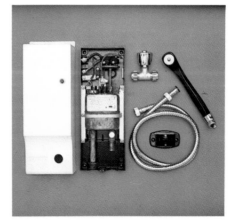

1 *An instant electric shower heater usually comes as a kit of parts. Installation involves plumbing and electrical skills*

2 Remove the cover and mark the position of the fixing holes, and drill for fixings as required. Knock through for connecting wires

3 Cable entry to heater is best made through the rear. Ensure this is correctly wired, tightening the cable clamp securely afterwards

4 The double-pole linked switch is located safely on the other side of the wall and connected to the heater via the wall aperture

5 Pipe connections near to the heater can be tailor-made to fit. Use capillary fittings up to the point the heater fitting is used

6 Interrupt the cold water supply wherever is most convenient, using a 'T' connector. In a loft, lag the pipe well

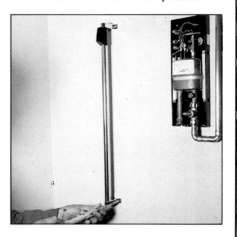

7 Mark the shower rail position and screw the rail firmly into position, with the top of the rail no higher than the heater

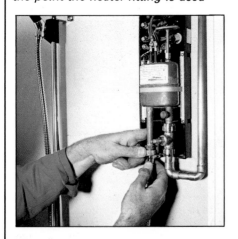

8 Connect the flexible hose to the water outlet of the heater, turn on the water mains and the flow tap and then check pipework for leaks

9 Repeat the procedure with the heater on. Where water pressure is too high, the restrictor may need adjusting to reduce the maximum flow

10 When tests have been completed to your satisfaction, finally replace the cover and connect the two neon spade leads

WASHING MACHINES

- **THE RIGHT SITE**
- **HOSE CONNECTIONS**
- **USING GULLIES**
- **WATER SUPPLIES**
- **WASTE PIPES**
- **SOIL STACKS**

Left: Though the way in which the hot and cold water supplies are connected varies from machine to machine, hoses are often used at the machine end. This gives you more flexibility in your choice of site and permits easy removal for cleaning

Though an automatic washing machine is a boon to any household, many people are discouraged from buying one because it has to be plumbed in—both to the water supply and the drains. But providing you choose the site carefully and set about the work in a logical order, the job is not half as hard as it seems.

The work can be divided into four stages: positioning the machine; connecting up the cold water supply (probably hot, too, though many machines are cold-fill only); installing a branch discharge pipe to the drains; making the electrical connections. The last step involves plugging into a socket outlet or fitting a fused connection unit.

Choosing a site

Your first decision here is in which room to site the machine. In the UK, the choice is normally between the kitchen and bathroom, both of which have hot and cold water supplies and drainage outlets. Alternatively, you could site it in a utility room.

You have next to consider the type of machine, the space that will be needed around it, the existing layout of the room and the design and materials used in your plumbing system.

Of these, the plumbing system must inevitably take priority. It is no use choosing the ideal space-saving site only to find that you cannot then plumb in the machine without demolishing the house.

Drainage: In the UK, for a washing machine in a ground floor kitchen, the most suitable outlet for the discharge pipe is a back inlet gully, separated from the main discharge stack and connected to the main drain by a branch underground. This is often easier to break into than the main stack and, as it is usually there to serve the kitchen sink discharge pipe, it is likely to be in the most convenient position already.

In older houses, the sink waste sometimes discharges over an open,

trapped gully. You will probably be allowed to run the washing machine discharge pipe to here also provided that the end of the pipe is below the grid. If in doubt, seek professional advice.

If the pipe has to connect to the main stack, the latter will need a branch fitting. Though this is relatively easy to fit to a plastic stack, on the older, cast-iron or galvanized steel types the job is best left to an expert. Indeed, it is probably better to take the opportunity of replacing the stack with a new one. A connection to an existing hopper head taking bathroom waste water (see page 285) may not be allowed.

Water supply: Breaking into the hot and cold water supply generally presents less of a problem, as the final connections to the machine are usually made with flexible hose. Nevertheless, the supply must be near enough to the site to allow you to keep pipe runs as short—and as uncomplicated—as possible.

In the UK, a cold-only supply might come direct from the rising main (usually the easiest arrangement if the machine is in a kitchen), though some water authorities do not allow this.

A hot and cold fill machine is best supplied via the cold water storage cistern or tank. In this case, as with some showers, low water pressure is sometimes a problem on upper floors or in flats and bungalows. Manufacturers 303

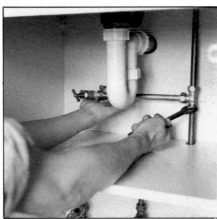

1 *Having isolated and drained down the pipes, sever them with a fine toothed hacksaw. Make the cuts as cleanly as possible*

2 *With careful planning, you can keep the run simple and the number of joints to a minimum. Use compression or capillary joints*

3 *With some types of valve, the flexible hose ends may simply screw on, as here. With other types different fixings will be needed*

generally specify a minimum 'head' of water—that is, the distance from the base of the storage tank to the point where the supply enters the back of the washing machine—and you should bear this in mind when choosing a site for your machine. If you cannot meet the minimum head requirement, consult both the manufacturer and your local water authority.

Most modern automatic washing

machines can also be connected directly to mains pressure supplies.

The pipe run must be arranged so that the branches do not cross one another, with the stop valves easily accessible. When you are planning the run, consider the best place to fit tee pieces to the supply pipes; it may be better to have a slightly longer run in order to avoid disturbing existing fixtures and fittings.

Breaking into the supply

Having chosen your supply pipes, turn off the nearest stop valves and drain the pipes by opening the taps at the end of each pipe run (see pages 15 to 18). With cistern-fed supplies, if there

A. Below: *A typical completed installation. Note that in some areas, taking the cold supply direct from the rising main is not allowed*

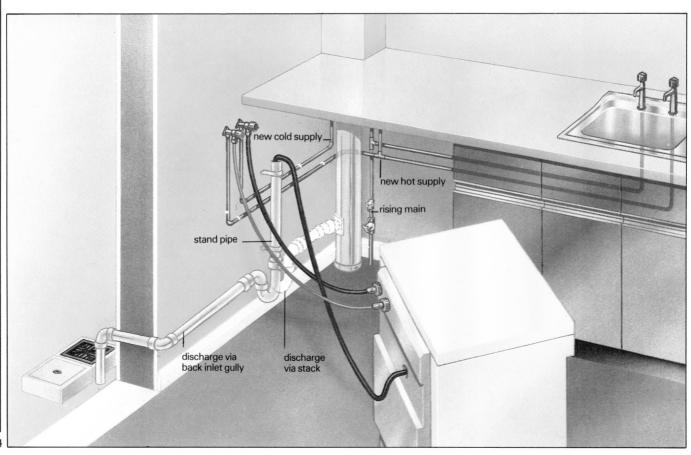

new cold supply

new hot supply

rising main

stand pipe

discharge via back inlet gully

discharge via stack

are no local valves, look for a cold supply stop valve on the pipe running out of the base of the storage tank and a hot supply valve on the cold supply pipe running into the base of the hot water cylinder.

If you still have no luck, you must tie up the ball valve on the storage tank and drain down the system. It is sensible to turn off the boiler or heat source before you turn off any water services. If you are taking the cold supply from the rising main, turn off at the mains.

To break into the supply, you must either cut out sections of pipe large enough to take tee fittings or remove and replace existing fittings. Opt for whichever gives the simpler pipe run.

Using the former method, measure and mark the cut sections very carefully against the tee fittings. Be sure to allow for the extra pipe taken up by the joints. If there is a joint already near a cut section, it may be easier to loosen this, make one cut and remove the pipe altogether (fig. 1). You can then trim it to the new length required on the bench. Make the cuts with a fine toothed hacksaw, ensuring that the pipe ends are kept square.

Having prepared the pipe ends, fit the tee pieces. If you are using compression joints, the best method is described on page 309.

Connecting to the machine

Somewhere between the tee pieces and the washing machine inlets, stop valves must be fitted so that the supply can be disconnected at any time. Some manufacturers provide these with their machines while others leave the choice of valve entirely up to you. Suitable fixing points for valves are normally the wall or the side of a unit.

Mark the points clearly then measure back and fit pipe runs—using 15mm copper tube in the UK—between these and the tee pieces. Where necessary, support with wall brackets every 1.2m. Fit the valve holders to the ends of the pipe runs before you fix them to the wall.

Finally, screw the valves provided into the holders and secure the flexible connections to the machine. On no account should you attempt to shorten the flexible fittings supplied with the machine: these are designed specially to length in order to balance out irregularities in the water flow.

If you are fitting your own valves, simply fit these to the ends of your pipe runs and connect them to the flexible hoses (see fig. 3). But as above, make sure that the valves are so positioned that the hoses do not cross or kink.

4 *Back inside the house, connect the waste trap for the standpipe at the point where the discharge pipe comes through the wall*

6 *Finally, when you are happy that everything is functioning as it should, make good the hole in the wall with appropriate filler*

In both cases, test the pipework and all joints for leaks at this stage.

Installing the discharge pipe

For the pipes themselves, follow the sizes and plastics type which is specified in the manufacturer's handbook. In the majority of cases, these will be 32mm PVC with solvent welded joints.

Connection to a back inlet gully:
The simplest way to connect to a gully is to run the pipe just below the surface of the grid. To do this, replace the grid (if it is a metal one) with a plastics type, and cut a hole in it of the right size to take the pipe.

Alternatively, you may want to take this opportunity to replace an old gully (whether back inlet type or not) with a modern plastics back inlet gully. To

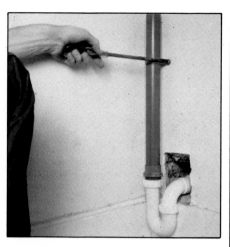

5 *Cut the standpipe to the required length, screw it to the trap and fit the support bracket. Now is the time to check the run for leaks*

7 *Roll the washing machine into place being very careful that you do not tangle the flexible hoses or press them against the wall*

do this, start by digging away the soil around the gully so that you expose the upper part (fig. B). Remove the water in the trap beside it with a plunger.

Next using an angle grinder and cutting disc, cut away enough of the pipe to accommodate your new PVC gully fitting. Bear in mind as you mark up for the cut that the new gully must finish above ground level and be far enough away from the wall to allow you to fit the discharge pipe (fig. A). Before you sever the pipe completely, support the gully from below to take the weight of the trap.

Remove the old gully and fittings above the cut completely. Then bed a PVC-to-clay pipe adaptor over the cut end of the drain run using rapid-hardening cement; hold the adaptor in place for 305

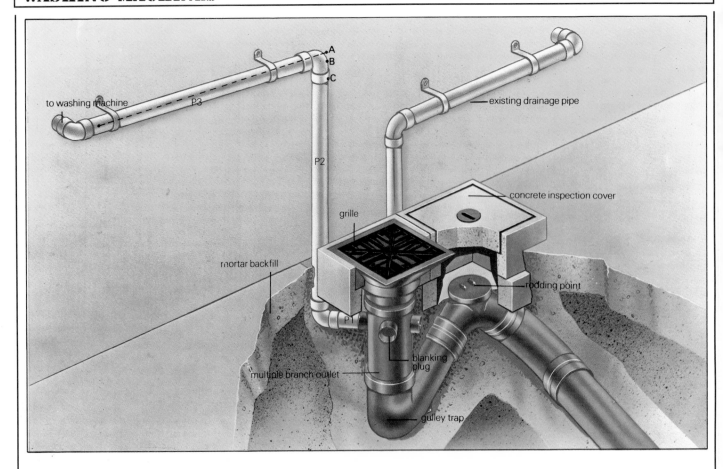

to washing machine

P3

A
B
C

P2

mortar backfill

grille

existing drainage pipe

concrete inspection cover

rodding point

P1

blanking plug

multiple branch outlet

gulley trap

a few minutes to ensure a sound bond. Next, shovel some almost-dry concrete into the hole and bed the gully trap on it with the trap outlet fitted into the adaptor. Finally, check that the hopper fits at the required level, assemble the components after lubricating the joints and backfill round the gully with fairly dry concrete.

Connecting the discharge pipe to the back inlet may call for a little trial-and-error. Start by connecting the bend and short length of pipe P1 (see fig. B), adjusting the length of P1 so that P2 stands out from the wall the correct distance to accommodate pipe brackets. Then fit P3 and its bends, so that the fall of the pipe is between 18mm and 45mm per metre, and so that the lower bend is vertically over the bend connected to P1. Finally, cut and fix P2.

Now continue the pipe run through the wall following the same cutting and measuring sequence. Do not permanently solvent weld the joints until you have checked the run.

After the run has been fitted as far as the wall, fill in the space between the gully and the wall with a 1:3 mortar so that the concrete gully frame is held firmly in place. Finally, solvent weld the gully hopper joint and fill in the ground around the gully with a concrete mix.

Connection to a stack: Aim to run the discharge pipe to an existing branch outlet boss. If this does not have a spare outlet, then you can either fit a new multiple connector in this position, or a boss adaptor (of the type that can be fitted to an existing stack) to a length of plain stack pipe—whichever allows the discharge pipe to have sufficient fall. If you buy new components, make sure they are compatible with the existing ones—shapes and sizes vary slightly from brand to brand.

If you are connecting to an existing spare outlet, simply cut away the blanking plug and fit the new pipe in position. A boss adaptor is almost as easy to fit: consult manufacturer's instructions. A new connector is a little more tricky: the old connector will probably have to be sawn off, and the new one may not be big enough to bridge the gap. You might have enough 'slack' in the stack to take up the gap, or you may need to fit a slightly longer piece of stack pipe.

Other countries: You can connect to existing drains in the same way as described above. You can even connect to a basement floor drain, as long as this is connected to a sewer or septic tank. However, do make sure that you

B. Above: *On ground floors you may want to connect the discharge pipe to a back inlet gully with a multiple branch outlet*

are complying with your local building ordinances—if you are in any doubt at all about how to connect to your drainage system, get expert help.

Final connection
At this stage, you should have run the discharge pipe through the wall and almost to the site of the machine. The final connection is made as shown in fig. A with a 'P'-trap and stand pipe fitted to the discharge pipe length. The height of the stand pipe will be specified in the machine's handbook; in most cases, the outlet hose from the machine simply hooks into the top; the air gap stops back-siphonage.

In some circumstances, you may be able to connect the machine's outlet hose to an existing trap or waste pipe without the need for a standpipe. Sink traps are now available which incorporate a special connector for a washing machine outlet hose; alternatively, a self-cutting waste connector can be attached to a convenient point on an existing waste pipe, and the outlet hose can be attached to this.

WORKING WITH COPPER PIPE

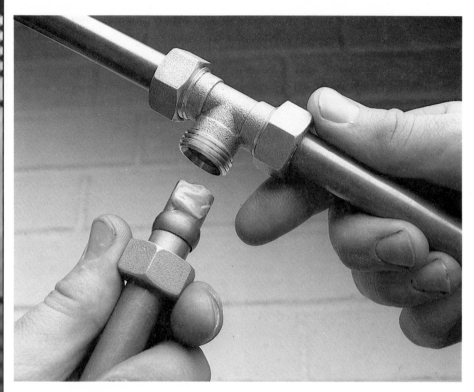

- ● PLUMBING TOOLS
- ● ESTIMATING RUNS
- ● CUTTING PIPE

- ● REMOVING SWARF
- ● JOINING PIPE
- ● CHANGING TAPS

Copper is now the most widely used material for pipework. And unlike old lead pipes, is quite easy to work with. Once you know how to cut, bend and join it, a whole host of home improvement projects become possible.

The sizes of copper pipe used in domestic plumbing have gradually become standardized—typically 15mm for the rising main from the entry stopcock to the cold-water storage cistern in the attic and for the pipe used to supply outlets such as sink and basin taps, and 22mm for pipes to bath taps and the hot cylinder.

Although any new pipe or fitting you buy will be metric, the existing pipework to which it is being joined may be in an imperial size—especially in an older house. Joining copper-to-copper pipework in the two types is not difficult, provided you remember that imperial ½in. (*inside* diameter) is equivalent to metric 15mm (*outside* diameter), ¾in. to 22mm, and 1in. to 28mm. The 15mm and 28mm pipe sizes

can be joined to old ½in and 1in pipe directly using new 15mm and 28mm pipe fittings respectively, but you need special adaptors to connect 22mm pipe to old ¾in pipe.

Tools
Few specialist items of equipment are really necessary for the more straightforward plumbing jobs such as cutting pipe and making simple types of joint. Most of the items can be found in every handyman's toolbox—you need a good quality hacksaw with medium-fine blade, a flexible steel 2m rule, wrenches, adjustable spanners, files, and steel wool.

It is often possible to get round the need for making your own bends by planning the pipe runs in advance, and by a careful choice of fittings.

Pipe bending is not a particularly difficult skill, but usually requires the use of a bending spring to avoid compression fractures on the inside of the curve.

Measuring and cutting
The first task is to estimate the amount of pipe required for your project. This can be done by using scale plans you have prepared or better, from direct measurement of the run using a flexible steel tape. For really complicated pipe runs, use a length of string instead of your tape measure. Lay it along the pipe route, then lift it and measure its length. Always double-check all measurements.

Cutting copper pipe
At its simplest, cutting copper pipe requires only a straight eye, a firm grip and a hacksaw. But in order to avoid problems later on, you should make sure that each cut is as clean and as straight as possible.

If a great deal of cutting has to be done, consider investing in, or hiring, a pipe cutter (fig. 7). It is recommended for use only on the thickest-walled piping as there is some tendency for the cutting area to be crimped if thin pipe is being cut. This might impede water flow later, resulting in noise-inducing turbulence within the pipe.

First, using a fine-toothed flat file, straighten and smooth out the cut edge. Any ragged edges that are left will probably cause leaks later on, so if you cannot get a good finish, leave it and cut the pipe again.

Next remove any swarf (metal shavings) from the outside rim and clean up the inside surface with a round file.

As the edge becomes smooth, angle your file so that you bevel the pipe end slightly (fig. 5). Finally, thoroughly clean the finished pipe end with steel wool or a wire brush.

Joining the pipe
Copper pipe can either be joined with screw fittings or with soldered joints. Soldered joints are cheaper and have a neater appearance, but they can only be used once the techniques of using a blowlamp have been mastered.

Screw fittings are much easier to use and you are unlikely to need many for a simple pipe run.

The two types of screw, or *compression* fittings used in plumbing are known as *manipulative* and *non-manipulative* (fig. A). The former, which require special tools to flare the pipe ends are rarely used by handymen.

1 Carefully unroll a length of tubing from a supply coil, straightening as you go. Wider tubing is available only in pre-cut lengths

2 Measure off the required lengths for each section of piping. Cutting marks can be pencilled, or scored with a nail or screwdriver

3 Use a medium-fine bladed hacksaw to make a clean and square cut, essential for good jointing later on

4 Larger pieces of swarf are more easily removed by knife, but take care to avoid injury as the swarf can be extremely sharp

5 Hone down the outside edge using a broad-blade flat file, taking care not to distort thin-bore tubing while doing so

6 Smooth down internal burrs using a round file, and then complete the preparations by cleaning the joint region

7 If you choose to use a pipe-cutter, insert the pipe up to the cutting mark and adjust the tension of the cutting wheels

8 Gradually tighten up the cutting wheels while rotating the pipe-cutter, and continue until the pipe is severed completely

9 Use the deburring tool accessory to smooth off the inside of the copper tubing and to straighten a crimped edge

Making a compression joint

To make a compression joint, you need a pair of grips, adjustable wrenches or open-ended spanners. Plumber's jointing compound or PTFE (polytetrafluoroethylene) tape is sometimes recommended, but is not necessary for making compression joints watertight.

Make sure the pipe ends to be joined with the fitting are both clean and slightly bevelled. Dismantle the fitting to remove the capnuts and sleeves and place these in order on the piping—setting the sleeves about 12mm from the pipe-ends. If your sleeves are tapered, position them with the slope towards the fitting. If you are using jointing compound, apply this to the inside of each capnut before slipping it on to the pipe-end (fig. 10).

Each pipe in turn is pushed home against the internal stop of the fittings while the capnut is tightened by hand (fig. 12). Apply a coating of jointing compound to the male thread on the fitting before you do this. While you are tightening, be sure not to disturb the seating of the sleeves.

As each capnut is tightened, the sleeve—or compression ring as it is sometimes called—bites into the pipe beneath and spreads out against the coupler to form a watertight seal. The degree of tightening is important. Although it is not possible to be precise—follow the manufacturer's suggestion if in doubt—a turn or so after hand-tight is normally sufficient. Over-tightening can cause severe problems.

A. *The two forms of compression joint for joining pipework, with the non-manipulative type above the manipulative type. Description of parts: (a) capnut, (b) coupler, (c) gland sleeve or 'olive', (d) brass cone insert.* **Below:** *Fitting together a non-manipulative joint*

10 *Sealing compound can be used on internal and external surfaces of a non-manipulative joint, ensuring a watertight but adjustable bond*

11 *The capnut and gland sleeve are slipped on in logical order and the pipe inserted as far as possible within the fitting*

TIP FROM THE TRADE

Q How can I cure the occasional slight leak that occurs when I make compression joints in copper pipe? I have tried sealing compound, but it is not entirely satisfactory.

A First, check that the pipe is properly seated in the compression ring; it will not seat properly if you have cut it crooked or if it is too short and has had to be forced home. Second, check that in cutting the pipe you have not slightly flattened it into an oval shape. In either case you will probably have to cut a new length.

12 *While ensuring the pipe remains firmly butted to the internal stop on the fitting, hand-tighten the capnut*

13 *After hand-tightening, restrict use of a spanner to one or two turns to avoid causing damage to the olive or the pipe*

Shower mixer taps

Replacing troublesome pillar taps with a shower/mixer tap set can quickly and cheaply transform the facilities of your bathroom.

Make sure the water is turned off before you start work, and see that the heating is switched off. Trace along pipework to find the stopcocks for both hot and cold taps. They are usually situated near the cold water storage tank.

The connection of the new tap set makes use of existing components in the case of older style piping. Remove old taps carefully, noting the arrangement of the components. These are illustrated below. The backnut is threaded onto the tail pipe. The capnut is screwed onto one or other of the shanks of the new tap and draws the lipped tail pipe into place. A seal—of hemp or fibre—is sandwiched between the tap shank and pipe-end to make the joint watertight. This seal, usually seated within the end of the tail pipe, must be replaced. The seating needs a good clean out'if jointing compound was used with hemp in the original joint. Repeat the use of jointing compound if hemp is again used.

A straightforward non-manipulative compression joint is all that is needed if you are joining the new tap set directly to copper piping.

IMPORTANT NOTE

Always check with local Water Authority that the kind of tap you propose to install is compatible with your existing plumbing. Local by-laws lay down certain requirements which must be observed.

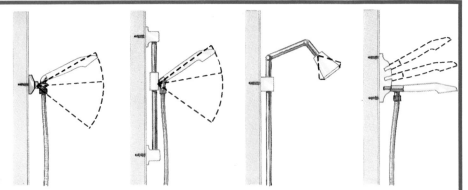

Some alternative methods of fixing the shower head which may influence your choice of shower/mixer set. A handset is useful for close-quarter rinsing and attaches to the wall usually by a fixed socket (left), slider socket (centre left) or fixed-angle socket (right). Some users prefer a fixed rose (centre right)

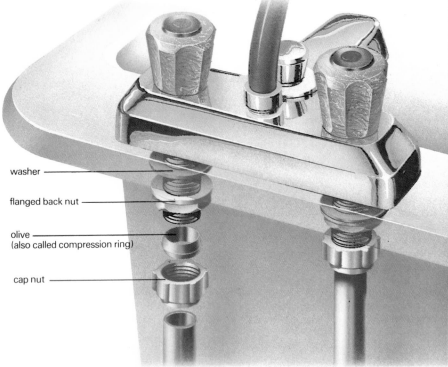

washer

flanged back nut

olive (also called compression ring)

cap nut

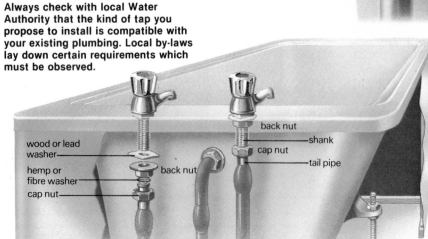

wood or lead washer

hemp or fibre washer

cap nut

back nut

back nut
shank
cap nut
tail pipe

Above: *A modern shower/mixer set fits between the space of the two taps, so check this distance before buying. The set comes complete with shower handset and handset fitting, hose, and the rubber seating and its fittings.*

Left: *To dismantle the old taps, first turn off the water and water heating. Prise off the tap handles (they can be stubborn), then use a wrench to loosen first the capnut—to disconnect pipe from tap—then the backnut plus washer to remove the tap from the bath*

GARDEN DRAINAGE

- ● **DRAINAGE BASICS**
- ● **PLANNING AND LAYING FIELD DRAINS**
- ● **BUILDING SOAKAWAYS** ● **LAYING PIPES**
- ● **DRAINING DRIVE AND PATH SURFACES**
- ● **RETAINING WALLS**

A. Below: *Where garden drainage is inhibited by a topsoil with a high proportion of clay, and where a planned structure or patio is in danger of flooding, the construction of an underground soakaway is an ideal solution and very simple to build*

Good drainage is essential for successful gardening. Poorly drained soils are sour and acid, requiring frequent applications of lime. And a wet soil is also a cold soil, retarding the growth of shrubs and plants. In extreme cases, the heave and shrinkage of clay sub-soils as they absorb and lose water can cause cracking in the fabric of the house. Less damaging, but still annoying, poor drainage causes doors and windows to jam at certain times of the year as the weather varies.

In temperate climates where the rainfall is moderate (about 500mm to 750mm per annum) and well spread thoughout the year many drainage problems can be solved by gardening, rather than constructional, methods. Raising the level of flower beds above the adjacent lawn or paving and adding peat, sand or compost to 'sticky' soils is often sufficient.

If pools of water form on an old lawn, it may merely be that the soil has compacted from years of traffic. This can be cured very easily by lifting the lawn, double-digging the soil underneath (adding new soil if necessary) and then re-sowing or returfing.

But in areas where the topsoil contains a high proportion of clay, or where the rainfall is exceptionally heavy, more drastic measures are needed. In all cases you should aim to have the water table (the level of water permanently in the ground) at least as low as the bottom of your house foundations—unless, that is, you have a below-ground basement, when you will have to settle for something less.

To establish the depth of the water table, simply dig a narrow hole the same depth as the foundations (about 1m in the UK) then cover it over and leave it for two or three non-rainy days. If it starts to fill with water, your water table is too high.

Drainage basics

There are three basic methods of laying garden drains, whether they are to be below ground or behind a retaining wall.

The cheapest, but the one with the shortest life, is to dig a trench about 600mm deep by one spade's width, and half fill it with bundles of brushwood.

The next best method is to fill a similar

trench with about 225mm of rubble. Use bits of bricks, broken concrete or large stones, but do not use old gypsum plaster which will only disintegrate and clog the bottom of the trench. If you have no rubble left over from other jobs, the cheapest source is a demolition site.

The best method is to fill a trench with a 50mm layer of coarse gravel, then lay a row of 75mm or 100mm diameter pipes surrounded by—and covered to a depth of about 100mm with—rubble. Pipes come in a wide range of materials and can be either perforated or unperforated. Perforated pipes are available in plastic, concrete and pitch fibre, the latter being especially easy to use because they are

light in weight and fit together with snap connectors. If you use perforated pipes, lay them with the perforations towards the bottom of the trench so that the water seeping into them takes a minimum of sediment with it.

Unperforated pipes come in plastic, concrete, and the traditional and inexpensive clay (field pipes). If you use unperforated pipes, leave a space of about 10mm between each pair, with a 'roof' over the gap made from broken roof-ridge tiles, pieces of slate or heavy polyethylene sheets of the type used by builders.

Whichever type of drain you choose, four things are important:
● The slope must be consistent. If part of

1 When calculating the size of the hole remember that it is difficult to dig a very small hole. Use a fork to shift a sticky soil such as clay

2 To create straight, square sides you must dig them with a spade; to help the soil slip off, dip the spade in water before you dig each clod

3 Once the hole is completed and the soil has been well tamped down, mix up a stiff batch of cement and 18mm all-in ballast and lay it thinly on the base

4 Next, mix up a sharp sand and cement mortar with a little plasticizer added to stop the mortar drying too rapidly and cracking as a result

5 Start laying the bricks so that there is a small gap between each one. For speed, leave the centre of the base bare then complete it after the walls

6 Continue to build the walls of the soakaway in a honeycomb pattern until you reach the height of the hole, then allow the mortar to set

the drain is steeper than the rest, sediment will lodge where the drain 'flattens out' or stops altogether.
● Only a gentle slope – anything from 1:60 to 1:100 – is needed. If you lay a steep slope, the water will rush along it leaving a rim of sediment to cause problems later. Where a sharp fall is unavoidable – for example to enter a stream or sewer – lay the bulk of your pipes in a gentle slope and finish with a vertical drop so that silt cannot accumulate.
● Always start laying at the lowest point and work your way uphill. This is the only way of getting a consistent fall.
● Above the brushwood or rubble you must place a layer of finer material to

filter out the soil which otherwise would clog the drainage system. Use 150mm or so of cinders, coarse sand or very fine gravel. Then you can fill the rest of the trench with topsoil.

Planters and retaining walls
The most effective method of draining a small garden is to divide it into naturally self-draining areas. On a sloping plot you could make a series of terraces between 1m and 1.5m high, depending on the slope. On flat ground you might divide the area into planter boxes with paving or lawn strips between. Either way you improve the appearance of the garden, as well as its drainage.

Retaining walls at the feet of terraces (fig. C) need to be strong because a large weight of soil is bearing against them. Dig the foundation trench 450mm wide x 300mm deep. Use pegs driven into the ground and a spirit level on a long straight-edged board to endure that the top of the foundation will be level; otherwise the masonry will slope and look odd. If the ground slopes across the width of the wall, you may have to step the foundation in order to keep it below ground level.

In the bottom of the trench pour a concrete foundation 150mm thick by the full width of the trench. Use a mix of one part cement to four of 18mm all-in ballast

B. *The best way to drain a large area is to install a field drain. The most efficient shape is a herringbone, and for very large areas this can be repeated. The cheapest drains are of brushwood, next best is rubble, and the best are of perforated or unperforated pipes*

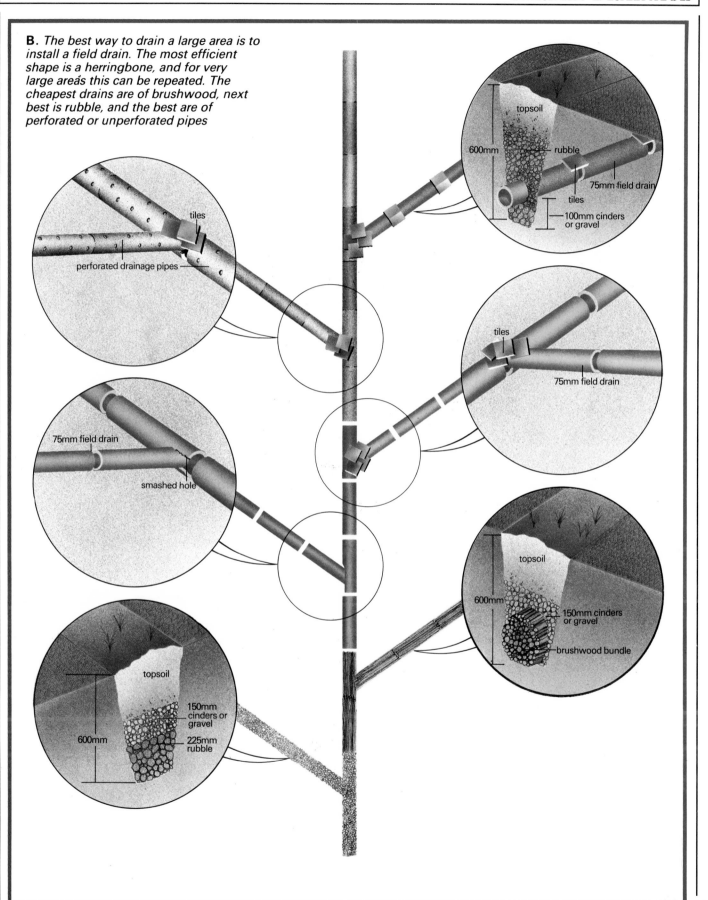

topsoil

600mm — rubble

75mm field drain

tiles

100mm cinders or gravel

tiles

perforated drainage pipes

tiles

75mm field drain

75mm field drain

smashed hole

topsoil

600mm

150mm cinders or gravel

brushwood bundle

topsoil

150mm cinders or gravel

600mm

225mm rubble

(shingle). Up to about 1m high, the masonry can be vertical. Above that, it should slope backwards by about 15°, and the foundation should be sloped to suit (see below).

Lay the first two courses of brickwork—or an equivalent depth in other materials—below ground level so that the concrete foundation will not show should the surrounding earth settle or subside. Brickwork should be laid in English bond (a builder's manual will help) for maximum strength, and in a long wall should be further reinforced by 330mm (one and a half brick) piers at 2.5m intervals, the piers being bonded into the wall.

As you go along, provide weep holes every 2m or so—one row just above ground level and a second row about four brick courses higher. To do this, you reduce the wall thickness to half a brick at the point concerned, leave the mortar out of a vertical joint, and fill the area behind with rubble.

Remember also to leave an outlet hole for the drain which will run behind the wall. This can be laid by any of the methods described above.

Pre-cast concrete blocks are also suitable for retaining walls, and are somewhat cheaper than bricks. Buy the sort that is made from cement and dense aggregate, not the lightweight blocks used for interior work. A handy type for retaining walls is the 450mm × 225mm × 225mm hollow block.

In a long wall, or one retaining a large garden, blocks need reinforcing at intervals corresponding with the piers used in brickwork. So every 2.5m or so, drop two 12mm steel reinforcing rods down the holes in the middle of the blocks and fill

the holes with concrete, well tamped down. Concrete coping slabs along the top of the wall will hide this reinforcement and keep water away from the steel, as well as giving a neat finish.

Planters can be of brick, stone, pre-cast concrete blocks, plain or coloured dry walling stones or even heavy timber—for example old railway sleepers, which are sometimes available cheaply.

Planters of up to five brick courses high can be of loose-laid materials, although the joints will require constant weeding and maintenance. Up to about ten brick courses, single-skin (half-brick thick) brickwork or blockwork is strong enough, provided that you lay them in stretcher bond pattern. Above that height, double-skin (one whole brick thick) masonry is the bare minimum needed.

Single-skin planters are easily drained by providing weep holes in the bottom course of bricks. Over 1.5m or so, you simply omit the mortar between adjoining bricks. Fill the bottom of the planter with rubble to about 100mm deep, then use a finer material as described above before filling with topsoil.

Weep holes alone will also serve to drain double-skinned planters up to about 3m square. Above that, planters should be drained in the same way as retaining walls (see above).

Field drains

In large flat gardens converting the garden into a series of terraces or planters is a back-breaking job, involving moving tons of soil. Unless you have cheap secondhand bricks it is also extremely expensive.

A simpler method is to instal a field

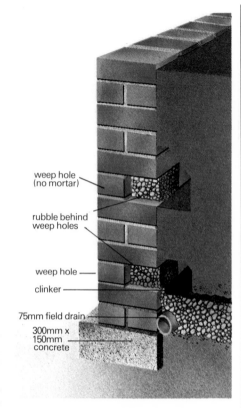

weep hole (no mortar)

rubble behind weep holes

weep hole

clinker

75mm field drain

300mm × 150mm concrete

C. Above: *Small gardens can be divided into self-draining terraces. The retaining walls need to be between 1m and 1.5m high, with weep holes every 2m or so*

drain system under the whole garden as shown in fig. B. It should if possible slope away from the house, and the subsidiary drains should meet the central one at an angle of about 45°.

There are several ways of laying out such a system. In slightly uneven sloping

7 *To insert a drainage pipe into the soakaway, remove a brick from the wall then position the pipe and finish the wall with half bricks as necessary*

8 *To support the concrete roof of the soakaway, start by cutting some corrugated sheet steel to size then lay it over the tops of the bricks*

9 *Next construct a timber formwork around the top of the soakaway, relying on bricks and battens rather than nails to hold the structure*

314

ground the subsidiary drains can follow the natural 'dips' in the ground. In flat ground a herringbone pattern, as shown, is effective. In really heavy soil, or a huge garden, two herringbones can be laid side by side with their central drains turned to meet each other near the outfall.

To establish a consistent fall in your drains, equip yourself with a long and reasonably straight batten. Give this its own 'fall' by fixing a small wooden block to the underside at one end only. A batten 3m long with a 38mm block, for example, will give a fall of 1:80.

With the gravel bed spread in the bottom of the trench, lay the lowest pipe first. Then lay a second pipe one batten's

length away. With the block on the first pipe and the other end of the batten on the second, the batten should be level. Check this with a spirit level.

Once you are satisfied that the two pipes are correctly placed you can use a builder's line stretched taut over them to align the pipes in between. Afterwards transfer the block end of the batten to pipe number two and work uphill over the next section.

With the central drain laid you can start on the branches. If these are to be narrower – for example, 75mm instead of 100mm – the first branch pipe will have to be aligned by eye, but after that you can proceed as before.

Outlets

The simplest method of disposing of the surplus water is to run the drain into a nearby ditch or stream. If the outfall pipe is much higher than the stream, you can prevent scouring by pouring a short concrete channel, starting below the outfall pipe and sloping down to the stream, for the water to splash on.

Another method is to dig a soakaway, as described below.

A third method is to connect the outfall pipe to the domestic sewage or rainfall/sewage system, which is sometimes allowed in the UK. This method should be used, however, only if your garden is tiny. The average domestic sewer line is

10 Mix a large quantity of cement and 18mm all-in ballast with a little plasticizer and shovel it carefully into the formwork until it is full

11 When you have half filled the formwork, place a suitably sized piece of steel reinforcing grid on top of the concrete mix

12 Next, continue to fill up the formwork with the concrete and use a shovel to dig out all the pockets of air which would weaken the roof

13 Using a sufficiently long piece of timber, spread and tamp the concrete until the surface is level and fill up any gaps before the mix goes off

14 After 24 hours the concrete should have set hard enough for you to be able to remove the formwork. Jar it free and carefully remove the timber

15 Before you bury the soakaway, place stones around the edge in the gap between the walls and the bricks to stop the gap becoming filled with earth

only about 100mm diameter, and the volume of water coming from even a medium-sized garden in a heavy downpour could make the system back up and overflow, with messy and unhygienic results. Always check first with your local authority before using this method; in the UK you will need permission, and it is illegal in many other countries.

Soakaways

Failing a simpler method you can dispose of the surplus water by running it into a soakaway from which it will permeate the surrounding ground.

Soakaways work well in soils containing a high proportion of gravel, sand, chalk, limestone and some types of crumbling clay, but less well in tightly-packed, small-grained clays, rock and similar ground. If your land has a clay subsoil or a hard 'pan' of rock half a metre down, try breaking through it—you may find a more permeable material below. In all cases you should site a soakaway as far from the house as possible.

Calculating the correct size for a soakaway depends not only on the soil conditions but also on the rainfall likely in your area and over how many days it is spread. A heavy downpour will run quickly across the surface, for example, while slow persistent rain will soak in and make the soil sodden.

As a very rough guide, allow for 15mm of rain over the whole catchment area served by the soakaway. If the catchment area is 20m × 10m, the volume of water will be $20 \times 10 \times .015$, or $3m^3$. This means the soakaway could be 1.3m square by 1.8m deep. This calculation, however, is for a temperate climate with 500-750mm of rain spread over 115 days; in areas of heavier rainfall, the size could well be increased by half a metre all round.

The simplest soakaway is a pit filled with pieces of rubble into which your drain is run. Dig the hole at least 300mm deeper than is needed for the rubble. Tamp the rubble down well, pour a few centimetres of concrete across it, and fill the hole with at least 250mm of topsoil—enough for grass or plants to grow.

For a more capacious soakaway dig the hole and line it with bricks, laid in a honeycomb pattern as shown in fig. 6 so the water can seep out between them. With the drain led in through one side, mortar a continuous row of bricks around the top edge of the soakaway. Then cover it with old corrugated iron or asbestos-cement sheets, supported on a couple of boards. Pour a concrete slab at least 150mm thick over the sheets and, when it is dry, replace the topsoil (fig. D). Returf or sow grass seeds to disguise the slab.

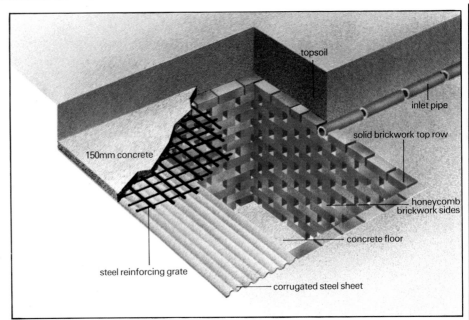

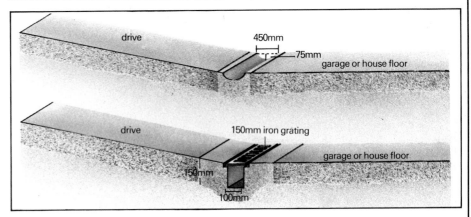

D. Top: *A soakaway provides a simple way of disposing of surplus water*
Above: *Where a large drive slopes towards the house, instal a drain*

Discharge downpipes

In some countries, though rarely in the UK, the downpipes from roof drainage systems do not run into an underground system but instead discharge on to the ground beside the house. In this case a small concrete splash block will help divert the water away from the house, and prevent splashing water from spraying the side of the house.

Driveways and paths

In the UK, driveway drainage is not usually a problem. But if you have a large driveway or other concrete area sloping towards the house, it will pay to do what is done in countries with heavier rainfall: cast a small drain across the drive at its lowest point to divert the water sideways and away from the house.

At its simplest the drain could be merely a shallow depression about 75mm

deep × 450mm wide which can be driven across to enter the garage. At its most elaborate it can be a 150mm × 100mm square sided channel with a row of iron gratings inset across the top.

Small paths running beside the house should be sloped sideways to carry water away from the house. To do this you tape a 12mm offcut of wood under one end of your spirit level as you place the shuttering for the concrete, thus making one row of boards a consistent 12mm lower than the other, automatically.

Alternatively, you can slope a path (or drive) towards the gulley into which the roof drainage empties. The concrete guard around this gulley is often a one-piece concrete casting, mortared in place. It can usually be chipped free with a cold chisel, allowing you to make a small outlet underneath it for any surplus surface water.

When laying any drive or path, make sure also that your concrete does not bridge the damp-proof course in the house wall—in masonry houses it is usually about 150mm above ground level.

INDEX